More Praise for Whole Child/Whole Parent

"If I were being sent to a deserted island and could only take one book in this entire catalog, this would be the one. Whole Child/Whole Parent has its own place on the nightstand next to the bed, and if I'm not too exhausted to read only one page, I do so—knowing that those few moments have enriched my life and given me guidance and inspiration which will make the life of my family blossom. I am humbled when I think of the contemplation which went into this volume. . . . I am inspired by this book, as are many of my customers, who have written to tell me how they've grown from it."

—The Chinaberry Bookstore, San Diego

"Highly recommended . . . has become one of the most turned-to guides (used by parents of many persuasions) for advice and inspiration."

—*Booklist*

"A pre-eminently wise, loving, and practical book."

—*Publishers Weekly*

"Whole Child/Whole Parent is a splendid book. It combines concrete practical suggestions for the new parent with special emphasis on parents' underlying attitudes and beliefs. Thus the author avoids a stultifying 'how to' approach, directing mothers and fathers to focus instead on how they perceive reality and relate to other persons. When parents are in touch with this fundamental of their own experience, their children must benefit. Within this context of values, the author suggests many ways parents can respond to their children. . . . She offers so many good facts and suggestions that even people without children are bound to profit from reading her book."

—Ann Belford Ulanov, professor of psychiatry and religion
at Union Theological Seminary and author of
Religion and the Unconscious

"I must say I am delighted with it. . . . I have on my desk right now several letters asking for the kind of information and spiritual guidance which this book promises, but which I had been feeling was not available anywhere. Polly Berends has done a great service, creating a workbook that will be of inestimable value to parents, and of great help to religious leaders like myself if they are truly aware of the need for expanding consciousness and not just instilling doctrine."

—Eric Butterworth, director of UNITY New York and
author of *You Make the Difference*

Praise from Parents:

"I can hardly contain the joy and elation that keep welling up from within me as I read Whole Child/Whole Parent. *It gives me a 'feeling of wholeness' along with a sense of 'it is possible—loving is possible.'"*

"It would be difficult to overestimate the positive influence you, through your book, have had on my life. . . . The practical advice it contains is valuable, but the spiritual insights are invaluable.*"*

"Books by Dr. Spock, John Holt, and Piaget share space in my library. But not until I found your book did I realize what parenthood could mean, the spiritual depth it could attain, and the inner growth I could foster within my child and myself by being a 'loving' parent to my child."

"Watching my little girl blossom, less hindered than she might have been otherwise by my errors, I am extremely grateful to you for sharing what you have learned."

"In the past few years as a mother and La Lêche League leader I have read a great many books about childrearing, but never have I encountered one so calming and yet so inspiring as yours."

"I want you to know that six *years and three children later your book is the one that I seek out more than any of the others. . . . In its pages I find the highest level of guidance during those times when my foggy and worn consciousness can't quite get to the truth."*

"Through it [Whole Child/Whole Parent], *my life has been given something which I could not seem to find anywhere else. My way of looking at everything is forever altered."*

"Thank you for writing such an enlightening and rare book. It is rare because you have shown how the spiritual and practical must in fact work together."

"I can't tell you what reassurances and joy your Whole Child/Whole Parent *has given to me. It is my daily bulwark against all manner of panics and preoccupations, and I'm very grateful to you."*

"I have never read anything on parenting which came close to it. The book is so positive, encouraging, and helpful."

"I just thought you would like to know how much of a source of solace, reassurance, bearings, and gratitude this book has been to us all. There are so many trendy, how-to books around which espouse one or another groovy way of 'dealing with life.' Obviously your book stems from a spring deeper than most."

"All three children are benefitting, with me, from the thoughts you bring us. Our 18-month-old twins, a boy and a girl, are so active right now: many days my 'wholeness' seems to disintegrate completely. But theirs remains, and your book reminds me of that, renews my perspective, and makes me look forward to another day with them. I have read it at least four times. . . . [Re. child-birth] Your chapter 'Special Delivery: Parentbirth' is the most positive, sensitive correct attitude. . . . So many teachers pass on nothing more than 'heroics' to the pregnant couple. . . . Your thoughts on sleep—being peaceful, turning the children over to love and just beholding—have given me and my dear children so much joy at bedtime. True, I am ready to let go at the end of the day just for some quiet and my own rest. But now I know how to 'let go' peacefully—and they know it. Inevitably I leave them smiling. Thank you, thank you!"

Praise for other books by Polly Berrien Berends

Gently Lead: How to Teach Your Children About God While Finding Out for Yourself

"First in Whole Child/Whole Parent *and now in* Gently Lead *Polly Berrien Berends proves herself the very best guide I know for teaching the art of spiritual direction for children. The most common question of parents is how to provide for the spiritual education of their offspring. Here is the answer. It is accurate, touching, meaningful, highly readable, poetic, and thoroughly capti-vating. Read it and the angels will rejoice."*

—M. Scott Peck, author of *The Road Less Traveled*

"This is the kind of spirituality that arises in the midst of life—at laun-dry duties and at bedtime—when one's children are learning to ride a bike, going to school, envying a sibling. It is substantial; it exemplifies the best of the feminine way."

—Ann Belford Ulanov, Johnson Chair of Psychiatry
and Religion, Union Theological Seminary,
author of *The Wisdom of the Psyche*

*"*Gently Lead *is a book I wish I had had in my hands when I was rais-ing my children. It is warm, nonjudgmental, and respectful of the mystery of God while making that mystery visible as God's works reveal themselves in everyday life."*

—Phyllis Theroux, author of *Night Lights*

Coming to Life: Traveling the Spiritual Path in Everyday Life

"A balanced, practical, and realistic guide to finding joy in the midst of questions and difficulties. The author draws on the universal religious wisdom of humankind to show that problems can be opportunities that lead us to fulfillment and love, which are the fundamental nature of reality. Her book is a mine of memorable quotations, examples, and stories that support this vision."

—Morton Kelsey, author of
Reaching: Journey to Fulfillment

"Deeply spiritual, but not 'religious' . . . wise without trying to be profound. It poses some of the great questions about life in a way that elicits answers within the reader. This is an important work."

—Eric Butterworth, author of
You Make the Difference

"In Coming to Life *our problems are not to be jumped over, but looked into. . . . This is sound psychology, for in it we see that our own life is our teacher."*

—Ann Belford Ulanov,
Faculty Member of the C. G. Jung Institute (NYC),
author of *The Female Ancestors of Christ*

"Polly Berrien Berends once again demonstrates her great gift of seeing daily experiences and the spiritual life as one. In this clear, insightful, and practical book, she invites all toward the source of meaning and truth."

—Gerald May, author of *Addiction and Grace*

Whole Child/Whole Parent

Whole Child/ Whole Parent

FOURTH EDITION

Polly Berrien Berends

Foreword by M. Scott Peck

Harper Perennial

A Division of HarperCollinsPublishers

A previous edition of this book was published by Harper & Row in 1975. Revised editions of this book were published by Perennial Library in 1983 and 1987.

WHOLE CHILD/WHOLE PARENT, Fourth Edition. Copyright © 1975, 1983, 1987, 1997 by Polly Berrien Berends. Foreword copyright © 1987 by M. Scott Peck. All rights reserved. Printed in the United States of America. No part of this book may be used or reproduced in any manner whatsoever without written permission except in the case of brief quotations embodied in critical articles and reviews. For information address HarperCollins Publishers, Inc., 10 East 53rd Street, New York, NY 10022.

HarperCollins books may be purchased for educational, business, or sales promotional use. For information please write to: Special Markets Department, HarperCollins Publishers, Inc., 10 East 53rd Street, New York, NY 10022.

First Edition

Library of Congress Cataloging-in-Publication Data
Berends, Polly Berrien.
    Whole child/whole parent / Polly Berrien Berends ; foreword by
  M. Scott Peck. — 4th ed.
            p.   cm.
    Includes index.
    ISBN: 0–06–092818-2
    1. Child rearing. 2. Child care. 3. Children's literature—Bibliography.
4. Parenting—Religious aspects—Christianity. I. Title.
HQ769.B515   1997
649'.1—dc21   97-9532

      99 00 01 ❖/HC 10 9 8 7 6 5

for Jan and Andy

Contents

Foreword

Whole Child/Whole Parent is a treasure house. It is many things, and all of them gems.

About the only thing it is not is light reading. Neither is *Walden Pond* nor *The Variety of Religious Experience* nor other classics. Polly Berends has her own way with words and makes this very important book about as easy to digest as possible. But it is not for the parent or other reader who wants a quick, easy fix. This is the real thing.

Now on to all the treasure.

It is the best book I know on the psychology of child raising. In ways that are gloriously general and ways that are strikingly specific, it tells us how children should ideally be regarded and responded to by their parents—or, for that matter, by any adult or caring person.

It does this because it reveals the essence of what human beings are all about. The author never allows us for a moment to be distracted by superficial appearances. Conversely, she unfailingly strikes at the heart of the matter. Polly Berends is a radical in the true and best sense of the word: She gets at the root of things.

Consequently she teaches us the "right attitude." The right attitude toward a child is that attitude which sees the child for who she or he truly is. And since the "child is the parent of the man," Ms. Berends is teaching us to see the essence of all human beings as true creatures of God.

Since this book is about essences, it is inevitably a religious book. Indeed, it is also, as far as I know, the one and only book about child raising written by a mystic. I hesitate to say this because *mystic*, like the word *radical*, has come to have a pejorative and dreadfully distorted ring in our culture, as if mystics were out of touch with reality. The opposite is the case. In all cultures, in all religions, throughout the ages, mystics have been those not only most open to the mystery of the world but also, as a consequence thereof, those who have penetrated most deeply into the mystery to discern an underlying unity, connectedness, and essential meaning to life. This is why Aldous Huxley properly entitled his book on mysticism *The Perennial Philosophy*, and why all of the greatest religious leaders—Jesus, Paul, Buddha, Lao Tse, etc.—have been mystics.

So *Whole Child/Whole Parent* is a deeply religious book, and while it is not specifically Christian, it is thoroughly Christian. Ms. Berends establishes with exquisite accuracy the connections between the hard-won wisdom of the best parents and the wisdom of the great sages of all times and all cultures.

So it is that this wonderful work is not merely about child raising (I use "merely" facetiously, as if child raising were not the most essential and important of human activities) but stands by itself as a classic of mystical and religious and psychological literature. It is not merely for parents who want to raise their children in the best manner possible; it is for all people, including all adults who want to raise themselves.

M. Scott Peck

"Why do elephants paint their toes red?"
"I don't know. Why?"
"So they can hide in cherry trees."
"I never saw an elephant in a cherry tree."
"See, it works!"

"How are you?"
"Perfect, thank you. I'm just traveling incognito."
"Oh? As what are you disguised?"
"I am disguised as my self."
"Don't be silly. That's no disguise. It's what you are."
"On the contrary, it must be a very good disguise, for I see that it has fooled you completely."

Introductions

Once I had a dream in which I was to receive a diploma as a spiritual teacher or guide of some sort. There were two of us being presented with such a certificate at the time. The other was a man—Swamibabagururishiroshirabbisoandso. He wore long colorful robes and had a fist full of degrees and papers. To receive his diploma he only had to step forward and present himself with his long titles, flowing robes, and abundant credentials. But before me there stood an enormous mountain of laundry. To receive my diploma I would first have to climb over this huge heap of laundry.

Introduction to the Fourth Edition

The first edition of *Whole Child/Whole Parent* was written in 1972–73, almost two and a half decades ago. By now our babes have become men, and I have nearly doubled in age and experience. The book's spiritual premise remains my bedrock. But subsequent life stages, further analytical work, years of study, and decades of working as a spiritually oriented psychotherapist have added layers to my way of seeing and being. When asked to revise the book for a fourth edition, I considered what to add that I wished I had known during my parental years. Besides that new material, I would reread and revise the existing text.

Rereading *Whole Child* for the first time in many years was bewildering. I was glad to find in it the spiritual convictions on which I still rely—but so cumbersomely expressed that I wondered what people had made of them and why experts had praised the book. Just then I received a copy of the Argentinian edition, several letters from grateful readers, and more lecture requests. Why?

Whole Child was the first and initially the only spiritually oriented book on parenthood, and the only one on the value of parenthood for the parent as well as for the child. While that might explain the initial readership, there have since been many more books, some *Whole Child*'s Godchildren, some easier reading. So, why had my book lasted? What does it offer that others don't? How could I revise it without writing an entirely new book?

I was a less than two-year-old parent and a no-year-old writer of adult books when I wrote *Whole Child*. In my early parental days, for which childbirth classes had *not* prepared me, I had found my spiritual perspective of critical importance. I wondered how other parents were surviving without one, and thought maybe in a catalog of books, toys, and equipment, I could pass on a few helpful spiritual insights. So the original idea was not for a book but a catalog. But as I have written in the preface to an earlier edition, the catalog idea, like the child in my womb, grew on its own into something requiring far more attention, skill, and understanding than I had. Between the time I signed the contract and when I began to write, my second child was born. With both boys still in diapers, I wrote mostly at night, sitting on our bed with my typewriter on a radiator. I was overwhelmed by the double challenge of childrearing and writing my first adult book. I was frightened by the magnitude of my unknowing.

I suppose *Whole Child* has lasted precisely *because of* that unknowing, which forced me to rely on the same spiritual foundation I counted on as a parent. The book was written out of my own groping, which for me means praying. When my husband took over the children to give me a few daytime hours of writing, I spent much of the time calming down. To do so I'd open the Bible and consider the personal relevance of whatever my eye fell on. Amazingly I kept randomly opening to the same two passages. One was about Ezekiel, whom God told to pack all his belongings and tunnel through the wall that surrounded the village. I inferred that my job, too, was to take my personal belongings and longings and publicly tunnel through the wall of ignorance. The idea that my work on my ignorance might help others with theirs was slightly comforting. The other passage stated simply, "Fear not, but let your hands be strong." It helped me to stop wringing my hands and to lift them to the typewriter keys. "Write anything" often came to mind. That's what I did. I just wrote what came to mind, a little here, a little there, until gradually a book patched itself together. So *Whole Child* was more lived through than written—diaper by diaper, doubt by doubt, question by question, grope by grope, prayer by prayer. Something helpful came through from beyond, in spite and *because of* my unknowing. Perhaps it is that if we listen something helpful can come through from beyond, in spite and *because of* our unknowing. Also, I believe people are more reassured by fellow gropers than by experts with all the answers.

Ideas in *Whole Child* that readers say they find helpful include:

• That life is a journey of spiritual awakening rather than an arena for success or failure.

• That you are not the only parent who wonders if having children was a mistake.

• That if you already knew how to be a parent you should be doing something else.

• That to be whole means not to be a complete person but to become aware of one's oneness with the whole.

• That this discovery takes time and is not achieved in less than a lifetime.

• That being a good parent does not mean being all grown up.

• That there is a Parent of parents to whom we can turn.

• That even if your childhood idea of God seems unbelievable, there is an idea of God that makes sense and can be counted on.

• That even if your childhood idea of prayer no longer works for you, there is a way of praying that can.

• That the fundamental wisdom of all ages and religions is the same and applies to the everyday challenges of parenthood.

• That the humdrum is the holy.

• That being a good parent does not mean being a perfect parent but rather a searching one.

• That if the impossible were possible and you could give your children a perfect childhood, you would have failed to equip them for life.

• That every experience, good or bad, can increase our own and our children's spiritual consciousness.

• That children learn more from our learning than from our telling.

• That parenthood is as much for the development of the parent as for the child's.

• That children raise parents as much as parents raise children.

• That picking noodles out of your toddler's hair will not be the story of the whole rest of your life, that your career is not going down the fallopian tubes in the meantime, that being with your child will enrich you and enhance your career.

• That spirituality is not just one part of ourselves and our lives but the deepest and most inclusive layer of self and life, its source and substance.

• That an ear to the ground is more important than uttered sound.

As the result of all of these musings, I have revised this book as follows:

Under the heading "Additional Reflection" I have added substantial new material about anger, marriage, dealing with today's teenagers, fielding children's dreams, the importance of having both a family and an individual life, the psychospiritual ecology of the family, and prayer.

I have also added shorter "Additional Reflections," some of which could be called "Do Overs." When children play jacks and the ball bounces crookedly, through no fault of the player, but rather from hitting a crack, they ask for a "Do Over." Parenthood doesn't give us "Do Overs," but there are many second chances even long after our children have grown up and moved away from home. So my "Do Overs" are really "What I Would If I Could Do Overs." I hope they will help others who are still engaged in childrearing. And while it is no longer my place to actively mother my sons, I trust that the inner version of me that lives on in them will grow kinder and wiser as a result of these belated discoveries. I know that is possible, because I have seen it.

I have edited old material mainly by simplifying and clarifying what I could without writing a different book. My assumption is that there is something about my original groping that is in synch with other parents' groping.

Over the years as my understanding has deepened my language has changed. I was shy about using religious language when I wrote *Whole Child*. Even now I avoid using *God* and *prayer* before defining them, because they are so loaded with questionable connotations. The God I learned of as a child was an invisible person in space. The idea of prayer I learned as a child was of talking to that space person. Up to a point these are fine ideas for a child, and sometimes I still find them meaningful. But often I find more meaning in the God described by Paul as that "in which we live and move and have our being—who (or which) is before all things and in whom all things consist." To me, the idea that there is an all-inclusive whole of which everything and everyone is an individual aspect, or of a Self to which each individual self belongs, is more helpful. It gives rise to an approach to prayer that I also find more helpful. Prayer becomes more a matter of listening than talking, of hearing than telling, a quiet opening at the bottom of one's self to the greater Self, a fitting of one's self into the whole and of letting the whole fill one's self. In writing *Whole Child*, drawing on the language of the world's great religions, I used "the Whole," "One Mind," "the One" to refer to this spiritual source, force, and substance of our being, and where we are. In later books, *Coming to Life* and *Gently Lead*, I added "fundamental mind." Recently I have found it meaningful to speak of "the Beyond Personal" as the basis and context of all personal and interpersonal life. These are all ways of saying "God." Ultimately religious language isn't necessary, but if one is able to understand it in a meaningful way, one can draw on the priceless experience, support, and inspiration of the great religious scriptures and traditions.

A word about *consciousness,* and about *spiritual consciousness.* In earlier editions of *Whole Child,* I spoke of consciousness as our essential characteristic, but while I wrote of the task of becoming increasingly spiritually conscious, I did not address explicitly the issue of what depth psychology calls the *unconscious.* There are two common usages of the word *conscious.* One refers to the awareness of the ego, the part of oneself of which we are presently aware and which we refer to when we say *I am a man, a mother, a New Yorker.* Ego consciousness reflects only that part of oneself which *Whole Child* calls "Me, Inc.," or what I have elsewhere referred to as our "lead side." Missing in Me, Inc.'s idea of ourselves are many unconscious "lag sides," which we learned as children to neglect or reject or which life has not yet called forth, but which we need over the course of our lives to consciously recognize and receive as part of our God-given being. The spiritual principles in *Whole Child* orient us toward this process, but they cannot spare us or our children from having to live through the process.

It is said that a little knowledge is a dangerous thing. The danger with a little spiritual consciousness is that just because we know *about* spiritual consciousness, our Me, Inc. self will think it has it and can do it. When we fall prey to this illusion, we tend to misuse the little understanding we have *against* unconscious parts of ourselves and against our children by positive thinking and willing, as if "I think, therefore I am." Spirituality is not something extra that we can superficially apply to life but something fundamental about life that applies to us and that we are here to discover. So I want to point out that by consciousness I mean our full *potential* to become aware of ourselves and our source, and emphasize that such realization only occurs through a process of awakening that involves an often painful facing and healing of energies, feelings, and parts of ourselves of which we were formerly unconscious or found unacceptable. The gap between Me, Inc. and our fuller self (which I have called the *Seeing Being* and which recognizes its oneness with the whole) is not only a gap in awareness between us and God. It is also a gap in awareness between us and our unconscious selves. It is as impossible to heal the gap between us and God without healing the gap between us and ourselves as it is to heal the gap between us and ourselves without healing the gap between us and God. This was always implicit in *Whole Child*, but in this edition I want to emphasize up front that spiritual consciousness is not something we can do for ourselves or to our children but a lifelong awakening process in which our children help us as much as we help them.

I hope new and old readers alike find this new edition helpful. I am indebted to you for your readership and amazing letters. I am grateful to many teachers and mentors, including James Jones, Harry Fogarty, Ann and Barry Ulanov, Thomas Hora, and especially Richmond K. Greene. I am grateful to all my past and present clients and students, and to each and every member of my beloved family. At HarperCollins I am grateful to my steadfast and longstanding editor Hugh Van Dusen, and to Associate Editor Kate Ekrem. Though we do not know each other personally, I am grateful to M. Scott Peck, whose wonderful foreword has so helped *Whole Child* make its way in the world. For friendship and help with this revision I thank Michelle Morin Woycik and Ann Tremaine Linthorst. I thank Dan, Lisa, Alex, Charlotte, and Ian Thomas for keeping me in touch with what it means to be young children and parents, for making me feel a part of their family, and for the well-trod path between our backyards. Heartfelt love, gratitude, and Godspeed to you all.

P.B.B., Hastings-on-Hudson
New York, 1997

Introduction to the Second and Third Editions

When *Whole Child/Whole Parent* was originally conceived, I had one baby and was fairly shy about speaking in overtly spiritual terms. In my own life I was looking to see how the spiritual insights I had long counted on applied to parenthood. Like any new parent I found parenthood hard. I got stabbed by diaper pins that popped open and experimented with a theory or two that either didn't help or proved merely distracting. But the spiritual insights validated themselves ever more clearly—and they proved so practical! I couldn't imagine how parents without this spiritual viewpoint could get by at all. So, as if I didn't have my hands full enough with one baby, I conceived again: of a book, a book baby. Almost immediately our second child was also conceived, and I was doubly pregnant.

As conceived, the book was to be a sort of catalog. Based on my experience as a new parent and my past as a children's book editor, I would put together a practical book about what I wished I had known (such as which diaper pins stay closed), and what I was glad I knew and was sure other parents would appreciate (e.g., the value of books, and which books, for preschoolers). In between, I would sneak in some spiritual ideas, which I didn't think many people would be interested in at first. So it would be a catalog of books and things and tips on using them, and here and there would be this smuggled spiritual perspective. The publisher planned to offer by direct mail everything recommended in this "whole child catalog." There was even to be an order form at the back of the book.

It seemed like such a great idea: direct mail for new parents, just when it was difficult to get to the store; an expert selection of books for young children; and all those smuggled nuggets of truth that I hoped some would find inviting enough to pursue further. As I write, it still seems a fine idea; it seemed fine then, too—until the day I signed the contract, when the book disappeared in my mind. It was a good idea; someone could make a fortune with it; it would even be helpful; *but I could not write it that way.* Placing so much emphasis on techniques and things without discussing forthrightly the spiritual principles that led to their discovery suddenly seemed misleading, even dishonest. So despite all my careful planning, the birth of *Whole Child/Whole Parent* came as a shock because, as with all babies, this baby (and how to raise it) was considerably different—and more spiritual—from what it was expected to be.

Doubts and fears notwithstanding, in due course, a book that surprised even me did get written and was successfully published. We all have ideas that we think are ours and serve our own purposes. Instead, over and over again, we can see that the ideas have a life of their own and that, after all, it is they that are putting us to use!

Whole Child/Whole Parent was originally prepared when I had two piles of diapers in my house. Now my children are older. Now diapers and pins seem too trivial to mention, and I was inclined to leave out all the material information specific to babies. Not only can you never step into the same river twice; you are also never the same person not stepping into the not same river again. So I found myself writing an altogether new book.

Many parents have written over the years to say that this spiritual book is the only truly practical book on parenthood they have ever read. Others have written that at first they read only about books, toys, and techniques—but that after six months they were interested only in the "spiritual stuff." Some have written that although their children were older, they found the principles still applied. Some even say that although they have no children, the book has been helpful in their own quest for spiritual understanding.

While I was stewing over my revise/rewrite dilemma I suddenly received a number of calls from people wanting to know when the book would be available again. It was clear that they weren't looking for anything other than the original. So it was brought home to me that while there are other books to be written, the old *Whole Child/Whole Parent* still had a job to do—one a completely new book, maybe even a better book, might not be able to do. In some ways this is a new book. It is much expanded, for in trying to spell some things out more smoothly and clearly I have had to add material to the text. I have also tried to be more inclusive of fathers and to make clearer the relevancy of these ideas to parents of older children. But the original book is here, and everything new was implicit in the original.

At the end of most chapters are sections called "Practical Information for New Parents," which include additional information particular to parents of very young children. For the most part, parents of older children will want to skip over these sections, as they are largely concerned with equipment, toys, books, and activities for babies and very young children. No attempt has been made to cover this information for older children because they have more individual tastes and interests. Also parents of older children are more experienced, and the children themselves are able to make their needs and interests known.

Rafts for Crossing

Quotations here and there in this book are intended to show the relevance of the great mystical teachings to the practical experience of childrearing and, at the same time, to bring to light the far-reaching spiritual significance of even the meanest momentary details of our experience.

We live in such a wonderful time. Almost all the world's great teachings are available in our own language. And each sheds light on the others! It is remarkable that so many wise ones independently have seen life in so much the same way and in such radical contrast to the views of those around them. They all have insisted that freedom from preconceptions is a prerequisite to spiritual realization. They all have maintained the importance of not confusing the teacher as a redemptive person with the redemptive teaching, or even the redemptive teaching with the redemptive truth. To be loving, to be wise—it is all the same: everything clung to has to be let go.

Pai-chang asked: "What is the ultimate end of Buddhism?"
Ma-Tsu said: "This is just where you give up your life."

—D. T. Suzuki, *Zen Buddhism*

Jesus said, "If any man would come after me, let him deny himself and take up his cross and follow me. For whoever would save his life will lose it, and whoever loses his life for my sake will find it."

—Mark 8:34–35

Buddha said: "Only he crosses the stream of life who wishes to know what is known as unknowable."

—*The Dhammapada*, trans. by P. Lal

He also said: "Monks listen to the parable of the raft. A man going on a journey sees ahead of him a vast stretch of water. There is no boat within sight, and no bridge. To escape from the dangers of this side of the bank, he builds a raft for himself out of grass, sticks, and branches. When he crosses over, he realizes how useful the raft has been to him and wonders if he should not lift it on his shoulders and take it away with him. If he did this, would he be doing what he should do?"
"No."
"Or, when he has crossed over to safety, should he keep it back for someone else to use, and leave it, therefore, on dry and high ground? This is the way I have taught Dhamma (teachings), for crossing, not for keeping. Cast aside even right states of mind,

monks, let alone wrong ones, and remember to leave the raft behind."

—*The Dhammapada*, trans. by P. Lal

The quotations in this book are but the sticks, branches, and grass that may be useful to some to build a raft for crossing over. Then the raft can be left behind. It is better not to get caught up with the raft itself and with questions about whether it is preferable to be Taoist or Christian or Buddhist. On the near bank it is easier to build a raft using everything buoyant that we can get our hands on. There is no advantage to using only maple or only pine. On the far bank no raft is needed and will impede our progress if we linger over it or try to take it along.

In fact, no one raft gets us all the way across, and in the beginning it is usual to ride on the raft of another. When you first find your way to the near shore you may meet someone who is willing to take you partway on his raft. This is your teacher. His raft is made of aged wood and driftwood gathered from up and down the river to carry himself—his life—and anyone else who wants to go along.

From the middle of the river a master's students can see all up and down the river those other rafts, ancient and new, which have been gathered under different lives. Some, left by ancient seers, have broken up and lie floating about for us to collect into our own new rafts. Out there on the river we are taught by our teacher to build small vessels of our own. *Whole Child/Whole Parent* is such a a student raft. Many teachers inspired me to build it. One of them was Thomas Hora, who gave me the precious idea that God is love-intelligence.

So there are three types of quotations in this book: age-old statements of truth from the world's greatest teachings, which in juxtaposition shed light on each other; new and recent insights and teachings that reveal the relevancy of these ancient truths to our life and times; and finally, as illustrations, anecdotes and quotations from the lives of individual children and parents. Included are stories from my students, clients, and friends as well as incidents from my own life.

Timeless wisdom, timely instruction, and daily experience all conspire to make us aware of a wise and loving God and our oneness with it. My gratitude for the teachings and teachers, including my own personal teachers, mentors, colleagues, companions, students, and family, is boundless.

Zen Mom

Child: Mom, how come you know so much about God?

Mother: I don't know so much. But I have been around for a while and been to many schools and studied with many teachers. There were Moses and Isaiah and Jesus and Buddha. There were many books and professors. But besides all those I have two private Zen masters who are always teaching me and making my learning into real understanding and love. I am very, very grateful for them.

Children: Tell us! Who are they? What are their names? You never told us about them!

Mother: Their names are Jan and Andy. It is you who are my masters.

Children [laughing]: Oh, Mom! We teach you? You're joking!

Mother: No, I am not kidding. You are my two wonderful Zen masters.

1
Wholeness

What he saw as One was One, and what he saw as not One was also One. In that he saw the unity, he was of God; in that he saw the distinctions, he was of man.

—*The Wisdom of Laotse*, trans. by Lin Yutang

I and my Father are one.

—John 10:30

Marrying and having a baby are part of our idea of fulfilling ourselves and becoming "whole." We expect somehow to have a fuller life experience and complete ourselves through having and raising children.

Generally we do not doubt that we can do this. These days we all prepare for childbirth, which we know we don't know much about, but there is very little preparation for what comes afterward, even though it lasts for years. Having been children ourselves, we feel ready to go. Merely by avoiding our parents' mistakes we expect to do better.

Yet so often parenthood turns out to be a mixed blessing. Many of us wait long years for a baby to be born, and as soon as she's born we begin wondering when she will ever grow up. So up she grows, and immediately we are pining for the days when she was just a little baby. Along the way we often let each other down. Sometimes we hurt each other. We don't live up to her expectations; she doesn't live up to ours. Yet even when our children are unhappy or the family is in conflict, we are never quite satisfied with the idea that unhappiness is "just a fact of life." Even if we are resigned to that for ourselves, we want life to be better for our children. Children make us want to do better, to be better. But to be better means, above all, to see better. And what having children shows us, first of all and again and again, is how much we don't understand, how much we don't see.

How difficult it is to be somebody's parent is one of the best-kept secrets around—along with that other one about being somebody's spouse. We all think we're supposed to know. Children don't know. Adults know. And because children don't know, parents above all *have* to know. So whenever it hits us—usually not until after our child is born—the idea that we *don't know* is both frightening and inadmissible. A successful journalist recalls:

When I became pregnant I was so happy. I was good at everything; surely I would be good at this too. But before three months were up, it began to hit me that this was going to be *very* different from all the other challenges I had faced. So I read. Three pages into Dr. Spock, panic struck. For every one thing Spock told me that I hadn't known before, fifty more previously unknown hazards were revealed to besiege my confidence. To keep from crumbling altogether I had to stop reading. I stopped just before the part about cesarean deliveries—just a short time before my child was born by cesarean section.

Whenever the going gets rough we each feel uniquely awful. *What's the matter with me? What is the matter with my child? What am I doing wrong? Why can't I get it right?* Few people dare to admit how tough it is—especially not if everyone else is doing fine.

Helping to keep the secret are all the books on childrearing, full of techniques for doing it better. Implied is that it *can* be done better, if we knew how, which the existence of such books implies we don't. So we read until we think we know. Then when our efforts don't work we are more convinced than ever of our inadequacy. This is pretty hard to take, since our whole purpose in becoming parents was to be "whole"—a "whole" parent having a wholesome relationship with a "whole" child in a "whole" family.

But what "wholeness" are we seeking? We have two or three separate beings—a parent or two, a child. What are they? What do we mean by using "whole" to describe them?

Wholeness, we are fairly sure, has something to do with love and understanding. We want to be loved and understood, to be loving and understanding. So we become parents, a circumstance in which love and understanding clearly are central issues. Why is it so difficult? How come hurt and confusion happen right where we are trying hardest to be loving and understanding? Is something the matter with us? Is something the matter with our children? With life? Or is there something mistaken in our *idea* of what it means to be a whole parent or child? What does it mean: whole child, whole parent?

Wholeness as Completeness

If you'll be m-i-n-e mine
I'll be t-h-i-n-e thine,
And I'll l-o-v-e love you
All the t-i-m-e time . . .

—"Zulu King," traditional camp song

We tend to think of ourselves as separate beings (I, the parent—you, the child) existing in relation to each other and trying to perfect ourselves as complete, "whole" persons. Parent and child alike are believed to be *completeable,* each in quest of wholeness, each to some extent *deriving its wholeness from the other.* Unconsciously, when we think of loving each other we tend to mean getting wholeness from each other.

But whether we call it love or not, there is a certain built-in contrariness to the idea of many would-be whole selves seeking to get personal completeness from each other. In breast-feeding, for example, the apparent situation is that the mother has got what the child has not. So the mother gives of her self, and the child gets. And what is the mother getting? A sense of personal completeness *and* a sense of self-sacrifice. On the one hand, she is fulfilling herself and being loving; on the other hand, she may feel secretly robbed and resentful. It takes so much time—much more than she thought. It's so tiring. Must she give up her whole life for her child?

When the child becomes more "self-sufficient," it is time for weaning. Now the mother is relieved and freed, and so is the child. Yet they may both feel cheated. The mother feels less whole, less of a mother if the child is weaned; she is less of a mother if he isn't! And while the child may seem reluctant to give up nursing, underneath it may be the mother's secret clinging that prolongs the nursing and inhibits the child's growing freedom and wholeness.

Fathers also experience such conflicts. A man wants a child to complete his marriage and his picture of himself as a whole father/husband; yet he seems to lose his wife (thereby diminishing his husband self) in the process. He wants his son to be a little man; but at the same time he wants to be in charge, to be looked up to and obeyed.

If we—parent and child—are indeed separate personal entities, each in quest of personal wholeness, such conflicts of self-interest are inevitable. As a doctor's healing work depends on somebody else being sick, so our ambition to be whole parents and raise independent whole children seems to depend on their being dependent on us. Our sufficiency seems dependent on their unsufficiency. Each of us in making our claim to personal wholeness is inclined to rob the other of his claim to wholeness. But where is the love in that? Where indeed? And where is the wholeness? If there is wholeness in any of us, what is this need to go around getting it from somebody else?

If you don't think the title of this book is *Whole Parent/Whole Child,* then you are the exception. Most people do. Implied is that *if* the parent is whole, *then* the child will be whole. *If* the parent knows how to do it, *then* the child will turn out okay. But then—oh, horrible thought and worse experience!—*if* the child seems not to be whole, *then* the parent must not be whole either. The nine-month-old next door is already walking, while our eleven-month-old hasn't taken a step. The manager of the supermarket says our seven-year-old has stolen a package of gum. From silly to serious, every difficulty suggests to us that the child is not whole, which in turn suggests that we are to blame, which in turn suggests that we are not whole. God forbid!

So we seek diagnoses, explanations for what's wrong with the child. If we can't take credit for our children, then at least please excuse us from the blame! *Thank goodness it's dyslexia! I thought it was my fault. I thought he was stupid, lazy.* Indeed, recognition of our children's special differences, limitations, styles of learning, and so forth can be very helpful. But there is another side as well. Secretly we are almost grateful to think that there is something really the matter with him, something only mechanical, something wrong with him rather than with us. So in a strange way, the very thing we started out in favor of (rearing a whole child) turns out to be something we are somehow also against.

There are all these hidden clauses—the fine print we don't see when we make this contract to have children and become parents. We act on assumptions and motives we aren't aware of and reap consequences we don't expect.

One mother has a wonderful governess who raised her as a child and now helps with her children. The children love the governess;

the governess loves and cares beautifully for the children. Any busy mother would be delighted to have such assistance and such loving care for her children. But this mother feels rejected and jealous! In her picture of her "whole" self she is the complete, perfect mother. She wants her children to love, depend on, and look up to her alone, for everything. But does she really want them to be afraid to leave her side? to find no love anywhere except from her? She sees how ridiculous this is. Yet the desire is very strong. Her desire to be the complete mother conflicts with her being a truly good mother.

Are we using our children? You bet we are. But while we are not as good as we thought, we are not as bad either—only mistaken.

The Myth of Me, Inc.

The real culprit is only a misperception of the goal we all seek, a mistaken idea of wholeness: the idea of the complete me, me embodied, me *in corpus* Me, Incorporated, Me, Inc. Seeing ourselves as separate selves, we aim to complete (become whole) ourselves. But each one's would-be complete me is a proposition mutually exclusive of everyone else's, and *in trying to build itself up, each Me Incorporated is always laying claim to the lives of others.*

Even though I knew better, when my son's first tooth came through early, I was proud. I was proud of him, and I was proud of me. It was perfectly clear to me how absurd this was. Yet there it was anyway. I said to myself, "This is ridiculous. It's *his* tooth. He didn't make it. I didn't make it. It just came." Then I called up two friends and bragged about the precocious tooth.

To Me, Inc. as parent, the child is necessarily either an annex or an accomplishment. In taking credit (or blame) for our children—even for giving them life in the first place—we are really "taking the life" of our children. It is no wonder that as our children take up the lives they have supposedly been given, troubles arise.

Jesus said, "A man's foes will be those of his own household."

—Matthew 10:36

Paul said, "The good which I would, I do not, but the evil which I would not, that I do."

—Romans 7:19

It is no one's fault that parents and children are frequently at their worst with each other. In a way this is inevitable, since it is in our families above all that we are always at our most. In our families we are especially concerned with this business of claiming complete self-hood. But we are not to blame. Neither can we through any process of civilization or technique become *personally* (as separate selves) any better. The very idea of a personally separate self, Me, Inc. (whether praiseworthy or blameworthy), is itself mistaken. Yet it is a universally held idea from which we all suffer and must transcend. However, it should also be added that Me, Inc. is not a mistake we can prevent or avoid or cancel, but a life phase that must be lived through. It seems that only by developing a sense of self can we discover the limits of the self, both our own and others'. Only in this way can we become aware of our need for, and the reality of, something beyond ourselves. Only then can we awaken to its ever presence and our oneness with it. So the advantage to be gained from all that is said in these pages is not a way of avoiding Me, Inc.'s mistakes. The advantage is rather the awareness of the possibility of awakening to our oneness with the whole—with a Beyond Personal Self of selves, with God—and some realization that this awakening process is happening and is the only thing of ultimate importance. Such an awareness does not prevent problems, but it can help us take advantage of and learn our way through them.

Me Gets Born

If a man thinketh himself to be something when he is nothing he deceiveth himself.

—Galatians 6:3

Judge not according to the appearance but judge righteous judgment.

—John 7:24

Judging by our senses—by what we see, hear, and feel—we get the impression that we exist separately from everything else. Experiencing ideas in our heads, strength in our arms, love in our hearts, life in our bodies, we infer that we *have* intelligence, strength, life. Like the circus clown who mistakes the place where light strikes the floor for the light itself and tries to sweep it up, so we infer that we exist on our own and that our good is something outside of ourselves. We seem to be "in here" while everything else is "out there."

But in so conceiving of ourselves as separate realities with our own intelligence, love, strength, life, we place ourselves in double jeopardy. For whatever we claim to *have* we also experience the *lack* of. The claim to personal knowledge brings with it the awareness of not knowing enough. With the belief in personal power comes the experience of powerlessness. With the experience of being autonomous comes the experience of fear and lostness; with the experience of being self-sufficient, the sense of insufficiency, helplessness, loneliness, fragility. In parenthood all this is compounded as we begin to view ourselves as responsible for yet another self.

What we call "self-consciousness" is actually a peculiar form of semiconsciousness. Eastern thought refers to the "illusory self." The New Testament speaks of "life according to the flesh" (2 Corinthians 10:2), which has nothing particular to do with sex, but with the idea of being a self contained in a body: Me *in corpus,* Me, Incorporated, Me, Inc. = Me Limited (Ltd.) = Me Desperado. Me, Inc. sees having and doing (or possessing and exerting power) as the primary issues in its survival. Judgment by appearance sires Me, Inc. in every one of us. It happened to Adam in the Garden of Eden. It happened to us when we were children. As parents we observe, even celebrate, the advent of self-consciousness as it occurs in our children.

Me Grows Up

At first, as babies, we do what we do, get what we get, and are pleased or displeased accordingly. But gradually we begin to make connections between what we feel and do, and between what we do and what happens next. We begin to view ourselves as causing thoughts and events; simultaneously we begin to be our own cause célèbre—to be self-centered, and to view all other selves as adjuncts or adversaries. Through praise and blame, and push and pull, the whole world transmits its belief in the complete me to the child, pointing out to each of us that we are really something. Our senses confirm this impression. Here I am in my skin; there you are in yours. Parent selves will care for our child self until it becomes self-sufficient, whereupon we will take care of our "own" self. Thus Me, Inc. comes into its own and embarks on a long period of self-completion called growing up, gathering the strength and virtue to be personally powerful and good in its own right.

Me Gets Married

By the time Me, Inc. is full grown, it is aware of certain limits that it cannot overcome by itself. It isn't half what it thought it would be. So a new plan is conceived. Next best to self-completion—maybe even better—how about this? The addition of another self! How better to enlarge and complete the self as possessor than to annex another self? So Me, Inc. takes a big step: marriage. The corporate merging of two Me, Incs. Two half-selves will become one whole one. But which of the two will they both become? Ah, there's the rub! *Whose self do you think you are anyway? I thought you were for me—mine. But I thought* you *were for* ME!

Me Makes a Baby

After marriage what could better establish Me, Inc. as both power and possessor than the production of—ta da!—another self. Having each other isn't enough. And we're both feeling had. Whether we follow tradition and have children soon after we marry, or put career first and wind up hurrying to get pregnant before it's too late, we continue to associate having children with being whole persons. Two selves combine to make another self—a baby one. And surely this little one will be more manageable than that spouse one has turned out to be! So Me, Inc. extends itself two ways—both through having and through making or doing another self. The complete, self-sustaining self, self-proprietor and self-producer in business for itself. If only other selves, spouse and child included, didn't have the same objective, maybe it would work.

Ta Da!

At one year old he always came so fresh from his nap—all new and warm and flushed—smiling, bright and lovable with cherry red lips and fat folds over his wrists. Still leaning too far forward, he toddled forth pell-mell to see what was next. We thought his entry so spectacularly cute that one day somebody jovially announced it with a cry of *ta da!* It was even cuter when he took to saying *ta da!* himself. We liked it that he thought of himself as a good thing worth a little fanfare. But when he was in his high chair and couldn't leap into the room himself, he would hurl other things—spoon, food, cup, dish—across the room, gleefully crying *ta da!* and waiting for everyone to be pleased. For a time there we were all leaping about, because whenever he said *ta da!* we knew something was about to be thrown. It was harmless, humorous, inevitable, but looking back we can see—he came from his sleep to see what's what, and we said to him, "*You* are what's what." One confusion leads to another.

Unmistakable confusion is one of the surest effects of parenthood, and perhaps its greatest benefit. Built into the idea of having a baby is the idea of losing it. Built into the idea of making a baby is the possibility of wrecking it. But as confusion and anguish mount, we begin to ask questions. Initially we chalk up problems to poor technique, lack of equipment, bad luck, or each other's shortcomings. But underneath a secret sense of personal failure grows that we struggle in vain to conquer and conceal. After coming at the problem from every direction we are forced to question the premise that parenthood is something we could do right. When other parents confess their bewilderment, something in us whispers in relief, *You mean I'm not the only one? You mean it's only a mistake? I thought I was supposed to know better.* Once confusion is recognized and embraced as confusion, there comes a possibility of better understanding. Here is where the laughter and the joy of being a parent return again and again.

Wholeness as Oneness

Sooner or later, defeated and frustrated by all attempts to achieve wholeness as completeness, we are ready to welcome a different idea—the idea of wholeness as oneness.

Like waves on water, leaves on trees, beams from the sun, islands on the earth, everything including ourselves and our children can be viewed two ways. Superficially they appear to be separate, isolated, vulnerable, complete things. But looking deeper we find a oneness between each appearance and its underlying source of being: the island is really one with the earth, the leaf with the tree. Every aspect of the whole expresses the whole in unique ways, and the relationship of each to all others is harmoniously governed by the underlying reality with which each is one.

For us then *the quest for wholeness becomes not to acquire, not to accomplish, not to complete our selves, but rather to discover what it is with which we are one so that we can go ahead and be one with it.* Parenthood is neither the having of children nor something we do to children. Parenthood is a time when we are pushed to discover the nature of the whole and our oneness with it, a time when both our mistaken ideas about who we are and truer ones are brought to light. There is so much that is beautiful and good to wake up to. Our children drive us toward this awakening. We begin with what seem to be two or more separate selves having and doing to each other and trying to get wholeness from each other; but life forces us to look deeper for the fundamental reality from which we derive our uniqueness and which alone can harmoniously govern us in relation to each other. So this book is called *Whole Child/Whole Parent* instead of *Whole Parent/Whole Child* to indicate that our wholeness already exists and is not something to be given or forced upon or gotten or taken from each other in the future—but rather, now upon now, awakened to.

So we come to see that Me, Inc.'s goal of wholeness as self-completion is a fundamental mistake. Can an island exist apart from the land, or the beam from the sun, or the leaf from the tree? No more do we exist or love or know apart from whatever it is that we belong to. Does one island get its life from another? Does one sunbeam manage another? No more do we cause or control each other. Our efforts backfire not because we are bad or inept but because they are contrary to the truth.

No one can learn this from reading a book. It is a lesson to be lived through. When problems come up, it is not that we are at fault; it is only that some false idea is being proved false. Well, hooray! Proving what isn't is part of discovering what is! Parenthood is a rich, uncompromising time in which even our problems can be appreciated as valuable revelations. Every step of the way points out to us either what is true or what isn't. Clarification of what isn't tends to be painful; revelation of what is—beautiful, liberating. Both occur together. Realizing this eases everything and sets us to laughing and loving. Our children help us as much as we help them, playing out the distinction between what is and what isn't before us in clear broad gestures.

On entering the sixth grade a boy suddenly found his world and freedom sizably enlarged. He became aware of all kinds of new possibilities for himself. He made vegetable soup, baked cookies, took a first-aid course, and treated his brother's injury. Through it all there showed in fits and starts both the true and the false. On the one hand, he felt a tremendous sense of possibility and freedom, the burgeoning fulfillment of his potential, which was expressed as joy, increased assurance, generosity, gratitude, and huge bursts of goodness and love. He whistled constantly, and sometimes even in the middle of a "boring" task, he would burst out, "Do you know how happy I am?" He was grateful. But in other moments he took credit and felt powerful and important. This expressed itself as overexcitement, anxiety, demandingness, competitiveness, envy, bossing, jealousy, and boasting. Sometimes it was infuriating, sometimes amusing and touching. When we liked his cookies, he might say, "Aren't I great?" Ta da!

Like wheat and tares these two ideas grow up together. Sometimes we march in all heavy-footed, trying to yank out the weeds, trampling the wheat, and only breaking off the tops of the weeds and sowing their seeds. Other times we stand back. Then we see that the wheat is strong and true and that the weeds will die out as the wheat grows. In this beholding we understand ever more clearly our own confusion. We notice that whatever ideas govern us also govern our children. Their behavior is like a wind sock indicating the direction of our own attention. As the years go by we find ourselves telling them less and learning more from them. We also see that they learn better from our learning than they ever did from our telling.

Additional Reflection: Reviewing the story of my young cookie-maker and the passage about wheat and tares, I recognize that at the time I intellectually knew better than I actually was able to do or be. If I had it to do over, I'd stand back even more, let wheat and tares grow, and do even less correcting and instructing. We have seen that Me, Inc. has to develop before it can be transcended. When he says, "Aren't I great?" being aware of Me, Inc. can help us to respond in truthful ways—"Well, I *really* love your cookies. Thank you! As a matter of fact, I do think you're great, and what's more, I love you." We can help to preserve our children's impression that the good of cookie-making has something to do with learning, chemistry, aroma, flavor, crunch, and giving rather than with impressing and pleasing. But it's not necessary to be too quick to point out the problem with bragging and calling attention to one's self. At times that may be helpful, but it can also suggest to the child that nothing he does is good enough, or that there's something wrong with everything he does—in fact, with *him*. It can cause him to develop an overly harsh inner critic. Anyway, he's supposed to be developing his Me, Inc. Having a sense of one's self is a prerequisite to recognizing and relating to others. So it's far better for him to feel he's a good Me, Inc. than a bad one. And how is he supposed to understand that he and his worth are not the issue in everything he does when we are only just beginning to find out that this is also true for us? Where did he get the idea that there was a connection between his worth and his cookies in the first place? Hmm. How much longer would it take before I began to see that sometimes I only saw him as my expression of me? Take time to enjoy the truly scrumptious cookies and the emerging young cookie-maker. Don't waste a single crumb.

Love and Intelligence: At Odds

Our hearts are restless until we find our rest in thee.
—St. Augustine

With what fundamental reality are we one? When we feel separate, what is it we feel separate from? At the root of all our yearnings—to marry, to have children, careers, friends, possessions—we can recognize two primary urges: the desire for love (which is synonymous with goodness) and for understanding (which is synonymous with intelligence and order). In all our strivings to be whole, it is always love and intelligence we seek: to express, to be met by, to dwell in, to find at the heart of life and self. Wanting this for ourselves, we have children; having children, we want it for them. Over the years I've come to see that *our urge is God's surge,* that at the bottom of even our most inappropriate impulses and behaviors is the healthy surge of the Divine in us. In order for our urges to find healthy expression we must discover their connection to the divine surge, their fundamental, spiritual significance. Meanwhile life is a bit confused and confusing, but very worth sorting out.

The Desire

Parent and child alike seek love and intelligence. From the beginning we recognize these urges in our children, who, fed, bathed, and exhausted, nevertheless will not sleep unless genuine love is present, who even in taking apart everything they can get their hands on are looking for some knowable and reliable underlying order—security.

As women we not only want homes (love) but also careers (intelligence). As men we not only want careers but feel we are missing out if we are not sharing, caring, loving parents as well. We who stay with the children rightly want it understood that this is intelligent as well as loving "work." We who "go to work" are equally concerned with finding love as well as achievement.

As parents the quest for love and intelligence shows up in the demand for both love and authority. All childrearing theories emphasize that a balance of parental love and authority is the key to raising whole, happy children. On the side of "love" are freedom, permissiveness, gentleness, generosity, cooperation; on the "intelligent" side, discipline, structure, firmness, security, independence. We all agree that both are necessary. We all try—and nobody tries harder than parents—to express both. Yet we find no amount of effort and no theory sufficient to actually endow us with the love we need to be loving or the knowledge needed to approach our children with anything even faintly resembling authority.

The Experience

The child ran from one parent to the other. "May I go? May I do such and such?" she would ask. There was never a simple yes or no—always a negotiation. "It's up to your mother," her father said. "It's up to your father," her mother would say. "He says it's up to you," said the child to her mother. "She says it's up to you," she said to her father. She quickly learned to wheel and deal. "It's all right with her if it's all right with you. It's all right with him if it's all right with you. So, please?" Each parent wanted to be both nice and right, both loving and intelligent. Neither wanted to be blamed. So finally an answer that was no answer came. "Well (sigh), dear (sigh), you do what you like; but you know what we think." So the "choice," such as it was, ultimately fell upon the child, and it was always a choice between guilt and resentment. "Why *are* you pouting?" they'd ask. "We said you could choose." The parents wondered why she seemed unhappy. No one wondered more than she. "What's wrong with me?" she puzzled.

So often what's loving and what's intelligent seem to conflict. To be "nice" turns out to be not nice; to be "right" turns out to be wrong. We want to be nice *and* smart, taken care of *and* respected. Where love is called for, we are short-tempered or apathetic; where authority is required, we feel uncertain. Strangely, our "love" is met with rejection, indifference, ingratitude, resentment. Strangely, our careful, "intelligent" plans are beset with chaos and rebellion.

Yet we are fundamentally unable to abandon our conviction that both love and intelligence are necessary and possible. Something in us recognizes that both are vital, essential, part of our very nature. We know we are not mistaken in our restless seeking for both love and intelligence.

The Meaning

It is the belief in Me, Inc. that divorces love from intelligence. It is only in conceiving of ourselves as separate that love and intelligence become separated from each other as well, divided into nice but dumb, shrewd but cold, masculine/feminine, work/pleasure, weak/strong, and in parenthood, strict/permissive, gentle/firm, loving but wishy-washy. Me, Inc. *on its own* can only conceive of love and intelligence as something to be done and had, to, from, for, by, and against others. In each of us, Me, Inc. necessarily functions *on its own behalf,* perverting love into exploitation, corrupting intelligence into a battle for power.

> To celebrate their wedding anniversary one couple traditionally shared a private, elegant dinner at home. One year to free the wife from cooking they agreed to go out for dinner. The wife made reservations at their favorite restaurant. But to surprise her, the husband secretly arranged for a catered dinner at home and canceled the reservations. They were both surprised. The dinner was perfect but the evening was not. She was disappointed by his surprise; he was surprised by her disappointment. The next year again they planned to go out, and the husband made reservations. But this year the wife secretly prepared her husband's favorite dinner at home and canceled the reservations. Again, for both, surprise and disappointment. Each was outgiving the other. They were taking giving from each other.

In trying to express ourselves as both loving and intelligent persons, we often prevent genuine love and intelligence from finding expression. There is self-expression and Self expression, expression of Me, Inc. and expression of the underlying One. Whenever we are unhappy together we can expect to find Me, Inc. in the act of promoting its self at the expense of others' selves, often under the guise of love. Whenever harmony occurs, we can be sure that the emphasis on Me, Inc. has been lost in the discovery of our oneness with the underlying whole.

> *He who loseth his life for my sake, shall find it.*
> —Matthew 10:39

> *Before Abraham was, I am.*
> —John 8:58

Love and Intelligence: At One

> It was one of those days. I had something important to get done. Yet from the time the children came home from school until 9:30 P.M.

there arose one conflicting demand after another. The music practice that needed supervision, the bike with a flat that had to be retrieved, the uniform that had to be purchased and the badge that needed to be sewn on it before the meeting, the dinner that had to be eaten early to get to the meeting on time, the second sitting that resulted thereby, the ungrateful complaints because everything was so rushed and chaotic. By bedtime mother/saint was rapidly turning into witch/martyr. Over and over I muttered to myself: *"Why do I always have to be the one . . . ?"* At 9:30 when I went to tuck my son in bed and saw his laundry on the floor, I did a number. It began with tsks, sighs, and humphs, and ended with a speech full of phrases like *after all I had done, how could he,* and *the least he could do . . .* I concluded irrelevantly by asking just what it was he thought I was for anyway. As if that was anything he was ever meant to consider.

He stood before me with tears of outrage. "Can I say something?" he said, spluttering.

"Of course," I answered, already sorry.

"I know I should have put my clothes away," he said, "but the way you said that was so . . . so . . . *self-saying!"*

Self-saying! He had hit the nail on the head. All evening all that I had set about to do was really *self-saying*—to express me as a personally competent, intelligent, good, loving, wise, hardworking, successful, creditable, admirable, appreciable, complete self. Ta da! It all came together—and fell apart—in my absurd little speech. The coincidence of mistaken idea and bad experience was unmistakable. Also clear was its perversity. As I wished to show myself to be good, nice, loving, here was an exposé of the hidden self-seeking nature of that love and how it inevitably yielded only anger and hurt. As I sought to appear intelligent and wise, here was an exposé of the actual stupidity of my "wisdom." What I had done and how I felt and what I wanted were no true basis for the picking up of dirty clothes. On the contrary, the more I made myself the issue in picking up the laundry, the more it would be suicide for my son to comply. So my self-righteous demand for order was in effect producing chaos. Was that stupid? Or what? Then what was the real issue in the tidy disposal of dirty laundry? Now there was a good question. Order, peace, freedom, purity—I could feel my Me, Inc. self subside as the value of these spiritual qualities washed over me. Did I really wish to become loving and wise? Did I really wish for love and wisdom to be expressed as goodness and order in our home? Then these qualities, not others' thoughts about me, were what I would have to value above all. Only then would they be allowed to take shape in our lives.

Once more I saw that there was much to be understood. But I was filled with gratitude that one way and another what I needed to see *was being made clear.* The speed with which the atmosphere changed amazed me. My son and I were laughing now. Relief and love filled us. How loved I felt knowing that the truth I couldn't grasp refused to desert me. How relieved I was to think that it would never abandon my child either. How beautiful was the way we were being brought along together. Who or what had inspired him with the insight about my self-saying day? Wouldn't that same source of inspiration (which was teaching me through him) also teach him about his own self-saying whenever he was ready? Wasn't there, somewhere in the background, a wise and loving Parent of us both?

Before we marry and have children we may never have asked the question, *What is love?* We continue to operate on Me, Inc.'s misassumptions until our experiences as spouse and parent bring us up short and expose the fact that our idea of love is exploitative. Love is not a sentiment or a feeling. It is not something we have to give or can get from each other. It is not a fair trade. Love is a mode of perceiving, a way of seeing. Ultimately it is *the* way of seeing. Anything less than love is not knowledge; it is opinion or belief, and it is always mistaken. Love is the accurate perception of the nature of being and our oneness with it. Love is intelligence. Intelligence is love.

As impossible as it is for separate selves to be loving to each other, it is impossible for love not to take place whenever we recognize our oneness with our fundamental source and force of being, which is itself love-intelligence and to which the name God is given.

> *In the beginning was the Word, and the Word was with God and the Word was God . . . and the Word became flesh and dwelt among us . . . full of grace and truth.*
>
> —John 1:1, 14

> *Love-intelligence is the basic attribute of God, the most fundamental aspect of divine reality. It becomes manifest every time we let it.*
>
> —Thomas Hora, *Existential Metapsychiatry*

Water is the truth about a wave. Everything else—its shape and size, its place in space, its duration in time, its force and speed—have nothing to do with the lasting truth of its being. In its wetness it is one with all water. Dryness or firmness is the truth about land. Similarly in its solidity, an island, which appears to be floating, is one with all land.

Superficially each wave is separate and largely surrounded by air. But the underlying truth is that each is entirely supported by the water from which it came, of which it is made.

As water is to wave, as land is to island, so awareness is to us. The capacity to be aware is the truth about us. It is our definitive characteristic: to be increasingly aware, conscious. In consciousness we are one with all consciousness. Consciousness is seeing; it is the awareness of whatever truly is. Because the substance of truth is idea and the substance of an idea is spirit, all true consciousness is spiritual consciousness.

> *He is before all things, and by Him all things consist.*
>
> —Colossians 1:17

As ideas, *baby, child, teenager* are all limited, just as *wave* is a limited representation of the idea of water. They all imply incompleteness, weakness, dependency, unconsciousness. But the truth of the child's being is whole. Essentially he cannot be half-true any more than a wave can be half-water. Therefore perfect consciousness is the truth of the child's being. Everything else, anything less, no matter how convincing it seems at the moment, is transitory and untrue. Whatever passes away is insubstantial. True substance is that which can be substantiated. True love is substantiating. Love takes place as we distinguish between the substantial and the insubstantial, the true and the untrue, allowing the untrue to fall away into nothingness.

The Waking of the Seeing Being

> *There is a Hindu myth about the Self or God of the universe who sees life as a form of play. But since the Self is what there is and all there is and thus has no one separate to play with, he plays the cosmic game of hide-and-seek with himself. He takes on roles and masks of individual people such as you and I and thus becomes involved in exciting and terrifying adventures, all the time forgetting who he really is. Eventually, however, the Self awakens from his many dreams and fantasies and remembers his true identity, the one and eternal Self of the cosmos who is never born and never dies.*
>
> —R. H. Blyth, in *Games Zen Masters Play*, selected
> and edited by Robert Sohl and Audrey Carr

To grow from babyhood to maturity is not a matter of changing from baby to adult, but a coming to light and to life of what is already so. It is not a matter of the baby becoming what she wasn't or isn't, but rather of becoming what she is: a conscious consciousness, a Seeing Being.

Truth is what *is*. *Is* is now. *Is* is always now. *Was* isn't. *Will be* isn't. Only truth always *is*. Anything that passes away is not truth. Only that which always *is* is truth. The helplessness and limitation that define a baby as a baby will pass away. The only quality of the new baby that will grow is consciousness. All of the foibles that define us as persons will pass away; the only quality that will remain is consciousness. None of us is or ever really was Me, Incorporated; we *are* Seeing Beings.

This is no less true for us as parents than for our children. As we repeatedly encounter the fact that we are not perfect parents, we feel discouraged. Again and again we have to face the fact that we cannot by any personal, willful effort be perfect parents and raise perfect children. We may try to settle for less. Give up. Compromise. Be "realistic." But the choice is not between being perfect or imperfect parents. The choice in parenthood, as in everything else, is between acting for our selves and being here for the sake of spiritual realization; for seeing what is.

So learning, awakening, "coming to" rather than accomplishing is the issue in parenthood. Whether we understand this before our children are born is not so important. Whenever it dawns it liberates us. Thus the moment of our greatest shame or despair may be the turning point where the love we could not do and the wisdom we could not acquire begin to take over.

To bring forth love, which is idea(l), depends on awakening, which is not a doing or a having but a dawning. Love is not done. Wisdom is not had. But the more we understand what being is, the more fully we become its expression. True seeing is loving. God translates itself through our seeing into being.

The Clown and the Light

The clown notices the spot of light upon the stage floor. He deems it desirable. He is right. The light is good and it is necessary to his life and happiness. He should, *must* have it. But here his understanding fails him, for he does not understand what he sees. The light spot seems pretty, warm, shapely maybe, a thing he wants. Or maybe he wants it to shine on him. He tries to scoop it up—perhaps to stuff in his pocket or hold for a hand-warmer, or make himself more noticeable. So he crashes around on the stage with pan and broom, trying to sweep it up, falling all over the place, hurting himself, acting a perfect fool. But in the end, perhaps after falling off the stage and through a drum in the orchestra pit, he despairs. In our story, he drops his hands to his side and looks up sadly only to find the light streaming into his face. He looks around—light is everywhere. He sees and is guided by it, so that now he can move around freely, safely, gracefully. What has happened here? The clown and the light are one. They were always one. The light illumines; the clown sees. The illumining and the seeing are one. The spot of light on the ground was not the light, but it did signify the light. The clown, by seeing, also signifies the light. What he was trying to get was all the time what he was: a Seeing Being.

Son, thou art ever with me, all that I have is thine.
—Luke 15:31

Parenthood is just about the world's most intensive course in love. We are not parents merely to give or get love but to discover love as the fundamental fact of life and the truth of our being and thus bring it into expression. Parents and children—children all—we embark on this journey together. It is a far different journey from what we may have thought—through the twilight zone of the myth of Me, Inc. to the realization of the Seeing Being. Even though we still struggle, it helps to know this. Like one who wakes having turned around beneath the covers, we grapple ignorantly in the darkness beneath a blanket of ignorance—sometimes frustrated and angry, often afraid—while all the time the perfect light of day is streaming through the window. Suddenly, stretching, blinking, in moments we find ourselves in the light aware of only the good in ourselves, in each other, and all around us. In love.

The path of the righteous is as the light of dawn
that shineth ever brighter unto a perfect day.
—Proverbs 4:18

In his later years, when India had become electric with his message and kings themselves were bowing before him, people came to him even as they were to come to Jesus asking what he was. How many people have provoked this question: not "Who are you?" with respect to name, origin, or ancestry, but "What are you?—what order of being do you belong to, what species do you represent?" Not Caesar, certainly. Not Napoleon, nor even Socrates. Only two, Jesus and Buddha. When the people carried their puzzlement to the Buddha himself, the answer he gave provided a handle for his entire message.

"Are you a god?" they asked. "No." "An angel?" "No." "A saint?" "No." "Then what are you?"

Buddha answered, "I am awake." His answer became his title, for this is what Buddha means. In the Sanskrit root budh *denotes both to wake up and to know. Buddha, then, means the "Enlightened One" or the "Awakened One." While the rest of the world was wrapped in the womb of sleep, dreaming a dream known as the waking life of mortal men, one man roused himself. Buddhism begins with a man who shook off the daze, the doze, the dreamlike inchoateness of ordinary awareness. It begins with a man who woke up.*

—Huston Smith, *The Religions of Man*

Hui-Neng said, "If you come for the faith, stop all thy hankerings. Think not of good, think not of evil, but see what at this moment thy own original face doth look like, which thou hast even prior to thy own birth."

—D. T. Suzuki, *Zen Buddhism*

Buddha said, "Be a lamp to your self, be like an island. Struggle hard, be wise. Cleansed of weakness, you will find freedom from birth and old age."

—*The Dhammapada*, trans. by P. Lal

Jesus said, "You must be born again."

—John 3:7

2

Spirit

Meister Eckhart said, "The seed of God is in us. Given an intelligent and hard-working farmer and a diligent field hand, it will thrive and grow up to God, whose seed it is; and accordingly its fruits will be God-nature. Pear seeds grow into pear trees, nut seeds into nut trees, and God seed into God."

—*Meister Eckhart*, trans. by R. B. Blakney

In the beginning was the Word.

—John 1:1

Getting the Idea

Parenthood is surely among the most beautiful of all phases of human existence. But it is good to examine what we are looking forward to when a baby is on the way. It is easy to imagine ourselves charmed by the cooing infant or the earnest child bursting with sweet questions, and certainly that is all part of the wonderful way it is. But how many times do you picture yourself vaulting the table and saying evenly, "Oh no, darling, you'll have to drink your milk before you can get the macaroni out of the bottom of the glass." My list of things I never imagined saying when I pictured myself as a parent has grown over the years. "Please, don't put any more pennies in the pizza dough." "Please do stop licking the sofa." Or, in a busy parking lot, "Please *don't* untie my wraparound skirt while I am tying your shoes." At how many ten-minute intervals in how many nocturnal hours will you rise cheerfully when your not-quite-housebroken toddler crawls into bed with you, pulls off his diaper, and announces brightly, "I have to pee"?

A sense of humor helps, but there is only one way to look forward to all this with realistically happy anticipation, and that is to have a pretty clear idea of what's in it for us.

Spiritual awakening is the point. It is the driving force, heart's desire, and lifelong task of both parent and child. It is the purpose of our being together, and the only workable way. To say that parenthood, childhood, or human lifetime is a spiritual journey does not mean that it is otherworldly. Truth is either supremely practical or it isn't truth. In fact, the practical, the incarnate, is where the true is realized and gains specific expression. Only as we see how truth applies to, or is revealed in, our most mundane experiences can any realization be said to have taken place. Occasionally we start with a truthful principle and then see it expressed in ordinary experience. Usually it is problematic experience that drives us toward truth.

Suddenly we have a baby who poops and cries, and we are trying to calm, clean up, and pin things together all at once. As fast as we learn to cope, the frontiers change. Now perhaps we have a teenager we can't reach. But even when we are no longer new or expectant parents, conception is a good place to begin. Even when our children are older, we still remember the marvel of conceiving and bearing a child. What a big e ent it was, is. But who did we think we were? Who, what, do we think we are? What is conceived at the time of conception?

Conception

Mostly it is said that we *get* pregnant, *give* birth, and *have* or even *make* babies. But if getting, giving, and having are all we understand of this process, both we and our children will be miserable. Having children doesn't make us parents. It just makes us busy. It takes becoming fatherly, motherly, parently to make us parents. Conception begins when we first conceive of the idea of becoming parents. Now we are responsible for learning what being parental means and redefining ourselves accordingly. We can use *at least* nine months! A good question to start with is: What's so great about a baby coming? What's so great about becoming a parent? Many of us have children before considering these things. But it's better to give the idea a little thought as soon as it occurs to us, as soon as we conceive.

Parenthood Is for the Parent

Even during the early so-dependent years, our children's dependency on us is fairly superficial. We say the child in the womb is completely dependent on his mother, but he is not depending on her to mother him—she is merely the environment within which he is taking place. As long as this environment is adequate, his progress toward birth goes on, regardless of whether the mother knows much about motherhood or children. She isn't doing the child: she's housing it.

After birth, the essential situation is only slightly different, though our experience is vastly different. Childhood, too, is a temporary condition to be outgrown, and it is given to our children themselves to hunger and thirst after whatever they need to help them do this. As parents, we are still mainly their environment—though now a more obviously mental and spiritual one than a physical one—and the caretakers of this environment.

In short, we do not mold, make, raise, or bring up our children at all. We can help or hinder, but our basic responsibility is mostly custodial.

So who needs whom? Of course the child needs the parent, and we are well aware of the damaging effects of ignorant, irresponsible, or overzealous parenting. A less obvious yet existentially critical fact is that we need our children. Some develop motherly and fatherly qualities without children, but many of us need our children to awaken us to these qualities. Motherliness and fatherliness are qualities necessary to our fulfillment and of more lasting value than most childhood lessons. We develop them for the sake of our children, but they benefit us most of all. The gain is not the having of children but the discovery of love and how to be loving.

> *Each man to himself, and each woman to herself, such is the word of the past and present, and the word of immortality;*
> *No one can acquire for another—not one!*
> *No one can grow for another—not one!*
>
> *The song is to the singer, and comes back most to him;*
> *The teaching is to the teacher, and comes back most to him;*
> *The murder is to the murderer, and comes back most to him;*
> *The theft is to the thief, and comes back most to him;*
> *The love is to the lover, and comes back most to him;*
> *The gift is to the giver, and comes back most to him—it cannot fail;*
> *The oration is to the orator, the acting is to the actor and actress, not to the audience;*
> *And no man understands any greatness or goodness but his own, or the indication of his own.*

—Walt Whitman, "A Song of the Rolling Earth
(A Carol of Words)"

> *If Tao (the Way) could be made a present, everybody would have presented it to his parents. If Tao could be told about, everybody would have spoken to his brothers about it. If Tao could be inherited, everybody would have bequeathed it to his children and grandchildren. But no one could do it.*

Pregnancy

If it is primarily the idea of parenthood that is conceived at the time of conception, then pregnancy is not merely the time when a child develops in the mother's womb. Even more it is a time for the concept of parenthood to develop in the parents' consciousness. So mother and father are both pregnant—with seeds of parenthood. It is well to make use of the nine months of pregnancy to prepare not only for the child but also for parenthood. Even if we do not have children, once we have conceived of the idea of being loving, parently, we are pregnant; and we remain pregnant until realization has taken place. In this sense we continue to conceive and remain pregnant long after our children are born.

When we are pregnant there are necessary preparations to be made, techniques to learn, information to be gathered. But it is not enough to prepare only for delivery, and to think only of things to get and do for the child. We need to look deeper for the underlying issues in the lives of both parent and child.

The Necessary and the Essential

There is so much to think about, so much to buy, so much to read, so many books on childbirth and childrearing. It's easy to go overboard and drown in confusion. How can we tell what's important and what isn't? It helps to make a distinction between necessities and essentials.

Esse means to be. We are *essentially* Seeing Beings. Therefore our harmonious being—every aspect of it, even the most mundane—follows from our coming to see what is. If we are approaching life as Seeing Beings, then no matter what confronts us, we approach it not from the standpoint of good and bad, right or wrong, even of how or how not to, but *what is* and *what isn't*. For such discernment it is useful to discriminate between *the necessary* and *the essential*.

Considering the deeper essential issues of being puts things in perspective and orients us toward what is really necessary and has to do with the essence of our real being. Simultaneously it enables us to deal with the temporary but time-consuming trivia of parenthood with maximum intelligence and less fuss. For example, the Seeing Being has a lasting essential need for peace, while a protective sleeping place is only a temporary necessity. Understanding this distinction enables us to select a simple, safe, affordable crib for the time being. Awareness that the Seeing Being has a lasting essential need for love but only a temporary need for constant attention enables us to give up a little sleep and social life in favor of a little more baby time. It also enables us to release our children to an ever wider circle of love without feeling that we are abandoning them or they are abandoning us. The idea(l), the essential, the true, is eternal and spiritual. So while doing whatever is momentarily required, it is helpful to keep sight of that which is of lasting significance. This makes momentary difficulties more clearly momentary, and saves us from overblowing small things and going off on tangents and wild goose chases. Your parents are coming for the first time since the baby was born, and you want everything to be perfect. But your fussy baby won't give you a moment to prepare the special meal you planned, and you are feeling frantic. Understanding the difference between the essential and the necessary, you recognize that showing off your culinary, social, and maternal skills at once is not the point. Your parents are happy to stay with the baby while you run out for a pizza. By the time you return she has smiled her very first smile at your father and fallen asleep in your mother's arms. "Shh," they say, beaming. "Don't wake the baby." Keeping sight of the essential, spiritual significance of whatever is before us keeps us on course toward the fullest realization of our essential spiritual being—ours and our children's.

When our diapering days are over, the diapers, which seem almost to take command of our lives for a time, become too trivial to speak of. But for parents there is something essential taking place in our involvement with the trivial. The necessary and the essential touch. As we lay our pleasures and customary life aside to get up at night for our babies, we are repeatedly pushed toward the discovery of what is essential—and what isn't. We move back and forth from the necessary to the essential, from the Word to the Word made flesh, from seeing to being, from the basic idea to its "practical" expression. Diapers, pins, maternity clothes, cribs—for new parents these are a starting point. For parents of older children, or any of us whether parents or not—the basic principles remain the same. There will always be necessities, and they will always be points where the essential is to be discerned and expressed.

Getting Ready

While trying on maternity clothes or while bending down to tie your round wife's unreachable shoes, consider what parenthood is.

What in essence is a parent? Not how should it be done or how will it feel, but *what is it?* Not what is happening to one's body or sex life, but *what does it mean?* What is going on in the long run? Is this a career change, and from now on you will be a gynecologist or an obstetrician or a neonatologist or a child psychologist or a pediatrician? Oh, a parent! Well, what is that? One who fosters the growth of the child? Okay. Then what essentially is a child?

When she has outgrown being a fetus, she becomes a child, and you will be busier than you can imagine with her bare necessities, but all the time she will be outgrowing childhood. What will she be then? What is it about the child from the very beginning that becomes increasingly evident rather than less so all her life? You experience this essence as vitality when she kicks inside your belly, pressing against limits. When she is born she will look at you, and you will see this essence peering out at you. Where did it come from? What is it? How are you to care for and nurture that Seeing Being?

> *Unto us a child is born*
> *Unto us a son is given*
> *Not out of us*
> > *by us*
> > *from us.*
>
> *Not we are going to make*
> > *we are going to have*
> > *we are going to get or produce*
>
> *But unto us a child*
> > *is born*

The discerning shopper. While buying things for the forthcoming baby, waiting for service—even just while brushing your teeth—practice being parently to a child of God. Apart from hugging, cuddling, nursing, burping, diapering, *what is parentliness?* Behold the child, the good child, the God child, in everyone. Everyone is someone's good child—at least at the outset. The good parent keeps sight of that essential goodness and is always inviting it forth and paving its way. Learn to pay silent respect to the lovable child in everyone, *especially* when it is not at all apparent. Disassociate all seeming imperfection, foibles, bad traits from the essential reality of each individual—yourself included.

Forgive them, Lord, for they know not what they do.

—Luke 23:34

Buy a bathtub or figure out some bathing arrangement in which she can be washed as necessary and *become aware* of her oneness with love. Set up a diaper-changing station at which to change her dirty diapers a thousand times while a thousand times sighing or a thousand times marveling at and welcoming forth her essential purity, goodness, perfection, and *amazing consciousness.* Get a highchair where you will clean up a thousand spills while a thousand times fuming or a thousand times acknowledging that it is love and intelligence that feeds you both and does the work. Buy a baby seat to put him down in and from which he can *see* what's happening. Make, buy a few toys, a mobile, a music box, a soft light. All the better to taste, chew, touch, hear, *and see* with, my dear.

Set up a crib or other sleeping arrangement to put the baby's body in so he may get the sleep he needs. That's the necessity. But what is the essence of bedtime and sleep? Here at the crib you and your child will need to discover that life goes on even when you are apart. Here you both discover and meet your need for peace. Go on from here. This perspective will help you make a good choice regarding crib or bed, and to avoid bedtime struggles—or to live through them gratefully.

Closet Cleaning

The most important factors in the life of their children are not the school, the television set, the playmates, or the neighborhood, but what the parents cherish, what they hate and what they fear.

—Thomas Hora, *Existential Metapsychiatry*

Before the baby comes and you are too busy, get rid of all the old clothes in your closet—the ones you've been saving in case they might come back into style. Get rid of all the old junk in the basement and garage—the things you were going to fix up but have replaced with something better. Do the same with worthless old-fashioned or fashionable ideas. At least drag them out and try them on. One woman told me that for many years she had two wardrobes, the clothes she liked and the ones her parents wanted her to wear—her "Peter Pan–collar wardrobe." What are my preconceptions? Whose mental preconceptions are they really? What are my mental pictures of my child and myself as a parent? What are my worries? Where did they come from? God? Society? My parents? Have they any essential truth and value? Or are they just troublesome assumptions?

Wishballs, Follies, and Wishing Prods

You may or may not throw out your old football when you clean your closet. It makes no difference. But watch for wishful fantasies. Notice how these productions feature yourself: Metrogoldwyn Me, Inc. the madonna, Metrogoldwyn Me, Inc. the good old dad. Metrogoldwyn's modern ecologically minded liberated unisexual family. What if your daughter isn't interested in playing with dolls? Worse still, what if she is? What if your son wants a doll? What if he doesn't? During pregnancy a football is neither necessary nor essential. So when your wife says, "We're pregnant," if your first urge is to run out and buy a football, *question that.* The idea that you and your (if it is a) son or (if it isn't) daughter will be companions is fine. But the thought that this must take shape as football is something to kick out of your mental closet.

> *Because we think that we "know best" many parents not only dictate the way our children's message is to be delivered, but even the message itself. All of which leads to confusion, discouragement and finally to failure.*
>
> *Because he thinks he "knows best" many a parent not only dictates the way his child's message is to be delivered, but even the message itself. All of which leads to confusion, discouragement and finally to failure. Instead, the parent should ever encourage the child's individuality, patiently removing every obstacle in its way, remembering that each one's message comes from God—is divine; and that the child's true self, like our own, is from eternity—two rays of divine light of exactly the same value, but pointing in different directions.*
>
> —Nora Holm, *The Runner's Bible*

Things That Go Bump in the Day

Fears are thoughts about what shouldn't be. We fear for our children. We don't want anything unpleasant to happen to them. But, we say, we need to be "realistic." Some unacceptable, dread fears seem too awful to think about, but there are others that we consider more or less acceptable. Acceptable fears are small ones that seem inevitable. We expect "our share" of these to come true, and so we prepare for them with ointment, vitamins, and a healthy attitude, confident that we can deal with them as they come—preventing some, coping with others.

The list of acceptable fears includes colic, diaper rash, cradle cap, teething, reactions to injections, the need to suck, getting buckteeth from sucking, spoiling, food allergies, attachment to bottle or breast or security blanket, terrible twos, and sibling rivalry. Most we accepted so long ago that we do not even question them or recognize them as beliefs. We call them "facts of life." Moreover, we are constantly being bombarded with fresh suggestions and endless embellishments on the old. An advertisement for a skin preparation begins, "When your baby gets a diaper rash . . . " *When,* it says. Not *if,* but *when!*

So these are fears made acceptable. There are so many that we could just get eaten up by fear. They cannot simply be ignored, avoided, denied, or thrown out of our mental closets. But we can question them. Nobody escapes all these problems, but hardly anybody is afflicted with them all either. And there's nothing on the list that everyone experiences. Evidently, while some discomforts are usual, none is an absolute necessity. So then it must be possible for babies to grow up without suffering many discomforts that we have always taken for granted. How about that?

Fears are thoughts about what should not happen in the future. As such, like wishes, they are fantasies. They haven't happened yet, so in a way they aren't real. Yet we are preoccupied with them. During pregnancy we need to examine our preoccupations. At least we can haul them out of the recesses of our mental closet and look them over, asking some of the same questions that we ask of our old clothes. Are they becoming? Do they befit us? On closer inspection, will they hold up or are they falling apart and ready to be shed? If they are falling apart or unbecoming and we still treasure them, what is it that we are really valuing? Does Me, Inc. have some vested interest in these ideas? Are they costumes for Metrogoldwyn Me—the hero? the martyr?

Dwelling Place for a Seeing Being

In his ship Scuppers had a little room. In his room Scuppers had a hook for his hat and a hook for his rope and a hook for his spyglass and a place for his shoes and a bunk for his bed to put himself in.

At night Scuppers threw the anchor into the sea and he went down to his little room.

He put his hat on the hook for his hat, and his rope on the hook for his rope, and his spyglass on the hook for his spyglass, and he put his shoes under the bed, and got into his bed, which was a bunk, and went to sleep.

—Margaret Wise Brown, *The Sailor Dog*

As long as we are pregnant, our children live within our physical bodies. We are never more intimately connected than at this time, yet scarcely ever again will we have so little knowledge of each other. At the birth of our child, suddenly and at long last, we will face each other, an overwhelming experience that defies description. Fathers are likely to be almost more overcome by this than mothers, as the child "becomes a reality" for the first time.

Yet no matter how dramatic the experience of childbearing seems, from the child's side perhaps the move from womb to room is not as tremendous as we are inclined to think. The child remains what she has always been, a perfect, unique idea—spiritually whole, unending, unbeginning. On a material plane, where she is an immature being seeking maturity or the realization of this ideal selfhood, the move from womb to lap is not so huge either.

Keizan said: "Birth cannot alter the mind, embodiment cannot transmute Original Nature. Though the essential and the physical bodies have changed, mind is as it has always been."

—*Zen Poems, Prayers, Sermons, Anecdotes, Interviews,* trans.
and ed. by Stryk and Ikemoto

In the womb or out, young children live almost entirely within the limits of their parents' consciousness. The very young child is subject mainly to *experiences* and *encounters* (see page 109) that are largely governed by the ignorant or enlightened consciousness of his parents. He lives as much in us after he is born as he did while still in the womb. We are his environment as long as he is a child.

Therefore, as we prepare a room or corner for the coming baby, it is well to seek the highest possible awareness of the idea(l) individual and its idea(l) dwelling place, and then to consider how the qualities of this idea(l) dwelling place might be translated into terms the child can appreciate. What ideal qualities do we wish him to encounter, to be surrounded by? What will best serve him on his path toward realizing his ideal selfhood? Disregarding the newborn's apparent weakness and limitation, and considering only his ideal, spiritual selfhood, his potential, it is clear that the proper environment includes peace, beauty, order, simplicity, joy, and love.

Without this perspective it is easy to get the impression that a baby is something to be taught and entertained through constant sensory bombardment—the more the better—and to give too little thought to what message is being brought to the child through his senses. A little exposure to advertising or a stroll through a few stores can lead to tremendous expenditures of time, money, and effort in decorating our children's rooms in a way that quickly proves inefficient, unsafe, inconvenient, monotonous, unpleasant, and impossible to keep orderly. Covered with cute, busy things, the walls crowd in; the floors are dangerously cluttered with toys and toy parts; the bed is a sort of padded cell, littered with things that he only pitches over the side. His bedroom, where he needs to find peace, becomes a restless place where nobody likes to be.

By keeping his essential, spiritual nature and needs in mind, we find guidance for preparing a room where he can be truly at home. If we cultivate an awareness of peace, beauty, order, and love, these qualities will be reflected in the decoration, furniture, and arrangement of the child's nook or room. The idea is to *address everything in the room to the ideal child, not only to the material one,* to keep in mind the spiritual or essential issue behind each aspect of the room and its furnishings:

• *Floor:* security, ground of being, freedom. Make sure it remains unhazardous, uncluttered, spacious in appearance.

• *Walls:* security, protection, privacy, but again also freedom. Do not let them become confining, oppressive, or overly cluttered.

• *Light fixtures, windows, curtains:* light, illumination, seeing, understanding. Choose things that help him to see beyond his room, not only things that merely catch his eyes and capture his attention. There are so many cute things available that it is easy to wind up with an overly busy and confining room in which the view from the window is almost the last thing the child will discover.

- *Toys:* fulfillment, unfolding consciousness. As with lights and windows, it is the function of toys to lead children beyond themselves, not merely to entertain.
- *Bed:* peace, stillness, letting go. It is not a cage or a playpen or a learning or achievement center.
- *Arrangement:* simplicity, order, efficiency, unity.
- *Decor:* beauty—again, toward seeing beyond.

Such a room will be joyful, not merely exciting (and therefore not soon boring). It will be cheerful and lovely, but not overly stimulating or startling. It will emphasize becoming rather than having, seeing rather than sights, understanding rather than doing. And love—how does a room reflect love? That cannot be pinpointed. It is the overall result of a consciousness of true goodness—the goodness of the child and the goodness of life as they are met in us, the parents, tonight.

Of course, the child is not brought peace or love or security or beauty or vision by the room at all. It is in our consciousness where he encounters these realities. Much stronger than the messages that come through his senses is his immediate spiritual encounter with whatever is governing our consciousness. Just as what the nursing mother eats determines the quality of what her infant receives from her breast, so the quality of what lies in our hearts determines what our children encounter. Preparing the room itself is not so important, except as a spiritual exercise for the parent. Our children can go anywhere, sleep on anything, do with nothing, and still be happy and grow beautifully if their earthly dwelling place, the mind of the parent, is love-filled.

Additional Reflection—Uses of Children's Bedrooms

Keen appreciation of these issues not only helps us to design and furnish our child's bedrooms but also guides us to use them as:

- *A place of solitude.* The bedroom is where a child first learns to be alone, and develops her capacity to dream and imagine. Here is where she can best discover a source of inspiration, solace, and creativity beyond herself and her parents, and begin to learn to receive and trust it. Here she can learn that she herself is good company, a discovery that will protect her from one of the most insidious social values of our time and one of the most poisonous infections most parents pass on: the belief that one's value depends on others' admiration and acceptance.

• *A place of refuge and reorientation.* When your child is older and getting out of hand, and it occurs to you to send her to her room, let that be understood not as a punishment or a banishment but as a time for healing and for feeling better or for finding "a better idea." Let her choose books or toys to occupy her attention. Pioneering pediatrician and psychoanalyst D. W. Winnicott observed a stage in young children's development when they need to learn to "be alone in the presence of the mother." If your child seems to feel abandoned, offer to stay with her—but quietly, as a presence standing by until she is sure of your love and at home in herself.

If you send her to her room, also send yourself to yours. Before seizing the chance to get things done unimpeded by your child, take a minute to prayerfully open yourself to the Beyond Personal source and force of all doing, of all being, of love. Jesus said, "The son can do only what he seeth the father do—The father worketh, and I work—It is not I but the Father within me that doeth the work." Usually when things are getting out of hand it means that there is a power struggle going on. "Getting out of hand" means "not being under my control," which is a belief that being a parent means being controlling. If you are feeling you can't be or do or have what you need unless your child does exactly what you think she should, she will be feeling she can't do or have what she needs unless you do exactly what she thinks you should—even that she can't be unless she *doesn't* do what you think she should. So our shoulds hit the fan. Since it's our should in the first place, peace is likely to be restored only with the discovery that there is a higher power in charge, the Parent of both parent and child, that loves, guides, and provides for us both, and not at each other's expense.

• *A private domain.* When your child is older and chooses to be alone in her room, respect her privacy. As much as possible, do not enter without knocking and asking and receiving permission. When she is much older and her room is a mess, remember that it's her mess, and that before she can sort out her things she may need years to sort out her thoughts and feelings. You have a right to insist that she not leave her things in the living room, which is family space, but it is better not to keep making her feel that *she* is a mess because her room is a mess. She already thinks she's a mess, and needs to know you understand that sometimes life *is* sort of a mess, that you have confidence in her ability to sort hers out eventually, and that you are available *if* she wants to talk. If, once in a while, you decide to clean up her room for her, let it be as a loving gift, not an angry judgment.

A messy room was a big issue in my childhood and adolescence, and I have one particularly bad memory of that. I was going to my first dance and I was very anxious. I suppose I tried on everything in my closet, put nothing away, and left the many projects I was always in the middle of all over the floor. But I dressed, I went, I danced, I survived, and came home excited and exhausted. My parents were asleep, so I tiptoed to my room, only to find that someone had gathered up my entire mess and piled it on top of my bed. I felt hurt and lonely that night.

Name and Identification

As our baby's arrival draws closer we begin to think more and more about the baby per se. We need to buy clothes—but for a boy or a girl? At first they are just babies—boygirls and girlboys—anyway.

Don't worry about raising boys to be boys and girls to be girls, just whole, individual, unique children. The ideal man/woman is as gentle as a woman and as strong as a man. As a father you are called on to develop some of your feminine qualities. As a mother you will find this baby requiring of you some traditionally masculine ones. Differences between boys and girls can be acknowledged, but they do not need to be taught. To emphasize group or sex membership is less a means of identifying uniqueness than of stereotyping sameness. Positive and negative group identifications dull the child's sense of uniqueness and worth. Let's see how God will be, what shape God takes as this entirely individual child. Let's see.

When I was preparing for our second child's birth I sat down one day, propped open the Bible on my bushel belly, and opened to the passage that speaks of not hiding one's light under a bushel. It reminded me to think of the baby as a point of divine light, rather than a body. It reminded me to think of the birth as a revelation rather than an expulsion. For a boy, we had selected Andrew as a name because of its gentle sound. Finding this passage in the book of Luke, which itself means light, we now added Luke. Andrew (sturdy, steadfast, stout) Luke (light). The next day our whopping son was effortlessly brought to light. And indeed he has proven to be a sturdy, steadfast light.

Let your light so shine that men may see your good works and glorify your father which is in heaven.

—Matthew 5:16

As the birth draws near you will hear about pushing. Even when the time comes and you are pushing, meditate on the idea of letting. Letting to be born. Letting sleep. Letting be. Letting mature. Letting be revealed.

This little tiny light of mine,
I'm gonna let it shine.
This little tiny light of mine
I'm gonna let it shine.
Let it shine, let it shine, let it shine.

Hide it under a bushel? No!
I'm gonna let it shine.
Hide it under a bushel? No!
I'm gonna let it shine.
Let it shine, let it shine, let it shine.

—Negro spiritual

In him was life, and the life was the light of men. The light shines in the darkness, and the darkness has not overcome it. . . . The true light that enlightens every man was coming into the world. He was in the world, and the world was made through him, yet the world knew him not. He came to his own home, and his own people received him not. But to all who received him, who believed in his name, he gave power to become children of God; who were born, not of blood, nor of the will of the flesh, nor of the will of man, but of God.

—John 1:4–5, 9–13

Hearken to me all which are borne by me from the belly, which are carried from the womb; and even to your old age I am he; and even to hoar hairs will I carry you; I have made and I will bear; even I will carry and will deliver you.

—Isaiah 46:3–4

What is it that sires and conceives and delivers and is expressed in us? What is it that husbands and wives? What sisters and brothers and mothers and fathers us and our children? What is our essential nature? What are we here to realize?

Special Delivery: Parentbirth

Traditionally childbirth has been thought to be a more or less painful experience for the mother to endure with more or less grace depending on the degree to which she is fearful, brave, or lucky. With anesthetics came the possibility of doing away with the experience of pain altogether. For several decades nearly every woman in the United States who could afford it slept through the childbirth, waking only in time to be introduced to her baby by a doctor or nurse. Fathers were more or less uninvolved. The mother was pregnant; the mother would give birth.

Now the idea of staying awake and having both parents present throughout labor and delivery has gained favor, partly on the ground that it is better for the child, partly because of a growing desire not to miss the wonderful event. With this change in attitude numerous techniques have been developed for avoiding pain while staying awake, for dealing with pain, and for being a cooperative participant in the baby's delivery. For some, pain-accompanied tensions based on fear of the childbirth process are alleviated simply by being told what's going on or by having a helpful partner or close friend present. Breathing and relaxing skills help others pass more comfortably through labor and delivery.

Regardless of delivery techniques, there are (and always have been) some for whom the moments of childbirth pass harmoniously and with surprising ease, and many for whom they seem difficult and dreadful. It is generally believed that these differences can be explained by medical science. But no theory has turned up yet that applies consistently enough to be counted true. Many advocates of conscious childbirth techniques believe the answer lies in the parent's skill in executing them (both mentally and bodily). But results are spotty when it comes to the record of easy versus difficult births. Some of the best-prepared mothers have the worst labors; some of the least prepared breeze through with no complications.

Choosing to be alert and awake during the moments of child-birth is surely positive. It is certainly better to view birth as a healthy, happy event than as a sort of hazardous emergency sapping the strength of the mother just before the demands of motherhood are placed on her. But further changes in viewpoint cannot be ruled out as long as disharmony remains.

As Thou Sowest

The very act of observing disturbs the system.

—Werner Heisenberg

For whatsoever a man soweth, that shall he also reap.

—Galatians 6:7

Some say the greatest variable in scientific observation is the scientists' own preconceptions, and that these preconceptions are actually reflected in the phenomena being observed. If we believe the sun revolves around the earth, a bigger, more powerful telescope may only augment our experience of that belief. If phenomena themselves are influenced by the viewpoint of the beholder . . . !—then any technique employed by the mother during childbirth may only augment her experience of her unconscious beliefs. If the belief is erroneous, truer understanding can occur only after the belief is recognized and relinquished—or at least questioned.

It is at least clear that all experience includes a mental factor that is worth taking into account. To leave your house, you first head for the door. But suppose as you near the door you become more con-cerned with the door itself than with passing through it. (Oh, what a beautifully carved door!) Perhaps you fear that the door will not open or that you personally will not be able to open it. (Oh, what a huge, heavy door!) Depending on the degree and nature of your conviction, you may soon find yourself pausing to admire the carvings, frame, latch, knob, wood grain of the door, or struggling with the lock, trying to bash down the door, or calling for help. As long as you remain fas-cinated with the door, you cannot pass through the doorway. Thought precedes progress; if thought does not pass through the doorway, neither will you—not unless someone forcibly gets you through.

This situation is analogous to the experience of many parents and children at the time of birth. After a healthy pregnancy and happy anticipation of the birth, many mothers (prepared and unprepared) experience long, painful labors in which both they and their children seem stuck in the doorway.

Only through letting go of one idea does it become possible for another one to occur. The object is to realign one's thought with what really is. What then is the essential event of childbirth?

A common assumption is that childbirth is the bodily separation of the mother and child from each other. But perhaps on an idea(l) plane, the moment of childbirth is something else entirely. It is at least something more. The true event that from the side of the child is called childbirth is from the side of the parent, parentbirth. Perhaps, then, delivery is not a matter of expulsion but of revelation, since what is essentially happening for both ourselves and our babies is the further coming to light of what we already truly are. Perhaps it is as we reach for the idea of parenthoood that the child is finally released.

In a way the moments of birth are as significant in the lives of parent and child as passing through a doorway is in any journey outside. It is only a matter of moments, a mere transition, and yet during pregnancy the whole focus of many of us is on labor and delivery. We spend the days of pregnancy preparing for childbirth, when it is parenthood with which we will be largely concerned from the moment of delivery on.

Perhaps it is impossible for a child to be born to a woman who still thinks of herself as a pregnant woman, just as it is impossible to pass through a doorway while focusing exclusively on the door. And isn't it also a mistake to think of childbirth as something between mother and child, since it is also the father's parenthood that is brought to light in the moment of delivery?

Since the true event of childbirth takes place in consciousness, we need to concern ourselves during pregnancy not merely with childbirth or embryology but with heightening our consciousness of motherliness and fatherliness, seeking to become parently in thought and mode of being. Reliance on a childbirth method does not preclude understanding, but the basic issue during pregnancy remains preparation for parenthood.

During labor, too, we need to center on these qualities of parentliness and on the real nature of the event. Such attention keeps the event in perspective and prevents us from becoming disproportionately involved with the door instead of the vista before us. This also helps to free us from pain—both physiological and psychological, both during and after birth—and fosters an atmosphere of peace and gratitude in which to greet the child.

A child is being born! We are here to welcome her. She is bringing new love, light, wisdom, and purpose into our lives. We are witnessing vitality and intelligence and power for good at work. We are becoming parents! We are about to begin to learn to love and give as we have never been moved to love and give before.

Besides expediting the birth process, such an orientation is also beneficial for the arriving child. Whether or not the labor goes smoothly or with a little distress is of small consequence. For most the result will be fine regardless. But for the child it is clearly more important to be welcomed into the arms of a consciously parently individual than someone skillful at pushing or pulling babies out into the world. And the relative value of these two orientations is no greater for the newborn child than for the newborn parent.

Additional Reflection: Two Very Different Deliveries

I was blessed with two wonderfully smooth and happy pregnancies, but the two labors and deliveries were as different as night and day. With the first child I experienced fifty hours of back labor, which was as excruciating as it was unproductive, and which the doctor pooh-poohed as being not "real" labor and not really painful. When at last he injected a hormone to augment the process, he said, "And now you will see what real labor is like," implying that now I would experience "real pain." In reality, the induced labor was a tremendous relief. Now for the first time there was a space between the contractions, a pain-free moment or two—and in a short time the wonder of meeting and holding and looking into the eyes of my big beautiful eight-pound fifteen-ounce son took place, along with an unprecedented sense of truly wondrous love.

But in the first months that followed I suffered what I now suppose were postpartum blues. They centered not on my new life as a parent or on my son but on the difficult labor. Hadn't we taken child-birth classes? Hadn't I breathed, panted, and relaxed as I had been taught? Hadn't I learned that back labor was psychosomatic? Hadn't the doctor said it wasn't real labor or real pain? I felt hurt, angry, betrayed, and baffled. Was there nothing on which one could count? Was there nothing on which my son would be able to count? I searched for what I was to learn from the experience. One day in med-itation a favorite Bible passage came to mind: "Trust in the Lord with all thine heart, and lean not unto thine own understanding." Here at last I found something that helped. I realized that with all the empha-sis on childbirth technique, during the labor I had completely forgot-ten to pray or meditate. I had not trusted in the Lord with any of my heart. I had leaned utterly on my own understanding and skill.

Nearly two years later I was in labor again, trying to center myself, heart and soul and body, in God. Beside me, perhaps in an effort to distract me from pain, my husband and the obstetrician sat chatting. They were talking about radial tires, which was only distracting me from my meditation. I didn't want to hurt their feelings or be a prima donna, so I said nothing. But when they went out for coffee, I men-tioned to the midwife that I was trying to pray but that the chitchat was making it difficult. "Oh!" she said, and briefly disappeared. My hus-band and the doctor did not return until it was time for the birth, and I think she must have told them to stay out. Throughout the labor, whenever I opened my eyes, I found that midwife praying beside me and, though I had some back labor, it took less than five hours for my nearly eleven-pound baby to be born.

"It's a whopper!" said the doctor, dancing around with the baby.

"But what is it?" I asked.

"It's a whopper!" he shouted. "The biggest baby I've ever deliv-ered."

"But is it a boy or a girl?"

"A boy," he said at last, handing me my son.

The name of my midwife turned out to be Mrs. Eccles, which is also the abbreviation of Ecclesiastes. I don't know about you, but when-ever I think of Ecclesiastes, I think of "a time to be born." It doesn't matter whether back labor is real labor or not, or whether it is psy-chosomatic or the result of a tipped uterus. It does matter that sooner or later we are born and reborn not only as children and parents of each other but as conscious children of God. Being aware that this is what needs to happen is helpful in every situation.

> *Before she was in labor she gave birth; before her pain came upon her she was delivered of a son. Who has heard of such a thing? Who has seen such things? . . . Shall I bring to birth and not cause to bring forth? says the Lord; Shall I, who cause to bring forth, shut the womb? says your God.*
>
> —Isaiah 66:7–9

> *i am so glad and very*
> *merely my fourth will cure*
> *the laziest self of weary*
> *the hugest sea of shore*
>
> *so far your nearness reaches*
> *a lucky fifth of you*
> *turns people into eachs*
> *and cowards into grow*
>
> *our can'ts were born to happen*
> *our mosts have died in more*
> *our twentieth will open*
> *wide a wide open door*
>
> *we are so both and oneful*
> *night cannot be so sky*
> *sky cannot be so sunful*
> *i am through you so i*
>
> —e. e. cummings, *Poems: 1923–1954*

Additional Reflection: Since, in our time, there are many single parents and increasing numbers of gay parents, the fact that each of us has both masculine and feminine, fatherly and motherly potential needs to be emphasized. While it is desirable for every child to have a relationship with both her father and her mother, and while every effort needs to be made to make this possible, the child who can't may nevertheless have the benefits of both fatherly and motherly upbringing. All parental love and wisdom has a Beyond Personal source. It comes through us, not from us, and it can find its way through many others besides the actual birth parents. So if, for whatever reason, one parent or the other is absent, someone else, or several someones, may step forth to play an important role in our child's life. Most of all, we can and need to look to the Parent of parents to supply us, whether mothers or fathers, with both the motherliness and fatherliness that is needed.

Getting Used to and Sustaining the Idea

Eating and sleeping become suddenly heightened concerns in any home with a new baby. *Struggle* describes what goes on in most families. Eating and sleeping are both forms of nourishment, and the following pages are loosely concerned with these issues and their significance. Worthwhile questions to consider are: Who is being nourished? With what? By whom? What is the sustenance that truly sustains and nourishes this idea that has become our child, and this idea that we are? What nourishment helps us and our children to become more fully what we really are?

A Mountain Is a Mountain, and a Baby Is Not Quite What We Expected

> Ch'ing-yuan said: "Before I had studied Zen for thirty years, I saw mountains as mountains, and waters as waters. When I arrived at a more intimate knowledge, I came to the point where I saw that mountains are not mountains, and waters are not waters. But now that I have got its very substance I am at rest. For it's just that I see mountains once again as mountains, and waters once again as waters."
>
> —A. Watts, *The Way of Zen*

Almost everything we encounter has two meanings: its apparent meaning, which is what we first experience through the senses, and its deeper meaning, which we can come to understand in consciousnes. Discordant experience slowly forces us to awaken to the deeper meaning.

Materially we may experience rock as an obstacle—dangerous, harsh, slippery when wet—whereas, looking deeper, we find qualities of steadfastness, strength, reliability, security, protection, immutability.

The difference is in the viewpoint. With the material perspective also comes the dualistic: To Me, Inc., self and rock conflict. (Will the mountain conquer the climber? or the climber conquer the mountain?) Mastery, control, power, dominancy become issues.

But to the Seeing Being the same rock calls strength to mind and reminds us that we are safe, supported, upheld, secure, and can count on one infinite underlying reality. Which viewpoint is true? What produces conflict, injury, discouragement, or frustration must be false; what brings us peace, harmony, strength, or assurance must be true. We are not quick to learn, *first* hitting our heads against the wall, *then* wondering what hit us.

Now substitute the baby for the rock. At last, we hold her in our arms. So tiny, so cute, so weak and helpless! We can hardly wait to cuddle and feed and teach and care for her. All aglow, we take her home, and the crying starts and the sleepless nights begin. And she isn't cuddly, she's struggly! Instead of expressing beautiful parental love we seem to be engaged in some sort of Olympic contest in which she is winning the no-sleep event hands-down. Within a week we are so worried about the mess we are making of her life or so upset by the mess she is making of ours that we can only remember how cute she is when she is asleep.

But suppose we looked at her in a spiritual way. Suppose instead of tininess we saw life's vastness; instead of weakness, vitality; instead of helplessness, wholeness; instead of ignorance, intelligence and alertness. Suppose we could also recognize that these same qualities, which are the baby's true nature, are the fundamental truth about us and life as well.

When I was pregnant, I thought, "A baby is a baby and a mother is a mother." But when we came home I found a baby is not a baby and a mother is not a mother. Ever since I have been learning.

> *Twinkle, twinkle, little star,*
> *How I wonder what you are,*
> *Up above the world so high*
> *Like a diamond in the sky.*
> *Twinkle, twinkle, little star,*
> *How I wonder what you are.*
>
> —Traditional nursery rhyme

That is the question, isn't it? The supreme question for parents. *How I wonder what you are.* If we would be good parents—then parents of what? What are our children—these wonderful wonders? What are we? When we see what we are we shall be what we are. Lord, Lord, what on earth, what in heaven's name, do you have in mind?

> *O Lord, our Lord,*
> *how majestic is thy name in all the earth!*
> *Thou whose glory above the heavens is chanted*
> *by the mouth of babes and infants. . . .*
> *What is man that thou art mindful of him,*
> *and the son of man that thou dost care for him?*

> —Psalm 8:1–2, 4

> *It is not yet clear what we shall be; we only know that when He shall appear we shall be like Him for we shall see Him as He is.*

> —1 John 3:2–3

Like the rock, every child has two meanings. On the one hand, he is an image and likeness of his parents. As such he not only bears physical resemblance to them but will also evolve a mode of being that is the spitting image (and mainly a mirror image) of their mode of being. This is true for our children; it is also true for us. What is apparent (what seems real) to the parent and is thus the central issue around which the parent's life is conducted will also be the parent of the child's experience and way of being. Every child is thus a model child. To the parent then, the child becomes a teacher. Through his being as an image and likeness of the parent, the child explains (makes plain by bringing out into the open) the parental thought of which the parentchild is also an image and likeness.

Parenthood has two meanings. The weakness and helplessness of the child as an immature organism dependent for life, safety, sustenance, training, and education on a greater, stronger, more mature organism reflects an idea of parenthood that is an ego trip and a power play. To Me, Inc., haver and doer, the baby is only a smaller Me, Inc.— a possession and a project. This belief is constantly proving itself false in the parent/child experience through exhaustion, frustration, and discouragement. We lug, prod, stumble, and fumble over our children, which only and at last (if we have the least inclination to learn) proves to us that this is not what the child is and not what he is for; that this is not what we are and not what we are for; and that this is not what parenthood and childhood and family life are, and not what they are for.

At the same time that what isn't so is being made plain, we are also being shown and shoved toward what we really are and are for.

The truer meaning of the child is brought home two ways. Beautifully, quietly, amazingly (if we have eyes to see), right where there seems to be a little body produced by two big ones, we see *awareness* and *vitality* spontaneously taking place. We know right off the bat that the vitality (being) and awareness (seeing) are not something that we *did*. And we can only recognize and marvel.

Insofar as we do not recognize the child as a Seeing Being, the true spiritual nature of the child is bringing itself home to us in other, less pleasant ways: as problems and endless demands. When we have done everything *necessary*—provided food, toys, diapers, exercise—and she is still hungry and restless, we are brought face to face with the fact that her *essential* needs and being are spiritual. We can do all the right and loving things as diligently and perfectly as we like, but if our consciousness is filled with resentment or worry or frustration, she remains unsatisfied, uncomfortable, restless. Because she *is aware* of when love is present and when it is not. What the child *sees* determines her well- or ill-*being*.

Often at the time of birth we are so preoccupied with bodies—the mother's big one, the baby's tiny, breathing one—that we do not stop to consider what is the most outstanding characteristic of the newborn baby. Look at her eyes. Evidently they see next to nothing, and yet seeingness or alertness is what they express most of all. Clearly she knows next to nothing and yet clearly she is *conscious, aware, alert,* above all interested in seeing—not judging, not liking or disliking—just seeing.

This consciousness is her definition. Any mother thinking back to the first moments when she and her baby looked at each other can remember it—the wide-awake looking. This quality of awareness is most memorable because it more than anything else is the truth of the child. Even before she breathes, she peers. As the wave is to water, the baby is to consciousness. She comes of it (conception), is made of it, and to it already she seeks to return. Only insofar as she becomes fully conscious will she become fully herself.

This recognition on the part of the parent is basic to parental love. Indeed, we can find no more practical definition of love than that it is the realization of the truth of being of the beloved. The idea of love as a way of treating each other, as a feeling of worth to be gotten from each other, puts love on a have and have-not basis. Sooner or later such love is always experienced as loss (in fact, theft) on the part of both lover and beloved. Between parent and child it is tinged with anxiety, worry, frustration, weariness, and resentment on the part of the parent, and with insecurity, fear of abandonment, and depression on the part of the child. For the implication is always that the child is *un*whole, *in*adequate, *un*safe, *in*capable, even bad. The beloved is thus the belittled. And life as a context is also seen as *in*complete, *un*fulfilling, *im*perfect, and *un*reliable.

But now we are going about love differently. We recognize, affirm, and proceed as if our child really is perfect consciousness; and we treat everything else as transitory. We still deal with the immaturities—ministering, caring, correcting, comforting, teaching, serving as needed—but we do not affix them to our child. Instead, we consciously separate him—his true, perfect, conscious, whole self—from everything else that seems to be. In this way an environment of letting be occurs in which the child most effortlessly becomes what he truly is.

So also are the true meaning of ourselves as parents and the circumstance of parenthood and family life brought to light. The child we thought we bore bears us toward the discovery of ourselves as potentially spiritually conscious, Seeing Beings. Our children both demonstrate and force us to see that life in general, parenthood in particular, is less a matter of doing and having than of seeing.

The child is not the only one who is maturing. We, too, are on the path of becoming what we truly are, consciously conscious of the whole and our oneness with it. Since consciousness is our true substance, it is noteworthy that the word *substance* has Latin roots meaning "under" and "to stand," that is, to "stand under" or "understand." Love as the perception of that which is substantial is itself substantiating. To be loving is to be understanding. To be understanding is to be conscious. If the truth of the child's being is consciousness and we perceive this, then we have become more conscious ourselves. In perceiving the true substance—the consciousness of the child—we become ourselves more conscious, and thus realize and substantiate our own lives more fully. In the instant of perfect consciousness there is oneness—the realization that there is only one mind, one self, and that it is good.

So the child is the parent and the parent is the child and our time together becomes a joyful participation in the process of child-parent and parentchild together to see and express our true nature.

What Have I Done to My Life?

Parenthood always comes as a shock. Postpartum blues? Postpartum panic is more like it. We set out to have a baby; what we get is a total takeover of our lives. But even in the surprising early days there are many blessings to even a little spiritual awareness. We are eased of resentment, for we realize that we have not given up our lives for our children but that rather our life with them is part and parcel of our own path toward self-realization. Our uncomfortable sense of personal responsibility (blame, guilt) is eased, for we realize that each child is what he is: awareness seeking awareness. We did not make him; we cannot break him. Our children are freed of our overbearing, overzealous trespassing, for now we view them less as projects than as revelations. And we see whatever problems arise as opportunities for learning rather than as something wrong with them, or us, or life.

Assurances

For the many of us for whom the early days with the new baby are fraught with one trial or another, here are some assurances:

• For some people what you find difficult is incredibly easy. This does not mean you are terrible or ungifted parents or that you got a bad deal. It means that the difficulties *can* fall away.

• For some people what you find easy is terribly difficult. This does not mean that you are superior parents; it means that God is God.

• The really dependent days are so few that you could almost miss the whole course. Suppose you live ninety years and your child who is born when you are about thirty is utterly dependent on you for three and a half years. If you wish away those three and a half years, you may spend fifty-six and a half years mourning what you missed.

• Babies need peace more than sleep. Believe it or not, so do you. So don't struggle over sleep; just learn to be peaceful together.

• Babies need love more than food. So don't struggle over eating; just learn to be loving together.

• Give yourself over to parenthood for the moment. Learn what is to be learned. Enjoy what is to be enjoyed. See what is signified. What could be more important to long-range happiness than learning true peace, love, beauty, harmony? Money? Career? Tennis? There is a place for all these, but there's no rush about them.

• So look for peace, love, beauty, order, harmony unconditionally. Find them in the baby and in yourself. Enjoy being together. Together enjoy being.

• Good news! The baby doesn't want to die, and he does not depend on you to do all his living for him. Parents are servants, suppliers, helpers, and colleagues—not prime movers. Having loving parents can make all the difference in the smooth unfolding of the baby's life. But let's not exaggerate our own importance with illusions of guilt and pride. Our children need mothering and fathering, but we are not their only source of motherliness and fatherliness. The reason for being with our children is not only that they need us but also that we need to become what we are, motherly and fatherly. Hardly any experience could change our lives more beneficially or faster than a correct appreciation of the significance of parenthood.

• If you have a job outside the home, you can find someone loving to care for the baby; and when you leave, you need not think you are abandoning her. You are not her *source* of love. You are just one place that love is taking shape, one channel through which Divine love flows. You are not the only shape that love can take. She lives in your consciousness. You can guard her in your thoughts, knowing her to be in perfect health and in perfect love and care. What you can know, she can experience. The biggest task of parenthood is awareness. Parental consciousness can be maintained anywhere. This does not mean worrying and fretting and calling home every five minutes. As a parent, seek simply to be aware of parentliness.

• If you decide to leave your job to stay home with your child, do not worry that your career is going to pot. The time you spend bringing up your child will also bring to birth and raise many parts of yourself that will benefit everything you are and do for the rest of your life.

• New experiences such as the overwhelming one of parenthood do not exist so that we can put what we already know to the test or on display, but rather so that we can learn what we need to know. So don't worry about what you don't *yet* know. The new situation that demands new understanding of us is also the channel through which that understanding can come. The understanding we need is always available in the situation that requires it. Prior experience is not necessary. Urgencies are provided, and all we need is to be Seeing Beings, sincerely receptive to what *is* revealing itself.

> *My people will abide in a peaceful habitation, in secure dwellings, and in quiet resting places.*
>
> —Isaiah 32:18

Diet for a Seeing Being: Essential Ingredients

Almost invariably the arrival of the new baby brings about a tremendous involvement with food and feeding. Whether we are breast- or bottle-feeding, our entire lives are suddenly wrapped up in bodily processes. *Is it time for a feeding? Is the baby getting enough? Has she eaten too much? Hungry again? or just tired? I've been feeding her the whole afternoon, so I haven't even started to fix supper.*

What happened to parenthood? Is it nothing but maintenance? Somebody told us that babies are nothing but little eating and pooping machines. At the time we laughed at the joke—now we don't think it is a joke at all.

After a few months digestive difficulties abate. The breast/bottle struggle has worked itself out. The baby doesn't die; neither do we. Enter solid food—tidbits everywhere and little jars of this and that. Now on top of the concern with eating enough, we have the worry of whether or not he's eating the right things. Next he begins to feed himself—and his hair and his eyes and the highchair and the floor. Oddly enough he's a little shy of messing up his clean hands with the fingerpaints we paid good money for. He likes smearing squash and peas better. I used to toy with the idea of feeding my child in a different room at every meal. That way, I was sure the house would be thoroughly washed every twenty-four hours.

All this time the regular grocery shopping, cooking, and cleaning up go on, becoming more and more complicated as the baby becomes mobile and wants to play an active role in the kitchen. Somewhere along the way we've translated our lunch into an all-day snack, and though we never have time to sit down and eat, we are putting on weight. Our hungry baby woke us at 5 A.M.; here it is 10:30 P.M. and we're just starting to wash the dinner dishes.

But all the time we sort of know—we even say from time to time—that *there must be an easier way*. We can't quite believe it has to be so hard. Yet many of us never find the way—we simply endure. As with everything else, the answer lies in a right understanding of who we really are and what it is that we are really about.

We tend to think of our offspring in material terms. We "made" a baby, "gave" it birth, and now we have to feed him so that he can become big and strong. But *did* we make the baby? Did the baby make the baby? When we hold the seed of the sweet pea in our hands, or when we plant it in the soil, where is the colorful blossom? Is it in the seed? Do we stuff it into the seed? Can we say that it doesn't exist? No, only that it has not yet materialized. With the seed we participate in the materializing of an idea. What is the substance of an idea? Spirit. And what or where is the beginning or end of an idea? No beginning. No end.

> *Oats, peas, beans, and barley grows,*
> *Oats, peas, beans, and barley grows.*
> *Nor you, nor I, nor anyone knows*
> *How oats, peas, beans, and barley grows.*

—Traditional nursery rhyme

Yet here we are with this baby on our hands, stuffing her full of food as if that will make her into something more or other. It's as if we tried to make a sweet pea blossom from a seed by stuffing the seed with soil. But oats, peas, beans, *and babies* grow! It is written into the very nature of oat, pea, bean, and barley to grow into fruitful plants.

Nobody questions whether they want to do this, or can. So why do we doubt our children? When the farmer sows a nice, round, healthy oat and it doesn't grow well, he doesn't say, "What's the matter with this oat? It must be lazy or sick or emotionally disturbed in some way." He assumes that something is wrong with the environment in which he knows that oat is trying to grow. Then he sets about trying to perceive what is needed.

Parenthood is similar, although in two ways it's harder than farming. First of all, we have a less clear picture of what a healthy man or woman is than we do of a mature crop of oats. Second, the growing environment of the young child is not made up of soil and weather conditions; it's us—our consciousness. But in one way our task is easier than farming, for, unlike the oat, the child is constantly telling us what he needs.

What is needed for this growth to take place? As we have begun to see, the answer is not simply material food; it is spiritual nourishment. As mothers and fathers, our job is not to create but to nourish. In nutrition the concern is with maintaining life—strengthening, building up, and promoting health. And what is health? *Health* and *holy* have the same Old English root, the word *hale*, which means "whole." The difference between the words *healthy* and *holy* is only the distinction historically made between the physical and the spiritual. But a strictly physical concept of health is not whole; at best it is partial.

If we feed our children only food, no matter how much they consume, they will be at least half-starved. The body is at best a partial representation of a spiritual idea. Doctors correctly refer to the baby's breathing and the beating of his heart as vital "signs." They are not vitality, they have not vitality, but they express and signify the presence of vitality. It is the unfolding of the whole ideal self of the child with which we are concerned. Since the substance of an idea is not material but spiritual, it is obvious that spiritual nourishment is what the child needs. So we need a whole concept of the child and a whole concept of nutrition.

The ideal food for the ideal child must be love, since, after all, the ideal individual is above all a loving individual. There is a sense in which we can say that food makes the man. If we want our children to become peaceful, assured, joyful, and loving adults, they must be nourished with peace, assurance, joy, and love.

We don't have to look to the end result to see that love is the prime food for sustaining the life of the child. Our children are primarily spiritual and their nourishment is primarily spiritual. Whenever love is present, all is well. Whenever love is absent, nothing goes well.

Our children take us a step further. Even when we fondle and frolic with them, as well as feed and change them, if love is not a present state of consciousness, or if it is, the condition of our consciousness registers directly in the child's consciousness and is accordingly translated into well-being or distress.

Nursing Child

Like everything else, breast-feeding has two meanings: material and spiritual. On a material level, in theory at least, it is the most fussless way of feeding the infant. If it goes well, it can spare us messy feeding days. Many mothers feed their children nothing but breast milk until around five months. Then food is gradually introduced. By eight or nine months, babies are proficient with training cups and largely able to feed themselves. No bottles ever! Further, breast-feeding may be a mutually sensuous experience that gives the mother pleasure and a sense of importance while the baby has an experience of closeness, security, and oral pleasure.

That this may not be an entirely true or complete picture is suggested by certain frequent difficulties. Breast-feeding may not "go well." It takes more time than anticipated, which mother or father may come to resent, feeling either used or neglected or both. In proportion, as you find it pleasurable, you may be reluctant to give it up. In proportion, as you do not, your child's need to suck becomes a tyrannizing demand.

La Lêche League deals extensively with all these contingencies, and *Whole Child/Whole Parent* has nothing to add by way of technique or advice about what to do, whether to nurse, how or how not. But whether or not we breast-feed our babies, whether or not they are actually at the breast, whether they are tiny milk-sucking infants or ten-year-old pizza wolfers, whether they are feeding or sleeping, or playing or studying, or at home or away from home, *our children are ceaselessly nursing on our consciousness and being nourished or malnourished accordingly.*

This point cannot be made strongly enough. When asked if we will, or are still, or are no longer nursing the baby, we should all be laughing. *Whether we literally nurse the baby, she will be nursing; and she will never stop nursing as long as she is a child; and she will nurse not only from the mother's but also from the father's consciousness.*

For the sake of new parents we are focusing on the early days of parenthood—breast-feeding, feeding, and so forth. But the fact is that through all the years of childhood, and, indeed, through all their lives, our children will continue to nurse from our consciousness. If this doesn't make us quake in our shoes, then we haven't really understood it. But once we do understand it, after we finish quaking in our shoes, we can begin to seek and to find relief, harmony, beauty, and inspiration.

So what is the new parent feeding the new baby? Often mostly milk and worry—also discouragement, guilt, resentment, depression, and general uptightness. Fortunately the baby is not yet conscious enough to learn these things from us. He is so largely a material translation of his ideal self that most of the mental nutrition (or malnutrition) we pass on to him is translated into temporary physical terms. He is not conscious of our worry or nervousness as worry or nervousness, but in some way he is aware of whether peace is there or not; of whether love is there or not. Somehow he experiences or encounters our secret mental anguish and displays it to us as physical discomfort, struggling, spitting up, and so on. However, when we feed him on love—the true stuff of his true self—we see this translated into a physical state of peaceful well-being.

Nursing Parent

But we can only feed him what we have, and spiritually we can only "have" what we are aware of while we are aware of it. Once we reach physical maturity, our nourishment is more and more a matter of pure idea. As ideal selves, our fulfillment ultimately depends on our consciousness of the truth about ourselves. This means seeking awareness of love, peace, gratitude, assurance, generosity, joy. *This is really scary,* you say. *Now you tell me that besides all the things I have to do for the baby, I also have to be loving, grateful, assured, and joyful? All I am is exhausted, anxious, and overwhelmed!* To this I respond, wait a minute. How did you make the milk in your breast? The answer is, you didn't. You ate, and the milk came. As the source of yours and your baby's nourishment is the nonpersonal field and orchard, so there is a Beyond Personal source of yours and your baby's love, and all you have to do is take time to drink it in.

Having discerned that *all children are always nursing,* we arrive at yet another nutrition principle: that *the nursing child needs a nursing parent.* Nursing mothers have to drink plenty of liquids; nursing spiritual parents, both father and mother, need a nourished spiritual consciousness. If you haven't prayed in years, now is the time to start praying again, and I don't mean, "Dear God, please make her go to sleep!" I mean, at least as often as you grab a bite of food, at least as often as you go to the bathroom, take time to be still and to let go of everything, and to let go into God and to nurse on what comes.

> *Like newborn babes, long for the pure spiritual milk, that by it you may grow up to salvation; for you have tasted the kindness of the Lord.*
>
> —1 Peter 2:2–3

> *But I have calmed and quieted my soul,*
> *like a child quieted at its mother's breast,*
> *like a child that is quieted is my soul.*
> —Psalm 131:2

We can see that the baby is as much a means of nourishment for us as we are for him. We can foster his growth as a peaceful and loving individual only if we nourish him with love and peace. We can express love and peace only if we know love and peace. And we can know love and peace only if this is what we hunger for and feed upon in consciousness. Most of us would do more for our babies than we have ever been willing to do for anyone, even ourselves. In this way the child (seemingly so helpless) performs the mighty work of awakening in us a tremendous appetite for understanding and so brings us to the table of love.

We stand there in awful hunger, asking two huge questions. Our whole lives have been the asking of these questions, but only as we consciously frame them does the preexisting truth become a receivable answer. *To be loving we need to be aware of being loved.* But how can we do this? How, apart from doing or saying or thinking, how can we fill to overflowing our consciousness with love? How, apart from getting and having and doing, can we know that we are loved?

After long years of searching and studying, and not a little struggling, the following has brought itself home to me. It may be the most important idea expressed in this book; and yet it may seem meaningless, even irritating to some. If that is so for you, skip it for now. Wait until something makes you want to come back to it. For me, at least, it answers these questions: *How can we fill our consciousness with love? How can we know that we are loved?*

Song of the Seeing Being

The more we see that seeing is the issue in life,
the more we look at everything for what it has to teach us.
The more we look at everything for what it has to teach us,
the more we see that we are being taught.
The more we see that we are being taught,
the more we know that we are loved.
The more we know that we are loved,
the more lovingly we are seeing.
The more lovingly we are seeing,
the more loving we are being.
The more loving we are being,
the more we see that seeing is the issue in life.
[*start over*]

Seeing is being. Intelligence expresses itself as love. Awareness expresses itself as being. Knowing is loving. Loving is knowing. What we are feeding on in consciousness is what we are nursing on. What we are nursing on is what our children are nursing on.

Just as it is not possible to bring love into the life of the child simply by doing loving things, neither can we achieve a loving state of mind simply by believing that we should, or trying to think loving thoughts. In fact, we could just about drive ourselves and our children crazy trying to do that. But whenever the need for spiritual realization is recognized and the interest sincere, it becomes possible to nourish spiritual consciousness. Just being alert to the deeper significance of everything helps, and further study, prayer, and meditation are helpful and will prove necessary as they are understood and appreciated. Nothing can or needs to be forced, but when you are at the end of your rope and you hear yourself saying, "Oh, God," let that be a reminder. *Oh! God! Yes. I forgot. Here I am. What willest thou? What do I need to see?*

I have meat to eat that ye know not of.
—John 4:32

My meat is to do the will of him that sent me.
—John 4:34

Truly, truly, I say to you, the Son can do nothing of his own accord, but only what he sees the Father doing.
—John 5:19

Besides the Bible, I have found the books listed here helpful in nourishing spiritual consciousness. Different things are helpful at different times, and a book that seems offensive at one point may be helpful at another. And one book may be inspired by truth while another by the same author may not. So don't feel frustrated if you find some, even all, of these books inaccessible or uninviting. When a book seems too obscure or too "religious," just lay it aside and wait. There are other books and other ways. The same is true of prayer and meditation; there are ways and there are ways. The main thing is simply to be receptive to some spiritual nourishment, to give some attention to it, some quiet time, some attention.

Chute, Marchette, *The Search,* E. P. Dutton, New York 1941.
———, *The End of the Search,* E. P. Dutton, New York, 1947.
The Dhammapada, Lal, P. (translator), Farrar, Straus & Giroux, New York, 1967.
Fox, Emmet, *The Sermon on the Mount,* Harper & Row, New York, 1934.
Goldsmith, Joel, *The Infinite Way,* DeVorss, Marina Del Rey, Calif., 1954.
———, *Realization of Oneness,* Citadel Press, Secaucus, N.J., 1974.
Graham, Dom Aelred, *Zen Catholicism,* Harcourt Brace Jovanovich, New York, 1963.
Holm, Nora, *The Runner's Bible,* Houghton Mifflin, Boston, 1913, 1915, 1941, 1943.

Linthorst, Ann, *Soul-Kissed,* Paulist Press, New York, 1996.

Meister Eckhart, Blakney, Raymond (translator), Harper & Row, New York, 1946.

Nhat Hanh, Thich, *Peace Is Every Step,* Bantam Books, New York, 1991.

Prabhavananda, Swami, *The Sermon on the Mount According to Vedanta,* Vedanta Press, Hollywood, Calif., 1964.

Tao te Ching, Mitchell, Stephen (translator), HarperCollins, New York, 1988.

Underhill, Evelyn, *The Cloud of Unknowing,* Stuart & Watkins, London, 1946, 1970.

The Way of Life, According to Laotzu, Bynner, Witter (translator), John Day, New York, 1944, 1962.

Nursing Creature

Whether we happen to be parents or not, honest reflection reveals that we continue to nurse on our parents' consciousness long after childhood, if only in the sense that our parents' values, their perspective on life and on us, continue (positively or negatively) to be the central, governing concern in our lives. Struggle to reform our character, behavior, or experience is fruitless until the human parental thought of what we seem to be, whatever that may be, is replaced with an essential, spiritual understanding that we are children of *Our Father (and/or Mother) Who (or Which) Art.*

We are, after all, fundamentally nursing creatures. Our consciousness hungers for, but cannot produce, its own content. So it suckles constantly on some conscious or unconscious content, which in turn is transformed into our way of being alive and experiencing life. But consciousness is primary to all our being and experiencing. As Me, Inc., we cannot in any way personally reshape ourselves or our experiences, but as seeing beings we can learn to exercise choice over what we nurse on, and gradually discern what is true from what is false, which in turn reshapes us and our lives. As Me, Inc., most of the time we conduct our lives in terms of doing and having and feeling, but eventually we need to begin to *be aware of what we seem to be aware of.* Because *whatever it is that we put in charge of our consciousness, we are putting in charge of our life.*

Our children are not our children. We are neither parents of our children nor children of our parents. We are all God's children. To the extent that we are nourished in this truth our lives will be reformed and transformed.

> *And be ye not conformed to this world; but be ye transformed by the renewing of your mind, that ye may prove what is that good and acceptable and perfect will of God.*
>
> —Romans 12:2

Just who do we think we are anyway? Just who in the hell do I *think* I am? Just what—just who—am I trying to prove? The proof is in the pudding, or in the sticky situation.

> *By their fruits ye shall know them.*
>
> —Matthew 7:16, 20

Looking at ourselves and our children and at nursing in a spiritual light benefits both parent and child. Before, breast-feeding was an interruption in our life; it now becomes a welcome lull and a time for our own spiritual nourishment. While the child nurses, we may read or consider spiritual ideas, or simply take time to commune (become one with) certain spiritual qualities. Nursing becomes a refreshing rather than a draining time, a time of fulfillment rather than self-sacrifice.

In breast-feeding, once we are no longer anxious, the milk flows freely and does not sour the stomach. The baby, no longer surrounded by worry, becomes his peaceful, comfortable self. Now, though we enjoy them more, we may have fewer feedings, also fewer diapers and spit-ups, less laundry, and more sleep. We are suddenly struck by the fact that the milk (which we did nothing to make) *is there!* The love we wish to express and wish to receive is also simply there; like a child turning to his mother's breast, we sincerely turn our attention to it.

The work of nursing, preparing food, spoon-feeding, and cleaning up is also decreased to a large extent. Having greater faith in our child's wholeness, we don't manufacture seven-course trial menus anymore, or spend hours trying "to get him to eat." (One couple reported that they used so many pots and pans fixing supper for their baby that they had to wash dishes before cooking dinner for themselves.) All mealtime proceedings become more enjoyable—because it is more pleasant to be concerned with fellowship and generosity and love at mealtimes and because we understand that we need to express love.

Additional Reflection: It isn't easy. Recently I ran across a photograph that reminded me that I needed to say that. The photo was taken when my sons were about four months and two and a half years old. I'm nursing the baby and talking with the older child. It's a happy picture. The baby is nursing. The older boy is smiling. And I'm smiling. Yet I remember that inside I was feeling so anxious about trying to meet both their needs. It wasn't easy, so I prayed a lot until I knew that the coming of a second child didn't mean that the first would now only receive half of the love he had been receiving, that there was, if anything, only more love available to us all. The praying helped. But it wasn't easy. But it helped. But it wasn't easy.

Feeding the Whole Seeing Being and Allowing Him to Feed Himself

What is the wholesome food for the wholesome child? Since the child is not merely a body but a Seeing Being, the question becomes: *How do you feed a spiritual Seeing Being?* Food is necessary, but what is essential? In what way do the essential and the necessary become one in the feeding of the child?

In the discovery that there is a Seeing Being rather than just a body to be fed, many things already become clear that were formerly problematic. Almost as soon as she starts receiving solid food, she begins to want to feed herself. While she is unlikely to eat unless hungry, she is not simply feeding herself because her stomach is hungry. Her feeding, reaching, feeling the food, pulling it into her mouth, is learning. And it is learning almost more than the food for which she hungers.

When she is popping peas with her fingers rather than eating them, she *is* eating! Her seeing self is nourished through finding out what it hungers to know. This recognition already leads to many blessings. Before we feared *(Is she eating enough?);* now we are amazed *(How insatiable is her appetite for learning!).* Before we felt resentment and frustration *(So much mess, why won't she quit fooling around?);* now there is an atmosphere of love and a flooding in of intelligent ideas. Did we take squished peas personally before? We don't anymore. Were we frustrating her by trying to prevent her from doing what she starved to do? In this fresh light we find her experiments somewhat easier to put up with, and more ideas for nourishing her consciousness at less inconvenience occur to us.

Before we conceived of the child as a Seeing Being we were preoccupied with what she should eat and how to make her do that. After we recognize her as a Seeing Being we become aware that she is already constantly feeding and that there is something in her that knows what she needs. When she is older the same thing will apply to her interests, preferences, hobbies, and passions. We can trust her. We can trust life. We can entrust her to life. Life itself is working in her—one thing leading to another. "Sheep may safely graze."

Seeing that our children are trying to learn inspires us with many thoughtful ideas on how to prepare food that not only nourishes their bodies but also helps them learn what they are trying to learn. Realizing that they are not simply "playing with food" when they should be eating it, but rather learning, many "foods for thought" occur to us. Whether or not they get eaten, the peas in a pod are amazing; the star in the apple is a wonder.

Before the feeding fuss ends, we enter the underfoot phase: Someone's in the kitchen with Dinah. And she isn't strumming on the old banjo, she's clawing at our stockings, fussing to be picked up, grabbing and tipping over bowls and pans. Alone you could fix supper in five minutes, but she wants to be held. Ever try to operate an eggbeater with one hand?

Before you perceive the child as a Seeing Being, cooking is either a chore or an emergency. You are Dinah, slave to your child's physical needs and limitations. You would like her to stay out of your way while you get your chore out of the way so she can eat what you believe she desperately needs but won't let you fix. After you begin to look at both your child and yourself as Seeing Beings, your kitchen time together takes on a different meaning.

There are two reasons for including our children in our kitchen activities. One is that we can't keep them out and get anything done at the same time. The other is that this is one of the best places in the house for both parent and child to learn what we most need to know.

We all have certain material and certain spiritual work that can best be done in the kitchen. The child's task is to explore the material properties of her world and learn how to deal with them. And where could you find a finer, better-equipped learning laboratory than the average kitchen? Here such spiritual nutrients as love, humility, abundance, order, beauty, gratitude are concretely expressible.

The spiritually alert parent reviews every activity in an essential light. In the kitchen, without this perspective, as Me, Inc., we are giving up "our thing" to cook for others. Or we may try to become a gourmet and win praise. Either way the presence of a toddler underfoot or the absence of more help and appreciation become problematic. But when task and circumstance are viewed spiritually, essentially, the necessary work is easier and more fulfilling.

For the child the kitchen is a learning laboratory. Supplied with endless tools and activities just right for his learning needs, the toddler is happily busy with his work while we are freer to accomplish ours. What manufactured toy exceeds an old drip coffee pot for the baby who wants to grab and lift and bang and take apart and put together? No sandbox offers the two- or three-year-old more than the kitchen sink or a basin of rice with spoons and measuring cups. No museum, science program, or chemistry set offers the grade-school child so much as the freedom to bake and cook and experiment in the kitchen. No classroom, play group, or other family situation provides such regular opportunities for learning to work and love together as the kitchen. As the years go by and you see your children growing up and away, over and over you will seek meaningful communication— "before it's too late." When my children were young, we told more stories, sang more songs, shared more profound thoughts, exchanged more deep secrets, confessed more doubts and received more assurance, hugged and laughed harder, and were kinder and freer and jollier together drying dishes in the kitchen than anywhere else.

> *A monk told Joshu: "I have just entered the monastery. Please teach me."*
> *Joshu asked: "Have you eaten your rice porridge?"*
> *The monk replied: "I have eaten."*
> *Joshu said: "Then you had better wash your bowl!"*
> *At that moment the monk was enlightened.*
>
> —*Zen Flesh, Zen Bones,* compiled by Paul Reps

Jesus said, "Therefore I say unto you. Take no thought for your life, what ye shall eat, or what ye shall drink; nor yet for the body, what ye shall put on. Is not the life more than meat, and the body more than raiment? Behold the fowls of the air; for they sow not, neither do they reap, nor gather into barns; yet your heavenly Father feedeth them. Are ye not much better than they? Which of you by taking thought can add one cubit unto his stature? And why take ye thought for raiment? Consider the lilies of the field, how they grow; they toil not, neither do they spin: And yet I say unto you, that even Solomon in all his glory was not arrayed like one of these. Wherefore, if God so clothes the grass of the field, which today is, and tomorrow is cast into the oven, shall he not much more clothe you, O ye of little faith? Therefore take no thought, saying, What shall we eat? or, what shall we drink? or wherewithal shall we be clothed? For after all these things do the Gentiles seek: for your heavenly Father knoweth that ye have need of all these things. But seek ye first the kingdom of God, and his righteousness; and all these things shall be added unto you."

—Matthew 6:25–33

Man shall not live by bread alone, but by every word that proceedeth out of the mouth of God.

—Matthew 4:4

When a hungry monk at work heard the dinner gong he immediately dropped his work and showed himself in the dining room. The master, seeing him, laughed heartily, for the monk had been acting Zen to its fullest extent. Nothing could be more natural; the one thing needful is to open one's eye to the significance of it all.

—D. T. Suzuki, *Introduction to Zen Buddhism*

Of Purer Eyes

The baby cries. But we just fed him! He can't still be hungry. Maybe he's tired. Maybe he just needs a change. Oh, yes, see? Diaper rash. That was it, wasn't it? Or is it something else—something more . . . ? What's the matter with him? What's *wrong*?

No matter how well we cleaned our mental closet, worries come and worries go. Some worries precede problems; some problems provoke the worries; but they keep bobbing up and have to be dealt with somehow—responsively, lovingly, *continuously*. What a huge responsibility! What if we make a mistake? What if there's something really the matter and we don't do anything? We can feel our imagination running away with us. What if it *isn't* our imagination?

Nobody teaches little ducklings to swim, and nobody tells the water to hold them up. And what does the mother duck say, or do—or know? Not much. But when it is time she receives a message to lead her ducklings down to the water. What does she do then? She just wades in and the ducklings follow. One minute they are waddling awkwardly on the land. Next they are swimming. It comes so naturally. There doesn't seem to be any doubt. And unless it is polluted, the river does not let them down. Whatever it is about the river that can hold things up is fulfilled in the little floating ducks. Whatever it is about ducks that can float and glide is fulfilled in the river. And the unseen quality of buoyancy expresses and fulfills itself in its oneness with them both.

We have said that the child lives in the parents' consciousness. So let's say that in parenthood the water is love (which implies well-being) and the river is the individual consciousness of the parent. The duck is the child—fully equipped for floating (and thereby expressing love as well-being)—paddling through our consciousness. Love is there, abundant, sustaining. The child is whole. Love flows through us to uphold the child as long as there are no interfering pollutants in our stream of consciousness.

With the rest of the world we share many worries concerning our children's potential for ill-being and our own shortcomings as parents. There are two major mental pollutants: one is all the thoughts about what can go wrong; the other is Me, Inc.'s belief in itself—that we are or should be in charge. Two things the mother duck has that we seem to lack are confidence in the water and no illusions about herself. Conveniently for her, she is just too dumb to get confused.

The same self-starring Metrogoldwyn Me that we saw featured in wishes is often featured in our worries as well. We depend on some troubles as excuses. *So that's what's the matter with him!* she sighed thankfully. Who is relieved by the bad news? The self-blaming parent. Who is the self-blaming parent? The would-be superparent.

Watch and see how we sometimes count on little problems to break up the humdrum of everyday life. Everything is going fine, but nobody's noticing. We feel lonely with our children. The phone rings:

> "I just thought you'd want to know. Johnny has been throwing up all evening—ever since he played with your Suzy in the park."

"Oh, poor you! I'm sorry. What are his symptoms? Fever? Headache? Thanks. It was thoughtful of you to call."

Like Snow White with the poisoned apple, we bite and are immediately asleep and dreaming. In the dream we search for something. For what? Signs of sickness. We are watching and waiting for sickness.

"Hi, it's me. Suzy has it, too. Only she also has a rash. Oh, so does Johnny? Well, then they do have the same thing."

Now we are less lonely and bored:

"Who else were they playing with? Yes, I'll call them right away."

Now we are also more important:

"Got to go now. Suzy needs me."

It isn't enough to say to ourselves that just because another child has the flu, ours doesn't have to have it. We need to go further, beholding the essential, spiritual child in her truest, purest light—not as my baby with stuffy or not-stuffy nose and hot or not-hot cheeks, but that other lasting child, the Seeing Being floating in and expressing God. And we need to recognize and relinquish any tendency to seek credit or blame in relation to others or through our children, realizing, instead, the fact and fullness of our lives as expressions of divine love.

It is important constantly to seek awareness of our children's essential perfection. *Despite all appearances, rumors, diagnoses, and experiences to the contrary, we constantly hold in the forefront of our thoughts the perfect, whole, unmarrable, essential nature of the child and the power of love to bear us both up.* This is not mere wishful, positive, or magical thinking. We do not cause good any more than we make rivers pure by not dumping garbage into them. If we don't dump garbage into the river its purity remains evident. Wholeness, goodness, and perfection are the truth of essential being. By not entertaining contrary thoughts we allow this wholeness freer expression.

Rivers become polluted only when their essential purity and value are not appreciated. So even with rivers the real pollution is mental. This is only more true for parents. Even before the phone rings and our well-meaning neighbor gives us a lesson in precisely how to be sick, we are full of thoughts about various disasters, some of which we are sure will befall us sooner or later. The only question is which, when, how.

Like waterways, the rivers of our minds are already polluted and need purification. We need to recognize and rid them of old unquestioned beliefs (whether cherished, feared, or hated), and to exercise discrimination over the new ideas we admit into our consciousness.

But there is no purification without appreciation of purity. If we don't know what the river is, how do we know what doesn't belong there?

The baby is dirty all the time. We are constantly changing his diapers and wiping his bottom. Yet it's easy to see that he is pure. His mess has nothing to do with him; he doesn't even know about it. And his ignorance of the mess he makes has nothing to do with him either; he will learn. We are not deceived by the mess into thinking that he is either impure or stupid. We have never seen such purity! No matter what he does to sheets, diapers, clothes, or our laps, purity remains to us an obvious characteristic of the child's true self.

This purity we see—that's truth! The distinguishing we do between the purity and the mess—that's love! We deal with the mess twenty-four hours a day, but we do not allow it to become confused in our thoughts with the perfect picture we have of the child; hence, it does not interfere with love. And let's not confuse the love with the diaper changing, just as we do not confuse the baby with the mess. Love is not the diaper changing or the fixing of meals or disciplining or whatever it is that we must do along the way. *Love is the sorting out in thought of the perfect child from all evidence to the contrary.*

No matter how orderly and clean the parents may be, if they continuously include their child's waste products in their picture of the child, the child may become involved with his excrement too, perhaps smearing it or relieving himself in inappropriate places. Likewise the child who is held in thought to his errors will manifest them steadfastly. He cannot do otherwise. But a clear picture of the perfect child in the parent's consciousness, which sees (unsees) imperfection as irrelevant to the child's true being, allows the child to develop truthfully with the speediest and most effortless falling away of all irrelevant behavior.

The best way to separate people from their mistakes is to put a credibility gap between them. We begin by making a distinction between who they really are and who they really aren't, and then conduct ourselves as much as possible in relation to who they are instead of who they aren't. This goes for everyone—including ourselves. We can practice and prove it to ourselves with our children.

With diapers it's easy. But crying? Staying awake late? Hitting? Demanding? Whining? Being sick? It seems much harder as we become more and more concerned with what to do instead of what we need to see. But just as we can see purity right in the middle of the diaper mess, so also must we learn to see gentleness in the midst of violence, innocence in the face of guile, health where there seems to be sickness, perfection where imperfection seems to be, intelligence where there appears to be stupidity, goodness and the desire to be good right where willful badness seems to be.

These spiritual qualities of purity, innocence, intelligence, gentleness, and goodness are true. Whenever we see them, we see God (good). As we find them in our children, we discover them in ourselves. We begin to see that they are true—not as personal virtues but as the truth of being. When we see that they are true, we are conscious. Now we are one with what truly is. Discord, conflict, effort, ill-being give way to love. This love, this perfect consciousness, is now what we meet and express, just as the water at one with all water expresses fluidity, the essential quality of water.

Here we are with a fingerful of ointment in one hand and somebody's bottom hanging by two feet from the other. What kind of oil are we applying? What is going on in consciousness? We think of oil as both an environmental pollutant and, since time immemorial, the substance used for anointing the beloved and chosen of God.

> *Thou anointest my head with oil; my cup runneth over.*
> *Surely goodness and mercy shall follow me all the days of my life,*
> *and I will dwell in the house of the Lord forever.*
>
> —Psalm 23:5–6

Anointing is a way of honoring essential wholeness, perfection, and worth, an act of hallowing that really occurs in the mind of the one doing the anointing.

At the same time that we apply the necessary oinment, we can discard the notion that the baby has to have diaper rash because that's what babies do, along with the notion that the baby is the diaper rash.

("He's a rashy baby.") We can bathe our children, washing away impurities, and then oil them with fine ointment that no friction may occur. At the same time we can purify our thoughts, washing away fears that our children are not quite perfect, that love is not enough protection for them or sufficient fulfillment for us. The choice is not between the necessary and the essential; it is just here with the necessity that we are brought to conscious awareness of the essential.

Additional Reflection: I do not mean to imply that all illness is psychosomatic. But increasingly we are coming to know that there are psychic and spiritual dimensions to illness, and that wellness and healing can be augmented through psychic and spiritual awareness. Two recent news items impressed the fact of this growing awareness on me. One told of a major health plan that will now provide and cover the cost of "alternative" or "complementary" treatment. The other concerned a physician who has instituted a program at a major hospital in which patients receive both conventional medical and alternative care simultaneously. In an interview the doctor said it is important to seriously study such methods as therapeutic touch, biofeedback, meditation, and acupuncture, to see how and to what extent they are effective. He himself does not "know," but he is open, even to the point of learning and performing therapeutic touch as well as conventional surgical procedures on patients.

For me such openness means prayerfully maintaining what I call a "healthy credibility gap" regarding the power of every disease and diagnosis. No matter how serious a physical problem or illness appears to be, no matter how frightening the prognosis, I feel responsible for prayerfully acknowledging that what comes mysteriously may also disappear mysteriously. Even while cleaning up vomit or smoothing out bedsheets or bringing trays for meals in bed, even while driving to and from the hospital, I prayerfully try to put the afflicted person "on behold," to seek healing of my own fears and dire predictions, and to become a silently soothing and healing channel for divine energy and inspiration. When I come down with symptoms myself (and when my children used to do so), I also prayerfully seek to understand what the symptom itself might be telling me, what I might learn, what psychological state of mind the symptom might symbolize, what spiritual direction I might need to take. If the symptoms seem to be "winning" and I seem to be "losing," I do not hestitate to seek medical help, but at the same time I continue to prayerfully open myself to beyond-medical, beyond-psychological avenues of healing and growth. I think this is what the Bible means by "Enlarge the borders of thy tent," and without going into specific testimonials, I must say that I have personally seen and found it to be amazingly and concretely helpful.

> *And when the dragon saw that he was cast unto the earth, he persecuted the woman which brought forth the manchild. And to the woman were given two wings of a great eagle, that she might fly into the wilderness, into her place where she is to be nourished for a time, and times, and half a time, from the face of the serpent.*
>
> —Revelation 12:13–14

The "two wings" are spiritual consciousness: the ability to distinguish *what is* from *what isn't,* and having done so, to place *what is* in charge of our consciousness rather than fear of *what isn't.*

> Once I was bringing our cat to a vet for emergency treatment. All the while I was hating doing so, certain that there was a better, higher route and no real need for the animal to be sick. Yet it didn't seem right to be ungrateful either. I did not know much about prayer, but I thought about God and waited for some understanding. Immediately an idea came very strongly to mind: *Do what you have to do until you know what you need to know.* It was obvious that I had not thought of this idea myself. This was the first time it was perfectly clear to me that a prayer had been answered.

It is good to *do what we have to do while seeking to know what we need to know.* With problems we can often wait to do what we have to do until it is absolutely *necessary.* And before and during and after that point we can keep our attention focused on the *essential.*

As we do whatever seems necessary to cope with and cure difficulties, it is also important to remain open to learning from and transcending them. Keep sight of the essential, spiritual reality no matter what seems to be amiss.

I have seen the retarded child of a devoted parent who focused on the child's potential for consciousness float across barrier after supposed barrier, expanding and transcending not only his own diagnosed limits but the limits of medical consciousness as well. I have read of autistic children whose parents tirelessly and successfully drew them out of themselves because "what else could we do?" after all doors of help and promise were closed to them. In my own family I have seen both major and minor symptoms disappear as mysteriously and suddenly as they came when one of us grew desperate enough to turn to God with sincere receptivity.

Some difficulties can be seen through and annihilated. Sometimes even in the middle of fears come true they can be transcended. But the real wonder and joy and purpose of our being here is not to gain power over what isn't but to wake up to what is.

Zen Cow

Most times a cow is content to mill around in the middle of the pasture with the other cows. But when the idea of going beyond the pasture occurs to her, she begins to have trouble with the barbed-wire fence around the pasture. Or perhaps it is when she bumps into the barbed-wire fence that she begins to be aware of the freedom beyond and to know that she is confined. The fence goes all the way around all the cows. But this cow is having a problem with the fence at a particular point. It is this particular section of barbed-wire fence that is hurting this particular cow. This isn't her fault! It is just that here she becomes acutely aware of her confinement and begins to appreciate what freedom means. The cow does not get through the fence by chewing through the barbed wire or by complaining to the other cows or being angry at the farmer. But at some moment her vision of what lies beyond becomes clear and dear to her, and she just begins to go there. She becomes unaware of the fence. Following her vision, mindless of limitation, heedless of pain, she simply leans down the fence and goes. If we have a serious difficulty, or if our children do, then for now at least this is our place to break through the universal fence of ignorance. Sometimes where the fence is down, others find freedom, too.

Hui-neng said: "From the first not a thing is."

—D. T. Suzuki, *Zen Buddhism*

Lao Tsu said: "The nameless is the origin of heaven and earth; Naming is the mother of the ten thousand things."

—A. Watts, *The Way of Zen*

Job said: "The thing I greatly feared is come upon me!"

—Job 3:25

Paul said: "Whatsoever things are true, whatsoever things are honest, whatsoever things are just, whatsoever things are pure, whatsoever things are lovely, whatsoever things are of good report; if there be any virtue, and if there be any praise, think on these things."

—Philippians 4:8

Jesus said: "In the world ye shall have tribulation; but be of good cheer, I have overcome the world."

—John 16:33

John said: "Beloved, we are God's children now; it is not yet clear what we shall be; we only know that when he shall appear we shall be like him, for we shall see him as he is. And every man that hath this hope in him purifieth himself even as he is pure."

—1 John 3:2–3

Habakkuk said, "O thou who art of purer eyes than to behold evil, and canst not look on iniquity."

—Habakkuk 1:13

Lullabye and Good Night

A distinguished teacher was once asked, "Do you ever make any effort to get disciplined in the truth?"

"Yes, I do."

"How do you exercise yourself?"

"When I am hungry I eat; when tired I sleep."

"This is what everybody does; can they be said to be exercising themselves in the same way as you do?"

"No."

"Why not?"

"Because when they eat they do not eat, but are thinking of various other things, thereby allowing themselves to be disturbed; when they sleep they do not sleep, but dream of a thousand things. This is why they are not like myself."

—D. T. Suzuki, Introduction to *Zen Buddhism*

Many people have trouble going to sleep at night or waking up in the morning. A lot of us believe that sleep is something that we do. But sleep is not done; it is allowed. If we believe life is *doing*, we may be reluctant to wake up—it is so risky and exhausting to be alive. By the same token, we may be reluctant to sleep; even while yearning to rest, we may harbor the secret fear that if we stop thinking and doing, we shall cease existing. I knew a woman who could never sleep unless she fell asleep before her husband did. She equated being alive with being paid attention to. When *he* slept, *she* felt ignored, even afraid. If no one was paying attention to her, maybe she didn't exist. So while she was dying to get some rest, she had to stay awake. At least then somebody knew she existed!

If we have an exaggerated sense of responsibility for our children, we may keep them awake in the busyness of our minds. If we believe their lives are our doing, we may also be unconsciously involved in the process of trying to do their sleep. This is impossible, since sleeping is a process of letting go, something that is allowed. If a baby is busy, restless, struggling at bedtime, and yet you know he yearns to rest, see if you are not busy, too—with ten thousand thoughts. The thoughts can be anything—he's got to sleep, he needs it; he's got to sleep, *I* need it; I have to get some time to myself; maybe if I do this; maybe he wants that; why won't he sleep? Is it so? Then try to acknowledge that, at least for the moment, neither you nor the child has any needs beyond the awareness of love. Corny? Just try it.

> *The Lord is my shepherd, I shall [need] not want.*
> *He maketh me to lie down in green pastures.*
> *He restoreth my soul.*
>
> —Psalm 23:1–2

Turn the child over to love. Turn yourself over to the idea that love and peace are available. For just a few minutes do not *think* of what you have to do or what you want to do or what the baby needs. Whether or not you remain in the room with the child, for a brief time before and after bedtime, simply give some quiet thought to the possibility that love is. Behold the child not as a burden, or a body in need, or a responsibility too great, or a cherished possession, but as an expression of love. Behold yourself the same way, acknowledging that love is bearing you up and flowing through you unendingly. No matter what has to be done, allow yourself to be peaceful. Hold or don't hold the child, but be very honest. It is not easy to be peaceful. You are not being peaceful if your mind is racing. Cultivate peaceful consciousness; rely on the idea that love is sufficient. In that silence it may happen that love, the only discovery of ultimate importance, breaks in upon you as a reality. If this happens, the baby will surely be peaceful and you will surely find yourself refreshed for any task.

Learning to be even momentarily truly peaceful, still of mind as well as body, takes much practice. It tends to be especially difficult in the early days of parenthood, when our lives are so suddenly so different and we are worried about how ignorant we are. We are constantly fretting mentally, so the child may continue to be restless and his sleeping habits unpredictable and brief. Others may suggest to you that the baby is manipulating you and that you are spoiling him. Don't believe it. He doesn't know anything about power struggle. If you start a power struggle with him, even when you win, you lose. Because in the process you teach him that power struggle is what life is all about. So just hang in there and seek a still and loving consciousness, that stillness of mind into which love pours itself. Let the problems fall away, let sleep, let be.

> Unless the Lord builds the house,
> those who build it labor in vain.
> Unless the Lord watches over the city,
> the watchman stays awake in vain.
> It is in vain that you rise up early
> and go late to rest,
> eating the bread of anxious toil;
> for he gives to his beloved sleep.
> Lo, children are a heritage from the Lord.
>
> —Psalm 127:1–3

High and Lifted Up

Bed, highchair, kitchen counter—these can become the locus of power struggle, battlegrounds of wanting and won'ting, or they can be places where we are high and lifted up. In the morning we often do better. We say we are rested. I think we are more childlike: not certain of what the day will bring, we are more open to its will, less willful ourselves. But by the end of the day we are doers and don'ters, succeeders and failers, willers and won'ters, martyrs and victims. So what is bedtime, then? A time to lay down controllingness, the feeling that we are, or ought to be, in charge. It is an exercise in entrusting ourselves to a greater power; as we lay down our own ideas of what our lives are, we allow ourselves to be lifted out of power struggles.

So much of the toddler's work is physical. The physical navigating on the floor and around the furniture—the lifting of this and that—becomes tiring and deteriorates from joyful discovery to struggle. Then mercifully it's mealtime. Mealtime, bedtime, anytime can become part of the struggle—or an opportunity for rising beyond the struggle and for realizing that seeing more than doing is being.

Now is the judgment of this world, now shall the ruler of this world be cast out; and I, when I am lifted up from the earth, will draw all men to myself.

—John 12:31–32

SEAL LULLABY

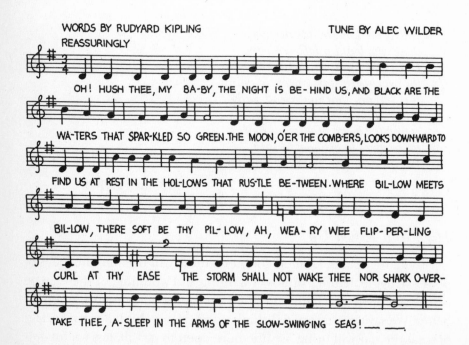

STAR WISH

TRADITIONAL
NOT TOO SLOWLY   TUNE BY ALEC WILDER

STAR   LIGHT,   STAR   BRIGHT,   FIRST   STAR   I   SEE   TO-NIGHT.

WISH   I   MAY,   WISH   I   MIGHT   HAVE   THE   WISH   I   WISH   TO-NIGHT.

*To thee, O Lord, I lift up my soul. O my God, in thee I trust. . . . Make me
to know thy ways, O Lord; teach me thy paths. Lead me in thy truth, and
teach me, for thou art the God of my salvation; for thee I wait all day long.*

—Psalm 25:1–2, 4–5

*Seek the Lord while he may be found, call upon him while he is near; let the
wicked forsake his way, and the unrighteous man his thoughts; let him return
to the Lord, that he may have mercy on him, and to our God, for he will
abundantly pardon. For my thoughts are not your thoughts, neither are your
ways my ways, says the Lord. For as the heavens are higher than the earth,
so are my ways higher than your ways and my thoughts than your thoughts.*

—Isaiah 55:6–9

*Wynken, Blynken, and Nod one night
    Sailed off in a wooden shoe—
Sailed on a river of crystal light,
    Into a sea of dew.
"Where are you going, and what do you wish?"
    The old moon asked the three.
"We have come to fish for the herring fish
    That live in this beautiful sea;
    Nets of silver and gold have we!"
        Said Wynken,
        Blynken,
        And Nod.*

*The old moon laughed and sang a song,
    As they rocked in the wooden shoe,
And the wind that sped them all night long
    Ruffled the waves of dew.
The little stars were the herring fish
    That lived in that beautiful sea—*

"Now cast your nets wherever you wish—
Never afeared are we";
So cried the stars to the fishermen three:
Wynken,
Blynken,
And Nod.

All night long their nets they threw
To the stars in the twinkling foam—
Then down from the skies came the wooden shoe,
Bringing the fishermen home;
'Twas all so pretty a sail it seemed
As if it could not be,
And some folks thought 'twas a dream they'd dreamed
Of sailing that beautiful sea—
But I shall name you the fishermen three:
Wynken,
Blynken,
And Nod.

Wynken and Blynken are two little eyes,
And Nod is a little head,
And the wooden shoe that sailed the skies
Is a wee one's trundle-bed.
So shut your eyes while mother sings
Of wonderful sights that be,
And you shall see the beautiful things
As you rock in the misty sea,
Where the old shoe rocked the fishermen three:
Wynken,
Blynken,
And Nod.

—Eugene Field, "Wynken, Blynken, and Nod"

I see the moon, the moon sees me—
over the mountain, over the sea.
Please let the light that shines on me,
shine on the one I love.

—Traditional camp song

As far as I know, all children are moonstruck. Even in the city where the lights blink and blaze insistently, where the sky is often only a straight-up chimney patch, even in the daytime, if the moon is out—just a pale, pale silver moon—the child will find it at once. "Oh, look, there's the moon!" Is the friendship between this round, clear wonder whose hand holds mine and the one in the sky (both with their whispers of faces) founded on a deep, inborn awareness of true calling? Does he already know, can he still remember, that the beauty and happiness of his whole life are to reflect a greater light? Does he already suspect that the darkness lies only in the shadow of turning away from the light in whom there is no shadow of turning? Does he already guess that in standing under (understanding) the light there is no shadow to be cast? See how he already casts about in the darkness for the light! This moonchild of mine keeps on reminding me that I must be moon for him as he is one to me.

> *Every good endowment and every perfect gift is from above, and cometh down from the Father of lights, with whom there is no variableness, neither shadow of turning.*
>
> —James 1:17

> *The child's wonder*
> *At the old moon*
> *Comes back nightly.*
> *She points her finger*
>
> *To the far yellow thing*
> *Shining through the branches*
> *Filtering on the leaves a golden sand,*
> *Crying with her little tongue, "See the moon!"*
> *And in her bed fading to sleep*
> *With babblings of the moon on her little mouth.*

—Carl Sandburg, "Child Moon"

> *There is a blue star, Janet,*
> *Fifteen years' ride from us,*
> *If we ride a hundred miles an hour.*
> *There is a white star, Janet,*
> *Forty years' ride from us,*
> *If we ride a hundred miles an hour.*
>   *Shall we ride*
>   *To the blue star*
>   *Or the white star?*

—Carl Sandburg, "Baby Toes"

LORD, BLOW THE MOON OUT, PLEASE

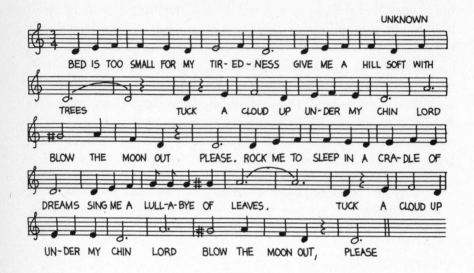

WEE BABY MOON

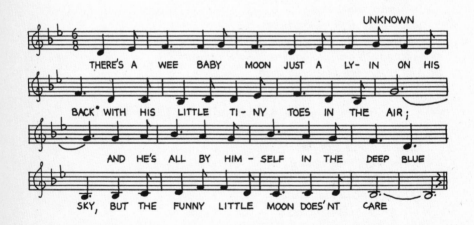

¹For a long time someone we know thought this meant that the moon had a lion on his back.

Additional Reflection: Fielding Children's Dreams

When our conscious selves sleep, the unconscious speaks up. Fears and feelings we didn't know we had, possibilities we haven't consciously entertained, parts of ourselves that have been pushed down or are just now ready to come to life stir and dance before us in what seem like fantastic films. Problems we haven't faced, ways of navigating through them that haven't yet dawned on us, are vividly presented. If we've leaned too far to one side of life or self, our dreams present the other side. Sailing through the night sea our ship of selves seeks to right itself, and find its true course. And I believe that the wind in our unconscious dream sails is the very breath of God, the Divine Spirit, seeking to guide us toward fulfillment.

As children, when nightmares frightened us, how many of us were consoled by our parents' soothing, "There, there. It was only a dream." Comforting it was, and helpful, too. Yet there was another side that was less helpful. Something of value was missed. How many of us repeatedly heard the words, "You're just dreaming. You're only imagining things." Looking back I am astonished at how most of us learned to ignore the guiding and healing potential of dreams. Since the age of reason, Western culture has tended to dismiss dreams as unreasonable and fantastic. But the work of Freud, Jung, and subsequent depth psychologists and sleep researchers is gradually making us aware that dreams are meaningful and necessary for psychic balance, growth, health, and healing. These days many people who were educated to belittle or ignore their dreams are finding some in-depth psychological dreamwork wonderful and helpful. But if *as a culture* we discover more of the nature and value of dreams, so that we just naturally respect and appreciate them, I wonder if so much professional dream analysis will remain necessary. A big part of dream analysis is simply remedial education to the fact that, like body temperature, rumblings in the stomach, and yawning, our nightly dreams are vital, necessary, and I would say divinely originated aspects of human development and healing. *Whole Child* is not the place to go deeply into all of this, but I do feel compelled to say something about the importance of children's dreams and how parents might field them.

When my children were small, I appreciated their dreams and was somewhat guided by what they revealed about their unconscious fears and the atmosphere in our home. But I responded to nightmares, like most parents, by switching on the light and saying, "See? There's nothing there—no monsters, no dragons. It was only a dream," and by changing the subject. I had little idea that dreams were not "just fantasies," not "just the product of an overactive imagination," and not "just wishes."

My grown children do take their dreams seriously. But what if when they were small, just as I felt their foreheads when they were fussy, or asked them if they were thirsty, or bought them paints when they showed an interest in drawing, or sat down to listen to their stories or latest adventures—what if each day I had invited them to share their dreams? What if when they had nightmares I had invited them to tell me *more,* to draw pictures of the dragon or to make up stories about what it could do or wanted or needed! What if, having comforted and held them until their fear subsided, I had exclaimed, "But wow! What a wonderful creature you dreamed up—what a wonderful, powerful, fierce part of you! I wonder how a person could make friends with that. I wonder what else it can do! Do you think he would let you ride him?" It's too late to run that experiment with my children, and I rarely work with child clients—but I wonder!

All I am recommending is that we *not* teach our children to demean or dismiss this important part of their being. Analyzing your child's dreams can be as harmful as dismissing them. So I'm not suggesting that you become an amateur psychoanalyst, or that you rush your child off to a psychoanalyst if he has a few nightmares. In fact, "bad" dreams are as natural, normal, healthy, and growth-promoting as "sweet" dreams. As the body's homeostatic and growth processes mostly function favorably without our being aware of them, most dreams do their work without ever coming to consciousness. For the most part, those we remember can also accomplish their purpose—*if* they are not brushed off as unreal, "only" imagination, or "mere" fantasy. By brushing them off we teach our children to brush off not only parts of themselves and dimensions of life but also a firsthand encounter with something grand and loving that is ever mindful of each of us. So do not analyze your child's dreams, only respond to them with positive interest, respect, and appreciation.

Should your child be persistently plagued by night terrors or nightmares, you may wish to consult an expert, just as you would consult a physician in the case of a persistent or raging fever. Whereas with physical symptoms you would take the child to the doctor, in the case of a prolonged spell of upsetting dreams you might take yourself to an expert, since children's nightmares can be manifestations of parents' unconscious problems. But in general all that's needed is to respond to the dreams your child brings you in a way that fosters her unfolding discovery of the meticulous, lacey meaningfulness and utter holiness of life in general and herself in particular.

You might encourage her to play around with her dreams *if she wants to*—to tell you more *if she wants to* ("What do you think happened next?"). You might validate her feelings ("That sounds so scary—fun—exciting!"). But the main thing is to listen, so that she will continue to feel that everything about her is worth taking seriously. Instead of dismissing a sweet dream as silly, or explaining why her fears were unfounded, just listen. One father and son used to spend time together each morning in the bathroom. While the boy watched his dad shave, they told each other what they had dreamed during the night. That's the sort of thing I'm recommending—not analyzing, psychologizing, or probing, just receiving, appreciating, and greeting with reverent respect the mystery of any dream your child cares to share.

Additional Reflection: *Letting Up, Letting Go of, and Letting Go Into*

Reviewing everything I have said so far, it occurred to me that two important things had been left unsaid: (1) It has been made clear enough that it is the parent as well as the child who is seeking to come to life, and that besides our objective children we have many unconscious inner children who also need to be born and lovingly brought up. But what has not been clearly presented is the way in which our actual offspring bring our inner children to our attention. (2) It has been stated that there is a Parent of parents to which we can and need to prayerfully turn, but not enough has been said about how to do that. Reflecting on these omissions I decided to include here the talk I have most often been asked to give in recent years. While these remarks repeat some of what has been said so far, they include many layers of understanding that I did not yet have or was too shy to mention when I first wrote *Whole Child,* as well as some gained since the publication of my *Gently Lead* and *Coming to Life* (from which I have also borrowed). The following Bible passage quoted earlier in the book sets the tone and expresses the whole point:

> *O Lord my heart is not lifted up, my head is not raised too high. I do not occupy myself with things too great and marvelous for me. But I have calmed and quieted my soul, like a child quieted at its mother's breast.*

> —Psalm 131:1–2

Often parents ask how to bring their children to God, but I like to speak first about how children bring *us* to God. If there's one thing I hear from parents today it's that they feel overwhelmed and at a loss. In many families both parents work. Many are single parents. Community and extended family are "out," yet parenthood is "in." The pressure we feel to be perfect parents in turn puts pressure on our children. Despite (or because of) the unprecedented number of parenthood books, many parents feel they don't know what they're doing. I believe we aren't meant to do what we already know how to do—that if we knew how to be parents we should be doing something else. Not knowing makes us desperate, which makes us think of God. So our desperate not knowing can help us with our spiritual growth, which is the key to helping our children with theirs.

The song says, *Row row row your boat gently down the stream. Merrily, merrily, merrily, merrily, life is but a dream.* Parenthood isn't always a gentle or merry experience. Yet the song applies. It says the power for our journey isn't us, that even when we lose touch with our inspiration we're actually being carried along, that our job is to go with the flow. We have to row to stay on course. But no matter what rocks, sandbars, whirlpools, or rapids we meet, where we are now is the way to the *next* place. It's not that we should always stay with our ship or never change course. But in order to tell when to do which things and how, we must hunker low, center ourselves, keep dipping our oars in, and find our oneness with the deep. If it seems too hard, we're either going upstream and need to turn around, or we're not letting it carry us and need to relax.

As for "life is but a dream," religions have long suggested that the purpose of life is awakening. Depth psychology, especially Jung's, has shown that events and people who show up in both our waking and dreaming life represent aspects of ourselves seeking wholeness, that how we relate to others depends on how we relate to our inner others, that awareness of the correspondence between conscious and unconscious life helps us with both our personal and interpersonal lives. So how do our darling/difficult, inspiring/crazing children teach and heal us? How can our individual and family lives enhance rather than hinder each other? How can prayer help? What sort? Who has time to pray anyway?

Some parents ask me about how to bring their children to God because they want to pass their faith onto their children. Others aren't sure if there's anything to religion, but, just in case there is, they don't want their children to miss out. For others it's because parenthood has made them face their helplessness, their ignorance, the limits of their love, their anger, even hate. They seek something better than themselves to rely on. They know their children need something more to rely on than their parents. Children shake up our beliefs and disbeliefs. Whether or not we believe in God, parenthood first throws us into the God position, then knocks us out of it. The idea that we "make" love, "make" babies, and the fact that they're so dependent on *us* for *everything* suggests that we are their very source and force of being—in other words, God.

But from their first night home, our children set about disabusing us of this idea. Just by being born they perform the great work of making us cry, *O, God!*—out of love, awe, *and desperation*. If we think we know what they need, they prove we don't. If we think our love is endless, they makes us hate them. If we swore *never* to do what our parents did, our children drive us to it. Little Davids all, with unerring aim, they slay our Goliath selves, our Godself images, by bringing out the overwhelmed child in us. It's wonderful how they free us, how after talking baby talk we're more open and childlike with others. It's awful how they expose our childishness. We're jealous of our children's attention to our partner (or our spouse's attention to them), hurt if they defy us, *retaliatory* when they won't "let us" do what we want.

If there's one thing we thought we'd be with our children, it's grown up. If there's one thing we vowed not to do, it's to put our "unfinished childhood business" on them. We know that trying to make them be what we failed to be would crush their spirit. But we find if we try to protect them from what hurt us, they become sissies. If we try not to tryrannize them as we may have been tyrannized, they become tyrants. Our efforts to be perfect fail and put awful pressure on us all. Joy drains away. Well, I want to stress that we *all* try to redo or relive our childhoods through our children, and to reemphasize that parenthood is designed to benefit both the children of the parent and the children *in* the parent. Trying to redo or relive your childhood, behaving childishly with your children, is not an avoidable mistake but an opportunity for healing and growth. Being good parents doesn't depend on our never being childish but on how we respond *when* we are. If we *could* be perfect parents, our children would be just as hurt and unready for life as if we were always childish. The best things they learn from us about life and about God for dealing with hurt, anger, evil are from seeing what we do *when* we feel like children.

The key is to *recognize* when we are in the child position. Often when we're at a loss, we hike ourselves up into the Almighty God position, becoming as powerful, big, and scary as possible. This reflex rarely passes through awareness. That we're momentarily frightened, overwhelmed *children* is inadmissible. When two kittens first meet, they bristle, growl, hiss, and swat in front while sometimes pooping with fear in the rear, looking so little and cute. It's not cute when we do. We're not picking on someone our own size. I recall my own desperate "Hell Hours" when I tried to fix dinner with fussy children at my feet before my husband came home. At such times we *feel* like desperate children, only we don't see or accept this. So instead we become *big bullies.* We say *if you'll just behave, I won't get so mad.* But this is asking the child to be parent, to set his desperation aside and take care of ours. He doesn't know that Mommy's only two now and wants him to be the grown-up.

We try to *act* grown up, but the desperate child inside bursts out disguised as Almighty God. Unless we receive our child feelings lovingly, we can't help siccing them on our children. We don't poop in our pants, but mean, "shouldy" things come out of our mouths. *Should* is the meaning of that other word for *poop.* There's no clearer sign that we're in the Almighty God position (which is really the overwhelmed child position) than when we're full of should. Worse than the Almighty God position is the Holy Mary Mother position. Nothing's more harmful than the idea that we should be "nice" all the time. Worse than overt bullying are underground shoulds that take the sneaky, snaky form of sugary manipulation and guilt trips. That's fighting dirty. The child feels like "should" for being so unaccountably upset and angry, for making Mommy sad, and being so "bad." The bumper sticker says, "should happens." The question isn't how to avoid that but how to deal with it when it happens. If we can accept our child-needs, then a desperate moment that could turn abusive can become an invitation to inspiration.

Sometimes when my children were rocketing about, feuding and fussing, I sent them to their room. If I did so from the Almighty God position, to punish or get rid of them, they either drew me into their room by going at each other, or they were back in no time, driving me mad. But if I did so from the child position, not to punish but for peace, theirs as well as mine—if I also took a moment to quietly turn to something beyond us all, the whole atmosphere changed. When I let go of them, they could let go of me. They'd get involved in their room, or maybe they'd come back. Either way the atmosphere was different, more peaceful or hilarious. When I left the Almighty God position of thinking that I had to run everything, when the hold between us was broken, the mental windows flung open to something bigger than both of us; peace would come. They learned to love such times. Sometimes they even came whimpering, "I need a quiet time."

I hope it's clear that we were learning to pray. As a story borrowed from *Gently Lead* shows, children take to this sort of prayer more easily than we do. My three-year-old wanted to draw a Christmas tree, but he didn't know how, so he asked me to show him. Usually I would have leaped at the chance to show that I knew something that he didn't. But that day I was not in the God position. Noticing that he had no paper and pencil, I said, "No. First, why don't you get a paper and pencil and then sit quietly and see if God will give you a good idea." "Oh, yeah," he said. "I forgot," as if, *well, of course, I just forgot for a minute that God can help me.* Off he went. Pretty soon I peeked around the corner and saw him sitting on the couch, eyes closed, short little legs sticking out, pencil in hand resting on the sketch pad on his lap, waiting for the good idea he was sure God would give him. Soon, back he came, eyes shining, with his drawing—a pile of triangles with a bunch of criss-crossed lines at the top—an unmistakable Christmas tree. Later I asked him to draw another Christmas tree for our family Christmas card. "Sure," he said, trotting off. This time when he came back he had drawn something that looked more like a Christmas elf than a tree. The star had become the tassle of a pointy cap. Not feeling at all like a failure, he said, "I started to draw a Christmas tree, but then God gave me a different idea!"

I regard *letting up, letting go of, and letting go into* as three stages of prayer (see also pages 228–238). In both of the above situations these steps can be seen: *letting up,* which is a personal step; *letting go of,* which is an interpersonal step; and *letting go into,* which is Beyond Personal. In my "Hell Hour" I first had to *let up* into awareness of the fact that I felt like a child who didn't know what to do. This is a step that my artist son did not have to take. He knew he was a child, so he accepted that he didn't know what to do. Next, in both stories, came the step of *letting go of each other.* In the "Hell Hour" I let go of the idea that my well-being depended on my children. In the drawing episode, both my son and I let go of the idea that his well-being depended on me. After that, in both episodes, there was a *letting go into God.* With the "Hell Hour" I did this letting go on behalf of all of us. In the drawing episode both my son and I consciously let go into God.

If you can *let up* the child in you, you can take two more steps: *letting go of* each other, and *letting go into* something Beyond Personal. Parents need a parent. Sometimes the parent is a child. But the child is not the parent. That children bring out our child-sides is potentially good. If you *let up* the child in you, you can *let go of* the idea that your child should parent you. Implied is that there's something to *let go into.* God. But what does that mean?

Lately we've heard a lot about the "inner child." Too rarely discussed is the possibility of finding a Beyond Personal parent. The idea of God as heavenly father or parent is modeled on the human parent. Unless we understand it metaphorically, this personal idea of God can be hard for adults to believe in. It conflicts with what we know about the universe. And it's difficult to trust a God in the image of our parents who, like us, were unpredictably loving/scary, present/abandoning. Paul's idea of God as that "in whom we live and move and have our being" is *Beyond* Personal, based on our experience of the environment, the air we breathe, the plants that feed us, the forces of gravity and buoyancy that support us *as long as we're at one with them.* I find it very meaningful. I believe if more was said about this God, there'd be more people in church. If *Beyond Personal* seems too impersonal, think of Moses's "I Am that I am," the Self of selves, which Paul, too, often expressed in terms of our being different parts of the divine body. I believe it is what Jesus meant by "I and my Father are one."

How does a Beyond Personal God apply to parenthood, to our children's dependency on us and our need for something to depend on? We know infants need air, food, and holding, *and* to be psychologically and spiritually inspired, nourished, and upheld. To provide oxygen for the unborn, milk for the baby, a mother only needs to do what she does for herself: breathe and eat. The better her food, the better her baby's milk. You don't try to produce milk for your baby without eating, or carry a child without centering yourself in the law of gravity. Yet when it comes to psychological and spiritual childrearing, we do. We try to say and do what's wise, but without accessing inspiration. We try to be loving, but without first accessing love. Yet we are no more *sources* of spiritual than of physical nourishment, inspiration or support. Rather we are *mediators* of Beyond Personal supply, channels through which what is needed can flow. To keep our babies physically alive, well, and safe, we must *keep* eating and centering ourselves. To spiritually feed, inspire, and support them, we must keep spiritually feeding, inhaling, and centering ourselves.

We serve as physical mediators for our children fairly easily. Once we ourselves were weaned—from personal umbilical cord, breast, and arms to direct reliance on the environment, from being children of persons to being conscious children of the Beyond Personal. Therefore we also wean our children fairly easily. Because we've found our oneness with these physical resources, we can entrust our children to them. We call children who are weaned independent, self-sufficient. But actually we *never* become independent. We only move from mediated to direct reliance on Beyond Personal sources of life support. When we walk, we are children of gravity. When we eat, we're children of the fruitful earth. In breathing, children of air.

We think of weaning as a stage of infancy. But life is really an endless series of ever deeper weanings from mediated to direct oneness with the Beyond Personal. Early physical weanings are parallel to, even stages of, far deeper psychospiritual weanings and realizations of oneness we face in later life. A Beyond Personal idea of God lends itself to an ecological view of this process that enables us to recognize many interdependent, mutually beneficial subsystems. It helps us to see family problems in terms of personal, interpersonal, and Beyond Personal systems that may be out of balance and trying to right themselves—for the good of the whole and its parts, for the good of parent *and* child. Instead of blaming ourselves or shaming our children, we can say, "What's trying to happen here?" When our child makes us childish, instead of feeling or making her feel rotten, we can ask what's being overlooked? What hurts that needs attention? Is some part of us that we *need* trying to come to life? Is God, through our child, refusing to let us go on without that part? Is life trying to wean us from dependency on each other to reliance on God? Yes.

One woman sought help because she mistreated her child. "I'm so needy!" she wept. After a while, she saw that while her needy behavior was illegitimate, beneath it was a real, legitimate need for loving attention—hers. This freed her from flipping back and forth between punishing herself and her child. Instead of asking, "What's the matter with me?" she learned to say, "Hey, what's up?"—to let up and see what the child in her needed. As she did this, she also grew more understanding of her son. When he had a spell of saying, "I hate you!" she heard it as, "Mommy, I'm hurting!" One day when he hurt his baby sister, instead of raging at him, she merely asked, "What happened?" "I think I pinched her too hard," he said ruefully. Instead of seeing everything in terms of right/wrong, should/shouldn't, want/don't want, she asked, "What's trying to happen here?" She wasn't religious, and I didn't use religious language with her, but by asking, "What's trying to happen here?" she was praying, so new inspiration could come in.

You don't have to hit people over the head with God, only to help them be comfortable with unknowing. Realization that parenthood is for our weaning and oneing, as well as our child's, brings us greater staying power. It makes us less anxious to run away and less clingy. It helps us let go when the time comes, enables us to flow a little more merrily and gently down the stream.

We're speaking of inspiration instead of respiration, spiritual instead of physical nourishment and gravitational support. Experts stress that children need a blend of love/authority, freedom/security, protection/permission. But they don't say how *to access it.* They tell us the great things *they* say and do but not how they arrived at them. Parenthood is like a popcorn popper where things are exploding and flying in and around you nonstop. No one can tell us what to say when our children defy us, or the perfect thing to do when they're frightened or angry. When your child says, "I hate you!" is he saying it's time to let go, or that he needs a hug? We can't be wisely loving or lovingly wise toward our child without breathing in, feeding on, and being centered in a source of wisdom and love beyond us both: God.

How can we breathe in, feed on, and center ourselves in God? How does a child—how did we—learn to walk? We were weaned from the personal to the Beyond Personal. How? We *let go of* parents (which is weaning), shifted all our weight from parent to ground, and we *let go into* the Beyond Personal force of gravity (which is a oneing). We knew nothing of gravity, and our first encounters were very bumpy. Yet, by so radically *letting go of* and *letting go into* what we didn't even know was there, we discovered an invisible force that supports, protects, guides, and frees us. Both physical and spiritual breathing, feeding, and walking depend on Beyond Personal support. In both we must take in what the Beyond Personal provides before we can express it. In both this can't be done ahead of time, or once and for all, any more than we can breathe in the morning for the rest of the day.

Why? When we're hungry for love, gasping for inspiration, failing, sinking—why *don't* we turn to the Beyond Personal? Because we still see love and wisdom in strictly personal terms. Either we have to take care of ourselves or find someone else to do it. When it comes to psychospiritual balance, nurture, and inspiration, we are in a sense still unweaned. We still see persons as the source of what we need. We talk of psychological *groundedness, centering, balance,* and *equilibrium,* but we forget that groundedness depends on a ground, that equilibrium and centeredness occur in or on something.

If we learned to breathe, feed, and walk *without lessons,* why not spiritual breathing, feeding, and walking? For one thing, the whole human race has found its oneness with certain physical forces, so our parents trusted them, and could entrust us to them. And as *unknowing children,* we were open to Beyond Personal guidance. Realizing our spiritual oneness takes a lifetime, but if we understand that this *is* the task, we can set about weaning ourselves of the need to be fed or carried by our child, and seek our oneness with the true source of what we both need.

When a child *lets go of* Mommy or Daddy, and *lets go into* the force of gravity, she does not have *to let up* into awareness the fact that she is a child. So she naturally approaches everything in a "let's see," learning way. That's why she even learns from the spills she takes and why *letting go of* and *into* is so easy for her. Letting up the child is a step we need to take that the child doesn't. It's hard for us not only because we have to let go of more and more, and because we must *let go into* on deeper and deeper levels, but also because we find being a child inadmissible. That's why *letting up* is so important.

When I was learning to swim I discovered a poolside drain just under the water's surface. If I laid back and stuck a finger in it, I could secretly hold myself up. "Look! I'm floating!" I'd call. But I knew I hadn't let go of the side. I knew I hadn't fully let go into the water. I knew what I was hanging on *with* and what I was hanging on *to* that I'd have to let go of before I would truly float. Letting go into God is harder. Even if we dare to let go of what we consciously cling to, and to let go into the seeming void of the Beyond Personal, our unconscious selves still cling. So we don't let go *of* everything, and we aren't letting go *into* with our full psychic weight. Thus we don't feel the force of the Beyond Personal, of God, under us.

It's hard! Buddhists say, "Everything clung to has to be let go." We merely have to let go. But of *everything!* This means *letting up* all shameful childish feelings and parts of ourselves that we're used to holding down and hiding. It means *letting go of* all familiar supports including family and fully *letting go into* the unknown—precisely when we feel most threatened and alone. It's counterinstinctual. Jesus said, "Those who lose their life shall find it." *Simple, but not easy. It can't be done, but must be lived. It takes at least a lifetime.* He also said, "Unless you become as a little child you will never enter the kingdom."

The Bible says, "A little child will lead them." Children lead us to be aware of the child in us who needs God. Sometimes I think that's a scribal error, and that it should say, "A little child will *drive* them." But it's this inner child who, if we recognize and are gentle with it, can gently lead us to God—which is also the best and only way to spiritually lead our children. Think of the man on the cross. "Father," he said, *letting up* the child. "Forgive them," he said, *letting go of.* "Into thy hands I commit my spirit," *letting go into.*

Practical Information for New Parents

If you are a new parent, you may be overwhelmed by the many new things you have to deal with and the variety of products designed to help you. This section provides guidelines to make things easier for new parents. Topics include baby clothes, equipment, feeding, and books on childrearing. None of these things is truly important and there is no "right way" to do anything. But discerning what's best for you is easier once the issues are understood.

Get Ready, Get Set

Equipment purchased ahead of time is better kept at a minimum, but in preparing for your newcomer, you'll want to consider the following:

Birth Announcements. In hospitals babies are automatically footprinted on arrival. If you remember to ask in advance or at the time, it is usually possible to have an extra print made that can be photocopied and glued onto announcement cards you have already addressed.

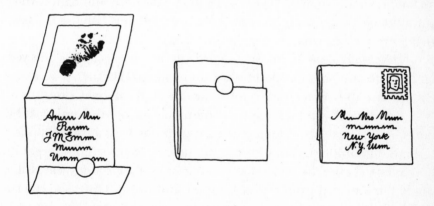

Baby seat. A sort of book stand for babies to eat, sleep, be awake, and travel in—a place where they can see what's going on and be a part of things without straining to hold their heads up or being held. So handy that it's hard to imagine what parents ever did (with us!)

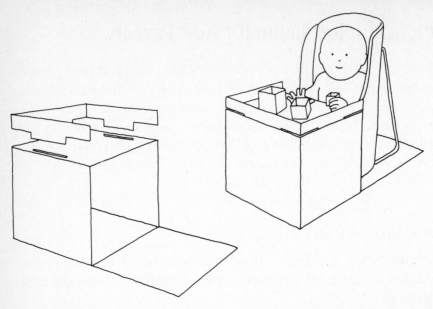

without them. Dinner is ready and your baby won't sleep? Put her on the table in her baby seat. You'll have a more peaceful hot dinner, and she'll soon be lulled to sleep by the conversation. For the wide-eyed two- to five-month-old who wants to use his hands, the seat has one drawback: dropped toys fall out of sight and reach. Turn a cardboard carton on its side to make a knee-hole desk. Various combination seats are available: baby seat/car seat, baby seat/carrier, baby seat/high-chair/stroller. See what exists; choose what you like.

Comfortable chair. A rocking chair with armrests *is* all it's cracked up to be for nursing and lulling babies to sleep. Whether it rocks or not, be sure to have a comfortable place to sit in the baby's room.

Baby bath. If you have enough counter space by your sink, a baby tub is handy. First baby? Then you may want one with a back support. If there's not enough room for the tub near its water supply, forget it. It's easier to bathe the baby in a tub at waist level, but not to carry the whole thing to and from the sink. Heavy and sloshy. Once she can sit up, she'll have more fun in the big tub. Meanwhile the kitchen sink makes a fine tub. The regular bathtub is fine if you don't mind kneeling. In just an inch or so of water, she can lie on her back, kicking and splashing freely. If you bathe with her, the water can be deeper, and she can float again with your help.

Changing table. Buy or improvise. As long as the mattress is in the high, infant position you can use one end of the crib. If you have one, an auxiliary portable crib for trips can serve as a changing table.

Changing mat. An extra and portable changing station is handy. A rubber sheet will do, or a vinyl-covered foam-changing pad with raised edges to keep the baby from rolling off. A *safety strap* is a good idea. If your setup doesn't come with one, improvise.

Indispensable dispenser. Mount a toilet paper dispenser near your diaper-changing station and forget about tissues, tidy wipes, cotton balls.

Get Dressed

Considerations in buying clothing include:

• Ease in putting on and taking off.

• Ease of changing diapers (should have snap or zipper crotch or be open at the bottom).

• Ease of care (should be no-iron, machine washable, machine dryable, or drip-dry).

• Season of birth (warm or cold) and the usual temperature of your house.

• Size of infant (a big newborn of eight or more pounds at birth will wear newborn-size clothes only briefly, if at all). Babies grow fast, so don't overdo on the initial wardrobe.

• Effectiveness—comfort and freedom for the baby—warm enough? cool enough? doesn't ride up, fall off, come undone, bunch up, stop circulation, fall over face?

• Looks? A word about *boy and girl clothes for babies.* Boy suits with separate tops and bottoms wind up with pants below and tops above the belly. Brrr! Better are one-piecers, or two-piecers that snap together. Little dresses are almost irresistible and come in drip-dry fabric. Don't fall for one that needs ironing or she will very likely outgrow it between the first washing and the first ironing.

Layette clothing sets with knitted cotton kimonos, nighties, pants, and tops are generally not useful. Within a few days of the baby's birth, you find which of these works best. Everything else is either a drag to put on or doesn't fit comfortably.

Stretch suits are best at first, provided it isn't too hot. If you have enough stretch suits, you don't need anything else. They meet all the criteria for baby clothing and can replace nighties, booties, sweaters, and undershirts. Long-sleeved, footed, snap-crotch stretch suits are useful year-round. Short-sleeved, legless romper and sunsuit versions are available for hot weather.

Nylon-tricot infant suits cost more and are outgrown sooner than stretch suits, but they dry in no time at all—two minutes in a dryer, about thirty minutes on the line (squeeze in a towel first). One or two are a boon for the clumsy early days when everything may be wet before breakfast.

Cotton-knit nighties (with a drawstring bottom to keep the gown from riding up) are cheap, a breeze for diaper changing, and can be washed and dried at hot temperatures. You may get extra mileage out of these gowns when your child is learning to walk. No good for crawling because the child crawls into the chest of the gown, but great for beginning walking when nonskid bare feet are an asset.

> *Wee Willie Winkie runs through the town*
> *Upstairs and downstairs in his nightgown,*
> *Rapping at the windows, crying through the lock,*
> *"Are the children all in bed?*
> *Now it's eight o'clock."*

> —Traditional nursery rhyme

Undershirts are a needless bother. Since you are constantly picking up the baby under the arms, any undershirt that isn't pinned to the diaper rides up and becomes a constricting wad across the chest and under the arms. But if pinned, they soak up the wetness. Undershirts mean double laundry and extra dressing. For warmth, an easily donned and doffable sweater, jacket, or blanket is handier.

A *bunting* is useful in winter. Best are ones with hoods, mittened sleeves, and no legs. A sack bottom makes diaper changing easy and allows freedom for kicking without kicking off the carriage blanket. Also a good place for an extra tissue or diaper. Sleeved ones are best because they allow the baby to move her arms without becoming uncovered. Get a machine-washable one with a hood that ties snugly under the chin and does not brush constantly against the baby's cheek. Such brushing makes some infants want to nurse at inconvenient moments.

When it's time for standing and walking, bare feet are the best nonskid base. In winter, toddlers need some kind of footgear for toddling on cold floors. Footed stretch suits are slippery. Booties fall off as fast as you put them on and are slippery. Moccasins fall off because they tie too high (above, rather than below, the anklebone). Shoes are awkward. Some sleep suits come with nonskid soles. Or sew pieces of leather elbow patches to the bottoms of footed pajamas.

Coated bellwire is good for keeping booties and mittens on. Bend and tape the ends for safety, weave through booties and mittens just below the child's ankle and wristbones, and twist. Especially helpful between one and two years when children *will* shake their mittens off only to cry for you to put them on, only to shake them off again.

Night! Night!

The main issues in choosing a child's bed are budget, space, safety, appearance, and durability. Your lifestyle matters, too—whether you travel a lot, whether or not you plan to have more children.

Cradles, baskets. These are outgrown very quickly, but can be handy as a temporary or auxiliary sleeping place. In the early days of night feedings, it may be handy to have the baby next to your bed at night instead of in a separate room—though there's nothing wrong with letting an infant cuddle, feed, and even sleep with you in your bed. Also handy for trips, though babies small enough for baskets can also be safely bedded down on normal adult beds with a bolster on either side, or in a big deep bureau drawer. Many carriages have separable baskets that can serve as small beds.

Cribs. There are three basic types: portable inexpensive, standard moderately priced to expensive, and unusual and expensive. There is something to be said for each. Check *Consumer Reports* for quality and safety. Before buying a standard crib, here are a few other considerations.

If you can avoid bedtime power struggles, you don't need a crib much longer than a year and a half. After that, crib sides aren't needed for safety, and it's best for the child to find better reasons for staying in bed than not being able to get out. Unless you plan to keep the child in a crib longer than two years, standard cribs are larger than necessary. Smaller cribs are fine and leave more floor space for play.

Whatever crib you choose, look for simplicity and openness as well as sturdiness, safety, and convenience. A bed, not a safe deposit box or classroom. If there is anything to be learned in bed, it is the art of grateful retirement, peaceful sleeping, and cheerful waking.

Small collapsible cribs are inexpensive and adequate for babies up to at least two years. Their collapsibility is handy for trips and storage, but they can also serve on a permanent basis. The mattress can be placed in two positions. Thick, firm mattresses are preferable to thinner ones if the crib is to be used on a daily basis. Fitted knit sheets are available for portable cribs.

If you decide on a *standard crib*, don't buy a double drop-sided one. They are more expensive, less sturdy, and you will fall into a routine of picking up the baby from only one side.

Unusual, expensive cribs range from worst to best. Worst are fussy, ugly, and cluttered with built-in toys that are supposed to expedite early learning. Overlooked is that beds are for sleeping. Unless space is a problem, cribs that convert to junior beds are no bargain since junior beds are unnecessary (see below). But we had one that converted to a small sofa and was soon a favorite place for story-reading.

Of course, no bedstead is really necessary. Around the world more people probably sleep on the floor than in beds. I happen to appreciate the idea of getting off the ground (see "High and Lifted Up," p. 78) that a bed suggests, but you don't really have to have a bed for that to take place. A mattress on the floor works fine and presents no danger of falling.

Moving from crib to bed. Junior beds with guard rails are unnecessary. Since you'll need one eventually, a regular twin bed makes sense when your child is ready to leave his crib. Place a chair beside the bed near the child's head. If he rolls onto the chair, his feet will land on the floor, and he'll wake up enough to climb back into bed. At first you may also want some pillows on the floor by the bed. If you're supercautious, put the mattress on the floor until the child is used to having no sides. Within a week he'll have a built-in sense of the limits of the bed. By then you'll have seen how nice it is to sit by the bed for a song or story, so you'll probably leave the chair there anyway.

Bedding. How much you need for the early days depends on your laundry facilities and savoir faire. If you're a rank beginner at diapering, you may need extra bedding. On our first day home, we ran through all the bedding before noon—two crib sheets, four receiving blankets, three rubber pads, and four nighties. We had no washing machine, so we did hand laundry until the humidity verged on rain. But after the first day we never got to the bottom of the pile again.

Even if you are a beginner with no skills, a few tricks can help to keep the laundry level low:

• Don't wake a sleeping baby for a change.

• Until the baby learns to move around in bed, it isn't necessary to change the whole bed just because there is a damp spot in one corner of it. Move the baby instead.

• Let the baby sleep on a small pad of cottonized rubber on top of the sheet. For small spit-ups or wettings, just change the pad.

Knitted, fitted crib sheets are useful as long as the baby stays in a crib, so if in doubt, buy more (three to six) rather than fewer. They are soft to sleep on, a breeze to launder. If you like to tie-dye, try a crib sheet. Two crib-size *flannelized rubber sheets* should be sufficient. If the mattress is vinyl covered, you don't need these, but you may want them to soften the mattress surface beneath the sheet and to avoid having to wash off the mattress. Four to six so-called *puddle pads* are handy for sleeping on (see tips above), and as lap pads and changing places. They can be bought precut in infant supply stores, or less expensively, off the bolt to be cut to size with pinking shears. Don't put them in a very hot dryer. *Mattress pads* are optional. Some people use them to soften the mattress surface or instead of a rubber sheet. But flannelized rubber sheets are adequate and more practical.

Bedmaking. Once the baby begins to move around (about a month), bedmaking arrangements need to be revised. There are two approaches. One is to make the baby, to dress him in warm enough clothing so that it won't matter if he stays covered or not. The other is to make up the bed like a real bed, with tucked-in top sheet and blanket. If you follow the babymaking approach, you need *thermal sleep suits* for cold nights. Disadvantages are that the suits are expensive, a bit cumbersome for diaper changing, and a bigger deal to launder. For the bedmaking approach, you can use season-weight pajamas and toss on or take off extra blankets as needed. The bedmaking approach is easier except that most ready-made top sheets and blankets for cribs are too narrow. Top sheets and blankets need to be wide enough to tuck in well under the mattress on both sides. Otherwise the child becomes uncovered and tangled up. Ideal dimensions for a 5-inch-thick standard crib mattress: $5^1/_2$ feet long by $4^1/_2$ feet wide for top sheets and 5 feet by $4^1/_2$ feet wide for blankets.

A washable *quilt* is unbeatable. Lovely patchwork ones can be inexpensively made by covering a ready-made, synthetic baby blanket with drip-dry cotton—patchwork on top, a plain print on the bottom. The whole thing may be stitched together on a sewing machine, with a grosgrain border 3 inches from the edge. We received one that was almost magically useful. As a cover, it was stiff enough so that our children could turn under it without becoming tangled up; and it was light enough to stay across their shoulders if they inched their way toward the head of the crib. Place on the floor to serve as a playpen. It is soft enough to cushion yet stiff enough not to crumple under the child.

Or you can make a special *blanket* with fake fur or scraps of cotton appliquéd to a cut-down blanket. Make a happy-faced clown from old scraps of cotton, a fake fur teddy bear with print paws and button eyes and a soft velvet or kid-glove nose, a fake-fur kangaroo with a print pouch for a stuffed baby kangaroo. To prevent raveling, machine stitch around the edge of each appliqué. Fold and iron along the stitching, baste or pin, and sew with invisible stitches to the blanket.

Glow-in-the-dark stars and moon on the ceiling are nice when the lights go out.

Bedtime Books

Here is a list of some of our favorite bedtime books:

Catch Me and Kiss Me and Say It Again
Goodnight Moon

Goodnight Richard Rabbit
Jamie's Story
Ladybug and Dog and the Night Walk
The Little Fur Family
Lullabies and Night Songs
Midnight Moon
The Sailor Dog
The Runaway Bunny

Yum! Yum!

Highchair. Besides safety, the main issue is cleanup. Buy one with a detachable tray (for washing in the kitchen sink) and with a space between the back and seat (for easily sponging off squashed food). The bigger the tray the better, as there are many other things to do in highchairs besides eating. Trays that extend back under the arms catch more of the inevitable spills. It should be possible to set the tray in several positions (nearer or farther from the child). Try taking the tray off and putting it on once or twice to see if it goes easily. Make sure that, when mounted, the surface of the tray is level. This seems obvious, but we had one with slanted arms. Everything slid toward the child and wound up in his lap. Chrome and vinyl are easier to clean than wood. You may want a convertible highchair. The top half converts to a child's chair, the bottom to a child's table.

Pyrex pie plates make good plates for preschoolers who have outgrown baby "cereal" dishes, but who still need sides to help them load their forks and spoons.

Clothes pins can convert anything—towels, cloth diapers and napkins—into bibs. Fasten with clothes pins. With two clothes pins you can fashion yourself an apron out of any hand towel.

The child who wants to feed himself has important problems to solve. At first the whole loaded fist arrives inside the mouth. But it cannot be opened there. How to remove the hand without dropping the food? Not easy, and not neat. Let him practice with pieces of banana, cheese, macaroni (it dissolves even if swallowed whole), toast, sandwich cubes, and omelets. These can be managed without teeth. Remember that babies do not have to be made to eat, nor do they only like what's bad for them.

The most important thing about the meal is the friendly, peaceful coming together. As your child grows, try the following "Foods for Thought":

- *Fresh green peas in the pod*—a miracle of abundance and mystery any two-year-old can appreciate. A great resource for the wonder of package opening and healthy (unsticky) nibbling, and perhaps talking a bit about growth and how the peas got there.
- *Corn on the cob.* A whole ear to husk leaf by leaf until she discovers the silk and, at last, the amazing row-by-row kernels.
- *A pumpkin.* On Halloween a one-and-a-half-year-old and his mother made a jack-o'-lantern. The process filled nearly a whole day of waking time. The child mostly watched from his highchair, delighting in the revelation of the seeds ("What do you suppose is inside?") inside the huge, round, orange ball. While the mother carved the face, the child sort of sorted the seeds from the meat. They roasted the seeds for a snack and cooked the pumpkin meat (with brown sugar and butter) to eat that evening by the glow of the candlelit jack-o'-lantern. The second year he was too busy to sit, but enjoyed choosing a face, did a little scooping, and still appreciated it a lot.
- *Apple.* If you want to teach your child about God, show her some divine handiwork. An apple sliced horizontally in half reveals a five-pointed star of seeds. Ever tried to draw a star? Then marvel at the perfection of this one that came by itself. Try this with a *pear.* "Hey! How did those seeds that look like a star come there? On the tree there came a bud, and the bud became a flower, and the flower became an apple, and I am eating that apple! If I eat its seeds, will a tree grow?"

The *highchair* is not only an eating place but can also be a place of quiet refuge, heightened concentration, and change of pace and perspective. At the end of the day when she's restless and tired, and you are fixing her supper, let her sit beside you in her highchair. She'll like being high enough to see what you are doing, to "help," or to play with some kitchen tools. At the end of a meal when she wants to get down but you would like to finish eating first, give her a puzzle to work in the highchair. Highchairs are wonderful for creative projects that might otherwise be hazardous to your home. Watercolors, crayons, or water-based markers—very young children enjoy these with more concentration and less mess in the gentle confinement of the highchair.

Kids in the Kitchen

The *potato and onion bin* is fun for children under one year old and leaves a relatively easy mess to clean up. Onions are fascinating to peel, and potatoes are great rumblers and rollers.

An old-fashioned metal drip *coffee pot* is the world's best first puzzle and stack toy.

Clear some low *cupboards* and *drawers* for the baby. Putting in and taking out *pots, pans, colanders, strainers, plastic containers,* or just opening and closing the doors themselves are absorbing and edifying activities for tiny hands.

Until label peeling is discovered, *canned goods* can be used for blocks—especially fun if you happen to store them on a *turntable.*

Kitchen utensils—spoons, spatulas, tongs, measuring cups, egg beaters, whisks, egg slicers, cookie cutters, potato ricers, and butter knives (be sure that it is not a sharp or serrated knife) make a fine modeling set when play-dough age is reached.

Cookie cutters that aren't too sharp are good for cutting sandwiches, watermelon, or apple slices. *Would you like to eat a triangle or a semicircle today?*

The *kitchen sink* with a trickle of running water and some ladles, cups, sieves, or toy boats will last for hours. Educators say water play is important for children.

Helping means being like Mommy and Daddy, which is a goal of children. Before age two they can already appreciate the challenge of:

- *Washing* unbreakable dishes and vegetables and *drying* silverware
- *Sponging* off cabinets and *dusting*
- *Unwrapping* a stick of margarine (while you season a casserole, put it in the oven, peel the potatoes, and wash his hands)
- *Peeling* off the outer layers of one onion (while you peel and finely chop six)
- *Breaking* the yolk of an egg before you beat it, and *dumping* ingredients into the pan
- *Telling* you when the spaghetti water starts to bubble
- *Throwing* anything away or *putting* recyclable things into appropriate bins
- *Carrying* things from here to there (little ones love missions and cooperative efforts)

- *Putting* the bread on top of, and *wrapping,* sandwiches
- *Sorting and putting away* utensils

And so on. The more we recognize what our children are trying to learn, the more appropriate ideas occur to us at appropriate times. We will be blessed a hundred times in priceless companionship and incredible beauty—for there is nothing quite so grateful or so lovely as a child who is merely being allowed to learn.

Worse than not allowing our children to help is expecting too much or insisting. This happens, too. You hear people hissing things like, "Can't you do anything right? You're no help at all!" Watch a child try to put a cloth table mat on the table for the first time. He'll try to lift it from the bottom edge, not realizing that the material will flop down. So much has to be learned. If he hasn't come to hate the failure connected with his efforts to be helpful, eventually he will indeed be a help.

What? No Books on Childrearing?

The best thing to read when trying to raise a child is the child. Even more important is to learn to read ourselves. From books that tell us how to deal with problems we often only get the problems. Problems can be contagious. See how easily our children catch them from us. Most problem-solving books for parents start with the idea that the child has a problem. They tell us how to fix the child, or else. But it's better to approach problems as mere confusions and symptoms. Problems arise from mistaken beliefs, assumptions, or expectations. We have these not because we haven't read the right books with the "right" answers but because we haven't discovered the right questions.

What we call our children's "problems" are mainly reflections of our confusions, which register on the child just as a thermometer registers a fever. Nothing you do to the thermometer changes the illness. You can shake down the thermometer so that the fever doesn't show, but the fever is not affected. Even if we shake our children into behaving (and sometimes in frustration some of us do literally shake them into obedience), nothing constructive will have happened. The problem is not in the child any more than the sickness is in the thermometer.

When a person who has had a fever becomes healthy again, he can put a thermometer in his mouth and it will not register a fever anymore, only health. That's how it is with our children. As we gain healthy understanding, they stop registering our confusions as behavioral or emotional symptoms.

We must not *blame* ourselves when our not knowing and confusion are reflected disharmoniously in our children. Perhaps the biggest occupational hazard of parenthood is the belief that we are supposed to know everything. Children are children so they can become adults; parents are parents so they can become understanding (which is the same as loving). Learning seems to be the point of it all. The first step is to recognize and accept our not knowing and confusion.

Likewise we need not fear that we can wreck our children with what we don't know. The thermometer isn't sick just because someone's fever is registered on it. Neither is the baby. In fact, until the child is about two years old, there's a sort of grace period in which symptoms of parental error disappear in the child the instant the errors are corrected in the parents' thought. As the child becomes more self-aware, he begins to take on the parents' errors as his own mistaken beliefs. But even then, any crucial progress has to be made in the consciousness of the parent.

Recognition that parenthood is as much for the parents' growth as for the child's also helps us to be easier on our children. The child is like a hand mirror in which we can perceive and correct our mental image of ourselves and life. Our children are not images of our selves but of our thoughts. The image itself cannot be faulted or corrected, nor can we even fault or correct ourselves as image makers. In the child as mirror we see neither our true selves nor the child's, only the reflections of our beliefs. So it's no use to view what we see with fear or guilt or blame or any thought that gives reality to the image. The image has value only in that it makes plain our unconscious confused beliefs and priorities.

To try to correct the child by merely regulating his behavior is like painting a smile on the reflection of an unhappy face in a mirror. To correct or try to change our behavior alone is like putting a lipstick smile on the unhappy face itself. Both actions are absurdly superficial; only genuine understanding and awareness can transform the face and its reflection into a genuinely loving smile.

Our children need to be comforted, cared for, encouraged,

trained, protected, instructed, reprimanded, forbidden, facilitated, and prevented. But we must also have regard for their right to be wrong or, more correctly, for their ability to learn to be right. As long as their mistakes are not dangerous to them and do not impinge on others' rights, we must allow them the freedom to learn. Respect their learning process. Children who are constantly corrected and "fixed" lose confidence in themselves and in life. Such children wind up thinking of themselves as needing to be fixed. As teenagers many of them come to believe that they need "a fix." (See also page 129.)

> *The kingdom of heaven may be compared to a man who sowed good seed in his field; but while men were sleeping, his enemy came and sowed weeds among the wheat and went away. So when the plants came up and bore grain, then the weeds appeared also. And the servants of the householder came and said to him, "Sir, did you not sow good seed in your field? How then has it weeds?" He said to them, "An enemy has done this." The servants said to him, "Then do you want us to go and gather them?" But he said, "No, lest in gathering the weeds you root up the wheat along with them. Let both grow together until the harvest; and at harvest time I will tell the reapers, Gather the weeds first and bind them in bundles to be burned, but gather the wheat into my barn."*
>
> —Matthew 13:24–30

The field is each person's consciousness. The seeds are truthful, fruit-bearing ideas; the weeds false, hindering ones. We are all the sowers striving, servants sleeping, and reapers discerning. The enemy is ignorance passing for knowledge. The farmer is the One Mind. The harvest is the reunion of the individual mind with the One Mind in consciousness. For us "the time for the harvest is now." The time for our children is also now, but that is their business, theirs and the farmer's. As parents, our main job is not ripping up weeds but tending the wheat.

3

Happiness

Verily I say unto you, Whosoever shall not receive the kingdom of God as a little child shall in no wise enter therein.

—Mark 10:15; Luke 18:17

And a little child shall lead them.

—Isaiah 11:6

Let both grow together until the harvest; and at harvest time I will tell the reapers, Gather the weeds first and bind them in bundles to be burned, but gather the wheat into my barn.

—Matthew 13:30

Wheat and tare, the Seeing Being and Me, Inc. coexist in us. By the time we are parents, Me, Inc. is full grown and proving itself false, ever more untenable, coming to the end of its rope. Like a bud breaking apart to make way for the flower, Me, Inc. is having more and more trouble keeping itself together. Now along comes our child to make the increasingly difficult seemingly impossible. Unaware of our true nature as Seeing Beings, Me, Inc. struggles in us—angrily, fearfully, futilely—to be self-sufficient, now even self-sufficient for two! Caring for a child repeatedly forces us to confront our insufficiency and to let go of Me, Inc. Yet what a tender mercy this is! In the child, Me, Inc. is just beginning; so for a time the Seeing Being shows through more clearly. If we know what to look for, we can see it. And what we are able to see is what we are free to be. In this way the wheat outstrips the tare and the weed dies back, never to be missed.

Work and Play

Does the newborn already experience himself to be one thing and life or other people another? When his blanket is unwrapped or he is lowered too quickly into bed, he flails his arms, and perhaps cries. Does he feel his *self* unwrapped and exposed? Does he feel his *self* falling from some goodness? Maybe his startle reflex shows that this sensation of being a separate self comes as a sort of shock, even that it feels wrong. With the experience of being a separate self comes the experience of limitation and the desire to overcome it—to sit, to walk, to crawl, to run, to fly; to find security, connection, freedom, love. To be happy.

Having entered upon the experience of being a separate self, he also embarks on the struggle to get his self taken care of or to become an adequate separate self, one that can take care of itself. But on a deeper level he remains a Seeing Being. Though he does not know what he is searching for, or even that he is searching, we can see that everything he does is part of a search to understand what he is, what life is, and how the experienced separation is to be overcome. He wants to make a connection, to see how he fits in and into what.

Play: The Serious Side

Well timed and at their best, toys are a means through which a child experiences certain spiritual qualities. Through playing with puzzles and blocks he experiences unity; through learning to walk or riding a tricycle he experiences freedom; through music and art, beauty; through books, meaning and truth; through pets and friends and family, love.

Experience is not really an adequate word. It is *through* experience, through the senses, that the child meets up with spiritual qualities. But we only need to watch a child's face light up with surprise and delight to realize that these events (literally *e-venire*, "forthcoming") are really taking place in consciousness. Increasing awareness, however rudimentary, is happening. Through various sensory experiences the child is made aware of, and on some conscious level participates in and appreciates, certain spiritual realities. Happiness does not come from the experience but from the awareness.

Perhaps *encounter* describes it best. He is not conceptually aware, yet there is clearly some conscious recognition taking place. If you put a piece of a puzzle in his hand, and use his hand to fit the piece into the puzzle, he has a sensory experience of unity. But if nothing clicks in his consciousness with some semiconscious question of his, then there has been no encounter and no real event. Nor will he register delight. The happiness lies in the happen-ness.

> The toddler at the beach at sunset, surrounded by a vast panorama of sky and sea, cannot see it; he is totally preoccupied with the pebble, the wavelet at his feet. His eyes can see it all, but his consciousness cannot recognize beauty, grandeur, vastness, order, harmony, all the formless realities which make the scene so breathtaking. However, his appreciation can grow; indeed, it must if he is to fulfill his potential. That expansion of consciousness to the realization of aesthetic and, finally, transcendental values is the essence of our human growth process.
> —Ann Tremaine Linthorst, *A Gift of Love*

So, while much of the child's learning occurs *through* his senses, the learning itself is taking place in consciousness. It is not purely sensory; it cannot be called instinct. Encounters are spiritual events that take place when sensory experience and spiritual reality meet in consciousness. Whether evoked by pebble, or wavelet, or sky, encounters are moments of oneness—the oneness of seeing with being—in which the Seeing Being supersedes strugglesome Me, Inc. When this happens there is always an explosion. It may be an explosion of light, *de*light, on the child's face, or an eruption of laughter.

Children do not laugh only at what is funny but even more often at what they find *wonderful.* One-derful. By the fact that they find it so wonderful we recognize the depth and truth of their yearning. They search constantly for encounters. It is the absence of encounters that renders any toy or activity a bore or frustration. Encounters are what motivate and please a child at play. Whenever they break upon her, we see that she is happy. For a moment the sense of gap between self and what it belongs to is overcome, and the Seeing Being rejoices. Without quite realizing it, but without doubting it either, she has a momentary sense that the unity, beauty, truth, freedom, love she innately desires (because they are the truth about her, too) are *so. That's* the joy of play.

Because the child's work with her toys brings happiness, we call it *play,* and we buy more toys. But *having* toys is not the fun; the toy is just a means. This is evident from the fact that children lose interest in a toy (or in the treasured pebbles from the beach) as soon as they have learned all they can from it. Whatever does not offer them a conscious encounter does not interest *or animate* them either.

So again we observe that the child is primarily a spiritual, Seeing Being. Even as she is being mis-educated to be Me, Inc. and take care of herself, she is vitalized and rendered happy only by what she *sees.*

Work: The Lighter Side

My meat is to do the will of Him that sent me.

—John 4:34

As our Me, Incs. grew up we learned to divide our lives into categories of "work" and "play." Work is seen as unpleasant, play as pleasant. As full-grown selves looking out for our selves we forget that happiness has something to do with seeing. Dividing our lives into work and play, we find joy elusive. Where has it gone? Our children bring it back to us by showing us what it is. Just when we had begun to notice it was missing!

Our children remind us that happiness depends on learning. Unity, freedom, beauty, love, are not things Me, Inc. can *have* but ideas that can only be real for us as we consciously realize that they are so. A good toy is one through which a child encounters spiritual realities through experiencing their effects. It is the encounter that is happy. As adults, we need to move beyond encounter to conscious realization. Yet somewhere during Me, Inc.'s growing up, the joy of conscious encounters has become confused with the things or experiences that facilitate them. ("Why don't you take better care of your things? I laid out good money for that toy, and now you've broken it!") So distracted, instead of moving smoothly from experiencing to encountering to seeing, we become involved with trying to acquire things or set up situations in which we can *have* the experiences. Detached from spiritual principles, these efforts fail, and from the failures we infer that the spiritual principles themselves are not so. But the true self, the soul in us, goes on yearning for its truly happy, spiritual fulfillment, the conscious overcoming of our sense of separation.

Beyond Work and Play

> *In thy presence is fullness of joy, and at*
> *thy right hand are pleasures forevermore.*
>
> —Psalm 16:11

A child is not a toy, but as we have seen, a toy is not merely a toy either. Like good toys, children concretely express certain spiritual qualities. We know they do not possess or understand these qualities; we know that we have not put them there. Yet there they are. Marvel at it! The incredible fact of them—peace in the sweet sleeping and still watching, love in the fearless expectancy of good, intelligence in the alert searching, vitality in the perpetual activity, unity in the working together of all parts and functions for good. Where did all this come from? What is it if it isn't so?

As a good toy invites a response from the child, children invite us to be involved with spiritual qualities and elicit them from us. Children confront us with the fact of goodness and the necessity and possibility of expressing more goodness. In proportion, as we give ourselves over to this possibility, we begin to experience the overcoming of the self/other gap, much as the child experiences unity when he consciously participates in fitting a puzzle piece into a puzzle. On the child's level it is a matter of spiritual encounters; for us a matter of consciously realizing the underlying truth that is the one nature of self, other, and life itself. In this way, Me, Inc. and its struggles diminish, increasingly replaced by the Seeing Being who is at home in, and at one with, the reality of love-intelligence.

In the last chapter we considered how the necessary becomes a point of conscious contact with the essential. The toy, the child, the task are all concrete points of expression for infinite spiritual reality. Thus being with our children can lead us toward the spiritual realization we have in fact been seeking since birth.

As parents we may begin to perceive the true nature of play as work and discover that the purpose and happiness of both are the recognition of underlying spiritual principles. Through this discovery, we can become as happy in our so-called work as parents as is the child at play.

> *Our attitude toward the newborn child should be one of reverence that a spiritual being has been confined to within limits perceptible to us.*
>
> —Maria Montessori, *The Secret of Childhood*

Toys, Playtime, and Learning

Our ongoing parental task is to do the necessary while keeping sight of the essential. Until recently toys were usually associated with childish pleasure, feeling good, and love, in contrast to books and lessons, which were associated with work, intellectual success, and discipline. Recognition that children's play is learning has led to a huge proliferation of educational toys. Side effects are parental confusion, budgetary distress, domestic clutter, and rampant materialism. With older children the availability of all sorts of lessons and educational experiences adds to the confusion. Now we're supposed to provide both fun things and educational things. If we aren't tempted to buy what our children want, we think we should buy it because they *need* it. Fresh standards are needed for selecting appropriate toys and opportunities at appropriate times.

So much seems necessary. Even when we succeed in the struggle to meet all these "needs" our success backfires. Our children can have everything, yet be discontented and dissatisfied. In fact, the more we provide, the more they seem to feel unloved. The more educational opportunity we provide, the more apathetic and disinterested they seem to be. They don't seem to try, or they try and fail. Or they succeed and are unhappy (the success is a failure).

If such is our experience, we need to ask: What is the motive behind our scramble to provide our children with everything? If the motive is *essential*, that is, if it is consistent with the truth of being, then the best can be expected. If the best isn't happening, there must be something essentially false about our underlying motivation. We can be sure it is some plan Me, Inc. has hatched for itself.

So what is our motive? It seems simple: we want our children to succeed and be happy. We associate success with personal intelligence and power, feeling good and happy with being personally loved. But is feel-good pleasure a true expression of, or motivation for, love? Is success a true expression or motivation for intelligence? Are we as selflessly concerned about our children as we think we are? There are two ways in which parents exploit children as the supporting cast in our Metrogoldwyn Me, Inc. productions. One is based on a false, personal, feel-good idea of love; the other on a false, personal idea of intelligence as power.

False Love and Toy Buying: The Hedonistic Motive

Give her what she wants so she'll feel loved (and so she'll love me in return). We are often seduced by this false motive. Watch for the thought that precedes the thought of going out to buy or do something special for your child. Often it is Me, Inc.'s desire for acceptance, either from the child or through the child from others. So then we are not really giving but getting. Also, to the extent that we look upon our children's lives as remakes of our own childhood, buying things for them is like buying them for ourselves. Either way the tendency is to define love in feel-good terms. We equate not feeling good with not being loved. If our children feel (or look or act) good, we feel (that we are) good. We equate feeling good with being loved. So we try to love ourselves through our children by making them feel (or look or act) good.

False Intelligence and Toy Buying: The Ambitious Motive

Buy it for him to help him get into Harvard—to increase his IQ. If you don't buy enough educational toys, he'll have a low IQ. The flip side of materialistic feel-good pleasure-seeking motivations for buying toys to show love is a kind of intellectual materialism that says we must provide toys, experiences, and lessons to make our child smart. If he doesn't learn enough before he is four, he will never get into (the) college (of our choice). Whereas formerly parents saw themselves as providers and caretakers of the child's physical and emotional well-being, with the discovery of the preschooler's intellect we now see ourselves as having to be early-learning specialists too. The belief is that the child is a sort of empty thing to be trained and stuffed with knowledge; otherwise he will fail. Fail? Our exaggerated sense of personal responsibility turns the discovery of the preschooler's potential into a frustrating, discouraging, anxious, exhausting, conformist, competitive frenzy.

Just as the so-called loving motive for buying toys may conceal a selfish motive, behind the so-called educational or intelligent motive is also an essentially selfish ambition. Through the success of the bright child we expect to demonstrate how knowing and smart and successful and powerful *we* are as both the source of, and the force behind, the child.

The Love-Intelligent Approach to Toys and Learning

With both false motives, love and intelligence are confined to the very narrow context of self and other (Me, Inc. among Me, Incs.); love as a feeling to be gotten from each other, and intelligence as a personal power to be used against each other (success, competition, comparison). In this narrow context everyone is either a tool or an adversary, and neither love nor intelligence is possible. Love becomes exploitation; intelligence becomes conquest. So then love is unlove; and clearly any intelligence that defines love as something that love isn't must be unintelligent. So these ideas of love and intelligence are clearly unloving and stupid. If we provide our children, via toys and tools, playing and learning, with such perverted ideas of love and intelligence, is it any wonder that there is a certain perversity to the result?

When does the light-obsessed clown become happy? (See pages 8, 20, 291, 339–340.) Only when he sees. At that moment he is no longer a fool; he is both intelligent (seeing) and endowed with and able to express—that is, to be—every goodness he sees (freedom, creativity, harmony, etc.)—he is at one with love (loved). Now love and intelligence are not something he gets from, or has at, the expense of another. The encountering of both love and intelligence is one event. *Love-intelligence takes place where the tendency of life to reveal itself is fulfilled in the essential nature of the individual to see and express what is being revealed.* It is what makes loving participation with others possible. Appreciation of this liberates us to discern both the loving and the intelligent response to our children's quests for love and intelligence. We no longer distract them through materialistic or dualistic misapprehensions of what wisdom and learning or love and happiness are all about. A discerning parent reports:

> I think it is better to show love by meeting needs than to keep telling my son that I love him. Right now he is learning to tie his shoes. He is old enough, so even though it's hard for him, sometimes I insist. But once in a while when he's tired I still do it for him, and I have noticed that while I am tying his shoe, he says, "I love you, Mommy." When he says, "I love you," I know he knows that he is loved.

The Idea(l) Gift, the Idea(l) Toy

If we recognize child's play as the seeing work of the Seeing Being, intelligent questions arise when we consider providing a particular toy or experience. What idea does this toy express? What will our *giving* of it express to our young Seeing Being? What does it mean to me? What does it mean to the child? Is the idea being expressed a good one? Is there a better way to express this idea?

Most toys are unnecessary, and can even be obstacles to a child's learning and happiness. When a child is given the notion that he needs to be entertained, learning comes to a halt. If we keep in mind that the value of play is learning, and that toys are tools of learning, we will be more successful in choosing appropriate ones. Children learn quickly. If we treat them as objects of our affection by tossing objects (toys) at them when we're at a loss for love, we teach them that they are themselves no more than objects. Painful object lessons.

Particularly with young children an idea is sometimes more clearly expressible through things than by word. But when it comes to love there is often a better mode of expression than through things. Sure, a gift of a toy can express love. But a smile when you see her, a minute of helping her do something she's trying to do, a minute of letting her do badly by herself something you could do better in ten seconds, the loving refusal to meet an illegitimate demand, a moment of abandoning everything just to listen to what she has to say—no toy can equal the power of these gifts to show her that she is loved, lovable, and loving.

> I was inspired by a mother I saw. Her son came running to her, fretting and frowning, all frustrated over something. Undisturbed by his disturbance she smiled the loveliest smile at him. I saw his face change, relax. Before anything had been said, his problem had shrunk. Now they could talk about it—if he could remember what it was.

Sometimes people give our children things without our approval. It may be the gift itself or the excessiveness of the giving that troubles us, but what others give our children is no big problem. Gifts from others—or from Santa Claus—can be appreciated by both parents and children as demonstrations that parents are not the children's only source of good.

The Idea(l) Teacher

As the nursing child needs a nursing parent, so the learning (seeing) child needs a learning (seeing) parent more than a teaching one. We do not have to make our children learn; we only have to allow and encourage them in their learning. We do not have to dictate what they should learn; we only have to discern and respond to what it is that they are learning. Such responsiveness is at once educational and loving.

If we approach parenthood as seeing rather than knowing parents, if we approach life as essentially a process of realization rather than an arena for success or failure, pleasure or pain, our children will not be distracted from the seeing/learning work that is their natural inclination. They will learn ceaselessly, and whenever they understand something they will sense that they are loved. No child who is learning is doubting that he is loved. Every child who does not doubt that he is loved is learning. Such children naturally develop their potential to be both intelligent and loving.

> *All things work together for good to them that love God.*
> —Romans 8:28

Life itself is loving and guiding (teaching) us along. The more we regard our children as Seeing Beings rather than projects or possessions, the more we see that this is so. All things work together in favor of realization to them that love truth. Observe how all things are working together to show our children what they so eagerly want and need to see.

At first the baby is mainly reaching with her ears and eyes. She almost seems to focus her eyes with her ears, using hearing to aim her face at you when you talk, peering out for you through those incredibly sincere, intelligent, unfocused eyes.

When she begins to "speak," you see this same reaching for focus—a sort of generalized groping for the specific. She sees you, smiles, and then her whole body reaches for the means of communication. Her shoulders and arms and legs come forward, she exhales through rounded lips, and a soft "Ho" comes forth. Answer softly, "Ho," and her face lights up. Your first conversation!

Slowly the hands come into play—first as unrecognized servants of the mouth, then more and more as a means of reaching out to explore what she now sees and hears.

Reaching is the crux. Everything follows from the reaching, meticulously and minutely ordered in favor of progress. At a certain period a baby will open and close his hand several times when reaching for a desired object. He does not know to raise the hand and bring it down upon the toy. We watch compassionately as his opening fist actually pushes the toy farther from his grasp. Soon he becomes frustrated. But meanwhile something wonderful happens. In striving to reach the toy, he draws up one leg. The beginning of crawling! The very inadequacy of his grasp initiates discovery of the possibility of mobility!

Ain't Misbehavin'

Intelligent seeing leads to loving responding. Instead of shouting at the child, the seeing parent asks himself, "What is trying to happen here?" and thus is able to work with, rather than react against, seemingly inconvenient or "mis"behavior—sometimes lovingly helping; sometimes lovingly not helping; sometimes lovingly allowing; sometimes lovingly forbidding.

> At a certain point diaper changing became almost impossible. Our baby was suddenly overcome with the desire to see what was behind his head. He'd look up, crane his neck, and arch his back, so that you really had to fight to get a diaper on him. But he wasn't just being ornery. He was trying to do something. What was it? One day he looked up, craned his neck, arched his back. He reached with his arm, then with his leg—reaching, reaching. I didn't know what he was reaching for. I don't think he did either. But it turned out to be the beginning of turning over. No one was as surprised as he was when—plop—he suddenly found himself on his tummy!

We don't have to know every stage of child development to be responsive rather than hindering. The key is to recognize our children's reaching as an impulse of life itself seeking expression. Then we can trust and respond in the most helpful, least interfering, most meaningful manner. We can gauge our response by the baby's reaction. A "ho" back to the "ho-ing" baby may evoke a smile or laugh of pleasure that seems to mean *mission accomplished. We have reached each other.* From "ho" we may go on to repeated, one-syllable, explosive sounds—"Buh! Buh! Buh!"—which bring almost startled laughter. But "Hey diddle diddle" is still too complex—just part of the background din that doesn't penetrate consciousness. From the lack of reaction we see that nothing has registered, that no *encounter* has taken place.

Sometimes we bring an out-of-reach toy within reach to relieve the striving baby before he becomes discouraged. But sometimes instead, perceiving the link between reaching and crawling, we place our hands beneath the soles of his feet, helping him to discover the possibility of pushing off toward the desired toy. Truth itself guides us both through our seeing—if we are looking to see.

The Responsive Parent

The seeing parent is freed from reacting for or against things simply on the basis of pleasure/pain or success/failure and self/other. When we perceive what in essence is taking place, the necessary response that is both loving and intelligent becomes clear—even if what takes place is troublesome. As Seeing Beings we recognize that what we want to do or have is less important than what we understand. We are less inclined to take things personally or to distract our children from learning by suggesting to them that life is a strictly inter-personal experience. We know that in any situation it is what is signi-fied and whether or not we see it that is important. This insight transforms our experience and provides a sound, love-intelligent basis for responding to our children.

Child [on telephone, crying]: Hello, Mom? I forgot to bring my homework, so I have to stay after school and miss basketball again.

Ambitious or Pleasure-minded Parent [inward experience: fear, hurt, anger, worry, embarrassment, guilt; inward thought: *Oh, no! He's going to fail! He's got the same problems I had. What shall I do? Who is to blame?*]: What? Again? Won't you ever learn? It's your own fault! Where's your homework and what if I bring it right away? I'm going to dock your allowance. Why don't you do better? How do they dare? This is going to show up on your report card, you know. Your father won't like this one bit. The coach is going to be mad. Other children don't do this. What's the matter with you? What's the matter with that woman? I'm going to have a talk with that woman.

Seeing Parent: Too bad. I'm sorry. But it is a lesson. I know you have been trying not to be forgetful, but it has been hard for you to be organized. Maybe this will help. Maybe from now on it will be easier to remember. Won't that be good?

From looking at the concrete, everyday moment in the light of the spiritual, from looking at the necessary in the light of what is essential, from viewing our children and ourselves at work or play as Seeing Beings in the process of realization—at every juncture what is at once immediately practical and in the long run most helpful is revealed to us. When it comes to responding to our playing/learning children, certain practical guidelines and priorities emerge. Each follows from, and is subsidiary to, the other.

1. The Parent as Model. Insofar as we approach everything for what it has to teach us (rather than what should or shouldn't be or what is pleasing or displeasing), we reinforce our children's innate conviction that life is a learning place and that learning is our purpose in life. Thought is parent. The thought that parents the parent is parent to the child. If *seeing what is* governs the parent, it will govern the child as well. Since Seeing Beings are what we really are, to really see is the same as to be. Children of learning parents are resilient, creative, interested, and efficient in their learning. They are comparatively free from hurt and failure in relation to others because they are not learning to compete or please but to see and thereby to be.

2. The Parent as Beholder. Insofar as we behold our children as Seeing Beings rather than as pleasing/displeasing or succeeding/failing ones it becomes evident to us that they are both good (lovable) and learning (intelligent). They are neither obedient nor disobedient, neither smart nor dumb, only relatively aware or unaware. A benefit for the parent is freedom from reactions of fear and anger, pride and guilt, credit or blame, and, in their stead, a growing firsthand appreciation of infinite goodness infinitely taking place. A benefit to the child is the preservation of his sense of worthiness. The beholding parent recognizes that a sense of worthiness is the child's greatest possession and so protects it by never calling it into question. Beholding means "holding to being." We constantly uphold the child in consciousness in the light of what is. Put your child and yourself "on behold." The beholding parent is able to be both patient and firm in a nonpersonal way. (See also "Worthiness," page 123, and "Discipline," page 218ff.)

3. The Parent as Preparer of the Way. By perceiving the child as a Seeing Being we understand that while we do not have to make our children learn or be happy, we do have a role in making way for the learning. We are relieved of the enormous burden of thinking we can make or break our children. The child is relieved of being pushed and prodded ambitiously or "spoiled" and distracted by materialistic overindulgence. She is relieved of being pressured to be good at everything, and freed to follow, passion by passion, her unique path toward individual fulfillment. Lovingly recognizing, allowing, and facilitating the learning child in his learning also makes possible both greater freedom and discipline.

4. The Parent as Preparer and Maintainer of the Learning Environment. We can take a cue from Maria Montessori. She saw that the way to facilitate learning is to set things up in such a way that the child can find and reach and select whatever he needs to help him in his learning— as much as possible on his own. Looking at the home as a learning environment, it is helpful to keep two objectives in mind: access and invitation; freedom and order.

Access and invitation. With the youngest children, this may be as simple as providing a low table for their work, a stool from which to reach the sink, a bottom drawer of kitchen things they can easily get at, a bookshelf that displays the inviting covers of the books rather than just the narrow spines. Especially with older children, access often means simply helping them find time for everything worthwhile. Partly it means not distracting them—for example, by constantly switching on the television to bring them under control. Setting aside space and time for quiet learning and creative enjoyment is part of access and invitation. Older children can be helped to make and keep to schedules, rather than being constantly reminded and scolded. Keeping a dictionary near the dining table is another concrete example of access and invitation. Let's look it up!

Freedom and order. Freedom and order are two sides of the same coin. In Montessori classrooms the "prepared environment" is where everything has an intelligent place and there is an intelligent and intelligible procedure for maintaining order. Children are taught simply that they may play with anything in the room (as long as someone else is not using it) for as long as they like, but when they are finished, before taking out anything else, they must return it to its proper place. The beauty and simplicity of this is stunning. It can be applied beautifully to the orderly home. As children grow, different accommodations have to be made, but new parents may wish to see also pages 150 and 168.

5. *The Parent as Teacher, Guide, and Companion.* Notice how low on the list comes the place of parent as teacher. While willingness to help our children learn should never be denied, it is best for both parent and child if the child is allowed to learn on his own whenever possible. This means not neglecting but being present in a somewhat removed way. Rather than either neglecting or overdirecting, the seeing parent recognizes various ways of participating in the child's learning. If you think of learning as a path, you can picture yourself walking beside her rather than pushing or dragging or carrying her along. Over*seers* only in a spiritual sense, we participate in our children's learning mostly through seeing beyond, appreciating, respecting, encouraging, and celebrating whatever it is that they are trying to learn. Only sometimes, and less and less, do we actually instruct or help or demonstrate—and then as nonpersonally as possible.

> Once my son came to me with a math problem that he could not solve. He had filled two sheets of paper already, but he was stuck. He explained the problem to me, but I couldn't understand it. Even when I did understand it, I still had no idea how to approach it. Whom could we call for help? One call was made, but no one was home. "Anyway," my son admitted, "we're supposed to do it ourselves." Well, he could go to school and say that he had not been able to do it. But then realizing that there was no other mind to rely on, I remembered the One Mind. I thought, he doesn't know how to solve this problem. I do not know how to solve it. But he does not have to rely on himself or on me or on anyone else. The only mind there is can reveal to him what only it knows. "I have confidence that an idea for solving this problem will come to you," I said. "Let's sit down here and see." We sat at the kitchen table and waited. I read. In a minute he picked up his pencil. A minute later he shouted, *"Oh!"* and began to write furiously. When he came home the next day, I asked if his solution to the problem had been correct and whether others had been able to solve it. He answered yes to both questions. "But guess what?" he said. "I was the only one who solved it the short way."

The One Mind seeks to fulfill itself in each individual consciousness. Intelligence and love take place strictly between individual consciousness and reality, not between personal minds. While neglect of a child's potential can be harmful, the more prevalent parental error today is too much pressure to achieve and perform.

6. *The Parent as Supplier of Tools, Toys, Equipment, Lessons, and Experiences*. Most assistance should not be given in the form of toys at all; but where toys are appropriate the main guideline for what and when is *reach*. Month and age criteria are uselessly arbitrary and part of a detrimental tendency to question the unique perfection of our children and compare them (and ourselves) with each other. The time to introduce a toy is when our children are in fact or in principle reaching for it. Look beyond their reach to the spiritual realization being sought. Their desire to walk is the quest for freedom; their love of bright pictures and music is a quest for beauty; their urge to speak is the quest for truthful understanding; their wish to be held is the quest for love. We need only watch our children to perceive what is most helpful, and when. The child whose essential spiritual perfection is constantly beheld in his parents' consciousness will concentrate raptly, and develop speedily, securely, and happily. At the same time, such parents are readily inspired with ideas for the right activity or toy at the right time. Partly it is a matter of improvising, partly of offering our children real tools instead of toys. Mostly it is a matter of maintaining a good work/play environment both spiritual and material.

Worthiness

A sense of worthiness is a child's most important need. The American self-made-man ethic says that we are what we make of ourselves. This is an improvement over Old World class systems that said you could never rise any higher than your father. But the implicit converse—that you are nobody until you prove yourself to be somebody—is troublesome. The suggestion is that self-worth depends on external measurements such as money, power, and popularity. Children's worthiness is often mistakenly measured by compliance or achievement.

Comparisons are always being made between ourselves and others, between our children and others' children. When these comparisons favor others, we tend to feel unworthy or ashamed. This has a serious effect on our human relationships. As long as we measure our worthiness in relation to others, we are constantly at odds with each other. It may be subtle, but often we are either putting others down or feeling put down by them.

I knew two teenagers who were descendants of royalty and who always seemed to stand out in a crowd. People often commented on how natural, attractive, assured, and graceful they were. While teenagers frequently seem self-centered and ill at ease, these two were poised and good-humored. They excelled academically, yet appeared to be free from both fear of failure and excessive ambition.

How was this possible? They had never had reason to seriously question their abilities or essential value. Evidently they felt almost no need to prove themselves. They did everything with excellence, not to prove anything, but because excellence befit them. A sense of superiority is not the same as a sense of worthiness, and these children had to develop a higher regard for others. But watching them it was easy to appreciate the value of growing up without questioning one's essential worth. Every child is a prince or a princess in the kingdom of God.

How can we raise our children with such a sense of worthiness? Just recognizing its importance is helpful. But there are ways to cultivate an attitude of confidence in our children's worthiness and convey it to them.

Freedom and Independence

Basic to an awareness of self-worth is a sense of competency. This is less a matter of achievement than of not doubting our capability. If we perceive our children as capable, so will they. An old aspirin ad showed a young woman protesting, "Mother, *please!* I'd rather do it myself!" The mother was hanging onto the headache of trying to run her grown daughter's life. Having a parent like that was a headache to the young woman.

A four-year-old I know will tackle anything with assurance and stay with it. She is also unusually comfortable with adults, starting up conversations with refreshing poise. One evening I was invited to her home for dinner, and the mystery of her assurance was solved.

After eating, the child was excused to prepare a surprise dessert. She had a step stool that she lugged around the kitchen, climbing up to open first this cupboard and then that one, choosing the ingredients for her "surprise."

There was no fanfare, no anxious glances from the watchers at the table. Once she consulted her mother in loud stage whispers. Agreement was reached that honey would probably taste better on yogurt than chocolate syrup. Before long, delicious individual desserts of yogurt, grapes, and honey began arriving at the table. Each had a cookie sticking up like a candle in the middle.

"Doesn't she ever try to go too far?" I asked.

"Sometimes," said her mother. "And sometimes we make more complicated desserts together. But mostly she's happy with ice cream or yogurt. She fixes yogurt with bananas or applesauce or raisins. She experiments with different combinations, and she likes to make them look pretty."

Most revealing was the mother's surprise at my enthusiasm for the idea of child-styled desserts. "I never thought much about it," the mother said. "She likes doing it, so she's just always done it."

Additional Reflection: Long after my children were grown, a wise and loving grandfather proudly showed me something his grandson had made. The grandfather was a master carpenter and engineer in charge of preparing a chain of theaters for different theatrical productions. At home he had a garage full of tools and equipment. That afternoon, his grandson had been with him, constructing a production of his own—a wheel-less "vehicle" that couldn't go anywhere, with "communicators" that couldn't transmit anything, and "switches" that turned nothing on or off. Though the grandfather could have put wheels on the vehicle to make it "really" go and wired the communicators and switches so they would "really" work, instead he just went about his own business, recognizing and reveling all the while in the real trip his grandson was taking and the real connections he was making. "Look what he did," he said. "And I said *nothing!* I told him *nothing!* Except for a board he asked me to saw, I did *nothing.* He did this all by himself." It will not be surprising if this child follows in his grandfather's footsteps, nor will it be a surprise if he goes off in some new direction of his own. God bless the child who's got his own and God bless the grandfather or the parent who doesn't mess with it.

Never miss an opportunity to allow a child to do something she can do, and wants to do, on her own. Sometimes we're in too much of a rush—and she might spill or break something. But whenever possible she needs to learn, error by error, lesson by lesson. The more she is able to learn by herself, the more she gets the message that she's a kid who can.

IQ: The Inhibiting Quotient

Retarded? Average? Gifted and talented? It's hard to say which label is more harmful. All children are gifted and talented. There is only one mind, so all manifestations of intelligence are *given*. True intelligence is neither had nor not had. Intelligence is awareness of what really is. All judgments made in the light of what really is are intelligent. In counseling a blind individual, it became clear to me that real seeing is seeing the real. In that light it was evident that by comparison to others she was not so radically handicapped as it seemed. If real seeing is seeing the real, and if the real is spiritual, then as long as we judge by appearances, we, too, are blind. The potential for seeing beyond appearances is no less in blind than in sighted individuals. Handicapped people may be less handicapped than we think they are, while the "advantaged" laden with ideas of self-sufficiency and superiority are more handicapped and weighted down than we recognize. Anyway, as the saying goes, "Kites rise against, not with, the wind."

To quantify intelligence and locate it in somebody's physical head and call it his (whether superior or inferior) is to handicap him. When you credit a child with having much intelligence, when you objectify intelligence *as* the child, you have disconnected that child from the source of intelligence. By changing the subject of his life from learning to self, you also confuse him about the purpose of intelligence. It is like thrusting a mirror between a reader and his book. He can't see himself and his book at the same time. When a child is identified as gifted and talented, he begins to think of himself as superior, which leads to many painful problems. When my children were invited to join a gifted and talented program, I said, "Not if it's called 'gifted and talented.'" They changed it to "challenge and enrichment," a name they gave to supplementary opportunities for lagging students as well.

True intelligence cannot be gotten or done. It can only be obstructed or unobstructed. When intelligence takes place in an individual, it is an event or coming to light of what really is. It is an awakening, a dawning or seeing. An intelligent event occurs when the tendency of reality to reveal itself is fulfilled in a moment of conscious realization. As the nature of light to illumine is fulfilled in individual seeing, so intelligence is fulfilled in understanding. Intelligence is a universal force seeking expression through individual consciousness. When understanding takes place it is not a matter of personal credit, success, or virtue, but of freedom, joy, beauty to be rejoiced in and appreciated.

> A preschool director commented that she used to have mostly children of families in which the wife was in her twenties and at home, but that lately there is a new breed of mothers who are thirty-five years old or older who are taking time off from their careers to have a couple of children. Asked whether there were noticeable differences between the children, she said, "Oh, yes. Children of young stay-at-home mothers tend to be quiet, 'nice,' at first fearful of leaving their mothers to take advantage of classroom opportunities. The children of older professional couples tend to be extremely verbal, extraordinarily bright, and outwardly poised, but nervous and subject to tempestuous times." Is this the choice? I'm not suggesting that mothers should not work outside the home. Indeed, in our day and age that is often a psychologically good, as well as an economically necessary, thing. But I think the preschool director was picking up on an all-too-prevalent and harmful motivation and its effect on children: the notion that life is for winning and proving and besting, a contest in which the children are only merit badges and trophies.

Hidden selfish motives—that the child be good (be pretty, behave, be close) for the parents' sake; or that the child excel, achieve for the parents' sake—backfire in various ways. I know this because in my therapeutic practice I've had too many adult clients who, having been "trophy children" all their lives, fall into despair and must struggle belatedly to find their true individual selves.

IQ tests measure something. Perhaps they record the flow and relative unobstructedness of a certain function of intelligence; maybe they measure interest, focus, and pace of learning; primarily they seem to record the relative earliness of language development, something largely determined by environment. But they cannot measure intelligence itself because intelligence is infinite.

Focused interest can have either a healthy or a pathological base. So-called idiot savants, intensely focused to the point of obsession, perform extraordinary, almost superhuman intellectual feats with seeming ease, such as instantaneously calculating on which weekday any date (past or future) falls. Yet they barely function on any other human level. Is that intelligence? In a way, yes; in a way, no. On the one hand, they demonstrate through utter single-mindedness an intelligent facility far beyond our usual level of realization; on the other hand, it seems that here narrow concentration is used unconsciously to screen out, and remain unaware of, reality in general. That cannot be considered true intelligence.

So-called gifted and talented children are frequently taught to use intelligence for personal power and superiority, for conquest and competition. But if true intelligence is awareness of what is, and if *what is* is infinite love, then is the conquering genius truly intelligent? If the so-called retarded individual, however unskilled and seemingly limited, nevertheless has a keen, simple awareness of goodness and finds joy and fulfillment in being good and useful, is he truly unintelligent?

If I were king of the schools, next to the nurse's office, where children are sent for health emergencies, I would set up an office for learning emergencies. I'd advise teachers to be on the lookout for fits and seizures of passion. Whenever interest rose like a fever in a child—whatever the interest and whoever "afflicted" (retarded, gifted, or average)—I would have the child sent to this office. If during math she doodles dinosaurs, if during writing she makes up a story about dinosaurs, if going to the library she selects dinosaur books, I'd consider her a bit flushed and in need of immediate attention. Unlike the nurse, whose concern is to bring the fever down, the resource person in the Office of Learning Emergency would be concerned with gently huffing on the glowing coal of her passion, hoping to kindle a self-sustaining flame.

Like the nurse, the resource person might send a note home to the parent: "Your child is feverishly interested in dinosaurs. Perhaps you might like to keep her home tomorrow morning for the television special on paleontology." He would also call on other resources—perhaps a session with a retired senior citizen volunteer, a special trip to the librarian, a recommendation to the teacher, who (if he hadn't thought of this himself) might assign an extra-credit project. Whatever the budget for special remedial or enrichment services, and such a service would be an affordable way of helping many children with a minimum of upheaval. Sudden passions would be seen as precious, critical opportunities for enhancing the child's sense of worthiness and possibility.

There is no such thing as a middle-of-the-road child; there is only a child who is standing in the middle of the road. An interest yet unkindled? A doubt about himself? A little valuing of his momentary interest and an opportunity to pursue it is enough to set him down the road at a gallop.

> In reviewing applications, I often spot a sudden change in a student's record. After years and years of substandard performance, suddenly one semester he seems to pull himself together and "get his act in gear." Over and over I have asked these students, "What happened?" Over and over the answer has come, "I don't really know. All I remember is that that was the year I" . . . built a canoe, bicycled through Nova Scotia, learned to juggle. Some success. Some interest allowed to come to fruition.
>
> —Dean of Students, Hampshire College

Shame and Blame

A child will behave according to what he thinks he is. Therefore, if he is addressed in terms like "You always . . ." and "You never . . ." and "You are such a . . . ," he will surely develop an image of himself as a "so and so" and continue engaging in "such and such." When correcting a child it is better to make a clear distinction in your own mind between who he really is and what he is doing, between his essential being and his behavior. Behold your children as innocent. Always assume that if they really knew better, they would do better.

As parents we are called upon to respond to various problems. Sometimes a firm and vigorous stand is called for, as when there is immediate danger of injury. Sometimes admonition is called for, the pointing out of a possible consequence. Sometimes we simply have to stand by and let our children discover consequences for themselves.

Sometimes reproof and explanation are appropriate. Sometimes psychiatric intervention is called for. But the child's goodness is never the issue; even behavior is not the issue; learning is.

In every instance something will be learned. If we view our children as stupid, naughty, disturbed, or guilty of their misdeeds, they will learn that they are foolish, faulty, or shameful. They will see us as judges from whom they wish to hide and interpret whatever we say as more proof of their unworthiness. If we view them as innocent, or at least merely ignorant, they will learn from their experiences, and they will continue to regard us as wise partners.

Write a no-fault clause into your family policy. Apply it to yourself and your children. With no-fault assurance, even if you have to yank your toddler off his feet to stop him from doing something, you will be able to do so with compassion and a sense of humor rather than anger. You will be able to issue warnings without insult, and to reprove without humiliation.

It is best not to reprove a child in public. Take him aside to offer respectfully the information you think helpful. Remember, the issue is not what should or shouldn't have been done but what needs to be understood. Assume the essential goodness of the child. As much as possible, be positive, nonpersonal, and concrete. Instead of, "No. Bad boy! I told you not to touch the scissors!" try, "Scissors are not a toy. They are for cutting. Here is something better to play with until I am free to help you cut that." Whenever you can, instead of giving directions, ask questions that lead him to discover better, more valid, truer alternatives for himself.

One afternoon I overheard our oldest child pestering the youngest. Repeatedly I told him to stop, but he couldn't. Finally it hit me that his pestering mood was as troublesome for him as for his brother. A feeling of compassion welled up. As I came out of the bathroom, he went sailing by. I grabbed him, pulled him into the bathroom with me, and shut the door so no one could hear us. "What *is* this?" I asked in genuine bewilderment and some amusement. Startled to find himself confronted with a question rather than condemnation, he jerked his head up and smiled. "That's the only way I can be happy," he said, sheepishly. "I can't find anything fun to do."

"Oh," I said. "Well, it isn't working very well, is it? I'm sure you can get a better idea. Let's see, what *would* be nice?" He was soon happily absorbed in a constructive project that he had thought of and I had helped him to set up. The pesterer disappeared and did not return that day.

Praise and Celebration

Surprisingly, praise can be as harmful as shame and blame. Personal praise suggests to the child that his personal worth rises and falls according to others' estimation of his accomplishments. In praising children we give them the idea that they are good because of what they do that pleases us. But then if we don't praise them, or when we praise others, they feel diminished and unworthy.

Praise also distracts the child from whatever he is doing by implying that the value of his activity is getting attention. It's a vicious circle. If a child has his eyes on his parents watching him learn to ski, he is likely to fall or crash into a tree, which may at once injure, embarrass, and discourage him. His skiing progress is impeded and his enthusiasm and self-confidence undermined. Whether it's manners or artwork, the principle is the same. A child cannot have his mind on seeking approval and on what he's doing at the same time. If his mind is not on what he's doing, he's unlikely to enjoy it or do it well. Paradoxically, the more a child's ego is bolstered, the more insecure, discouraged, and even incompetent he's likely to become. Good self-esteem occurs not when children think well of themselves but when, able to forget themselves, they are free to lose themselves in whatever they are learning.

It is good to express joy and to encourage our children in their growth. But there is a better way than to make a big fuss over them. When a child says, "I did it myself!" usually this is not Me, Inc. speaking. He doesn't mean, "Aren't I great?" but rather, "Isn't it great that I am able? Isn't it wonderful that this is possible for me!" In other words, he is grateful. Celebration characterized by appreciation and gratitude rather than praise and pride heightens the joy of discovery and increases the child's sense of possibility. If you wish him to grow with joy and confidence, do not let him become the issue in his own work and play. Let him be good-conscious rather than self-conscious. Instead of "What a great reader you are!" try "Reading is really getting much easier for you, isn't it? Soon you'll be able to read anything you like!" Instead of "Aren't you proud of yourself?" or "I am very proud of you," try "Wonderful! It sounds so lively now, and I can see that you really enjoy playing that piece!" (See also pages 217 and 267.)

Truthful Regard

Most of all it's good to consider what's right with our children, to focus on the true rather than the false. Truthful regard is the purest form of love and the most important aspect of parenthood.

> Robert is the older of two children. He takes everything personally and thus is constantly flying off the handle. Whenever he is reproved he tends to become angry or discouraged. Whenever he is helped he feels criticized. But nobody has to walk on eggs with his younger sister. Julie is spontaneously happy, cooperative, and her characteristic response to reproof is, "Oops! I forgot!" How can this be? They have the same parents. Or do they?

In a sense, Robert and Julie do not have the same parents. Julie's are more experienced than Robert's, less anxious, and still preoccupied with Robert. Robert is the plow. Julie saunters along in the furrow her parents have made with Robert. The real difference between Robert's and Julie's behavior lies in the way their parents regard them and the way, accordingly, that they view themselves.

Especially with our first child, we tend to take too much responsibility—both credit and blame—for everything. The more we want to be good parents, the more we tend to see ourselves as making or breaking our children. Experts alert us to all kinds of problems until we are constantly searching for what's wrong with our children, then trying to fix them. As in Robert's case, our efforts to make our children prettier or smarter or nicer only suggest to them that they are not pretty, not bright, not nice—in short, unworthy.

Overzealous parenting—or what someone has called "smother love"—undermines Robert's confidence. Like his parents, he views himself as a problem and life as a hazardous situation with which he is incapable of coping. Julie, on the other hand, is a revelation to her parents. Lo and behold, she cut her teeth—with no parental supervision! With a minimum of attention she is spontaneously cheerful, intelligent, and resilient. Her parents regard her as a constant source of pleasant surprise. She sees herself and life accordingly.

The child who lives in an atmosphere of truthful regard will know himself and others to be worthy. Then in the same way that a boat is seaworthy, he will float along—buoyed up, unsinkable—learning in due course to express his full potential as a loving, intelligent, assured individual. He is a see-worthy individual in a reliable, self-revealing world.

It helps to continually behold the perfect child right where the disobedient, failing, or disturbed one seems to be. The perfect child cannot be seen at a superficial glance any more than the flower can be viewed in the bulb. We must look deeper than skin for beauty, deeper than behavior for goodness, deeper than test scores for intelligence. Call it potential, or basic goodness, or divine spark—every good and necessary quality of wholeness is given to the child and does not need to be imposed on him by us, only beheld. What we can see, he can be.

Anyone who has ever raised a child from diaperhood has a perfect example. We change hundreds of diapers without being deceived by sight or smell or repetition into thinking, "Why did I have to have a dirty one?" In fact, purity is usually regarded as the baby's most outstanding characteristic. Indeed, in the end it is the child's own maturing purity that eventually does away with the need for diapers. It can happen quite smoothly. Those of us who, doubting, fall for the idea that we have to "toilet train" our children, learn the hard way that children are not *made* to use the toilet. Rather they just do when, sooner or later, it becomes perfectly clear to them that it is good to do so and that they can. Once they perceive the worth of the idea (provided they do not question their own worthiness), the idea itself takes charge of them and thereby of the situation. What we do or don't do, say or don't say, is not too important. But the way we view our children—and how accordingly they view themselves—is crucial.

View your child as a promise rather than a problem or a project. Enjoy him. When he is around, smile often. When he speaks, listen. When he proposes, consider. "Let's see. Would that be a good idea or not?" Tuck in his shirt because he deserves to be comfortable, not because he looks like a slob. See him not as a success or a failure, well- or ill-behaved, but as a fully equipped participant in the process of living and learning. When he fails, offer comfort rather than condemnation. "It doesn't matter. Now you know that doesn't work, so it won't have to happen again." Show respect for his effort even when his work is imperfect. Sometimes let him all but hang himself to discover something he needs to learn and above all demonstrate to him your truthful regard for others as worthy individuals to be loved and respected. Then he will do likewise. And no one who has truthful regard for others ever has time for self-doubt.

This is my beloved son, in whom I am well pleased.
—Matthew 3:17

Receptivity

Your road I enter upon and look around! I believe
you are not all that is here;
I believe that much unseen is also here.

Here the profound lesson of reception,
neither preference or denial. . . .

—Walt Whitman, "Song of the Open Road"

The baby's repeated craning of her neck suddenly results in her being able to turn over. But this is not at all what she had in mind, so her increased freedom comes as both a shock and a tremendous blessing. Likewise our children come as something of a shock to us yet bring a great blessing. To receive it we only need to become like the children themselves—humble, teachable, receptive Seeing Beings. This is best and happiest for our children, and for us as well.

In thy presence is fullness of joy; and at thy right hand are pleasures
forevermore.

—Psalm 16:11

We spend so very much time trying to get our work done—the laundry, dishes, bookkeeping, what have you—with the idea that once all that is out of the way we'll be able to "devote our full attention" to our children. Yet in rare moments when our sense of self-importance is diminished or satiated enough so that we feel we can "take some time off," we suddenly find that we are uninspired. We sit down to "be with" our children and find the moments almost awkward. It must mean that our idea of "being with" is invalid in some way.

As Me, Inc. we are inclined to believe that the purpose of being with our children is one-way: We take care of, train, educate, and entertain *them*. This narrow outlook leads to our feeling taken advantage of by our children and feeling we never have enough time for ourselves.

Until they learn otherwise, though children do not consciously know that seeing is happiness, they also never doubt it. They are learning machines, ceaselessly seeking new understanding of anything and everything. That is one reason they will not play with their toys and leave us alone for long. They love their learning work and feel loved through it. Furthermore, their learning is existential; they especially want to be learning what relates to their living. For the toddler this usually means whatever we are doing.

We, however, have long since divided our work and learning time into separate, mutually exclusive categories. "I have so much work to do that I don't have time to improve my mind anymore!" Medical science even suggests that children's brains are good for learning while ours are already deteriorating. But if we are not learning much anymore it is either because we no longer think learning pertains to us, or because we do not recognize what life is trying to teach us. For example, how many suspect that there is something for an adult to learn from changing diapers or folding the laundry.

What the child has to learn is more obvious to us only because so much of it is so physical. If we allow our one-and-a-half-year-old to "help" us fold the laundry he will learn something about buttons, zippers, snaps, where things go, the physical properties of cloth, what happens when you drop it, how easy or hard it is to carry compared with everything else he has ever carried, what clean clothes smell like, how a big towel can turn into a small bundle, how the small bundle you just folded can turn into a big towel again, plus any songs we care to sing or stories or related or unrelated facts we care to pass on. If we are cheerful and responsive, he may also go on assuming that orderliness is an agreeable aspect of reality and that it's a joy to be together.

And he may *not* yet begin to think that he is only a nuisance.

The learning child unconsciously assumes two things that are crucial to learning. The first assumption is that *there is nothing standing between her and happiness except what she hasn't learned yet*. At least for a while, she does not think that having or doing something else would be nicer. As long as she's learning, she's happy. She lives to find out. The second assumption is that *whatever comes along next is the next thing she needs to learn*. She does not doubt the fulfilling nature of life. These two assumptions are crucial to receptivity, and receptivity is crucial to learning.

So what might we learn when we are trying to fold the laundry (which we may think is a bore) and the task is being made more difficult by the fact that our toddler is aggressively in the way? Perhaps it is to relearn how to learn. And this is one thing our children can certainly teach us. Another issue in folding the laundry is orderliness. If this is the task before us, then a right appreciation of orderliness may be what we need to learn. Or perhaps interruption by our child can help us realize that love is an even higher priority, or that love and order do not in conflict with each other. Perhaps we need to learn that peace is not achieved by our taking charge of life but by letting life take charge of us—or that the humdrum is the holy.

The possibilities are infinite, and we can discover some new dimension of reality and self in each situation before us. Perhaps while the child is exploring the physical properties of cloth or material, we will discover that what we do is *im*material, or that life is *un*foldment and that expressing life (in this case love, order, humility) is fulfilling. When we understand whatever there is for us to understand while folding the laundry, we will either be happy folding laundry or else we will be lifted into some other task altogether.

Like us, our children will become fulfilled, happy adults only in proportion as they come to understand and express life aright. We cannot teach them what life is or what orderliness is, even if we come to understand it ourselves; one day they will have to find out for themselves, just as we are doing. But they enter this world with a natural expectation or unconscious appreciation of order that we can help to foster and become conscious. Then when our children become searching adults, order will be one of the realities they seek to discover and understand.

But orderliness is only a small part of what we teach our children.

The unspoken lesson for us all in our right appreciation of even the smallest tasks is that life—every minute detail of it—is significant and meaningful and worthwhile, that receptive understanding is the secret of happiness.

> *Lay disciple Ho said:*
> *"My daily activities are not different,*
> *Only I am naturally in harmony with them.*
> *Taking nothing, renouncing nothing,*
> *In every circumstance no hindrance, no conflict . . .*
> *Drawing water, carrying firewood,*
> *This is supernatural power, this marvelous activity."*
> —Huston Smith, *The Religions of Man*

> *Paul said: "Set your affections on things above, not on things on the earth."*
> —Colossians 3:2

> *Jesus said, "Suffer the little children to come unto me, and forbid them not: for of such is the kingdom of God. Verily I say unto you, whosoever shall not receive the kingdom of God as a little child shall in no wise enter therein."*
> —Mark 10:14–15

> *Suzuki said: "'Childlikeness' has to be restored with long years of training in the art of self-forgetfulness."*
> —Eugen Herrigel, *Zen in the Art of Archery*

Additional Reflection—A Time for This and a Time for That

When I first wrote *Whole Child* I was particularly concerned to help overwhelmed, in-shock parents discover parenthood's value for the parent. All through the book, particularly in this chapter, I emphasized that parenthood isn't just self-sacrifice, that being with your child isn't a waste of your time, of your life; that even the "work" of wiping up spills and tying shoes can be fulfilling. All that *is* important not only for the child's sake but also for the sake of the parent. I believe this message is even more needed today.

But in this edition I want to add another message that was not included earlier: That even while being a parent there are other things to attend to—marital life as well as parental life, individual life as well as family life. This holds true for every member of the family. All these lives and all the selves and subselves they entail need attention and care. Without this message there is a subtle danger to the other one. If the focus is too much on parenthood and on our children, the danger is that the marriage, the individual, and many parts of each individual family member will be orphaned and die of neglect. Therefore, I want to present some other less apparent children who need time and attention. In keeping with the book of Ecclesiastes, I want to say that even while we are busy with our actual child there is *and there needs to be* "a time for this and a time for that" as well. There is

A Time for Putting the Child First. D. W. Winnicott observed that it is almost instinctual for mothers of newborns to identify with the baby to the exclusion of everything and everyone else. He says that although this intense preoccupation meets almost all descriptions of neurosis, it is normal and necessary for the infant's healthy development. During this period the mother's world shrinks to a very small circle of just two persons, herself and her child. This close two-person relationship is necessary at first, but if clung to too long, it becomes problematic for the child, the mother, and everyone else in the family.

During this period husbands often begin to feel like abandoned children. If sex is also reduced they may begin to demand it, with a hungry infant's intensity as well as with the strength of a man. For them it can be helpful to realize that this state is *necessary but temporary.* Understanding the necessity may open the father, too, to greater involvement with the baby. Understanding the temporariness may help him to be more patient with the mother even if she seems to have lost interest in him for the time being.

It is also important for the mother to understand that the presence of a new baby and her involvement with the baby places a strain on the family, not only on her other children if there are any, but especially on her partner. This awareness may remind her that the baby is not the only one who needs attention, that her partner, including his child part, also needs attention. It may also help her to recognize an overwhelmed child part of herself and to give it the attention and the freedom it needs. It may remind both partners that there needs also to be—

A Time for Putting the Marriage First. It is not only mothers who may be overly "wrapped up" in their children. This can happen to fathers and to marriages as well, and not only during the baby's infancy but through the whole period of childraising. Dr. Barry Ulanov points out that it is a bad sign when parents stop calling each other by name or speaking of each other as husband and wife and begin to call each other "Mother" and "Father." When they no longer see themselves and each other as whole individuals but only as parents, their adult relationship, their marriage, is jeopardized. Both now alternately behave like demanding, needy children and like patronizing, controlling, managerial adults toward each other. Now there are three babies on hand, all abandoned, all squalling—both in and out of bed.

The sooner we recognize the presence of our own baby selves the more responsibly and *responsively* we can attend to them. The marriage, too, is an important baby. Marriage doesn't simply happen at the altar. It is a baby that may be born at the altar, but then needs a lot of care and attention, protection, nurturance, and upbringing. Couples who understand this know that even in the early days of parenthood it is important to set aside time for the marriage. If having a baby is hard on the marriage, certainly a bad marriage is bad for the baby.

For the sake of both the children and the adults in the family, it is important for couples to reserve time for being alone together—not in your particular way or my particular way, just some way that you both find easy to be together. A regular night out, a regular walk, some regular fun, some "time *out*" together eases the abandoned child in each partner and builds the sort of trust and maturity that lead to mutually meaningful, intimate sexual intercourse, and constructive discourse about sharing family responsibilities—in short, a fully developed, grown-up marriage. Partners in such a marriage also recognize that there needs to be—

A Time for All Sorts of Relationships. Within the family this means having not only family times but also times for each parent/child pair to be alone together. Each child needs time alone with each parent, and vice versa. There are times and stages when a particular child prefers and needs to be with a particular parent (and vice versa). But even then, perhaps even more then, it is important to set aside private times for both preferred and less preferred relationships. One family I know has "car time." Every evening when the father comes home from work, he and his two-year-old daughter spend time alone together in his parked car. One day I noticed they were also having "car time" in the morning. He said, "Yes. On my days off we have two car times. That's when my wife gets to blow-dry her hair." What form your time with your children takes is up to you and your child, and may change according to different stages and circumstances. But it is important for each pair to have its share of private time together—and to have it often.

Nonfamily and extended family relationships also need time. Some couples give each other a regular "night out"—a time for being with personal friends. Particularly when there are young children who require constant care, the gift of time out with adult friends refreshes parents for their parental tasks and strengthens the marriage. If one parent is the primary caregiver while the other is the primary breadwinner, the caregiver's night out also provides the breadwinner and children with an important chance to build stronger relationships. And, without getting into the issue of gender relationships, it can be said that having a relationship with each of two different adults who approach things differently is important for the child's development. Parents who recognize and value each other's differences also recognize the importance of having—

A Time for Individual as Well as Family Life. Traditionally, the living of family and individual lives has been divided along gender lines. As primary breadwinner the man did all the individual living, developing his individual skills and fulfilling his individual potential at work. As primary caretaker the woman did all the family living within the home. This is not an entirely accurate picture in that various cultural mandates often squashed rather than developed the man's individuality in his career, while the more private family situation often provided women with enhanced opportunities for individuality. But in general, at least on the surface, men were aimed in the direction of fulfilling their creative intelligent individual potential through achievement, while women were aimed in the direction of fulfilling their feeling, loving potential through service to the family. Now all that is changing.

Women are aware of the need to fulfill their individual potential, and (close on their wives' heels) men are discovering the need to fulfill their family, or relational, potential. For the time being, this is problematic, because our culture has not yet caught up with these changes. Breadwinners feel left out of the family; caretakers feel their individual creative selves are going down the fallopian tubes (especially as they see other women moving ahead with their careers). All kinds of experimental solutions are being tried: parental leave from jobs for both men and women, job sharing, role switching, each with its pros and cons. But in the end, I believe the problem can be solved best through recognizing that all persons, male and female, need both an individual and a family life, and that they need to live these aspects of their being not during different stages of their lives (e.g., the man gets to live his family side only on weekends or after he retires, the woman her individual side only after the children are grown) but to some extent all along the way.

Appreciation of this dilemma leads to the realization by both men and women that they need to claim for themselves and to give each other a time for the living of both their family and their individual selves on a regular basis. Again and again I see wonderful benefits occur when a woman who is the primary caretaker of the children takes up a little more of her individual life, for example, through a part- or full-time job outside of the home, the taking of a course, the pursuit of some passionate interest or talent. Her depression lifts, her presence with her children becomes more joyful, and the conflict in the marriage is reduced. Again and again I see wonderful benefits occur when a man who is the primary breadwinner takes up a little more of his family life, through spending a little more time with his children and just hanging out and feeling his feelings. Such couples also recognize that they need to claim for themselves and give each other—

A Time for Solitude as Well as Togetherness. Elsewhere we've spoken of the end-of-day "Hell Hour" in many homes. The primary caretaker, who has traditionally been the woman, is tired, as are her children, which makes fixing dinner difficult and stressful. The primary breadwinner, who has traditionally been the man, is also weary. Both breadwinner and caretaker yearn for some "downtime," and each looks to the other to provide it. At the end of the day the breadwinner looks forward to being taken care of and allowed to relax, but so does the caretaker. Whoever has been with the children all day may want to talk to an adult for a change, while talking may be the last thing that the one who has been out in the world all day wants to do. Either one may want to tell the other about his or her day. But since the children continue to need care, one adult must remain "on duty." Both have been "on duty" all day. So conflict arises about who should be on- and who should be off-duty with the children. Thus, one Hell Hour gives way to another as everyone's needs seem to conflict.

The deterioration of happy anticipation of end-of-day downtime into disappointment and anger ruins many an evening of family and individual time—and many a marriage. Couples who recognize both partners' need for downtime and alone time, for quiet time and talking time, are able to claim it for themselves and give it to each other. Obviously one of the two must wait, since young children rarely leave both parents alone at the same time. But as long as we know our turn is coming, we *can* wait. Likewise, couples who recognize the need for both solitude and togetherness can claim and give each other both. For instance, a mother of young children made the following Saturday "deal" with her husband. She loved to go running. He agreed to take care of the children for two hours while she jogged to her session with me. After the session, he and the children would pick her up in the car. Then she would drop him off at home for two hours of alone time while she and the children did errands or went to the park. He developed new parental skills and grew closer to his children during her alone time. Both returned from their alone time refreshed for each other and for their various caretaking and breadwinning tasks. Grateful for each other's gift of alone time, the couple grew closer.

On a daily basis, reliable rituals can be established. After only a fifteen-minute walk, a shower, or a chance to read the paper, couples are more ready to deal with the children or to listen to each other. The important thing is not how much alone or together time each needs, or who gets it first. What's important is for both partners to have both kinds of time and to know that they can count on having it with some regularity. People who understand this are also flexible and generous, because they also understand that they need to claim for themselves and to give each other—

A Time for All Kinds of Things and All Kinds of Feelings. The best-laid plans of mice and men and couples often don't work out. As the bumper sticker says, "Sh—t happens." Things, crises, meetings, job changes, illnesses, deaths, and deadlines happen that interfere with our plans. And *life* happens! Moods, spells, phases, enchantments, and disenchantments overtake us and make us feel unable to hold up our end of whatever bargains we've made with each other. We are constantly growing, changing, and facing new frontiers. We all have lead sides and lag sides, conscious and unconscious partial selves. Life aims to bring all aspects of ourselves to maturity. People who understand this also realize that they need to give time and attention to new parts of themselves as they make themselves known.

Lag, undeveloped, neglected, or rejected sides of ourselves are often rather primitive, frustrated, and babyish. Like babies, they express themselves powerfully, demandingly, *but not clearly,* because they don't have language. To understand what they need, you have to devote time and attention to them. A baby has one way of expressing his needs—*waah, waah, waah!* When a baby cries, we trust that he needs something. But what? Is he hungry, tired, wet, sick, in pain, afraid, lonely, frustrated? Often we don't know. So we pick him up, offer food, check the diaper, walk and rock him, experiment with this and that until he is peaceful. When an older child is upset, often we don't know what's the matter either—and neither does she. She may know what she *wants* but not necessarily what she really *needs*. So we take her aside, spend time with her, experiment until we have a sense of what her need is. Then we can see how it can be met. We need to approach our own upsets, depressions, sadness, and anger the same way.

As grown-ups with grown-up responsibilities our tendency is to override these feelings and to expect our partners to do the same with theirs. But the more we ignore them, the more they press for attention, becoming ever louder and more demanding of parental attention from others. The need and its "urge-ency" is genuine. Our urge, whatever it is, is at the bottom, the surge of God in us, pressing for recognition and life as a necessary part of our inner family of selves (see also page 230). If we suppress or ignore this urge, it will only have to press harder, in increasingly disturbing ways, for parental care from others who are not, in fact, our parents—including our spouses and even our children.

When we find ourselves in a *waah-waah* state, feeling unaccountably blue, angry, trapped, anxious, or overwhelmed, it is a good idea to treat ourselves as we would our children. Rather than ignoring our child-needs or expecting our partners to figure out and address them for us, it is better, as soon as possible, to give quiet, parental, and prayerful attention to them ourselves. If you're suddenly feeling lifeless, finding it harder and harder to be present to your adult tasks, arrange as soon as possible to take your baby-self aside. Pick it up, hold it, and be with it until you know who it is, what part of you it is, and what it needs. If you feel like a lump, give your self some lump time. If you feel sad, set aside some crying time. If you feel angry, set aside some fuming time. If you feel full of longing, set aside some longing time. The sooner you do this, the shorter the time needs to be. If you do this in a timely way, you will begin to understand your less conscious selves, and they will develop language for telling you more explicitly what they need.

Every marriage is part adult–adult relationship and part parent–child. But no marriage can last if it is only parent–child, because we are not in fact each other's parents and we can't both be children at the same time. Expectations that our partners should figure out and address our child needs (which we haven't even figured out) only make our partners feel like abandoned overwhelmed children themselves. People who recognize and respond to their own child-selves, as described above, are often able to give themselves what they need; less likely to have unreasonable expectations or place illegitimate demands on each other; and better able to make reasonable, meetable requests of each other—in both their child–parent and adult–adult relationships to each other.

Because we have many kinds of subselves, we have many kinds of needs. Often just a little change of pace or a different sort of activity or a change of environment is all we need. The more understanding and responsive we are to our own child-selves, the more understanding and responsive we can be to our children and to the child-selves of other adults. People who understand this also know that there may be—

A Time to Seek Help. If you find that you and your partner are spending most of your time in the child–parent position, and that your conversations all boil down to "But what about me? Who's taking care of me? When is it ever my turn? Why do we always have to do it your way? and *waah waah waah!*"; if there are rarely two adults and mostly just two children in the marriage, then it is a good time to seek help. Marriage counseling can help us to take turns and play fair, and for some couples that's all it takes. But since our relationships with each other can be no better than our relationship with ourselves, deep individual analytical work on oneself is what can make the greatest difference.

Seeking help used to be stigmatized, and many people are still ashamed to do so. Having marital problems often seems like failure and disaster. But if you understand that life is a journey of spiritual awakening, you can look at your problems as growth pains, and at seeking help at various points in your life as a wonderful part of the wonderfully mysterious process of becoming. Children whose parents understand this are blessed. No one can tell you what or when is the right thing for you to do. Each person and each couple must pray their own way through. People who understand this also increasingly realize that there needs to be—

A Time for Spiritual Searching and Prayer. Since I've written of this topic elsewhere, both in this book (see pages 81–92) and in *Coming to Life* and *Gently Lead,* there is no need to say much about it here. Yet this section would not be complete if I did not at least mention it. Of all the "times" listed here, the time set aside for spiritual searching and prayer is the most important. The ongoing health and unfolding wholeness of our selves and our souls (and the selves and souls of our children) depend as much on ongoing and fresh spiritual nourishment and inspiration as our bodies depend on physical nourishment and respiration.

Practical Information for New Parents

Included here for new parents are some guidelines for toy buying, improvising, organizing, storing, and play.

Toys and Things

The first and last thing to know about toys is that buying toys isn't important. Love, intelligent love, is enough. If you cannot afford to buy any toys, your children can still have every educational advantage.

We can buy all the best toys in the world and they won't help a bit unless we are present, maintaining without reservation the understanding, loving atmosphere vital to all children.

Not Buying Toys

It makes no sense to buy many toys for babies. Play is work, and the baby is supremely motivated to do this work, which includes a thorough sensory examination of all the properties of everything he can get his hands on. When this work is done, the object ceases to be interesting. It doesn't take long, because every baby is enthusiastic and works fast. So as much as possible, use things you find around the house—plastic measuring spoons, potholders, coasters. Baby food jars, plastic bottles, and boxes can be filled with colored water or split peas or beads or buttons *until* the baby learns to open or break them or *unless* she has an older sibling who doesn't know better than to do so for her.

From sitting to crawling is perhaps the easiest time of all. At this stage children enjoy and work diligently with almost anything you put in front of them—patting, pounding, picking up and putting down, putting in and taking out, over and over and over. From standing to walking to running, things start happening very quickly and busily. When she tries to walk, set up a walking tour. Arrange a few chairs and low tables so she can progress from one to the other while still holding on. Put a ball on one chair, some spools on another, a book on another, a favorite toy on another.

Each time you buy a toy, you make a commitment to finding a place for it, and picking it up frequently. Despite the fact that your child may have lost interest within a few days, she will keep dragging it out, and you may believe you have to keep it in case she regains interest or "grows into it" or is followed by a younger sibling who will be just as interested in the toy as she was . . . for about twenty-four hours.

Most toy purchases are a matter of parental weakness. If we pay attention, we can find many ways to amuse and educate our children (of any age) with things that are already in the house. Children like to use our "real" things because they are trying to grow up into real people who accomplish real ends.

Certain concept materials such as wooden parquetry tiles are worth purchasing because their beauty and precision are difficult to duplicate. But when you consider buying a toy, first make sure it is not something you can match with what you already have at home. Try some of the following *nontoys* (see also some of the books listed on pages 155–158 and 249–250):

Under one year old, try a *telephone*—the real one (if you have two) with the button taped down; *transistor radio*—children love turning the knobs and watching the dial move and hearing the stations and volume change; *jewelry box*—with only safe and durable things too big to be swallowed; children will lift the lid and close it, take things out and put them in, and examine endlessly; *kitchen drawer*—"This is your drawer," full of things to explore.

Over one year old, try an *old manual typewriter* or *tool box* minus sharp instruments.

Any desperate rainy day, try a *ball of string, roll of toilet paper* (just once or twice), *masking tape,* and a lot of *newspaper.*

Montessori teachers are masters at setting up worthwhile and inviting *nontoy activities* that leave the child free to learn without adult assistance or interference. In a good Montessori classroom you may find dozens of children working at the most mundane tasks with the most sublime expressions on their faces. On one tray are a small bowlful of walnuts, an empty bowl, and a pair of tongs. Another tray, also with two bowls, includes some small objects and a pair of tweezers. Each activity is self-explanatory and offers the child a practical skill. And their arrangement on trays helps to bring about a sense of security, definition, and peaceful order that could never be expressed verbally. Once the child has transferred all the nuts to the empty bowl (and probably back again several times), he will almost certainly replace the entire tray on the shelf from which he got it. (If not, this can be gently and firmly taught in only a few sessions.) The whole procedure is carried out by the child independently. Whatever they may lack in the garish appeal of commercial toys, such activities more than make up for in their appeal to the child's intelligence and innate love of discovery.

One of the loveliest Christmas gifts I ever heard of was a scrap of cloth with four buttons sewn on it. A two-and-a-half-year-old had sewn them on, taught secretly by her eleven-year-old sister. There are so many little things our children would learn with joy if we did not view them as dull work, too hard for the child, or too time-consuming for us. They are often happiest (and least bothersome) by our sides doing some modified version of whatever we are doing. How few toys we would buy if we really appreciated this.

Toy Buying

Choosing which toys to buy is a small matter compared with the task of discerning from moment to moment how to respond to our children in an intelligently loving way. When buying a toy seems called for, here are some things to consider:

- *Physical quality.* Is it sturdy and safe? Is it strong enough to last as long as the child's interest or as long as you think it should for the price you are paying? It is a mistake to stress the safety issue to the point of fear, but given what your child is likely to do with her new toy (bite it, fall on it, take it apart?), is it safe? Sometimes a cheap throw-away toy is the best answer.
- *Physical appearance.* Is it beautiful? There's no disputing tastes when it comes to beauty, but in general, is it nicely designed and harmonious in appearance? Is it inviting? Can you stand the sight of it yourself? Remember, it may be around and in sight for quite a while.
- *Span of usefulness.* How long at a time will the child enjoy it and how many times?
- *Educational value.* What does it teach, and is that worth learning? Is a toy really needed to teach this or is there a better way?
- *Your child's stake in the toy.* Does it meet a need or interest your child is manifesting *now?* Even the right toy at the wrong moment is the wrong toy. You can answer all the other questions by examining the toy, but this one can be answered only by watching the child.
- *Cost.* Balancing the price against all the above and in relation to your budget and space, is this toy worth buying?

Toys to Avoid

Many toys that seem worthwhile at first turn out to be disappointing. It is well to be circumspect about the following:

- *Terrific but too late.* Try to avoid buying things you wish you had known about six months ago. If he's already learned what your latest discovery teaches, the toy will not interest him.
- *Terrific but too temporary.* Some beautiful, well-made, and educationally sound toys that are worthwhile for preschools may be almost worthless at home because the child learns what they offer in a few minutes. At least in the beginning, children are not interested in *having* toys (possessiveness is acquired) but in what they can learn from them. As soon as the child has learned all he can from a toy, he will lose interest in it. Educator Glenn Doman estimates that the average toy designed for the average eighteen-month-old holds interest for about ninety seconds.
- *Babysitter toys.* Sometimes parents want to find a set or something that will "really keep her busy so I can get some work done." This hardly ever works because the motive is tantamount to an open invitation to the child to cling. But if you are looking for one "big" (meaning costly) thing that will last, try to test it out at a friend's house more than once. Consider where you will keep it and whether or not you have a good place for the child to use it. For example, a model garage or farm is easier to use and more interesting to the child if set at eye level on a table rather than on the floor. Some use-up activity items such as sewing cards and easy follow-the-dots with a set of colored pencils may occupy the child better, take up less space, and contribute more while costing less. Just think twice.
- *Redundant toys.* While a toy can teach much and be of lasting interest, it may be that the child can learn what it teaches with things around the house—for free. If so, you may prefer to save your pennies for something that can't be so easily duplicated at home.
- *Home learning programs.* As soon as your baby arrives you are likely to find yourself on a surprising number of new mailing lists, some of which invite you to subscribe to *their* home learning program for *your* baby. They may offer to send new toys each month pretested to suit the development of the child plus various books, publications, and charts. Some publications are full of helpful ideas and can be a real tonic, but first make sure the suggestions are compatible with your own philosophy. Avoid programs that claim to speed up the child's learning and may tempt you to push your child. Avoid publications that tempt you to compare your child with others. Avoid programs that arbitrarily send

preselected toys on schedule as part of your subscription. Direct mail is a big help, but retain your freedom to select and to buy or not buy. All babies and parents are different, so the time progressions of these programs may not apply to you and your child.

Organizing and Storing Toys

The physical environment in which the child works with his toys is important. No matter how selective we try to be, by the time our children are only a year old they have accumulated quite a supply. Unless we discover an orderly way of storing them, we will slowly go crazy from looking at, or trying to deal with, the mess.

It is important to find a reasonably effortless way of organizing and storing things. A jumble of toys only expresses possessiveness, which obscures the learning purpose of play. Some "mess" has to be tolerated for the child to be free to learn, but pure chaos works out to be tyrannizing rather than freeing.

Children appreciate order and, provided the order is *reasonable and apparent,* they can help to maintain it. They like finding things in the same place; they like knowing where things go. Order makes life easier. The only difficulty is finding a rationale on which to operate— not merely a place for everything but a sensible place for everything.

Most preschoolers will not play long by themselves. So you may find it nice to have a play area near where you spend most of your time. When there is a separate place for most toys, then the bedroom is easier to maintain and retains its sanctity as a place of quiet refuge, peace, contemplation, privacy. A few toys of current interest can still be kept there, as well as a good selection of books.

Wherever you keep them, generally speaking, toddlers' toys can be organized by category: small-parts toys and sets, small to medium single toys, medium to large toys, medium to large unorganizables.

Small-parts toys and sets can be stored in plastic containers or bins. Clear plastic kitchen containers come in all sizes, and you can see what's inside at a glance. When giving a small-parts gift, it's nice to give such a container as well. Frequently used sets such as Legos can be stored in stackable plastic bins and are thus easy for children to get at and pick up on their own.

Small to medium toys, such as yo-yos, balls, and flashlights, are almost as troublesome as small-parts sets. They defy organization and are easily knocked off open shelves. Shallow plastic bins make good "drawers" for these, and can be set on shelves or mounted on glides beneath shelves.

Medium to large single toys, such as a cash register, pounding bench, or xylophone, can have specific places on a shelf.

Medium to large unorganizables, such as dolls and stuffed animals, can be sorted into categories and stored in large plastic laundry baskets or large cardboard cartons (cover with contact paper, add rope handles). If placed on the floor beneath a shelf, they look neater and can be pulled out like drawers. You might want three boxes: one for cars and trucks, one for costumes, one for dolls, stuffed animals, and puppets.

Big *toy chests* are not very useful, except for long-term storage without use. Things get lost at the bottom and nobody wants to wrestle them forth.

Shelves, built up rather than around the walls, take up less play space. Besides, it's wise to have some things out of reach so that not everything can be spread out in aimless moments or at inappropriate times. Obviously things of greatest interest that need least supervision need to be stored within the child's reach, whereas those that need you (e.g., perhaps paints, glue) can be placed higher.

If most toys are kept in the bedroom, the *closet* may be more useful for toys than for clothes, at least while the clothes are too small to need hangers. Though it's good for children to have free access to their toys, having them in sight all the time may be a distraction that results in their moving from one thing to another in a superficial, unsatisfying way. Line your child's closet with storage shelves. She can still get at her things but is less likely to drag everything out.

Hooks are handy for tanglers and danglers that don't fit in elsewhere. And for some of the clothes you took from the closet to make room for the toys, provide hooks that she can reach: one for pajamas, one for bathrobe, jacket, raincoat. You'll be surprised at the daily difference it makes to both of you.

Pickup time. If you're overwhelmed by the task of picking up, imagine how it looks to your child. For a quick pickup and a chance for her to experience the cleanup as happy and rewarding, give her a shopping bag in which to put "everything you find on the floor" or "everything you find around the house that really belongs in your room." Then have a sorting session. It is as much fun for the child as a treasure hunt, and the sudden improvement makes the value of order apparent. When the idea that we are Seeing Beings is kept in mind, it is easier to know what to expect of her and how much help to give in restoring order. What will help her to see the value of order? A time to demonstrate, a time to enforce, a time to help, a time not to help.

A Place to Work

In fostering the best use of toys and playtime, a good place to work is as important as a place to put things away. The former is part-ly taken care of by the latter, since a little space is about all a child requires for her work. The only equipment that might be considered crucial are a child-size table and chair, and a step stool for upping her size.

A child-size table and chair are almost as valuable as a bed. While it's possible for children to work or read in highchairs or junior chairs at adult-size tables, they are more comfortable at tables and chairs that fit them. Activities last longer at child-size tables than at a big one or on the floor. The children can pick up what they drop, work standing up for a while, move around and work from the other side, and come and go and come again. A clean, visible, reachable work surface inspires constructive work. Greater concentration, independence, and freedom are possible. Heavy-duty plastic-topped tables available through educational catalogs are ideal, but almost any smooth surface of the right height will do. Cut down an old table. A large piece of ply-wood covered with matte-finish white Formica makes a superb counter/table/desk that can grow with the child to adulthood. All you have to do is change the base from short legs to longer legs. Or rest it across small chests of drawers. A good minimum size is 20 by 30 inch-es. Most important is the relative height of table and chairs. During the preschool years, 24 inches is a good average table height. Ten inches between chair seat and table is about right. Have extra chairs for playmates.

A step stool that brings the child up to sink, counter, toilet, workbench, and higher bookshelf level replaces the water table, play kitchen, and in many instances the long arm of Mommy and Daddy. Any sturdy stool will do. We had one that combined a two-step stair with a small rocking chair.

Kinds of Play

When the days are long, often what's needed is not a new toy or a change in the weather but a shift in subject, a change of perspective, another way of carrying on, of shifting gears. Only clear seeing can tell us what and when, but there will be times for . . .

Playing alone. While we try not to abandon our children or push them aside, we must nevertheless stand back as much as possible. Be available but not interfering. Help and encourage, but prepare to be ever more irrelevant as the child grows. It is also important to treat our children and their work with courtesy and respect, never unnecessarily interrupting a child at play any more than we would interrupt a fellow adult at work.

Playing beside each other. This is the most common mode of play throughout the preschool years. They do their work; we do ours—not interfering with each other unnecessarily but sharing the joy of working and learning. We keep each other company and are near each other in love.

Playing together. Doing the same thing together—from roughhousing, to artwork, to games, to cooking, or making anything together. Often an activity that requires two people is what first awakens the child to the benefits of cooperating. Whatever is happening, let it be characterized by gentleness and joy.

Planned play. With toddlers it is good to have some planned activities every day and some regular activities each week. Toddlers are too mobile and too thirsty for learning for us to respond adequately on an entirely moment-to-moment basis. Parent and child are likely to tire of each other at the end of any day in which there is no planned time. One nursery school child who had had enough of doing what he pleased said that he hoped at his new school they would not "make me do what I feel like."

A time of day that is often trying for small children is early morning. They wake so expectantly, glad to see us, eager to get on with life. But sometimes we almost wrestle the morning away.

It may be that a little sooner attention rather than all that later attention would be better—just a little help to get her started in her own "work." So set up something after she goes to bed—a project or a toy she hasn't seen for a while or all her cars lined up in a new place. Try reading one story right off the bat. Afterward you may find you can go your separate ways for a time. And give some thought to what she might do beside you while you work. Such thoughtfulness expresses love and can help free everyone for a happier day.

Going out. No matter how responsive we are, we almost have to have an outing each day to break the illusion of being each other's captive. If you are at home alone with your toddler for long stretches of time, you almost can't help revolving around each other. The more we think we are running our children's lives, the more we feel they are running ours. We wake up glad to see them, but by bedtime we are standing over our sweetly sleeping children, vowing that tomorrow we will give more of ourselves to them. But maybe less is the answer. Outings are great for changing the subject from me and him for and against each other to both of us in the big wide world, making discoveries side-by-side.

Outings give life a chance to take charge of us and diminish our conviction that we have to take charge of life. On any outing try to arrange for the child to do some walking or climbing on his own. While a ride in a grocery cart or a quick tour of a nearby pet store can be as good as a museum expedition, long shopping trips are a trial to be avoided when possible. Besides regular outdoor explorations, frequent library visits are tops. Make both as shouldless as possible. Most libraries are relaxed about children talking in the children's section. Try the firehouse, an airport, a pajama walk just before bed. And don't let the rain keep you in. Hardly anything is more fun than a pair of boots, an umbrella, a puddle, and permission to splash.

Active play. A time to allow for climbing. You are available now, so the safety gate can come off the stairs and he can practice. Dancing. Marching. Walking like a duck or an inchworm. He does things and you copy him. Indoors or out, just some running around and jumping and climbing. There is a time for peace and a time for pillow fights and being rowdy!

Quiet play. Separate private times. Quiet times together. Is there conflict and frustration? Then let's both go to our rooms—not as a punishment, but to get free, become quiet, and put something besides each other in charge. A time to be still together, to listen to the wind or what she wants to say. To look out the window, up at the stars, down at the street, into the woods. To walk once around the house before bed and hear the insect music. If we want to help them learn to pray, let's not teach them what to say but how to be still and listen when there doesn't seem to be anybody talking at all.

Books About Toy Making and Play

One last thing to consider before heading off to purchase a toy is a good practical book on homemade toys and play activities. The true crafts books on toy making are best reserved for enthusiastic grandparents and friends unless you already have the necessary skills or a helper to take care of your preschooler while you learn to carve or sew or carpent. But improvisational books on toy making and play activities provide well-tried ideas that can be done on the spur of the moment. One such book is worth a dozen toys and will probably cost half as much as one toy. (See also pages 249–250.)

> *Child Care Tips for Busy Mothers,* by Nancy Carlyle. Practical tips to make life with children pleasanter and easier. From coping with slippery-soled new shoes, to fingerpaint recipes, to long car trips. Sometimes silly, but mostly very helpful. Simon & Schuster.
> *The Cooperative Sports and Games Book,* by Terry Orlick. We all say winning isn't what counts, yet we find it difficult to say what does. Orlick shows how to face challenges and have fun together through playing games that nobody loses! Pantheon.
> *Easy Woodstuff for Kids,* by David Thompson. Woodworking is one of the most appealing and discouraging activities for preschoolers and their parents. Unless you are experienced with both woodworking and children, you are likely to set your sights too high. The result is either an unsuccessful project or a frustrated child, sighing, "I didn't make it. You did." *Easy Woodstuff* is full of projects manageable by almost any parent and preschooler. Especially nice are the numbers of things children can make and give as

gifts. Fosters appreciation of trees and nature, satisfying creativity, learning of basic woodworking skills, and resourcefulness. Gryphon.

The Everything Book, by Eleanor Graham Vance. Divided into "Things to Make" and "Things to Do," this is a real treasure chest of good ideas for parents, sitters, and grandparents. Among our favorites: directions for newspaper hats, boats, and giant trees; mice and dolls from knotted handkerchiefs; and an "impromptu dollhouse" from junk—sure to provide days of fun that you'd never get from a "boughten" one. Great for trips, rainy days, chickenpox. Handy throughout childhood. Golden.

How to Make Children's Furniture and Play Equipment, by Mario Dal Fabbro. Cribs, chairs, gyms, tables, sandbox, easel, playhouse, workbench—sixty plans for parents handy with power tools. McGraw-Hill.

The Incredible Year-Round Playbook, by Elin McCoy. A book of over 100 season-related crafts, games, tricks, and stunts that promote resourcefulness, awareness of nature, and good family times. Random House.

I Saw a Purple Cow and 100 Other Recipes for Learning, by Ann Cole, Carolyn Haas, Faith Bushnell, and Betty Weinberger, illustrated by True Kelley. An endless variety of things to do and make with young children. Includes play-dough recipe, finger plays, toys to make. Compiled by four experienced mothers. Little, Brown.

Just a Box? by Goldie Taub Chernoff, illustrated by Margaret Hartelius. Many things to make from the endless cardboard boxes everything comes in. A toothpaste-box alligator, oatmeal-box cradle, and so on. Scholastic Book Service.

Learning with Mother, by Ethel and Harry Wingfield. Books 1 (up to two years), 2 (two to three years), 3 (three to four years), and 4 (four to five years). Imported from England, these unassuming little books are unusually helpful regarding what to do with preschoolers. Arranged according to chronological development, the sequence is good, though many children will be ready for things sooner than the books suggest. As small activity books they don't contain many things to do, but each idea suggests a dozen other ways of helping your child to learn. A Ladybird Book. Penguin Books.

Making Things, by Ann Wiseman. A good craft and toy-making book that is mostly for older children but good to know about. Includes a wide variety of activities from printing, to xylophone making, to carving wooden whistles. Little, Brown.

A Parent's Guide to Children's Play and Recreation, by Alvin Schwartz. First published in 1963, this book is not quite up to date in the materials and prices it mentions. Nevertheless, it is an exceptionally useful introduction to the activities most children enjoy, with rough guidelines for when, and suggestions for how, to provide appropriate equipment inexpensively. Collier.

Play and Playthings for the Preschool Child, by E. M. Matterson. A useful book brimming with suggestions for providing young children with a good play/learning environment. Ideas for the handy parent-with-a-hammer on building shelves, benches, gym equipment (doesn't give specific plans, just ideas to improvise on). Very useful presentations of the value of various kinds of play. Penguin Books.

The Playgroup Book, by Marie Winn and Mary Ann Porcher. A superb book about all the things preschoolers like to learn from doing. A highly useful resource for preschool parents, whether or not you have a play group. Penguin Books.

Puppet Party, by Goldie Taub Chernoff, illustrated by Margaret Hartelius. All kinds of simple hand puppets made from paper bags, socks, paper plates, and cups. Scholastic Book Service.

Three, Four, Open the Door, by Susan M. Stein and Sarah T. Lottick. At once just about the most conscious and practical book of activities for young children: what they accomplish, how to do them, and when. A well-thought-out response to society's growing awareness of the young child's ability, eagerness, and right to learn. Wonderful for parents or teachers. Follett.

Toy Book, by Steven Caney. Instructions on how to make and get the most out of more than fifty toys and experiments. Many are for children older than preschool age, for whom much of the fun will be in the making. But the preschooler is growing up fast and in the meantime such things as soap crayons, tube telephones, sand combs, and a creature cage are wonderful. Workman.

What to Do When "There's Nothing to Do," by staff members of the Boston Children's Medical Center and Elizabeth M. Gregg, illustrated by Marc Simont. Six hundred and one truly practical play ideas that really work with younger children. Expresses very well the possibilities of learning and playing without buying a lot. Dell.

Workjobs, by Mary Baratta Lorton. Jar tops, safety pins, rice, and such can help preschoolers help themselves to language, math, and happy hours. Described as "activity-centered learning," *Workjobs* is a mind-opener for the home. So often we don't recognize learning when it is taking place. We fall for workbooks that bore or frustrate and overlook the educational potential of everyday materials and situations. This is a catalog of child-proven activities that respect child's play as learning work. Photos and straightforward text demonstrate a variety of learning games easily assembled from ordinary grocery-bag fallout. Addison-Wesley.

4

Freedom

We never had tears over broken balloons because, knowing that they would rise when the string was released, our children always wanted to let go immediately. As parents we had some trouble adjusting to this. While we secretly lamented the "waste" of our money, the children marveled at the freedom of each bright, rising thing. After a while they learned to hold onto their balloons a little longer and more tightly. So the kids are learning to hold on, while we are learning to let go.

—parent

And ye shall know the truth, and the truth shall make you free.

—John 8:32

The urge for freedom is universal. From infancy on, whenever limitation is experienced we desire to overcome it. The new-born infant, unable even to hold up her head, so restricted physically, is completely dependent on her parents. As she learns to feed herself, to walk and climb, she finds increasing freedom, from both her own limitations and her dependency on her parents. Each increased freedom augments her awareness of freedom. You can see that she desires freedom and rejoices in it. There does not seem to be a period in the human life span during which freedom increases so rapidly as in the first three years. Why? How can we facilitate our children's quest for freedom? What can we learn from our freedom-seeking children that can free us—to live more fully, to be fuller selves?

False Freedom

Me, Inc. can conceive of participating in reality in only two ways: by having and by doing. So we tend to approach freedom in two ways: by wanting (and not wanting) and by willing (and won'ting). We want freedom to do what we feel like and not what we don't feel like. We seek freedom *from* others' expectations. We envy those we deem free to "do their own thing." Free time is time to ourselves, time out, time to relax or do as we please. Implied is a sort of being above the law. What law? Whose law? The law of others. On the other hand, we expect others to free us by complying with our expectations. We equate freedom with being in a position of power over others. So, freedom seems to mean being above the law or having the power to impose it on others.

Free to Be Me

We sense freedom involves both pleasure and order. Yet we experience a conflict between these aspects of freedom that result in little pleasure (except at the cost of order) and little order (except at the cost of pleasure). When we seek freedom as pleasure we achieve only enervating, enslaving, chaotic self-indulgence. So we try ordering, making resolutions; we try to get what's expected of us done so we'll be free to do as we please. Here we meet internal rebellion. The more we try, the more something in us resists. The more we succeed, the more bound up, uptight, joyless, *unfree* we become.

Free to Be Me and You

Most families experience a constant struggle to maintain freedom without trespassing and chaos, order without tyranny and conflict. A constant battle rages between doing what we feel like doing and what others think we should, and between family members over who is getting his or her way. Each one's freedom is experienced by the rest as his "getting his own way" at their expense. One's pleasure wreaks havoc on the others' order; one's order inteferes with the others' pleasure.

When freedom is identified with pleasure outside the law, being a good parent seems to mean letting our children do as they please. If freedom is identified with imposing order, then being a good parent means constanty telling them what they should do. Either way parents and children feel tyrannized—by the chaos or the conflict, and by the conviction that order is up to, or imposed on, us.

> *Parent:* You are bossing me around by making me boss you around by not doing what you should. If you would just do what I tell you in the first place, then I wouldn't have to keep telling you.
> *Child:* I think there's something fishy about that.
> *Parent:* I think you're right.

Parents who equate freedom with pleasure are prone to being overprotective, interfering, fearful parents or overindulgent, "spoiling" ones. In the first case, the child may be overly afraid to go forth and try new things, or he may be reckless and wild and wind up getting hurt or into trouble. Either way, he is not free. In the second case, he becomes demanding and self-indulgent. He assesses everything with the question of whether he "feels like it," and so is confined by his feelings to a very narrow world in which there is little freedom. His freedom to fulfill his potential and to participate in an ever-widening world is curtailed. He is bored stiff and constantly in need of entertainment. He has no idea what he'd like to do, only a long list of things he doesn't feel like or fears.

Parents who identify freedom with order may be overly strict, demanding, and shouldful. We want our children to do first things first, so that later they will be free to do what they like. No matter how sensible such arguments seem, they do not impress our children. Our goal may be to free our child to be all that he can be by training him to be disciplined. But right now he only feels pushed around, and he is learning that freedom is a matter of exerting power over others, which in turn means that he must not do what others want him to do. I overheard one despairing parent say to her son, "Asking you to hurry is like telling you to take a nap." Somehow children never do what they should, or they try but fail, or succeed but are miserable or obnoxious. They may feel mad as hops or guilty as hell; they may be bullies or sissies; they may try like the dickens or give up in defeat. But they aren't free.

I Will, Therefore I Am

All such approaches to freedom equate it with the exertion of personal willpower in a fundamentally chaotic or conflicting universe. Whether as wanting or not wanting, willing or won'ting—and whether selfish or altruistic, strict or permissive, individual or collective—the basic assumption is that life is a chaotic situation in which freedom depends on exertion of the human will and imposition of human order—especially on other human beings, particularly family members. As we fail to see—but often experience—the free will approach to freedom through will is both a preeminently tyrannical and chaos-producing idea. Wherever freedom is sought in vain, we can expect to find an underlying idea of personal willpower. Beneath it lie basic misperceptions of who and where we are: a body among bodies, a personal will among personal wills—Me, Inc. The idea that each of us is a body among bodies tends toward feel-good pleasure-seeking (wanting and not wanting) and a narrow, chaotic self-indulgent life outside the law. The idea that we are persons among persons, embodied wills among embodied wills, leads to power struggle (willing and won'ting).

Let Freedom Ring

The girl did not fall asleep readily, and when she was ten, she began to switch on her radio at night—which was against the rules. She rarely broke rules, and then only fearfully, switching the radio only "on," not turning it up at all. She could just hear it if she put her ear to the speaker. When the stations signed off by playing the "Star Spangled Banner," she'd climb out of bed and, shivering sleepily, stand obediently while "our national anthem" was played. With the volume so low, she couldn't hear it, and had to keep bending down to hear when it was over.

I knew a young lady of wealthy parents who ran away from home and was driving a taxi in New York City, living in Greenwich Village in squalor and misery. She said, "Well, I wanted to be free." I was able to show her that she was not free, she was only trying to be independent, which means she was still dependent since she was fighting against her parents by driving a taxi and living in poverty. That's not freedom, it's a struggle for independence, which is a state of dependency.

—Thomas Hora, *Existential Metapsychiatry*

The Child as a Model for Freedom

Jesus said: "Except ye be converted, and become as little children, ye shall not enter into the kingdom of heaven."

—Matthew 18:3

Jesus didn't say that children were getting into heaven, but rather that there is something about the way children are, which if we understood it, might free us to get into heaven. What is it? Are children free? In a way, no; but in a way, yes.

On the surface, there is hardly anything less free than an infant. She appears to be a very self-centered, body-oriented, tyrannical, and limited creature—helpless, weak, dependent on others in every way.

Yet, within a few short years, she has gained so much freedom that we can simply be amazed. From a weak, nearly blind, pleasure/pain–bound, ignorant, uncomprehending, powerless, speechless little thing, she becomes in no time a running, dancing, singing, talking, questioning, understanding, delighting wonder.

And talk about chaos! What is more chaotic than the crazy quilt of meaningless sensations that bombard the uncomprehending newborn? Yet in an unbelievably short time she has found order, meaning, and a way of orienting herself so that she can move freely about and have considerable dominion over her experience. For all she doesn't yet know and can't do, for all she still depends on others, before she even enters school, she has demonstrated a freedom to become free that is mind-boggling. Before long—already in fact—it is inevitable for her to experience conflict between what her developing Me, Inc. wants and what the world of other Me, Incs. seems to require. Nevertheless, as she transcends one limitation after another with incredible speed, she provides astonishing demonstrations of how freedom is realized.

What is the child's secret? It is a secret from herself. In fact, it is the secret of herself. She doesn't *have* the secret of freedom, but she *manifests* it. Like a messenger with an unopened envelope, she delivers freedom's message to us.

> *In inexperienced infancy*
> *Many a sweet mistake doth lie:*
> *Mistake, though false, intending true;*
> *A seeming somewhat more than view,*
> *That doth instruct the mind*
> *In things that lie behind*
> *And many secrets to us show*
> *Which afterwards we come to know.*

—Thomas Traherne, from "Shadows in the Water," in
Poems of Felicity

Children exhibit a freedom to become freer that we seem to lack. They also lack something that we have: self-consciousness or, more accurately, self/other consciousness. Besides purity and innocence, one quality we universally admire in young children is their *freedom from worry* about what others think or want of them.

During the largely un-self-conscious period of infancy and early childhood they demonstrate this purity, innocence, and *freedom* we so admire.

Is there a connection between children's striking lack of self-consciousness and their striking freedom to grow freer so efficiently? If you observe a group of young children at play you will see that the freest child is the least self-conscious one. See how his freedom to grow freer by leaps and bounds springs from his ability to look at life for what it can teach him, an ability directly proportionate to his lack of preoccupation with self in relation to others. He is not distracted by worries about what others think of him; he is utterly focused on what he is doing. His attention is not divided between what he is doing and what others may think about it or him. His self is not divided between what he desires and what he fears. And what is he doing? He is discovering underlying laws and his oneness with them. Through his undivided attention to seeing *what is, what is* ultimately gets its way with him and brings him new freedom. The tremendous effort he exerts is not willful but passionate.

Zen and the Art of Throwing a Ball

I heard a father marvel: "How did he learn to throw a ball so far? I didn't teach him! When did he learn? I didn't see him! Why did he do it? No one in our family is interested in baseball."

Everything that father thought was missing might have been a hindrance. Somewhere along the way in throwing a ball, the child had conceived of a possibility of freedom. Perhaps it first came through watching someone else. Perhaps once in flinging a ball he had really let it fly and surprised himself. At any rate, some freedom had been encountered and was now a possibility in consciousness. After that, as long as he remained un-self-conscious (undivided), he was able to give his undivided attention to the possibility of which he had conceived. Through his pure desire for freedom (and his sense of possibility) certain laws found the opportunity to gain power over him. Aiming himself toward a conscious possibility, he became subservient to it. Through his receptive and devoted consciousness, the underlying force of being itself organized and energized and utilized and coordinated everything in him to express *it*self in the form of the freedom of so beautifully letting the ball fly.

He must have practiced for hours on end, carried away and carried along by his interest in seeing what was possible. Confident that what he could conceive of was possible, he went at it. Sometimes the ball fell short, but he did not infer that he lacked power. Sometimes the ball went wild, but he did not infer that his goal was impossible or that there was no reliable order. Whatever seemed too hard only showed him that he had not yet discovered the knack. Whatever appeared chaotic only suggested that the order and his oneness with it had not yet been discerned.

Sometimes his shoulder hurt, but the hurt became a guide, directing him into better alignment with the hidden force he did not doubt. He looked at everything for *what is* and *what isn't*, so everything taught him, until he could throw the ball—far, fast, accurately, with remarkable ease. And he wasn't proud, he was thrilled; he didn't feel triumphant, he felt grateful; he didn't feel powerful, but assured; and he felt and was freer.

It was never that he had his way with the ball. Rather through his undistracted, passion-focused un-self-conscious consciousness the invisible laws of physics had their way with him. Through submission to the invisible laws he found what he rightfully and joyfully experienced as freedom.

Me, Inc. knows that freedom has something to do with law and order, but believes order must be brought about by willpower. Children show us that, on the contrary, freedom comes through finding our oneness with existing order and being subservient to, and consciously aligned with, it. Me, Inc. knows freedom has something to do with pleasure, but thinks it means feeling good and being above the law. The spontaneous child shows us that this pleasure is really a by-product of obedience to the law.

By feeling for and obeying the hidden laws of physics, we become free to navigate a bicycle creatively—no hands, standing on our heads, riding on only one wheel, almost anything we can think of—with minimum effort. To Me, Inc., such feats seem the product of power. Since we do not usually attribute our lack of freedom to ignorance, we do not expect to find freedom through spiritual consciousness. But the boy with the ball shows us again that we are Seeing Beings and that seeing is being, that whatever we can truly see, we can be. He shows us that life is after all fundamentally orderly, which is to say that it is intelligent, which is also to say that it is intelligible. He demonstrates that in any endeavor maximum freedom depends on maximum obedience to the fundamental order of being. Obedience means oneness.

Oneness with a fundamental intelligence is consciousness. Thus he shows us that *seeing is freeing*.

And ye shall know the truth, and the truth shall make you free.

—John 8:32

The Parent as a Freeing Agent

"I didn't teach him." "No one in our family is interested in baseball." We need not conclude that the way to raise a free child is to leave him alone. Indeed, somewhat neglected children often seem to thrive better than those with "overinvested" parents whose overbearing attention makes them self-conscious and distracts them from their natural explorations of self and universe. But better than a parent who merely doesn't distract is one who exemplifies, recognizes, trusts, facilitates, and fosters awareness of the fundamental intelligent order of life.

1. The Free Parent looks at everything with such questions as *What is being shown? What is really going on here? What is there for me to learn in this?* The more we see that the only obstacles to our freedom are our own limited and limiting ideas (rather than external circumstances or expectations), the more we reinforce our children's innate sense that seeing is freeing, and the less they are enslaved by the idea of having to fight against "outside" constraints. The more we seek to discover what the natural order of the day is than to impose our order on it, the more we reinforce the child's innate sense that his only hindrances are the limits of his understanding.

2. The Parent as Beholder of the Free Child. The child's freedom depends on her confidence—in herself as a "see-worthy" individual, in life as a fundamentally intelligible and orderly system. The more we recognize that seeing is being, the more eager we are to let our children see for themselves. The more we recognize that all life is meaningful, the easier it is to entrust our children to life as a gentle instructor.

The freeing parent is above all a seeing parent. As seeing parents we do not view our children (or ourselves) in terms of virtues and faults, but in terms of what is true and what is false. This way we are continuously freeing our true, unique children, rather than tethering them (or ourselves) with cords of guilt, shame, blame, or criticism.

3. *The Parent as Paver of the Free Way.* By understanding that the basis of freedom is fundamental, intelligent order, we are freed of confusion about strict versus permissive and license versus freedom. Whenever we are guided by awareness of what *idea* is being expressed and what the child is ready to *see,* it becomes clear from moment to moment when "laying down the law" fosters security rather than tyranny or dependency, and when "letting be" fosters confidence and learning rather than insecurity or self-indulgence.

4. *The Parent as Preparer and Maintainer of the Freeing Environment.* The substance of freedom is order. Thoughtful orderliness is one way to make way for the free child. Intelligent freeing order can be expressed in the management of household, time, the setting of priorities on a "first things first" basis. (See pages 150 and 193.)

> When her sons were small, children's book illustrator Cyndy Szekeres bought a playpen—for herself! She did her artwork in the playpen, thereby protecting it from the children while leaving them free for their more active work. This approach wouldn't suit everyone—but the basic idea makes sense.

5. *The Parent as Guide and Fellow Seeker.* As freeing parents we make the least of ourselves, factoring ourselves out as much as possible according to the child's readiness. We often ask before telling and, even then, more often show than tell how something can be done. The essential value of instruction is to awaken the child to a possibility for himself (not his dependency on a superior parent). The value of regulations is to help the child encounter a new freedom or to protect some existing freedom. We are fellow seekers of freedom with our children. All the attention we give to considering what is really freeing for the child enhances our own realization of freedom.

6. *The Parent as Supplier of Opportunities for Freedom.* The value of any activity is its potential to increase the child's awareness of freedom and of her potential to be free. Her interest in an activity depends on her sense that some order will be revealed and thus free her, or that some freedom will be achieved and thus help her discover some underlying order. Animals, gym sets, vehicles, trees and woods, indoor and outdoor activities, everything can be approached with freedom in mind.

Additional Reflection: The Freedom to Be Individual

An important idea implicit in all of this material, but which needs to be made emphatically clear, is that a child's most important freedom is the freedom to discover and to be her unique, individual self. In my psychotherapeutic practice I've seen far too many adults despair as they realize that they have spent their whole lives trying to be what their parents wanted them to be in the vain hope of finally winning a parental blessing that was, in fact, their birthright.

Long after the parents have died, their critical voice nags on inside these people. It says nothing they do is good enough, that they should have done better, or more, or been something else altogether. No matter what worldly success they achieve as what Winnicott calls "false selves," they feel empty, unfulfilled, "dead inside," or that "something is missing." And it is. What lies in the emptiness, what's missing and unfulfilled, is the "true self" or at least aspects of it. Weeping, these people recall passions and interests that flared up and died in childhood, doused by parental pressure, criticism, or indifference.

I must assure them again and again that what's dead or dying is only the false self, that the true one is trying to come to life. Most had parents who also suffered from false selfhood and sought to live through *their* children by making them into whatever *their* parents wanted that they felt *they* had failed to be. The long work of healing and bringing to life the true "inner child" depends on the healing of the hypercritical "inner parent." A new inner parent must be established to receive, encourage, trust, and set free and let be the true and unique and worthy child of God.

If we wish to spare our children such a painful journey with such wide detours, there are two important things we can do. First, we must work on ourselves, because we will not be able to treat our objective children any better than we treat our inner children. So we must learn to listen and respond to the voices of our own inner putdown and neglected selves. Second, we must seek to be aware of, and to trust, the God source of our children as it shows up in their passions. Each self is intrinsically whole, worthy, unique, God given and God driven. Each path aims to bring each self to its unique fullness.

Instead of trying to make our children into something, we need to focus above all on making way for what they naturally are. Looking at my grown sons today and looking back on our years together, I see that one of my greatest joys as a parent was watching their uniqueness emerge. I see that the best they were, are, and are becoming was there from the outset.

A Model for the Freeing Parent

The freeing parent is like an orchestra conductor. On the surface it seems that the music is made by the conductor telling everyone what to do at a particular time. But a good conductor does not merely tell everyone what to do; rather he helps everyone to hear the music. So he is not so much a telling but a listening individual. Even while the orchestra performs loudly he listens inwardly to the music. He is not so much commanding as obedient. He conducts by being conducted. By hearing, feeling, and losing himself in the music, he finds ways to help others hear and express it, too. He knows that music is not made by people playing instruments but by music playing people. By any and all means he endeavors to conduct his orchestra into a consciousness of what the music is. For this he is at once absolutely subservient to the music and respectful of the players as musical instruments. And he is always trying to factor himself out so that nothing comes between the music and its instruments, the players' consciousnesses. He knows that music makes the music.

This philosophy is well demonstrated by Isaac Stern in the film *From Mao to Mozart*. After years of prohibition from Western music, Chinese musicians were out of touch with it. Though they could play the written notes accurately, the result was not music. They couldn't express what they hadn't felt inwardly. Working with young adult students in a master class, Stern provides us with a model for parenthood. Is he strict or permissive? Praising or critical? Gentle or severe? He responds different ways at different times. He is never patronizing, and he is clearly attuned both to the music and to what the student is ready to hear.

Before a large audience, a student begins to play. "No!" he says, only moments into the piece. *How could he?* we think. *She must feel so humiliated!* But his interruption is not personal; it is musical. By refusing to let the student play unmusically he expresses confidence in her ability to play musically. An interpreter is ready to translate what he says, but this time he speaks the universal language of music by playing the passage over himself. What was merely skillfully played a moment before becomes beautiful and alive. *Oh,* we say. *Is that what it is! I didn't know.* "Ah!" says the girl. To another student he says, "Quite good. But now sing it, will you?" She sings expressively. "You see, when you sing, it is beautiful, because you are listening to the music," says Stern. "That is how we play the violin. We listen to the music and then we find a way to make it sound like that." Everything he does helps the student really hear and feel the music.

He says nothing to the very young child performers, only listens with evident appreciation. These children are growing up with Western music, so they hear and feel it. Teachers will give them technique. Music is teaching them music, which they will play in their own unique ways. So Stern keeps silent. A good conductor conducts by being conducted by the music. Love-intelligent parents are conducted by love-intelligence.

> *A true Master according to the Eastern tradition embodies truth for the disciple and transmits it directly as a lit candle can light another. He represents the reality which is present, but as yet imperfectly released, in the disciple, and his purpose is to help the disciple to realize, in the Indian phrase, the eternal Guru and Teacher in himself. When he has succeeded in doing this, the need of external Master and mediator is over. In short, the aim of the Master is to prove himself superfluous, since what he essentially is, the disciple is too.*
>
> —Hugh l'Anson Fausset, *The Flame and the Light*

Freed to Go

> *They shall mount up with wings as eagles; they shall run, and not be weary; and they shall walk and not faint.*
>
> —Isaiah 40:31

> *"Whither, oh whither, oh whither so high?"*
> *"To sweep the cobwebs from the sky."*
>
> —Traditional nursery rhyme

As parents of active children how can we apply and recognize the idea that seeing is freeing? Our small children's most obvious frontiers are physical. They want to overcome all limitations and the first ones they perceive are physical. They want to get up, then to go, then to go higher and faster and farther and upside-downer and arounder. If we keep sight of the spiritual motivation behind our children's physical activity, we can be waymakers rather than impeders of their growth.

At first their motives are so pure. They do not climb to compete, or to be physically fit. Neither do they climb to put gray hairs on our heads or to knock over our favorite lamps. They climb to see; they see to be free. This is the primary motive for most of their activity—until other motives are introduced.

We have considered two ways that we tend to use our children: for our own pleasure and for our own ambition. If we are not alert to these temptations we become hinderers rather than helpers in our children's growth toward freedom. To be freedom enhancers rather than hinderers we need to recognize and relinquish our tendency to use them and their activity for selfish motives, and behold their activity in the light of the idea that seeing is freeing.

Safety and Freedom: The Parent as Roadblocker

"Mother, may I go out to swim?"
"Yes, my darling daughter.
Just hang your clothes on a hickory limb,
But don't go near the water."

—Traditional nursery rhyme

The inclination to use our children for our own pleasure places roadblocks in the way of their freedom. With regard to their physical activity, it shows up in such ideas as daring/fearing ("Don't be such a chicken." "Oh, no! You're going to fall!"), pleasure/pain ("It'll feel so good/bad, comfortable/uncomfortable."), pleasing/displeasing ("Don't you want your father to be proud of you?"), wanting/not wanting ("He doesn't *want* to walk. I think you should carry him."), sickly/healthy ("You'll get sick from doing that!").

Such attitudes toward our children's physical activity can virtually stop them in their freedom-seeking tracks. Some parents inhibit their children with exaggerated fears of injury. Others pressure their children to exercise, compete, and "be a sport." Either extreme can spoil the freedom and joy of active play. The parallel for psychologically minded parents is fear of the child's getting "hurt feelings." It is neither necessary nor possible to consider all the many variations. But one experience worth extra attention is that of safety in relation to freedom.

New parents in particular are likely to worry when their children begin to run and climb. Parents of older children face the same temptation when their children begin to want to drive a car, go off on their own, and undertake new challenges.

How can the parent as a freeing agent also be a responsible custodian of the child's safety? We need to be careful about "Be careful!" Almost against our will this cry dominates our parental vocabulary. When our children returned from visiting relatives in Holland, we found that although they hadn't learned much Dutch, they did know many ways to say *be careful* (think of your . . . mind your . . . watch out . . . beware . . . look out . . .).

To some extent, this is unavoidable. If your child is backing off the bed, standing up in his highchair, teetering heedlessly at the top of the ladder to the slide, you have to warn. But some parents are so fearful of what might happen that they virtually keep their children prisoners. I've seen children over two years old sitting harnessed in strollers *next* to sandboxes *watching* other children play! Others allow their children to play but are so terrified by near and imagined dangers that they even become angry, shouting, "What's the matter with you? Do you want to get killed? It's your fault that you got hurt. I told you to be careful."

Such children are likely to become reckless and clumsy, or timid and hypochondriacal, or, worst of all, apathetic. We want them to be safe from harm, but not *full of care!* How can we maintain their safety without undermining their confidence and freedom?

The more we see our children as Seeing Beings, the more we understand their impulses toward freedom and how to keep them safe while entrusting them to life. The baby who crawls toward the open fireplace isn't trying to destroy himself. He is purely and rightfully interested in learning. Once he knows what *hot* means and that fire is hot, he will not try to crawl into the fireplace. *Yes, ooh—it's hot! Ouch. Hot! Not for touching!* is usually all it takes. We need to protect them from their ignorance, but we do not need to tie them to chairs.

I knew someone who grew up near the edge of a cliff. I asked him how his parents had dealt with that. He said, "The first day we moved in they took us right to the top of the cliff and dropped a melon over the edge. We saw it splat. From then on we made sure to stay back." Conversely, our family used to visit a country place with a high rock wall. As soon as we got there our sons made straight for that wall and began to scale it. The first time, I was terrified. I saw that they *knew what they were doing,* but I couldn't watch it. So I turned around and prayed, *they shall mount up with wings as eagles.* They had their share of scrapes and bruises, but they never fell off that rock wall. There is a time for protection and prohibition, and a time to prayerfully let go.

While we don't want to belittle or be negligent, it is good to help our children let go of pain. Most hurts arise in the process of learning. Often what hurts most is the disruption of learning. Children are glad when the pain passes so that they can go on learning. Without arousing fear or self-pity, we can comfort our children as needed and then help them let go of pain and carry on. Usually a comforting kiss or hug, followed by a quick change of subject, is the best medicine.

> One family refers to small injuries as minor mishaps. Their crying youngster receives a quick check and a generous hug. The parent says, "Did you have a minor mishap?" The child finds this idea more fascinating than the hurt. "Yes!" he says, running off to play. "I had a minor mishap with the stairs!"

> *Because he cleaves to me in love,*
> *I will deliver him;*
> *I will protect him because he knows my name.*
> *When he calls to me, I will answer him;*
> *I will be with him in trouble,*
> *I will rescue him. . . .*
>
> —Psalm 91:14–15

Bad experiences as well as positive ones are also teachers. Both can be freeing. *While positive experiences can deepen our awareness of the fundamental order of being, negative ones show us how we are misaligned with the fundamental order of being.* Therefore, while we protect our children from harm, it is best not to be too quick to come between them and a negative experience from which they can safely learn something on their own. The freeing parent asks: What is she trying to see? What is she ready to see? What will help her see it? What will this experience show her? Is there any serious danger? Allowing children to fumble through some things is freeing. (See also pages 188–190.)

The Boy and the Sponge

After ninety-three patient mop-up operations she found herself screaming, "Watch out! Why don't you look what you're doing?" Then she hissed, "I said don't *cry* about it!" so venomously that the crying grew louder. Nervous spills were becoming more frequent, and she was having self-hate headaches from suppressed fury and rampant guilt.

One day she visited a Montessori classroom and encountered for the first time the idea of the child-wielded sponge. Each child was carefully shown how to dampen and squeeze one out, how to sponge up a spill with light circular motions, squeezing out the sponge and wiping again. A chore? No, a freedom. Later she tried it herself.

"He had just spilled his paints for the fourth time in half an hour. I knew better than to get mad, but I felt angry and he was looking worried because he knew I was unhappy. I considered putting the paints away just to avoid another accident. Then I remembered about the sponge. I gave him one and said, 'How would you like to clean it up yourself this time?' He looked as if I had just given him a gift. He was so relieved. 'Oh, Mommy, I love you,' he said. I didn't know whether to be sad or happy—it takes so little, but most of the time you just don't see it. Now whenever he is doing something in which spilling is a possibility I make sure he has a sponge nearby. He still needs my help, but he is learning."

Freedom and Competition: The Parent as Sidetracker

The inclination to use our children to fulfill our own competitive ambitions can sidetrack them. Competition is so much the American way that we do not recognize many accompanying problems. Competition is not to be feared. But with freedom as the central concern it is possible for children to compete without being overly competitive and not to compete without feeling out of it. Competition can sidetrack children because it changes the subject of an activity from freedom and discovery to the false issue of selves against each other.

At first children run and jump for the joy of freedom. When competition and comparison are introduced the subject gets changed. The pleasure-seeking motive changes the subject to how we feel. The competitive motive changes the subject to how powerful we are compared to others. Winning/losing, succeeding/failing rather than freedom and joy may become the central focus and experience. Physical activity, sports, and recreation are associated in many people's minds with both freedom and competition. We equate being athletic with being competitive, and miss other possibilities.

In Holland more than in America I've seen boys and girls spontaneously sing and dance together—a lovely sight. Because Holland is so small, most children know dozens of the same noncompetitive singing and dancing games. They also just frolic. This happens in the United States, too. But there is an extraordinary emphasis on competition—on winning, losing, succeeding, *and failing*. Some parents pit their children against each other like fighting cocks. Addiction to competition is so great that when grade-school children, particularly boys, face free time, many of the most sports-minded find it difficult simply to play. If they can't compete with someone, they either become bored or begin to pick fights.

> On a school camping trip most of the children had a ball exploring rocks, climbing trees. But two highly competitive children were restless and bored until they found each other. While the rest hunted for frogs by the pond, these two played catch—back and forth, back and forth. They were not free to find the new fun, to make the discoveries that lay in wait in this new situation.

Whatever happened to tree climbing, fort building, exploring? Of course many children still do these things. But as parents it is well to be aware of the American tendency to equate energetic activity with contest. Our children's worth does not depend on their ability to trounce each other. And surely we can find ways of frolicking and adventuring in some joyful, free way that has nothing to do with adversary relationship. (See *The Cooperative Sports and Games Book,* page 155.)

Additional Reflection: A ten-year-old who loved baseball shied away from joining the local recreational league. His parents encouraged him to try it once. At the first practice another child said he was no good. Later he announced that he was quitting the team, and went to his room. Recognizing himself and his own insecurity in the boy, the father left him alone for a while. Later, he knocked on the door. "May I come in?" he asked, respecting the family rule not to enter without permission. "No," the boy said. "Son," said the father, "I know you are hurting, and this is very important. We need to talk about this. So I am coming in." When his son said nothing, he entered and sat with him on the bed. After a while he put a hand on his son's back and spoke of how people who feel bad about themselves sometimes put others down to make themselves feel better. He told of how much fun he had missed himself, of how many things he had given up for fear of criticism and of not being good enough. "You don't have to be on the team if you really don't want to," he said, "but I think you do. You love baseball and you're already pretty good at it. So you need to decide whether you want to let this one boy rob you of the freedom to do something you love, or whether you can understand that he was all mixed up when he said such a dumb thing, and not let that stop you."

Important points:(1) the father understood what was up with his son because he was belatedly working on the same problem himself; (2) thus he could both discern the urgency of the situation and focus on the real issue of freedom rather than false issues of acceptance, winning, and manliness; (3) he was able to speak as one having authority without talking down to his son; and (4) to leave the choice up to his son. The greatest help he gave his son was through the example he set by working on himself. As the boy was initially hindered by his father's unspoken fears, he was freed by witnessing his dad's increasing freedom to participate in life without fear of failing or being hurt.

The most freeing contributions we can make to our children are mental and spiritual ones. By constantly calling to mind the child's ideal self, his essential perfection, we preserve his freedom to grow. True freedom is not freedom from anything, but there is much bondage to be avoided along the way. While there is a need for protection and comfort, there must be freedom from fear. At the same time that there is a need for guidance and teaching, there must be freedom from domination. At the same time that there is a need for reproof and correction, there must be freedom from guilt and blame.

At the age of fifty, one man was still trying to prove himself to his parents by being what they wanted him to be. He constantly criticized himself as they had criticized him for never measuring up to what they expected. But he never knew what he wanted, because he didn't know who he really was. Trying to help him find his true self, I asked if he could remember any passions or interests he had as a boy. His first memory was that he had to play little league baseball, and that he hated it. He couldn't recall anything that he had really wanted to do. I said, "Suppose you could say to your little boy self, 'Surprise! You don't have to play little league anymore, because I know you don't like it.' What would you want to do after school instead?" He answered without hesitation. "I'd go fishing with Mr. James. He had no children and used to take me fishing. I loved that. I'd go fishing with Mr. James." I asked what they talked about when they went fishing. "Fishing," he said. Mr. James just liked being with him, and with Mr. James he was free to be and to like himself. No judgments. Just fishing and being together. It was a good place to start.

Some like baseball, some like fishing, and some like both. The important thing for parents is to keep sight of the fact that freedom *is* an issue, and not only the freedom to do, but the freedom to discover and be oneself. The child who is allowed to play and learn for the fun of it is free to come true. Parents who pay attention to their children's freedom also learn to be freer themselves.

Pennant
Come up here, bard, bard;
Come up here, soul, soul;
Come up here, dear little child
To fly in the clouds and winds with me, and play with the
*   measureless light.*

Child
Father, what is that in the sky beckoning to me with long finger?
And what does it say to me all the while?

Father
Nothing, my babe, you see the sky;
And nothing at all to you it says. But look you, my babe,

*Look at these dazzling things in the houses, and see you the
    money-shops opening;
And see you the vehicles preparing to crawl along the streets with goods;
These! ah, these! how valued and toil'd for, these!
How envied by all the earth. . . .*

Child
*O father, it is alive—it is full of people—it has children!
O now it seems to me it is talking to its children!
I hear it—it talks to me—O it is wonderful!
O it stretches—it spreads and runs so fast! O my father,
It is so broad, it covers the whole sky!*

Father
*Cease, cease, my foolish babe,
What you are saying is sorrowful to me—much it displeases me;
Behold with the rest, again I say—behold not banners and pennants
    aloft;
But the well-prepared pavements behold—and mark the solid
    wall'd houses. . . .*

Child
*O my father, I like not the houses;
They will never to me be anything—nor do I like money;
But to mount up there I would like, O father dear—that banner I like;
That pennant I would be, and must be. . . .*

—Walt Whitman, "Song of the Banner at Day-Break"

Additional Reflection—A Word About Adolescence

Today the threat of teenage substance abuse, suicide, and pregnancy is terrifying. Old repressive foundations of values and conduct
have crumbled, while new, better ones have yet to be established.
Parental relations can turn so raw and destructive as our freedom-
seeking teenagers in workboots trample the freedoms of others, worry
and anger us, and hurt themselves. I want to offer a few thoughts

about adolescence, the particular problems of today's kids, a guideline or two for preventing and responding to them. As misguided as teenagers' idea of freedom may be, they're right that freedom is the issue—the freedom to find out and become themselves.

Remember that your child is an individual, not a chess piece. She's the only person in the universe like her. The universe needs her to be her God-given self. She doesn't know what that is. Neither do you. Discovering and becoming herself is a lifelong process. Don't fall for the idea that this year, exam, or activity will make or break your child's future. Don't fall for the idea that she must prove she is as good as or better than someone else. Don't believe that if he doesn't make the team his life is over. Each child is incomparable.

In our society the pressure to compete and to prove oneself is persuasive and intimidating. The pressure reaches giant proportions in high school, when getting into the "right" college is touted as a life-or-death issue. The importance of being well-rounded, taking advance-placement courses and exams, and filling out impressive applications is heaped on our youngsters just when developmentally they need to feel their own way, find their own footing and stars to steer by. In jazz band, plays, art and shop classes, and clubs they are presented at last with opportunities to pursue more individual interests. At first they are eager to explore these options, but as the pressure mounts some youngsters are defeated or driven wild. To do it all *and* get into the best college means putting in a workday that is longer and harder than they may ever face again. I think the pressure is inhuman.

After band at 7 A.M., Student Council at noon, track at 4 P.M., and play rehearsal until 11 P.M., they still face daily homework and study for college boards. Some kids seem to thrive on it—at least for the time being. Others break under the pressure, give up, rebel, or run away. There's something wrong with the whole setup. It doesn't leave room for the hanging out and groping for themselves and each other that adolescents need.

It's more important for a child to find what's his than to become everything that others expect. It is more important to experiment than to triumph. Children need to feel we have confidence in them and in a life process wherein one thing leads to another. They need to feel respected and loved for whoever they are so far rather than only judged for what they aren't yet. They need to be trusted to learn from their mistakes, to feel hopeful that eventually things will come together even while everything seems to be falling apart. They need time to dream, feel, mope, grope, huddle, and muddle. Maybe they need to fall apart. They need to feel that problems are not shameful failures and faults, but turning points to new possibilities.

You'll find it easier to trust, support, and be responsive to your child's individual process if you remember that he's God's child and the only child of God like him, that the same God who dreamed him up can make that dream come true. "Underachievers" whose parents not only set minimum standards of behavior but also make room for their problems and messy process are often the first to find their own true vocation. Troubled children whose parents not only see to it that they do homework and chores, but also take time to listen to what's up when they don't, are more likely to accept help when they need it.

Be aware of the pressure your child is under. Don't add to it. The whole world will suggest to you that you need to put more pressure on your children. Don't believe it. On the way up, you can already begin to reduce the pressure by making way for your child's individuality. If you've fostered and nourished her own unique passions, no matter how tempted your teen may be to flee the pressure and experiment with awful behaviors, there will be a level below which she will not let herself sink. She'll lose interest in what's not fulfilling if she's already found something that is. On the way up you can already help her to make responsible choices by letting her know when she has a choice. Teach her that while sometimes we have to do what's expected even when we don't feel like it, there are times when we have to say, "No. Right now I can't. I just need to hole up." Teach her to keep custody of all aspects of herself, to respect that there is a time for this and a time for that.

Remember that high school is not the decisive turning point in your child's life, after which she will either go down the tubes or rise to great heights. Everything you read about college will conspire to make you believe you have to ride your children. If you do, they may have to buck you off. High school is not decisive. College is not decisive. I think it would be better not to go straight from high school to college. A lot less tuition would be wasted on beer kegs, and students who have kept house and worked on their own for a while have better firsthand reasons for furthering their education and more focused ideas of what they want to study. One teenager I knew had fun and was well-liked but just poked along academically. Her parents were puzzled, but trusted their headstrong daughter. She graduated from college with an adequate if undistinguished record, worked as a leader of a program for troubled teenagers, became the director of the whole program, and is now in the top of her graduate-school class.

A boy I once knew barely made it through high school. He joined the military, but was kicked out when he became a conscientious objector. He flunked out of college and became first a student and then a teacher of aikido. Now he is a peaceful man to whom many high-pressured businesspeople come to learn how to find peace. One executive asked how his well-educated parents had reacted to his wayward youth. "They thought I was crazy," he said. "But I always knew they loved me."

If problems occur, don't make them worse. You've done your foibled best to raise her, and even if she has problems, you may be the last one who can personally or directly help her. Adolescence is increasingly a time of preparing to leave home. Teenagers have to begin to know themselves as viable in their own right. So they *can't* take much input from parents. Even as we are dismayed to realize that we have somehow passed onto them our own unfinished business, we also have to recognize that for the most part it is their business now. As we had to deal with the world in which we found ourselves, now they have to deal with theirs. Their world inundates them with freedoms and demands, true and false, that are greater than, or at least different from, what we faced. It tells them to "go for it" all, but gives them little to go on.

You can't spare them pressure and confusion in high school, but you can try to understand it. And don't base future predictions on the basis of present confusion. Often it's the most individualized and creative kids who struggle the most in high school. They may be rude, hostile, inconsiderate, and irresponsible—especially if you try to straighten them out. They may infuriate and scare you to death. They may even get into serious trouble. On top of extraordinary school pressure and ordinary adolescent uncertainty, any extra problem (small or big) may prove to be too much. Even the child who has consistently managed to "do it all" may begin to show how impossible life feels by becoming impossible to deal with or talk to or live with.

No matter what happens, the most important thing is to keep the lines of communication open. Even if they don't want to use them now, someday they will. "Tough love" has its place, and maybe you realize that you've been too lenient. Maybe you do need to be tougher. But tardy parental "tough love" can work the wrong way and it may be time to let the world, the school, even the courts be the tough ones. You can set limits and boundaries up to a point. You can insist that the house be quiet enough for you to get the sleep *you* need, but you may not be able to make your teenager get the sleep *he* needs. For a while you may agree to wake him up in time for class, but at some point you may have to turn that responsibility and whether or not he flunks his first-period course over to him.

You can only discipline your children as long as they let you—and they may only learn to discipline themselves when you stop. You need to set standards for what happens in your house, and you may be able to form a firm and supportive alliance with other parents. But you can only ground, threaten, or bribe your teen as long as it works. No matter how outrageous and infuriating your children are, do not take their teenage behavior so personally or let the atmosphere become so angry that communication becomes impossible.

I know of three teenagers who ran away at the beginning of their senior year. For five days their parents had no idea where they were. Later I met with one of them. I asked why they had run away and why they had come home. She said when they looked at all the pressure they were facing they had felt hopeless and overwhelmed. They decided to run away and start a new life. "When we left we felt so incredibly happy, relieved, and free! But when we saw what jobs were available, we realized that life without an education would be the pits. So we decided to come home and finish high school." How was it when they got home? "Well," she said, "I was so lucky. When I walked in my mother threw her arms around me. She was so glad to see me. My friends are still being punished. Their parents won't even speak to them. I feel so sorry for them. My mom and I have problems. I have problems. And I know I really scared her. But the first thing she did was hug me. She was so glad to see me that she cried. It was the best gift she ever gave me. I know she really loves me." It was touch and go, but she did graduate. She hasn't found her way yet, but she has a job and is thinking about college.

Some problems have to come to a head before they can be addressed. Another teenager who was sent away to school also ran away. For days no one knew where he was. At last, he called home.

"Are you all right?" asked his dad.

"Yes. But I'm scared. There are police cars outside."

"Don't worry," said the father. "I'll call them off. Just tell me where you are."

"I don't want to tell you. I don't want to go back to that school."

"Okay. Just promise me one thing. I'll talk to the school, and you don't have to tell me where you are. Just promise that you'll call me every day."

For the next few nights the phone rang and a brief exchange took place.

"It's me, Dad. I just called to say I'm okay."

"Thank you, Son. Anything else you want to say?"

"No."

"Then I'll hear from you tomorrow?"

"Yes."

At the end of the week the boy came home. After that it was possible to begin to address what was troubling him. This boy was lucky, too. His father knew that the most important thing was to stay in touch. As this story illustrates, the answer is not to probe or pump our children, but just to keep loving lines of communication open. You may not be the one your child can confide in, but you may be the one who can help him find help when he needs it. Be honored, grateful, and welcoming even if your children only turn to you as a last resort. At some point you may be their only resort.

I trust this piece won't be misconstrued as recommending excessive permissiveness. I could say more about structure and the setting of limits and boundaries but I believe parents who choose to read this book are more inclined to over- than to underparent. Also, while the tendency of society to throw up its hands and let teenagers run wild is well addressed in other books, it seems to me that the opposite problem of putting too much pressure on teenagers, and on parents to add to this pressure, is somewhat overlooked. I've tried to offer some perspective and practical suggestions, but in the end, the only truly practical way is the spiritual way.

Our primary task is to work on ourselves. Only if we ceaselessly seek our own spiritual footing can we discern when to step in and when to stand back in relation to our developing youngster. Only by maintaining our own spiritual balance can we know when and how to lend what hand to our children. Only by finding our own way can we help them find their way. Only by discovering our own spiritual nature can we hope to keep sight of and help our children be true to theirs. Only by turning our selves and theirs over to God can we gracefully and responsibly release them to life.

Animals and the Freedom to Be Loving

When babies see an animal for the first time they exhibit total delight, recognition, almost a look of *hey, I know you!* Children sense their kinship with whatever is alert and alive. So they're very interested in what animals can do, how they live, how they treat each other. The child's first concern with animals is really a matter of self-discovery. Can a deer run so fast? Is that a possibility for me? Can a bird fly? Is this freedom possible for me? Can a beaver build such a dam? Then such a dam and a pond, perhaps even better things, can be built.

The possibility of freedom is unquestioned until contrary evidence intrudes. Conflict, tyranny, the struggle for mastery between human and beast, between beast and beast, come as a shock. It may be a frightening encounter with a big dog or the witnessing of a fight between two animals. Or the brutal treatment of a pet by its "master." Or an animal's fear of the child's touch. Or the child's sensing of a parent's fear. Such problems always come as news to the child. *Can and do they fight and hurt each other? Would they hurt me? Must we fight for power over each other? Are we not free to be together?*

Whatever confronts the child, he approaches with personal existential interest. Eventually he'll wonder as humans have always wondered: Which is true? Freedom and love? Or fang and claw?

> *And, behold, I, even I, do bring a flood of waters*
> *upon the earth, to destroy all flesh, wherein is the*
> *breath of life, from under heaven; and every thing*
> *that is in the earth shall die.*
> —Genesis 6:17

The Noah's Ark story is often the child's first exposure to the Bible and the idea of God. It is usually presented as a fang-and-claw story. Because man and the animals were bad, God killed them. God seems to have been made in the image of man, just bigger and stronger.

But the story can be viewed other ways. In the beginning, we are told, God made man in his own image, to have dominion over the earth and earth's creatures. A state of harmony is described—not dominancy, not man dominating animals through power, but a state where freedom and love have dominion. It is only when man (Adam) sets himself apart to be "like God" that the knowledge of good *and* evil and the need of *one* to dominate *the other* occurs.

In the life of every human being this experience begins in childhood with the emergence of self–other awareness, conflict, and the threat of punishment. Here begins the idea of fang and claw, of enmity between child and parent, humans and animals, and, according to depth psychologists, between one's conscious and unconscious selves. But is Noah's flood a punishment from God? Or is it the inevitable byproduct of the belief that one's freedom is contingent on the impingement of others' freedom, whether inner or outer others, whether animal or human. And is the flooding the end of life? Or is it the beginning of awakening to a new level of harmony and freedom between seemingly incompatible, inner and outer selves?

> But Noah found grace in the eyes of God . . . and Noah walked with God . . . and Noah did according unto all that the Lord commanded him.
> —Genesis 6:8, 9 and 7:5

Noah is described as a man of God, who sees life from God's viewpoint, goes about life in God's way, and lives according to God's wisdom. He is protected from fang and claw and flood through being at one with the fundamental order of being. Noah is inspired to build the needed ark, and the animals who board it two by two live peaceably *as one* under his roof, his consciousness of love-intelligence.

As our children encounter animals, and people with animals, and people who behave like animals, love-intelligence can remain the central issue. Then, as they encounter parts of themselves that seem incompatible, which perhaps would even like to kill each other, they can learn to build an ark of self in which these different aspects of themselves can be in love and productive.

> *Child:* When I meet people I can usually tell right away whether or not I'm going to like them.
>
> *Parent:* Maybe it's better to say that sometimes you can see people the way God sees them right away, and sometimes you know you'll have to look harder.
>
> *Child:* Yeah. Right. When I first met Kate, I couldn't stand her—but now she's my best friend. I guess sometimes you have to see people the way God does even when they don't see it themselves.

While our children will meet loving people and animals, they will also meet people (even their parents) and animals responding cruelly to each other out of fear and power madness. We can't, nor should we, protect our children from such encounters. To hide or deny conflict in the world is also to teach our children to hide and deny the conflicts that rage within them. It is better to help them face conflict and to discover that there are ways of resolving it.

We can help them to see love-intelligence where it is revealed, to see the need for love-intelligence where it is hidden, to express love-intelligence where it is welcomed, and to perceive that it is love-intelligence, not fang and claw, that can ultimately have dominion over the earth and within oneself. A child can understand that when people do not know how to be loving they are flooded with troubles. A child can be inspired by the power of love in the life of Noah—when animals who "normally" fight and eat each other were free to live together, safe from the flood.

Additional Reflection—When Good Children Meet the Big "Bad" World

Much as we'd like to protect our children from evil, they will meet it and need to learn how to deal with it. Unpleasant situations you run into together can serve this purpose. Suppose you're riding the bus with your child and someone shoves you, is rude, or even steals your purse. The first issue is what to do in the immediate situation. The other, with which we are mainly concerned here, is how to help your child afterward.

In the immediate moment you first need to size up the situation. Is there immediate danger? Is it too shocking for your child to witness, or something to be lived through and learned from? Options to consider are protect and remove your child, stand by your child and see what happens next, or turn to someone else for help. Options to avoid include retaliating in like terms, becoming helplessly passive, panicky, or overwrought.

Afterward talk over the incident. First give time for feelings. Start with your child's and your own. *I felt kind of scared—angry—and so on. How did you feel? Did anything like that ever happen to you before? When?* Then you might want to explore what the other guy might have felt, where he was "coming from."

Explore what the options were for action or nonaction in the situation, how you decided to do what you did, how you might have responded differently, and whether you wish you had. Ask your child what he would have done in your place. Talk about what he, as a small child, should do in a similar situation if you weren't there. Be very clear about when he should get help or run away.

Explore the place of blame and forgiveness. Help him to learn how to take appropriate action and set firm boundaries while still having compassion. Remind him that in any situation there is a greater power than himself or the other guy to which he can quietly and quickly turn for guidance and protection. Take a minute with your child to prayerfully "be still and know that I am God."

The Spirit of the Lord shall rest upon him, the spirit of wisdom and understanding, the spirit of counsel and might, the spirit of knowledge and the fear of the Lord. And shall make him quick of understanding in the fear of the Lord. He shall not judge by what his eyes see, or decide by what his ears hear, but with righteousness shall he judge the poor, and decide with equity for the meek of the earth; and he shall smite the earth with the rod of his mouth, and with the breath of his lips shall he slay the wicked. Righteousness shall be the girdle of his waist, faithfulness the girdle of his loins.

The wolf shall dwell with the lamb, and the leopard shall lie down with the kid; and the calf and the young lion and the fatling together; and a little child shall lead them. And the cow and the bear shall feed; their young shall lie down together; and the lion shall eat straw like the ox. The sucking child shall play on the hole of the asp, and the weaned child shall put his hand on the adder's den. They shall not hurt nor destroy on all my holy mountain; for the earth shall be full of the knowledge of the Lord, as the waters cover the sea.

—Isaiah 11:2–9

Additional Reflection—Loving What Comes Naturally

From the very beginning, Alex, the little girl next door, loved our old dog Marley. As soon as she could talk, whenever she saw the dog she would run up to her crying, "Ooh! Hug'em! Hug'em!" When she was ten, Marley, who was older than Methuselah, began to die. Alex came to love her good-bye. When Marley died, after she and her younger sister and brother had put flowers on the grave, Alex asked if she might bring something more to put there. Of course, I said yes. One day, about a month later, she brought a ceramic plaque that she had made and glazed in pottery class. Below a well-drawn picture of Marley were inscribed the words "She Was Loved," followed by three small pictures: a heart, a bone, and a heart.

Alex's responses to Marley and her death were completely spontaneous, and I believe they were religious in nature. The plaque she prepared in secret (even from her parents) and her gift of it had all the qualities of religious sacrament and ritual. It is quite natural for children to first conceive of, meet, and respond to God in nature. I did as a child, and I still do. Trees, skies, mountains, storms, sunsets, all, as the psalmist says, "tell of thy glory" and inspire awe, wonder, love, and a sense of mystery in children.

Animals, whether wild or tame, bring God closer, and afford intimate, startling encounters with some greater source of intelligence, vitality, and love. An animal's death, or the preying of one creature on another, evokes not only dark questions about death and fang and claw but also a prayerful reverence for life, respect for individual difference and freedom, and the loving desire to protect and care for all forms of life. Familiarity with the amazing habits of different creatures suggests that there is something huge and wonderful, to which each of us belongs and on which we can learn to count. At least we can be in touch with it.

The child who spends time in nature receives many of these messages directly, through hands-on sensory contact, without verbal religious instruction. In this sense nature is the best religious classroom and sanctuary. So it is very unfortunate, even potentially disastrous, that so many children in our time are growing up with little or no free access to the wild. It is therefore very important to make every effort to provide our children with such opportunity.

Humility and the Freedom to Love

"We were overanxious and overbearing . . . we tried too hard . . . smothered her . . . corrected her constantly . . . expected much too much . . . didn't let her be a child." Parents feel guilty about hard times they have given their children—things said and done in the name of love, later recognized and regretted. The first child often has overzealous parents, but sometimes it's the second. ("The first was a breeze. We didn't know a thing. We didn't even really care. It was so easy.") Is it worse to try too hard? Passingly maybe. But the answer is not to give up or feel guilty. Some problems come with progress. They can't all be avoided or circumvented. They have to be lived through. Humility lessens guilt and hastens understanding.

When a child begins to learn to walk, she succeeds in fits and starts, sometimes falling flat out, sometimes momentarily teetering upright. If she knew more, she might think it impossible and unfair. Had she heard of the law of gravity, she would seriously doubt it. Were she told of its supportive value, she would be incredulous. Yet, we know it to be reliable and, at least for walking, necessary and beneficial. We hardly think of the laws that enable us to walk, but we are aware of, and count on, them just the same. Without them, walking would be impossible.

The laws of classical mechanics that make walking possible are extremely complicated to master intellectually. Yet, without having even heard of them, we walk. Though we don't understand them, we abide by them. How did we master them? We didn't. They mastered us, and whenever we walk, from moment to moment, we give them mastery over us. Partly through colliding with them, partly from seeing others walk, mainly through an innate desire for freedom, each toddler finds his oneness with them. Now the very laws that first seemed no laws after all support, guide, and free him to walk.

And he made from one every nation of men to live on all the face of the earth, having determined allotted periods and the boundaries of their habitation, that they should seek God, in the hope that they might feel after him and find him. Yet he is not far from each one of us, for
  "In him we live and move and have our being";
as even some of your poets have said,
  "For we are indeed his offspring."

—Acts 17:26–28

How do children achieve the freedom of walking when their first experiments are met with so little success? Jesus' statement again comes to mind. "Except ye become as a little child." I think the he was calling attention to children's outstanding ability to *trust* and to *learn*. Young children expect to learn, they don't think there is anything better to do, and they trust life to teach them. Until self-consciousness develops, *because* they know that they don't know, they can learn.

Adults can't simply return to the childhood state of un-self-consciousness. But we can go forward toward conscious realization of our oneness with the whole, with God. Children help us rediscover the receptivity in which self-consciousness is replaced by the desire to discover this oneness—in other words how to learn. They show us how to "lose our lives to find them." What we need to lose is pride; what we need to find is humility. One aspect of toddlers' remarkable teachability is lack of pride. They may cry when they fall, but they are not humiliated. They may be disappointed that *this* walking attempt didn't work, but they do not think they are failures or that walking is impossible. So, after a few tears, they try again.

Children do not fall until they become interested in walking and begin to learn to do so. So falling is more a sign of learning readiness than of failure. We are hardly aware that learning is an issue in love. Our visions of parenthood were filled with loving images of ourselves and our children, yet now we are more often hurt and angry. We had not thought of love as a freedom, yet we don't seem to be free to love. Depending on who or what we blame, we feel angry or guilty that we've been failed or are failures. Toddling children show us that our troubles with love are signs of learning readiness. If we have more difficulty with love now, it is because we are readier than ever to learn to be loving.

They also show us that failures are lessons through which guidance comes. It is partly from tumbles that children learn to center and align themselves with the forces that make walking possible. Likewise our failures to love can guide and correct us—if we approach them as children, not with blame or shame, but with hearts and minds open to learning how, specifically, we are not centered in, or aligned with, love.

Sometimes a child becomes afraid of falling or angry with his momentary failure to walk. Briefly, he may quit trying. But soon his natural need to walk becomes more urgent than the fear or anger. It will become urgent; he must learn to walk. In our quest for love, sometimes we, too, frightened and angry, want to quit—to quit on each other, to quit trying to love, to quit on love. But as the hymn "Oh Love That Wilt Not Let Me Go" says, we can't quit on love because love won't quit on us; it drives us even when we want to give up. Toddlers show us the necessity and value of picking ourselves up and sticking with the task of learning to love. They also demonstrate there is something beyond us and each other that can be trusted to bring this about.

Once children have learned to walk at home, they can walk anywhere. By struggling and suffering a bit, they discover what walking is, what makes it possible. Thereafter they can walk freely everywhere. So they demonstrate that we may learn what love is, that it is, that we are in it, of it, and may learn to walk *in,* and express love everywhere. They move us to recognize that the struggle is worth it. Our children and families are worth it; we are worth it; the freedom to love is worth it.

> Problems are lessons designed for our edification. . . . The understanding of what really is abolishes all that seems to be.

> —Thomas Hora, *Dialogues in Metapsychiatry*

In contrast to Jesus' recommendation, "And ye shall know the truth and the truth shall make you free," it is written in Zen literature, "Search not for the truth; only cease to cherish opinions." These statements do not really contradict each other. Both suggest that the most basic freedom is the freedom to learn, to understand. Jesus' statement calls us specifically to that aspect of receptivity that may be called gratitude (appreciation of the truth as valuable) or prayer. The Zen calls us to humility or fasting. If we value the truth and set our hearts on it as Jesus says, and if we are willing to give up our personal minds as the Zen says, then the truth that is the one mind becomes ours, is what we are. Then, already, we are free.

Be a lamp to your self,
be like an island.
Struggle hard, be wise.
Cleansed of weakness, you will find freedom
from birth and old age.

—Buddha, in *The Dhammapada,* trans. by P. Lal

In clearness comes freedom from all pains; in those whose minds are free of
all pains, understanding is utterly steadfast.

—*The Bhagavad-Gita*

Practical Information for New Parents

This section includes childproofing the home, walks, trip tips, gym equipment, animals and pets—all loosely related to the issue of freedom.

Childproofing the Home

Good childproofing frees children to learn, parents from worrying and nagging, and homes from destruction and disarray. But there's no need to go overboard and revise the entire home to suit the unsteady toddler, no need to change your whole life for temporary stages. While it's sensible to make some adjustments and take a few precautions, there's no substitute for adult vigilance. At nine months your daughter may bruise her head on the coffee table when trying to walk; at one and a half she can open the door and dash out! Try to take reasonable precautions without going to fearful extremes.

Freedom is a good guide for discerning what safety measures to take. The more hazards that can be removed, the more freedom (from injury and scolding) can be enjoyed. Babyproofing is a breeze: you simply don't put the baby down where she might fall, where anyone might step on her, or where anything might fall on her. Toddlerproofing is another story. You need to protect both toddler and home while maintaining the freedom of both—of the home to be pleasant for everyone, of the child to freely learn and grow.

Most safety measures for toddlers and older children are obvious. For starters: put breakable and dangerous things out of reach. Close off places where children might fall. Install *safety latches* on cupboards and drawers containing dangerous or breakable things, but have some safe cupboards and drawers for them to explore. The pulling-out-and-dumping-all-over stage doesn't last long, and evidently something is learned from it. *Socket caps* are a must for protecting small children from poking things into open electric sockets.

Practicing Freedom

After hours of struggling, a restless, wakeful baby falls instantly asleep when put in the carriage and wheeled out the door. Is it the hum of outdoor sounds, the rocking of the carriage, or the change of scene that lulls the baby to sleep? Maybe. But I also think there is an important change in the parent. There is the difference between the parent who is trying to put the child to bed and the one who is taking a walk. The first says, "He won't even let me leave the room!" But who's not letting whom? The parent who is putting the child to bed is paying attention to and experiencing the child. The parent who is going on a walk is looking where she is going and experiencing the view. If the child falls asleep in the carriage, is the child letting the parent take a walk or is it that in taking a walk the parent lets go of the child? Over and over new parents report: *So I finally gave up and decided to take him for a walk. By the time I put on my coat and got the carriage out, he was already fast asleep!*

Long before children experience any conscious need for freedom *from* the parent, new parents experience a need for freedom from the baby and the demands of parenthood. Captivated by the baby's physical dependency we may feel trapped and imprisoned. Thus parenthood makes us acutely conscious of our innate yearning for freedom. Life is no good alone; but it is no good only together either. We cannot *get* along together unless we *go* along together. Take a walk. Quit running in circles. Shove off. Get the show on the road. Let the road take charge.

Trust in the Lord with all thine heart and lean not unto thine own understanding; in all thy ways acknowledge him, and he will direct thy paths.

—Proverbs 3:5–6

A man's mind plans his way, but the Lord directs his steps.

—Proverbs 16:9

Without a rightful perception of freedom on the part of the parent, the child's growing need for freedom (even so small a thing as the freedom to sleep) is frustrated.

> The first time we took our baby out for a walk I thought she would be annihilated—by the sound of a jackhammer, the fumes from passing cars. Greasy dirt fell from the air onto her beautiful, clean cheek. I tried to wipe it away, but it turned into a black smear. I wanted to send her back somewhere where she would be safe. I pushed the carriage across the street. Faces streamed by—mothers, storekeepers, drivers, teenagers, policemen, thousands and thousands of city dwellers who had actually survived babyhood.

Different parents have different illusions, but walks are good for most of them.

Baby Carriers

A baby carrier is a great way for parents and babies to be together without revolving around each other. Sometimes a baby and a parent seem to be holding each other captive. The child cries the minute he is put down, yet the parent suspects that his very efforts to put him down are precisely what are keeping him up. A carrier of some sort can help break this vicious circle, releasing parents to carry on with their work while allowing the baby to be unfussed with but close. Many babies fall asleep as soon as they are put in a carrier.

Back or front infant carrier. In Taiwan, this type of carrier is used everywhere all the time, worn on the back with the straps crossed in front, then divided again and tied behind the back. Used until the child is two or three years old, it replaces the carriage, frame-type back carrier, stroller, and even the babysitter. It folds to a purse-size nothing and is considered almost as indispensable as diapers.

In the United States we insist on wearing such carriers in the front. Though this is less comfortable physically for the parent, it makes it possible to see how the baby is doing. Wherever you wear it, an infant carrier can be a handy problem solver if you happen to live in a walk-up apartment, or if you're trying to houseclean when the baby is fretful, or for shopping, hiking, and cycling.

Back carrier with frame. For carrying on without a lot of carrying on, there is nothing like a back carrier with a light metal frame. Children in back carriers smile, laugh, and enjoy the view, or fall asleep without a peep. At home, when the baby is tired but not ready to sleep, you *can* quickly get the dishes, ironing, vacuuming, or leaf raking done with him on your back. He'll probably be asleep by the time you are finished and can be snuggled into bed without much fuss. When the guests are hungry and dinner is ready, you can wear him to the table to enjoy, be enjoyed, and probably conk out in no time flat. Like any backpacking, this takes getting used to. A five-month-old is ready for backpacking; a slightly younger baby could be okay if you sandwich in a pillow for extra support. Most find a twenty-five-pound baby the limit.

One mother's favorite early parenthood memory is of two under one umbrella, three hands on the shaft. She can't say which version is better—being one of the two under the one umbrella, or looking from under a separate umbrella at father and son—saturated, rainy-day colors, sunny-day laughter. The three of them so private and safe somehow, traveling dry and warm and cozy along the wet city sidewalks, the rain pat-patting. You can hear snow fall on an umbrella, too.

Walks

For children and parents, walking can be a wonderful exercise in freedom—a way of setting each other free, and finding freedom together. But, especially if you like walking yourself or need to get somewhere on time, it may take some new understanding before walking with your lagging, "carry me" toddler seems anything like freedom. For many parents and very young children walks are pure hassle. The children keep stopping, hunkering down to study things, while the parents are dying to keep moving. Some parents drag their children; others manipulate, baiting them with promises of what they might see around the next corner or what they will eat when they get home. Thus freedom to go walking together can feel a lot like a restriction.

Around two and a half or three years old the child, too, will probably discover that a walk is a way of going somewhere. Quite spontaneously, he will take your hand and walk along, viewing things as he passes them instead of stopping to study each cellar door, each fuel intake, and every balustrade. But first he simply must examine these things. Meanwhile, it's best to consider which kind of walk it's going to be before you set forth. If it's a walk-walk for *him*, plan to stand around a lot. His walk may be short in distance but long in time. It may take an hour and a half to go around the block at his pace. So if you want the walk to be short in time, don't plan to go far. And when you really need to get somewhere, take a stroller or carrier. Both kinds of walks are good and can be freeing.

Trip Tips

1. *Leave shortly before a nap time* or even when the nap is slightly overdue.

2. Will it be a long trip? Then *see if there is someplace to stop off that will be of interest to the child.* With a toddler, a picnic at a playground may be better than a greasy lunch and a wrestling match in a restaurant. A few minutes of sandbox, swings, and snack will refresh and settle much better than his first french fries in a restaurant where he doesn't know how to behave.

3. *Take some things along* to entertain the child and expedite maintenance.

- A roll of paper towels—standard equipment for trips.
- A wet washcloth in a plastic bag and a clean hand towel. Or some packaged wash-ups.
- A few Colorforms (flexible, vinyl shapes that adhere to smooth surfaces) to work with on the car window.
- Any toy that is of current special interest.
- A magic drawing board—those gray ones with acetate sheets on top. Draw with a wooden stick, and then erase by lifting the acetate.
- A story anthology from which to read or tell stories.
- A book of activities for children on trips.
- Diapers. (Yeah, well, sometimes they get forgotten.)
- Disposable (or not) spoons, cups, and plates. If you have these

along, you can pick up lunch in a supermarket instead of making a picnic or hunting for a suitable restaurant.

- Snacks and juice.
- Bib. Even for older toddlers a bib is handy for car-seat meals. A really big one keeps built-in children's safety belts from becoming too sticky to lock and release.
- Magnetic versions of games. Pieces don't slide off and get lost in the car.

Set Free

From gym sets to pets, from climbing like monkeys and flying like birds to capturing and releasing wild creatures, our children seek to find and understand freedom. The matter of when to provide what equipment or experience is best settled the usual way—by watching the child.

At first a few things to reach for will satisfy any gymnastic needs not met by a baby's incessant kicking, waving, and playing with her parents. Next comes the desire to get up and get going, very soon on her own. Then comes running, jumping, swinging, climbing, and the sky is the limit.

Jumper. A hanging sling-seat harness in which prewalking children can bounce and jump. Some find this too much trouble. Before our first son was born we were against this on the general principle that it was a contraption and he could learn to walk without it. But, at about four months—when his desire to be vertical became a passion—we tried it, and it gave him many squeal-happy hours. He could see better and turn around on his own. He jumped and jumped for joy until about seven months when he was stricken with the desire to go forward as well as up and down.

The first few tries last less long than it takes to saddle up. The child just hangs there, drooling on his toes, until he discovers the possibilities of turning and jumping. Mount it in the kitchen doorway while you fix supper. Play music; sing. And once in a while jump along with him.

Walkers are becoming obsolete, because of the many serious accidents that happen to children in them. Anyway there is no substitute

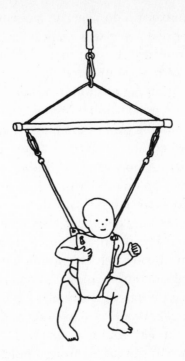

for walking around holding Mom or Dad's hand. I visited at the airport with a friend whose daughter had just learned to walk. At one corner of the waiting room was an escalator, toward which she repeatedly plunged. He'd carry her to the point farthest from the escalator, put her down, stroll along behind her as she plummeted back toward the escalator. We had a much better visit hiking back and forth with her than if we had tried to keep her still on a bench.

Indoor swing. Indoor gym equipment for preschoolers is often overlooked. Especially for city children who can't go outdoors unescorted, a good piece of gym equipment may replace years full of toys and, to some extent, make up for the lack of a backyard. *Doorway swings* are ideal. Unlike park swings, which must be used by children of all ages and heights, the indoor swing can be hung low enough for even a one-and-a-half-year-old to experiment independently. The most popular position for preschoolers is the flying position—hanging by their tummies, watching how the floor goes by. If the door frame is wooden the swing can hang from heavy eye-hooks. If the frame is metal a doorway gym bar will do. You can make one with a board and rope or buy a rubber belt swing seat, trapeze bar, or combination.

Mattresses. Old ones are cheaper than real tumbling mats and just as much fun. Cover with a rug or fitted sheet.

Indoor climbing gyms. Small indoor toddler gym/slide combinations are outgrown too quickly to be of much value. More useful and for longer is a real climbing gym of some sort. Again, this is extra nice for children with limited outdoor access. Gym/playhouse/slide combinations are available. A horizontal or folding ladder climber takes up less space and can also be used with a slide or as a playhouse scaffolding. See *Consumer Reports* regarding safety.

Impromptu and homemade equipment. Cartons and crates can do the trick. Especially if you live in an apartment, you need solutions for energetic indoor fun. If you are handy with a hammer and saw, there are books for building and improvising equipment. We made a sliding board that hooked over a stair of the bunk bed. It was put to an astonishing variety of uses. There are as many ways as days. But the time for them is now, and again now. And now again.

Outdoor gym sets. You can drive through miles and miles of suburbia and see hundreds of used-to-be-bright metal gym sets, and *nary a child* on one of them. You are more likely to spot the children under bushes, behind garages, in culverts and empty lots, and up in trees. Unless you can afford a high-quality wooden jungle gym, you're better off taking your child to a school or park plaground.

Swing. Anyway, since flying is the thing, how much nicer to hang the swing from a tree. The better the view the better the swing. The longer the rope the farther it swings. All you need is the right tree, a board or old tire, a bike tube to protect the branch, and a rope. I have very fond memories of sitting on the tire swing behind our house after dinner—not swinging, just scuffing, thinking, and watching the sun go down. If there isn't a good branch available, you can find other types of swing mounts (even one that attaches to a tree trunk) in some play equipment catalogs. If you don't have a yard, you can still have a tree swing at picnics. Just sling a rope over a branch. Make a loop low enough for your child to step on and knot it just above your head. A two-year-old can learn to stand in this loop on one foot. Tell him to reach as high as he can before stepping up. If there's enough extra rope dangling from the knot, you can pull the end of the line to give a nice ride. Remind children not to step off unless the swing is still. Let *them* tell *you* when they want to go higher.

> How do you like to go up in a swing
>   Up in the air so blue?
> Oh, I do think it the pleasantest thing
>   Ever a child can do!
> Up in the air and over the wall
>   Till I can see so wide,
> Rivers and trees and cattle and all
>   Over the countryside—
> Till I look down on the garden green,
>   Down on the roof so brown—
> Up in the air I go flying again,
>   Up in the air and down!

—Robert Louis Stevenson, "The Swing"

Animals and Pets

> Oh, a hunting we will go
> And a hunting we will go
> We'll catch a fox
> And put him in a box
> And then we'll let him go.

—Folk song

Beastly books. When the toad is in the hand or the pollywog is in the jar, it is surprising how attentive young children are. There are too many excellent animal books to presume to make a best selection, but do support each creaturely interest with a trip to the library or bookstore. Especially helpful when keeping creatures are three books by Caroline O'Hagan: *It's Easy to Have a Worm (a Snail, a Caterpillar) Visit You* (Lothrop).

Pets. Children of all ages benefit from having and caring for a creature of some sort. Preschoolers are too young to do so. Neither is it feasible for any household to maintain all the wild catchables and patables that capture the child's interest. Nor, alas, can many creatures long endure the tender, loving ignorance inflicted upon them. But whether or not you have a permanent family pet, brief visitations—of school pets on weekends, pets of vacationing neighbors, and wild foundlings—are a happy way to satisfy a child's interest and develop a love-intelligent reverence for life and freedom.

The study of animals and their habits and habitats provides startling revelations of the fact of intelligence at large. It is wonderful to observe and share with our children how meticulously it is given to each animal to know what marvelously to do. No need to belittle this intelligence by calling it instinct; nor to attribute it to the genius of the creatures themselves. The point is this: *Love-intelligence is always available, providing the needed idea and the needed skill in the needed moment.* Share the marvel of this with your child and let its significance sink in as a sense of security and confidence.

In watching a captive creature, the true object of attention is not the animal itself but the intelligence reflected in it. Try to see what each creature needs while in our care: a suitable environment, food, and, ultimately, to be set free in the care of the governing intelligence at large. A key emphasis needs to be on letting be. Letting be free. Letting be so. And, sometimes, letting die. Beautifully, the young child (still unpossessive of property or power) is spontaneously almost more overjoyed with setting free than with capturing. To let it come—to let it go—to let it be. Each temporary guest presents an opportunity to explore the freedom that comes with setting free. Catch a flying star. Put it in a jar. Watch it glow. Let it go!

> *A little light is going by,*
> *Is going up to see the sky,*
> *A little light with wings.*
>
> *I never could have thought of it,*
> *To have a little bug all lit*
> *And made to go on wings.*

> —Elizabeth Madox Roberts, "Firefly"

A well-balanced *fish tank* is something even a baby can appreciate. Vinyl ones are available for hanging over cribs, but they seem cruel and the fish do not survive there for long. A five- or ten-gallon tank

Captivating Captives

Creature	In what?	How long?
Caterpillar	In a jar with holes in the top, and inside a twig and fresh greenery of the proper sort (some caterpillars are very particular), sprinkled with water each day until the cocoon is built. Then keep some wet sand in the bottom of the jar for moisture.	Until there is a butterfly or moth—if possible release before it is ready to fly.
Frog or fish or insect or any waterborn insects' eggs	Gather with a jar full of the water in which you find them. From time to time scoop out a cupful of water and put in a cupful of new water from wherever you found them.	Until they hatch—then release or else do a lot of research on what is needed by a growing, captive whatever-you-have.
Fishlings	Catch in a bath towel and keep in a jar full of their own lake, brook, or seawater. Baby fish are wonderfully transparent: little more than eyes with locomotive ability.	Observe for an hour, then release where you found them.
Fireflies	In a jar with a little greenery to perch on inside, and holes in the top.	An hour of darkness.
Ants (about two dozen from the same colony), the bigger the better	In a thin plastic box (with tiny holes made with a pin heated red hot on the stove), or a jar with an upside-down jar inside (to make a narrow space so you can see tunnels). Fill with sand. Cover side with dark paper when you aren't looking so the ants won't be sneaky. Put in a drop or two of honey or syrup once or twice a week. If ants get through the holes (the advantage of big ones), stand your ant house in a little bit of water; they'll go back through the holes.	If you don't catch a queen, release in a week and a half.
Any insect or animal you run into	In a jar with holes in the top or in a creature cage.	Just for a close look—see, she can fly and needs more space.
A baby bird that has fallen out of its nest	Nothing; just lift it gently off the ground and place it in a nearby tree out of cat range.	Only as long as it takes to put it in a tree. Now be very still and watch its parents come to it.

outfitted with a light, bubbler, and filter system seems a good investment. It is especially nice if you can have a lighted tank in the child's
bedroom where she can watch the fish at bedtime, free of other dis-
tractions. See how they swim perpetually, randomly, not in squares or
in circles or straight back and forth within the confines of the tank,
free yet never bumping into each other.

In God we live and move and have our being.

—Acts 17:28

5
Unity

One in all,
All in One—
If only this is realized,
No more worry about your not being perfect.

> —*Buddhist Scriptures*, selected and
> translated by Edward Conze

Hear, O Israel: The Lord our God is one Lord.

> —Deuteronomy 6:4

For many people the least obvious aspect of reality is its underlying unity. We experience life as chaotic, unreliable, fragmentary, precarious, chancy, even meaningless. What order we perceive seems unreliable. Yet as living, Seeing Beings, it is unity we yearn for and are driven to seek.

We wish to find a basis for being at one with ourselves and each other, a viewpoint from which things make sense, and out of which we can live with confidence and trust. Not finding it, Me, Inc. tries to take all the apparent pieces of life and *make* them one. Experiencing ourselves as separate—un- or dis-united from the whole—we try to bring about unity ourselves. In families, our efforts to organize our lives and to bring about family unity are often as disunifying as a child's first handling of a puzzle.

There are two elements in our mental picture of family unity. On the loving side we look for family unity as mutual support, comfort, enjoyment, friendliness, warmth, and coziness. On the intelligent side we look for reasonable consensus, cooperation, and agreement. Yet we experience bewildering difficulty. Often the harder we try to effect unity, the more disunity—disharmony, dissent, disagreeableness, disaffection, dissatisfaction, and distance—occurs among us. Everybody wants to be the puzzle maker. Nobody wants to be someone else's puzzle piece.

Are we to conclude that family unity is unattainable? that we cannot live unique lives as individuals and still be at one with each other? Frustration and disillusionment suggest such conclusions. But inwardly we find them unacceptable. Even if we part company (storm out of the house, separate, divorce) we cannot abandon our quest for unity.

We need not abandon our hopes of having cooperative, respectful, and supportive relationships. But for such expressions of unity to take shape in our lives, we have to transcend the fundamentally disunifying idea that each of us is a separate self enclosed in a separate body: Me, Inc. The "family picture" conforms to whatever underlying concept we entertain.

For a unified, love-intelligent family picture we must seek our oneness with the underlying love-intelligent source and force of our being. In it alone are all its expressions—self, other, and their proper relation to each other—united. By it alone can the harmony we recognize as love be brought about. While we are born with the yearning and a sense of the necessity and possibility of unity, its discovery is a lifelong task. One of my favorite and most comforting Bible passages is Paul's statement that "We are placed on this earth that we might feel after and haply find God for in God we live and move and have our being."

Oneness with God or fundamental intelligence or the whole is not something we can just bring about once and for all. Realization of oneness is gradual and depends on our tracing everything and everyone and every aspect and phase of our life back to God—to that "in which we live and move and have our being," and which as Paul goes on to say, "is before all things and in whom all things consist." As long as we live, we are never done with this task of finding ever-deeper oneness with ever-deeper layers of reality. So it is wise to abandon perfectionistic expectations of ourselves and each other, and to settle down humbly to the task of "feeling after" God, happening by happening.

Even before much oneness is realized, once we have settled in for the long haul, the long grope, the unexpected seems easier to take, more meaningful and worthwhile. When our "reasonable expectations" make others' bristle, instead of shaking our heads, we cock them; instead of shouting, we listen; instead of accusing, we pray. In this way we are more likely to fit ourselves into the giant divine puzzle than to force each other into little, uncomfortable human ones.

Love and intelligence are no more separate from each other than we are from God. The outside of a glass gets its smooth curved beauty by conforming to the essential raison d'être (reason for *being*) of the inside as a vessel. The outside is defined by the inside. Likewise, love is the expression of the fundamental intelligent order of being. I believe there is an underlying universal intelligence, which tends toward love as its universal effect. Our yearning for love and intelligence is its impulse in us. So it is to that we need to turn for the wise inspiration that leads to loving expression. *Universal* and *unique* have the same root: *one*. Like the wave on the ocean, the *unique* individual is a place where love-intelligence takes specific perceivable shape, comes to a peak (where we can take a peek at it).

In the beginning was the Word, and the Word was with God, and the Word was God . . . and the Word became flesh and dwelt among us.
—John 1:1, 14

Jesus said: "I and my father are one."
—John 10:30

Through Jesus' conscious oneness with the primary and universal reality of love-intelligence, this primary reality gained full unique expression. Likewise, as parents who seek to be unifying factors in our families, our primary task and ongoing first priority must be to remain in constant, conscious touch with Beyond Personal love-intelligence.

Without awareness of the underlying One and our oneness with it, life is a muddle. Proceeding from the sense of separate selfhood, we try to impose love and intelligence on each other only to bring disunity into expression as friction, conflict, discomfort, and all that pains and saddens us. *On our own* we cannot do otherwise; our efforts to bring unity to our children cannot help being perverted with the selfish, exploitative counterfeits of love as hedonism and intelligence as power and control. But by seeking awareness of our individual oneness with the underlying One we invite love-intelligence to have its unifying effect on us, as individual love that is truly wise and individual intelligence that is truly loving.

Falling into Place

As the truly parently parent is the childlike parent,
as the truly nourishing parent is the nursing parent,
as the truly teaching parent is the learning parent,
as the truly freeing parent is the obedient parent,
so is the truly unifying parent the unified parent.

All things are done by love-intelligence, and apart from love-intelligence is not anything done that is really done.

One love-intelligent moment leads to another.

Some realization of, or at least devotion to, these ideas already helps us. It helps us as parents to recognize love-intelligence at work in our children and enables us to respond to them in ways that enhance their discovery of their oneness with it. So the one mind guides and governs the parent through the child, and the child through the parent, each of us as a unique Seeing Being in a unified and self-revealing universe of love-intelligence.

As long as the child is un-self-conscious he continues to be himself a place where the one mind is expressed as growing awareness of unity. In their puzzle solving our youngest children demonstrate how discovery of unity is possible in the midst of seeming chaos. If you present a child of less than a year with a knobbed wooden puzzle, he will lift out the pieces, his attention first attracted by the protruding knobs. That what appears to be one whole can become parts is a revelation to him. He is not concerned with putting the puzzle together again. Fascinated by the pieces, he ignores the puzzle tray. When the possibility of putting the pieces back into the puzzle occurs to him, he will try to push them in anywhere, oblivious that each has its own hole or that there is a relationship between the outer edge of each piece and the inner edge of its particular hole. Only gradually does he discover that he needs to align the pieces with the holes for the fitting together, the unifying, to occur.

With parenthood as with the child's puzzle—indeed with every aspect of our lives—there is the same discovery to be made: If you align the parts with the holes, the parts become whole and the whole becomes evident. What the child discovers materially about his puzzle we must discover spiritually about ourselves—that unity comes into our experience not by manipulating others but by aligning our thoughts and ourselves with the underlying whole to which we belong.

For adults, puzzles are often only a sort of intellectual activity, a fantasy confirmation of the sense of personal mental power. But the child's unconscious motivation is different. Not yet having learned to believe in disunity, he proceeds from an unconscious assumption that unity is. He is delighted with all demonstrations of unity, and they all have existential import for him. A Playskool advertisement nicely pointed this out: "Puzzles reinforce a conviction necessary to learning: that things make sense." The child's joy in his puzzles goes even further: He enjoys being part of (united with) the underlying sense of things. By fitting puzzle pieces into the whole, he also fits himself into the whole.

The Parent as a Unifying Factor

1. The Parent as a Rock

> *Everyone then who hears these words of mine and does them will be like a wise man who built his house upon the rock; and the rain fell, and the floods came, and the winds blew and beat upon that house, but it did not fall, because it had been founded on the rock.*
>
> —Matthew 7:24–25

The unifying parent is the unified parent. The more we are "at one with the Father," the divine parent the whole, the less likely we are to be at odds with each other or to set each other at odds with God. Being at one with the divine parent means being at one with love-intelligence. To find this oneness we need to bring every thought, word, action, the quality of our being, and our way of looking at everything into full and perfect alignment with what is love-intelligent.

We allow love-intelligence to take charge of us and we leave it in charge of everyone else. What is both loving and intelligent is true. Everything else is false. Seeing everything in terms of what is and isn't rather than what should or shouldn't be makes us evener, surer, firmer, more open and understanding. Our whole being demonstrates to the child that life can be counted on.

> *. . . look to the rock from which you were hewn, and to the quarry from which you were digged.*
>
> —Isaiah 51:1

> *So we being many are one body in Christ.*
>
> —Romans 12:15

> *Let this mind be in you which was also in Christ Jesus.*
>
> —Philippians 2:5

> *Jesus answered, "The first [commandment] is, 'Hear O Israel, the Lord our God, the Lord is One; and you shall love the Lord your God with all your heart and with all your soul, and with all your strength.' This is the first and great commandment."*
>
> —Matthew 22:37–38

2. The One-Seeing Parent as Beholder

And the second is like unto it; thou shalt love thy neighbor as thyself.

—Matthew 22:39

The more we are able to see each other as one with God or the love-intelligent whole, the more we are able to respond to each other love-intelligently. So it is that we behold each child as a point where the universal comes to a unique peak. We trust she is and respect her as an expression of love-intelligence in the process of becoming conscious. Whatever appears bad is regarded as false rather than as fault. So we treat it as having nothing to do with the essential child. Whatever is good is regarded as true and appreciated as an expression of God. Thus freer of parent-introduced self-consciousness, the child proceeds undistracted, a Seeing Being in the process of seeing.

One is one and all alone
and evermore shall be it so.

—from "Green Grow the Rushes,"
traditional folk song

3. The One-Knowing Parent as One Waymaker. Recognizing life as a journey toward conscious oneness with God, we constantly release and entrust the child to love-intelligence at large, thereby expressing our confidence that through lesson and revelation life will bring about the full reunion.

Wist ye not that I must be about my Father's business?

—Luke 2:49

How like an angel came I down!
How bright are all things here!
When first among his works I did appear
Oh, how their glory did me crown!
The world resembled his eternity,
In which my soul did walk;
And everything that I did see
Did with me talk. . . .

A native health and innocence
　　Within my bones did grow,
And while my God did all his glories show,
　　I felt a vigour in my sense
That all was spirit: I within did flow
　　With seas of life like wine;
I nothing in the world did know,
　　But 'twas divine. . . .

—Thomas Traherne,
"Poems of Felicity"

4. The One-Centered Parent as Custodian of the God-Centered Environment. Long before a child conceives of unity she can encounter and appreciate its value. Every aspect of the home, every task and activity, can be approached with the idea of making the fact of one love-intelligent force appreciable and expressible. Order, simplicity, efficiency, respect, peace, and privacy emerge as outstanding qualities of the God-centered home Whenever we sincerely ask what best expresses love-intelligence? what is love-intelligent? in the light of love-intelligence what's next? we will be guided by love-intelligence.

And ye shall hear a voice behind you saying, "This is the way; walk ye in it."

—Isaiah 30:21

5. The One-Pointing Parent as Teacher and Guide. The parent is a finger God points at God. We do not point to ourselves; we do not point at the child; we do not shake our finger in the child's face. Because he is of one mind with love-intelligence, he is taught the most important things by the one mind itself, through experience, inspiration, and by our example. When we must teach or explain or lay down rules, we remain focused on the one underlying and overriding love-intelligence and the child's ability to become aware of it. Thus we are able to establish certain love-intelligent standards within the home without becoming overly personal or domineering.

We are also able to discern what our children need to and can better discover through experiencing consequences. There is a time to pick up the child's room for her; there is a time to require her to do so; there is a time to do it together; there is a time to tell her how; there is a time to close the door and let her live with the mess until she tires of it.

> *Let your light so shine that men may see your good works and glorify your Father which is in heaven.*
>
> —Matthew 5:16

6. *The Parent as One Giving Hand.* The parent is one hand of God. Through this hand God gives the child many good gifts. Through the inspired, love-intelligent parent, God gives God's self. The parent who is aware of unity as a primary life issue is able to select and introduce toys, lessons, equipment in such a way that fosters the child's awareness of fundamental love-intelligence and her oneness with it.

Besides teaching necessary skills and providing pleasant experiences, the playthings and ideas at the end of this chapter are designed to help children encounter unity. In working with any of them the undistracted child also experiences the transition from apparent disunity to unity, from unreliability to reliability. She learns the impossibility of trying to force seemingly conflicting puzzle pieces together and instead to gently align them and to effortlessly allow them to fit into place. She learns that the water in which she sinks while struggling fearfully after all supports her when she gives up her struggle to go it alone and relies on her oneness with its buoyancy.

Children are not yet conscious of the significance of these experiences, so they do not yet become generalized as understanding. But these experiences foster positive expectancy and the development of adaptability and steadfastness. As children become more conscious, such experiences become evidence that unity and reliability are facts of life, that contrary experiences are transitory and instructive, that it is possible and worthwhile to make the transition from one to the other, that the way to do this is through understanding, and that understanding is the point.

> *Do not be deceived, my beloved brethren. Every good endowment and every perfect gift is from above, coming down from the Father of Lights, with whom there is no variableness, neither shadow of turning.*
>
> —James 1:16–17

Science

O Shiva, what is your reality?
What is this wonder-filled universe?
What constitutes seed?
Who centers the universal wheel?
What is this life beyond form pervading forms?
How may we enter it fully, above space and time,
names and descriptions?
Let my doubts be cleared!

—*Zen Flesh, Zen Bones,* compiled by Paul Reps

To drink milk will be the least absorbing activity in connection with the cup,
while he is conducting research on the nature of the cup. He examines the
outer surface of the cup, explores the inner surface, discovers its hollowness,
bangs it on the tray for its sound effects. Rivers of milk, orange juice and
water cascade from cup to tray to kitchen floor, adding joy to the experiment.

—Selma Fraiberg, *The Magic Years*

Science means knowledge. Our children's scientific interest is an aspect of their quest to know love—not as a feeling but as the by-product of a reliable underlying intelligence. Children are all scientists in the manner of the ancients, for whom science, philosophy, and religion were one. Their interest in understanding *how life is* is also an interest in their own being. Is life good? Is it a loving place to be? How does it work? What is it? What am I? How do I fit in?

On the surface, the evidence is conflicting. You certainly can't just look around and say that life is love. But it is equally false to stop with the contrary evidence. The conflict and confusion at the surface are just that—surface confusion that can be straightened out and harmonized by—and only by—deeper understanding. When we foster our children's natural interest in getting to the bottom of things, we augment their ability to recognize love. Because love and truth are aspects of one reality.

So the most important thing about our children's scientific explorations is not the acquisition of information but the discovery of life's fundamental intelligibility. Recognition that there *is* order behind every phenomenon also helps children learn to find their way through difficulties. As awareness of the whole resolves the seeming complexity of heaps of puzzle pieces into a coherent picture, one-mindedness over-comes life's tribulations.

In this world ye shall have tribulation: but be of good cheer; I have overcome the world.

—John 16:33

At first our children's unconscious but rightful motive for wanting to know what is so is the desire to be reunited with the One Mind through awareness; with goodness through awareness of good; with love through awareness that love-intelligence is. They are spontaneously drawn toward this reunion. Each revelation that intelligence is under-scores the secret yearning and hunch that they belong to, are one with, what is fundamentally good and loving.

Today's constant academic testing and competition intimidates us into pushing our children academically, which retards and distracts them from learning. Knowing the details of *how* things work is less important than understanding *that* they work—according to certain laws. Factual knowledge is constantly being revised in the light of new and deeper ways of seeing. So, in our time it has become possible to hear distinguished physicist David Bohm and neurophysiologist Karl Pribram agree publicly that, "In the beginning was the Word!" (1979 conference on "The Coevolution of Science and Spirit").

Overemphasis on personal knowledge can chain a child to the idea of having a personal mind and drive him apart from the one mind. When personal knowledge is overvalued, learning is difficult because what is already known must be defended even when it is erro-neous. Friendship and love also become difficult for the child who learns to pit his personal mind against others.

"Facts" need to be learned. But where discovering fundamental intelligence is the central concern it is easier for our children to remain open to new understanding. Such openness improves their academic effectiveness since new discoveries can be made only as old "facts" are relinquished. It is also easier for children to make friends when their self-worth is defined in the light of the One Mind rather than through besting each other. Thus one-mindedness enhances the possibility of our children fulfilling their potential to be both intelli-gent and loving. It help them continue to assume that life is harmo-niously ordered in favor of good.

Our main role in our children's explorations is attentive noninterference. We provide materials and opportunities but without predetermining what our children should make of them. This letting be attitude expresses our confidence in the meaningfulness of life and in the child as an understander. We regard our children as Seeing Beings rather than as doers and knowers. Recognizing that their most important task is to develop their faculty of perceiving, we are better guided in what to say, do, and provide to foster learning. We are less inclined to correct wrong answers or to do over what their unskilled hands can do only awkwardly. We are better able to point out and joyfully appreciate their discoveries.

Instead of	It will occur to us to say
That is very good (or bad).	It doesn't work very well that way.
You are very good (very bad).	Now you can see that thus and such is so (e.g., glasses break when they fall on the hard floor).
Oh, what a stupid (smart) child you are.	You have discovered . . . , or, Isn't it wonderful; this shows us . . . , or, What good pouring! or, That pouring was a little unsteady; perhaps it would be easier with two hands.
Don't (do) you know how to do that yet (already)?	You are learning. That was only a mistake. (See how smoothly it goes!)
Oh, what a lot you know! (You can say the whole alphabet!)	How wonderful! (The whole alphabet! That is the beginning of learning to read!) I see that you are finding out . . .
You can't (can) do that very well.	It is still a little difficult to manage such a . . . It's getting easier and easier to . . .
What a lucky girl you are!	Isn't it wonderful to see that such a thing can happen!

It's hard to say what's science and what's not for children. If nothing else, young children are certainly physical scientists. How does it feel? How does it taste? What does it smell and sound like, and do? Where did it come from? Where will it go? How did it happen? How does it work and what happens next? Everything children do, every mess they make, every toy they break, every tumble and every stumble they take is for learning's sake. So the question isn't what's a good scientific toy or activity for preschoolers. What isn't? To begin with, all they need is some scientific license and parental appreciation that science is what's going on. The cracking of an egg, the peeling of an apple are scientific revelations! Let the child play once with the peels, crack one egg and crumble the shell, squash a few round peas.

A child less than two years old went for a winter walk in a carrier on his father's back. Somewhere along the way the father made for the child his first snowball. So beautiful it was, scooped clean and white from beneath the surface and molded gently into a perfectly round, firm ball that just fit into the child's cupped and mittened hands. On the way home he slept on his father's back, still clinging to the snowball. The father tried to remove the snowball, but the child woke up and cried. So they brought the snowball inside, put it in the freezer, and the child finished his nap. That evening when the child was having his bath, the parents brought him his snowball. "It will melt," they explained. "Put it in the water and watch it melt. Snow is made of water. In the warm water the snow will become water again." He was not sad when his snowball went away. He was amazed.

Some things that seem to turn to nothing still exist. Some things that seem to be really aren't. Some things that seem not to be really are. Finding out what's what and what isn't makes life interesting. Is air nothing? You can blow up a paper bag or a balloon with it. You can put out a candle by depriving it of air. When you try to hold your breath, what happens? You can blow bubbles under water with air. Moving air cools, dries, and moves things. It helps things fly and boats sail. Blow up a bunch of balloons and see how light and easy they are to keep aloft. What's what? And what isn't? And who says so?

When I was a child I thought my kite would fly better if I flew it near the trees; I thought there was more wind near the trees because that's where I could see its effect. Naturally my kite got caught in the trees. I spent all day finding a way to climb that tree for the sticks from my broken kite, so I could make a new kite. And I did. And it flew, this time, from the middle of the field. What I learned from that experience still helps me with other experiences. When I'm hung up or stuck up a tree, when things aren't moving along as I expected, I remember that day.

Who has seen the wind?
* Neither I nor you;*
But when the leaves hang trembling,
* The wind is passing through.*
Who has seen the wind?
* Neither you nor I;*
But when the trees bow down their heads,
* The wind is passing by.*

—Christina Rossetti, "Who Has Seen the Wind?"

Our scientific children often ask us, *Why?* It is fine to answer these questions when we can, but knowing why is not of ultimate importance. While answering his why questions, also give your child this question: *What is the meaning?* What does it mean that we can see the work of the wind but never the wind at all? What does that signify?

> *The wind bloweth where it listeth, and thou hearest the sound thereof, but canst not tell whence it cometh, and whither it goeth; so is everyone that is born of the Spirit.*
>
> —John 3:8

> *For we look not upon the things that are seen, but upon the things which are not seen.*
>
> —2 Corinthians 4:18

There was hardly any toy he loved so much as his father's flashlight. Brighter than the light from any flashlight was the light in his face whenever he held one. One day, at two, he was "helping" by holding the flashlight while his father did some work in a semidark corner of the house. "Okay," his father called. "Would you please come back and give me a little light now?" The child ran happily to his father's side, shook the flashlight like a salt shaker or a watering can over the work, and then ran off to play again, clearly believing that his sprinkled light would continue to enable his father to see. How like the child we are, flicking little bits of love, little partial understandings at dark corners, and then being bewildered and disappointed at the lingering darkness.

Discipline

Neither children nor adults are greatly distressed by the tumbling of sand castles and block towers, or the failure of water to remain in a leaky or overturned vessel. Over and over the castles are built, gradually better and better, until the nature of sand and the laws governing its behavior are at least partially understood. For the most part progress is made harmoniously and the sandbox remains a pleasant place to play.

We understand that sand behaves according to reliable physical laws, so we do not teach our children to take its shifty behavior personally; neither do we too often take personally our children's ignorance of these laws. From the start we say "that's how it is" and "that's what happens when," so the child does not develop the notion that through exertion of his personal will he can somehow force it to behave differently.

We are not so enlightened regarding higher laws of being. As Me, Inc., we take life in general, our children in particular, and ourselves above all, very personally. Therefore, most of us have difficulty with our children in the area we call discipline. We have a whole battery of techniques that we fire at our children "for their own good," from old-fashioned, punitive insistence, to more subtle forms of manipulation, coercion, and bribery, to excessive permissiveness. Results vary from fearful compliance and passivity to anxious uncertainty to fierce anarchy and rebellion, often moving from one extreme to the other, especially in adolescence.

As our disciplinary effects fail we resort to every extreme. But no method is effective as long as the idea behind it is a belief in the power of our personal minds. Most disciplinary techniques are based on the idea that the parent's personal mind is the primary determinant of the child. We believe we are personally and causally responsible for the existence of our children and for the way they behave. This a very troublesome misperception.

In the sandbox we express a certain degree of faith in the sand as teacher and the child as learner, but we assume full personal responsibility for just about everything else. The less we know about something the more personal responsibility we assume. In ignorance we constantly violate higher laws of being and thus invite experiences of disharmony that reinforce our belief in lawlessness. Misinterpreting our own ignorance of higher law as the fact that there is no higher law, that reality is lawless, we assume responsibility for personally authoring, imposing, and enforcing law. When it comes to our children (whom we also believe we have authored), we even believe we *must* take this personal responsibility. But in adhering to this misconception, the biggest lesson we are teaching our children is that personal will (be it compliant or defiant) is the basic issue. This places us and our children in direct conflict with life and with each other.

In reality, of course, we too are but children in the sandbox. Our children and the situations in which we find ourselves are like the sand, relentlessly—but not maliciously—manifesting certain principles of existence. We are to each other both sand and fellow diggers in the sandbox. As diggers we are responsible only for discovering, obeying, and expressing those laws in our lives. But we are not *personally* responsible for creating them. We do not create the laws, nor can we vary them, nor force anyone to live by them. We are responsible only in that we are *able* to respond to the laws both in understanding and in our mode of being in the world. These laws are the truth about us; we do not make them true.

What does this suggest about parental discipline? How can we avoid the years of struggling, frustration, anger, disappointment, and even tragedy that plague so many well-meaning families?

Silent Knowing

It is important to remember that our awareness of fundamental truth makes the more difference than what we do or say. Carefully built sand castles will bewilderingly crumble until the builder understands the difference between wet and dry sand. Though from a material standpoint sand is characteristically shifting, in ideal terms it is constant; it is reliably shifty. It always expresses the laws of its being. The same is true of our seemingly undisciplined children. They are reliably disobedient, always expressing underlying laws of being. So it is important for parents to make a continuous conscious effort to discern the underlying meaning in any disciplinary situation—not the immediate facts or causes but the underlying principle.

We must maintain an unceasing vigil over our thoughts, distinguishing honestly our shifting personal moods and whims from reliable underlying law or truth. Little children are so easy to push around. Only as we understand the truth of any situation can we transmit it to our children without resorting to personal willpower.

What we truly understand is somehow transmitted to our children through consciousness and does not have to be spoken of or enforced at all. Insofar as we see that reliable underlying law operates in our lives, we can more easily and noninterferingly let our children live and learn. Our assured noninterference is conveyed to the child as a sense of confidence in both himself and life, despite all evidence to the contrary.

So the first answer to the problem of personal mind is silent seeking and knowing. This process involves letting go of our exaggerated sense of personal responsibility and receptively turning our attention toward the revelation of principle.

Demonstration

The second answer to the problem of personal mind is the demonstration in our lives of the principles we understand. This means simply practicing what we preach—which is easy if we really know what we're talking about; otherwise it is more difficult. We have dominion over our children much as we have dominion over the sand, not through domination but through understanding. Our children behave in accordance with our values, reflecting positively or negatively the ideas we cherish most. Any truths we fully understand and demonstrate in daily living will be picked up by our children. Even though children are not conscious enough to understand the principles per se (we are only beginning to discover them for ourselves), they are drawn to and will live in accordance with them, and thus joyfully experience their fruits.

But sometimes we do not know the law ourselves, much less the principle behind it. At such times, affirmation in the face of uncertainty is called for. We affirm that truth *is,* that the sand does behave according to law even though it is not completely clear to us why this particular sand castle has just caved in, or why at this particular moment our child is having a tantrum. Our difficulties with our children are no more personal than their difficulties with sand. Our difficulties are only with our ignorance of the nature and significance of whatever presents itself.

If we do not understand the laws behind the behavior of sand, we may try to force it to behave in accordance with our erroneous preconceptions, quite against its own nature, or fling it about in frustration. As long as we cling to the belief that the problem is with the sand, the sand will only be able to manifest our error. It will be shifty, unreliable, hurtful to the eyes. Likewise, when we run into difficulty with our children, we are often inclined to try to change the children rather than our thoughts, thus trying to force them to behave in ways that are contrary to the truth of their own as-yet unconscious being. At best this is bewildering. At worst, since the child, unlike the sand, is growing in consciousness, he not only manifests our error but sooner or later begins to adopt it as his own conscious, but false, belief.

Acknowledgment of discord as ignorance of truth is the first step toward relinquishing error and its problematic results. This one step releases our children from false lessons of personal badness. Affirmation that reliable truth exists, whether we know it yet or not, is faith. In our children it will be expressed as confidence, enthusiasm, and happy expectancy, the freedom to live and learn. In our own lives the practice of known or acknowledged principles leads to firsthand validation of them.

Thus with regard to discipline, removal of personal sense from parenthood means first of all the silent seeking and knowing of principle and, second, the modeling of it. But do knowing and exemplifying substitute altogether for teaching? No.

Spelling out the Law

Much bullying that passes for what has been called parental discipline is eliminated through silent knowing and demonstrating. Yet parents also have an important role as teachers.

Whatever is not communicated through silent knowing and example must be reduced to laws. Laws are a temporary measure necessitated by the imperfection of our understanding of principle and by the fact that our children are not yet mature enough to comprehend principles.

We must try to see that the laws we set forth are based on principles we understand and *live* by. Laws are an imperfect reflection of principle. We must be prepared to revise or relinquish any law in the light of greater understanding or the growing readiness of our children to move from imposed regulation to understood principle. If we recognize that the toddler's destruction of a flower is really a constructive effort to understand something, then instead of reprimanding and forbidding we can channel his efforts and foster discovery. Instead of "don't touch," we may offer him one flower from the centerpiece to dissect.

Likewise, we are ready to revise or relinquish behavioral laws as the child gains understanding. At first we must physically keep her from danger and keep breakables physically out of reach. But as the child grows, a progression occurs from protection and prevention to admonition and advice. More and more the child is allowed to discover things for herself through trial and error (depending, of course, on the possible danger).

From time to time, it is good to verbally express to our children the few principles we genuinely understand, but only as sowers, letting the ideas fall as seeds in consciousness, to sprout and bloom later. *It is important to do so in the most concrete terms possible.*

Initially this means not even using words, as in the physical protection of the physical baby from physical harm. Later it means expressing simple do's and don'ts. For example, when children first begin to play with each other they have great difficulty sharing. They do not understand the value of sharing. Yet, to pave the way we have to help them overcome the problem of fighting over cherished toys and to have a happy social experience. A helpful and effective law that can be set forth at such times is, "No one may take anything out of anyone else's hands." Such a principle-based concrete law enables the child to encounter for himself the underlying principles it benefits.

It is also wise to express laws as positively as possible. The best way to stop a child from banging the glass coffee table with his xylophone is by giving him something more interesting to do. While there is a place for taking a firm, stern, *No!*, in most instances, rather than telling a child what not to do it is better to suggest what he might do instead. One baby boy used to kick his mother while his diaper was being changed. The kicking became painful and also playfully purposeful. Saying "Don't kick" only fixed the idea in his mind and made it impossible for him to think of anything else. Then another idea occurred to his mother. "Kick leaves," she said, "not people." The kicking stopped. There was more than technique at work. The principle behind an effective technique is that truth is always to our good. "Kick leaves" distracted the child by suggesting an attractive new possibility. Sacrificing error does not mean loss but rather fulfillment. The living child is not interested in how not to live but in living.

Finally, *in formulating laws for our children the most important thing to keep in mind is the removal of personal sense.* Truth is the issue, not personal will or mind. There is little more important that we could do for our children than to spare them a too-persuasive indoctrination into an overly personal point of view. Bad and good behavior does not imply badness or goodness on the part of the child, nor is it bad or good because we say so or because we do or do not like it. In fact, there is not good or bad behavior at all. There is only what works existentially and what doesn't, what brings harmony and what brings discord. The opposite of true isn't bad; it is only ignorant. To keep our children from thinking that life is a matter of personal goodness and badness, it is helpful to delete the misleading personal words of "I" and "you," "want" and "don't want," when setting forth laws or instructions.

This means first of all viewing all discordant behavior as mistaken or unknowing and assuming that the child would do better if she genuinely knew better. Such a forgiving attitude facilitates learning. Instead of "Why did you do that?" or "You shouldn't do that" or "You are a bad girl!" or "I told you not to do that" or "Don't ever let me see you do that again!" we can say concretely, "Banging the glass on the table is a mistake. See? Now the glass is broken." (See also pages 119 and 302.)

Likewise, it is good to *delete "I" and "you" from all commands and positive rules and regulations.* Instead of "You have to do this because I said so," or long, drawn-out explanations that are meaningless to the child anyway, try "This is the time for going home" or "Now is the time for putting on coats." The experience of personal dominance is reduced, even if it remains necessary to pick up the child and bodily cart him off. Nonpersonal is not better because it is less offensive; it is less offensive because it is more truthful.

The True Disciplinarian

Behind laws stands the Law, which is greater and more perfect than the laws and which the laws must serve. Behind the Law stands principle or truth, which is purer and more perfect than the Law and which the Law must serve. Only truth is ultimately redemptive. Truth is neither personal nor impersonal. It is beyond- or transpersonal. Nonpersonal silent knowing, exemplification, and teaching fosters our own and our children's awakening to Beyond Personal truth.

The highest of these ways is silent knowing, which is the pure concern with pure principle. Another name for silent knowing is prayer. Its fruits in our lives are revelation and redemption. Its fruit in the lives of our children is the maintenance of a wholesome and happy environment for growth.

The second way to reach realization is through exemplification—the affirmation, practice, and demonstration of principle in daily life. In our lives its fruit is the discovery and validation of principle in experience as Law. In our children's lives this is the providence of healthy models of being and the maintenance of the desire and freedom to be healthy. Another name for exemplification is witness.

Finally there is teaching. On the highest level this means voicing realized truth in the presence of sincere interest. As parents it is mostly the concern with what to do or say *in the meantime*—until we know, until our children are ready to seek to know. This is the most confusing of all because it is the farthest from the truth, the most human, temporary, and contingent. It is made easier by the removal of personal sense, and it is largely replaced by silent knowing and exemplification. In our lives the fruit of teaching is learning. In our children's lives, it is easier growth.

So the true disciplinarian of us all is truth. The true discipline is the following after or seeking of truth. The best way to discipline our children is not to discipline them in the usual sense but rather to be ourselves disciples of truth. The true answer to the problems of discipline is thus discipleship.

> *Mountains and rivers, the whole earth—*
> *All manifest forth the essence of being.*
>
> —*The Gospel According to Zen,* ed. by Sohl and Carr

> *So we, being many, are one body in Christ, and every one members one of another.*
>
> —Romans 12:5

> *Kabir said: Behold but One in all things; it is the second that leads you astray.*
> —Lao Tzu, *The Way of Life,* trans. by R. B. Blakney

> *The One is none other than the All, the All none other than the One.*
> *Take your stand on this, and the rest will follow of its accord;*

To trust in the Heart is the "Not Two," the "Not Two" is to trust in the Heart.
I have spoken, but in vain; for what can words tell
Of things that have no yesterday, tomorrow, or today?

—Seng Ts'an, in *The Religions of Man,* by Huston Smith

Additional Reflection—Anger

In groping for family unity we often provoke and are provoked to anger. In earlier editions of *Whole Child* I said little about anger, because I knew little. My parents were loving and generous, but they weren't good with anger, so they couldn't help me with mine. One only expressed his anger in sudden, all-over-everything eruptions. From him I learned to fear anger. His. The other was never openly angry and never admitted to being angry. From her I learned to be ashamed of anger. Mine. Worst of all, I learned to equate *feeling bad* with *being a bad person.* So I didn't learn the value of anger or how to use it.

I learned that anger, mine *and* others', was to be avoided at all costs. My parents were better with anger than their parents. Our sons are better with it than we were. But when they were young we just had to muddle through anger. Sometimes it was pretty muddy. This is true for most people. Anger says "No!" Love says "Yes!" You can't have one without the other. Anger, like love, must be lived through by each human being over a lifetime, by humankind throughout history. Knowing that anger has a worthy place in life, and that it has to be learned, is helpful.

Anger is one of several aspects of our psychic being that begin with *A.* Like the letter *A* itself, *A* words are angular. They come to a point and are sharp, can be destructive or constructive. Sharp pointed things can poke, sting, stab, cut, wound, or kill, like a sword or dagger. But they can also write, carve, etch, sculpt, make openings, cut paths, discriminate, probe, separate, sew, and patch things together in new ways. A few road signs staked into the ground—*one way, wrong way, merge, caution: road under construction*—afford safer travel, fewer wrong turns and collisions. Likewise, well-placed *grounded, timely, and clearly stated* anger—*not now, not here, caution: person under construction*—averts interpersonal conflict, accident, and collision. Destructive anger usually takes the form of attack or abandonment. Each one leads to the other, neither to love. Constructive anger facilitates love, just as road signs facilitate safe and harmonious traffic flow.

If you fear anger you are also likely to be afraid of all forms of aggression, assertion, action, autonomy, authority—both others' and your own. All these *A* forms of expression are necessary and interrelated. If we have trouble with our anger, our children will not only have trouble with anger but also with aggression, assertion, action, autonomy, and authority—in other words, with "putting themselves out there." Freud called the impulse to put ourselves out there *libido,* which he saw mainly in sexual terms. Jung expanded libido to include all forms of self-expression. I call it *live-ido,* by which is meant the drive to become fully all that we essentially are. It is also *love-ido,* our drive to fully give, receive, and be received by each other.

We have existential needs both to receive and to contribute, both to take in and to *ex-press.* Ex-pression is also our function as contributing parts of the whole. To be lovingly received we must express ourselves. To lovingly receive others we must know how to receive their self-expressions, including their angry "No!"

Anger happens when there is frustration or disappointment, when our assertion meets danger and obstacles, when our *live-ido* or *love-ido* is thwarted or hurt. When we put ourselves out or put something forth and we meet with rejection, opposition, or indifference, it's painful. Right where the pain occurs, anger happens. *Ouch!* Knowing that pain underlies anger is helpful, because it makes us more understanding and kindly toward both our own and others' anger. There's a difference between anger and what it may make us want to do. Anger can make us want to do bad things. But anger itself isn't bad.

Elsewhere we discussed that *Our urge is God's surge,* and how at the bottom of even our most destructive and unhealthy temptations and behaviors is a healthy divine impulse toward wholeness and fullness of being (see also page 144). We speak of an "angry" wound or a boil, a "raging" fever. If a body part is injured, we say it has received an "insult." We know that pus, swelling, and pain mean that something is wrong in our bodies *and* that the body is attempting to heal itself, that white cells and plasma are rushing to fight off an enemy, that messages are being sent to the brain for help.

We know some pains are growing pains. Lengthening legs ache.

Budding breasts are tender. The ache and tenderness are signs of growth. We've learned to read some of these messages and thus respond to them. The symptom is a negative experience, but it is a postive sign of health trying to happen. We may have to manage a symptom, lower a dangerously high fever, lance a boil, alleviate pain. But we know we also need to deal with the disease behind the symptom. Likewise we need not only to manage our own and our children's angry symptomatic behavior but also to respond to what underlies it.

If your child is having a tantrum in the supermarket, you may have to forcibly carry him kicking and screaming to the car. But once he has calmed down, you need to be with him, try to get to the bottom of the anger, to see what the real need is. If we can read anger we have a chance to turn destructive energy and defensiveness into constructive energy and creativity, anger into shared love and individual growth. Even if we can't read it, knowing that it is a meaningful expression of a real need is already helpful.

One day I heard the two-and-a-half-year-old next door having a positive fit, screaming and ultimately threatening his father, who was watering plants. "And I'm going to hit you with this 'wake'!" he bellowed when he wasn't able to turn off the hose. "I don't think so," said his dad calmly. "Because I will take it away from you." When he finished watering he scooped up his son and carried him indoors. I was impressed that he hadn't seen his son's tantrum as "bad." "Oh, no," he chuckled. "He was trashed. After that he napped for three hours!" Such situations often end so badly. The child yells something, the parent takes it personally, and the situation goes from bad to worse, ending only when both parent and child are exhausted.

Some parents are so afraid of showing anger that they let the child "get away with murder." Others are so offended by a child's show of anger that they want to murder the child. Others crush their children with guilt by acting wounded. Still others terrify them with abandonment by psychologically *ice*-olating them in the deep freeze. Most of us channel-surf wildly through all these poor options. But this father has a different perspective. To him anger is like a runny nose or fever. He knows it signifies something. He correctly read his son's anger as fatigue. He could distinguish the "bad" behavior from his good but exhausted son. He firmly managed the behavior by taking the rake away, and, once he had finished watering, lovingly carried his son off to bed. It is noteworthy that this is his third child. His older daughters have already taught him a thing or two.

We can't read or respond to our children's anger unless we've learned to read and respond to our own. One mother came for help because she hated how angrily she treated her four-year-old son and her husband. "I've become my mother!" she wailed. When she felt abandoned, she attacked—when she felt attacked, she abandoned—and she was even harder on herself than she was on her family. Over time we uncovered the pain underlying her anger. We found the fear and hurt she had suffered throughout childhood from her mother's abandonment and volcanic wrath. Beneath that we saw her real need and healthy desire for love. Part of her was an adult. Part of her was a hurt, abandoned, and angry child.

The more this woman understood and responded to her own child pain, the less she depended on her husband and son to do so, and the less often she "lost it," attacking with searing rage or coldly abandoning. Now she could be firmer and gentler. When a second baby came, the son could not go near the baby without hurting her. When he wasn't hurting his sister, he was claiming to hate his mother, who began losing it again. I reminded her that pain underlies anger. I suggested that the next time he said, "Mommy I hate you," she hear it as, "Mommy, I'm hurting!" The next time the baby wailed, instead of yelling at her son, she asked him quietly, "What happened?" *A new thing!* After a thoughtful moment, he said, "I think I pinched her too hard." *Another new thing!* A new level of awareness. Though he still felt like pinching his sister, next time he wouldn't do it so hard. He didn't feel abandoned or attacked. He didn't feel rotten about feeling rotten. Now he could reflect on it. Soon he would make better choices—especially with Mom on his side.

Psychology has noticed that children's putting forth of themselves occurs about the same time as toilet training. It takes a certain degree of self-development to notice that one needs to poop and that one has a choice about when and where to do so. We must also have confidence in the safety and desirability of our choice.

Learning to use the toilet involves a complex psychological process of noticing what one is feeling, holding that feeling until one gets to a certain place, then letting the feeling have its way and letting go of something that one has produced. To use the toilet must become our idea rather than somebody else's. No wonder we say, "Oh sh—t," when we are angry. No wonder our angry child says, "You Doo Doo!" when she is frustrated.

Baby words for mother, father, and poop are remarkably similar. First comes Mama and DaDa. Later comes Doo Doo. When Doo Doo enters a child's vocabulary we can be sure that she recognizes both her own self and others', and that she's learning to assert hers. When the little boy next door calls me "Doo Doo," I feel almost as honored that he feels safe enough to put his feelings out there with me as when he throws his arms around me.

So anger is partly about autonomy, power, and control, which is why the "terrible twos," when children begin to assert themselves, are so difficult for many parents. As I've written elsewhere, parenthood first throws us into the God position and then knocks us out of it. The demands of parenthood first suggest that we have to be grown up, all-knowing, all-loving, all-giving. As all our knowing, loving, giving fails, our left-behind helpless, powerless, overwhelmed, hurt, *angry* child parts are evoked and become vocal.

At such times we believe all we need is more power. If we don't recognize when we are in this child position, it's impossible not to flip into the terrifying, wrathful, punitive, vengeful, bullying, Almighty God position or the even-worse guilt-laying Holy Mary Mother Martyr position. Either way we terrify and burden our children with the responsibility of taking care of *us!* Only by recognizing and dealing with the hurt and angry subjective child inside of ourselves can we hope to deal firmly and lovingly with our hurt and angry objective children.

The first step is to recognize when you are in the child position and to be with that child part and listen to what it feels. The second is to recognize and relinquish the, come to think of it, ludicrous idea that your children should be your parents. The third is to turn with all your feelings and needs to the Parent of parents—that is, to God, or, if you prefer, to the whole, to life, the Beyond Personal source of everything we need. We have already summed up these steps as *letting up* (the child), *letting go of* (others, i.e., your child or spouse or anyone else who seems to be letting you down), and *letting go into* (God, the Beyond Personal source and force of our being; see also pages 88–92).

These prayerful steps are helpful in any situation, but here we are looking at how they apply to parenthood and anger. You may have to do something to manage the situation at the same time that you need to address the child feelings—both yours and your child's. You may have to forcibly remove yourself from the situation before you can become prayerful. When my children were small and things were going haywire and I was starting to lose it, I found the bathroom was a very good place to go. Even children generally recognize the bathroom as a private place, and there is usually a lock on the door. So it is a good place to go to protect your children from your anger. Since anger is often about control, which is the same issue in toilet training, the bathroom is also a symbolically appropriate place for sorting out anger and flushing it away with new inspiration.

Prayerful Processing of Anger

First, deal with yourself. Let up your own feelings. What are they? Read them. What is the feeling beneath the anger? Do you feel powerless, hurt, embarrassed, abandoned? Are you expecting your child to parent you—by obeying your wishes instead of his own, taking care of your feelings instead of hers, making you feel good, remaining your baby instead of exercising his own budding freedom and authority? One graduate student and mother of three tried this. The family lived in a cramped student apartment. Her dissertation was due, but her children were climbing the walls. "Then my four-year-old found that if he squeezed his juice box it would squirt. I came into the kitchen and found him squirting juice everywhere. I wanted to strangle him, but remembering our talks, I took his juice box away, went into the bathroom, closed the door, and prayed. I noticed how powerless I felt, and I cried [letting up]. Next it occurred to me that maybe he wasn't squirting his juice against *me*, that he probably had no idea what a mess he was making, and that he wasn't responsible for taking care of me [letting go of]. Then I remembered that there was a higher power and that from God's standpoint it wasn't possible for my being to depend on his not being, or for his well-being to depend on my sacrificing myself. I couldn't see how that was so, but I acknowledged the divine logic of it. I figured my paper was either not so urgent or that there must be a way for me to write it—that God would work all that out [letting go into]. After that I felt calm and went back to the kitchen."

Second, deal with your child. Once you have dealt with your own feelings then you can see more clearly to deal with your child. The same steps of letting up, letting go of, and letting go into are helpful. When I was upset as a child, my mother often said, "What *is* the matter?" When I did "bad" things, I was often asked, "What's the matter with you?" Whenever such things were said to me, I said to myself, "Yes, what is the matter *with me?*" Over the years I've discovered more helpful questions. Better questions bring better answers.

"What is trying to happen here?" is a helpful question. The mother of the little squirt may have asked, "What is trying to happen here? Is he intentionally trying to drown me and my life in juice? Is he really trying to douse my career? Is he telling me that he feels pushed aside and needs my attention? Is life telling me to slow down, that being a mom as well as a scholar will develop me and even help me vocationally? That my time with my son will be shorter than my career, and that I don't want to miss it? Was he simply making a delightful scientific discovery that has nothing to do with me? What am *I* to learn here? That he needs more structure? or more freedom? That there is something for me to learn here at home or that I need to find someone to take him to the Natural History Museum while I finish my paper? Is this situation a symptom or a growing pain? His? Mine? Ours?"

"Hey, what's up?" is another helpful question. When we say, "Hey what's up" instead of "What's the matter with you?" or "Why did you do that?" we express two important messages. One says, *I know you. You are my good and beloved child. So if you're acting this way, I know you are hurting or in need.* The other is, *Here I am. Let's figure out what hurts and what you need together. I love you, and I'm here to help.* And by the way, it's better not to ask why your child did or feels something, because children rarely know. It's better to ask *what* are you feeling? They, too, need to learn to *let up* and eventually to be conscious of what their feelings are.

I'm not sure which questions the mother of the little squirt asked or what answers came to her in the bathroom. But I know what she said to her child. She wrote, "I went back to the kitchen and we cleaned up the juice together. I said that juice boxes are not for squirting and that if he needed to squirt we would find something better to squirt with. He looked interested!" She also finished her paper, and a week later the whole family went on summer vacation in the country. *Whew!*

Other Tips and Tales about Anger

Being a good parent doesn't mean never being angry. When you stub your toe it's natural to yell. When you stub your life it is normal to feel angry and it is even okay to shout. Just be honest about it. Describe your feelings and what hurt you, if possible without putting the other guy down. One mother, who was often overwhelmed and inclined to lose it, was inspired by an incident she witnessed at a friend's home. The toddler knocked over a whole gallon of milk. Instead of spilling her anger all over him, the mother cried out, "Oh no! I wish that hadn't happened!" "Me, too!" said the child. Then they mopped up the milk together.

No matter how hard you try, you will lose it sometimes. Don't be too hard on yourself about that. Feeling awful about losing it, about not being perfect, is only continuing to think about ourselves.

No matter how hard he or she tries, your spouse will lose it sometimes. Don't be too hard on him or her about that. When someone loses it she is hurting and feeling powerless. Don't be too impressed. Try to distinguish between what's her problem and what's yours.

Don't try to manage your partner's anger either by combating it or by warding it off. Anger is often about power and powerlessness. Rage tries to tyrannize. Running around trying to please and prevent someone from ever becoming angry is also tyrannical—and infuriating. We all want to have our way and avoid disappointment. When we don't, we feel angry. But we are all different and we think different things will make us happy. So in a marriage there must be times when we want different things, when it seems that one of us can be happy only at the other's expense. Now anger happens, and a new agenda arises: how to avoid feeling angry and how to avoid having our partner be angry at us. This is when marriages either fail or grow. Some people try to ward off their partner's anger by pleasing. We try to figure out what will prevent the other from ever becoming angry, to do what will please, to avoid what may displease. This never works. Being tiptoed around is just as insulting and upsetting as being stepped on. The more we try to please the angrier the other one becomes. What we don't see is how infuriating it is to have someone trying to control everything we feel, think, and do and to be treated as a dangerous person.

The opposite of tyrannical anger is not "nice"; it's signpost anger.

Signpost anger doesn't punish or manipulate. It informs. It says, *No, not this, not that, not here, not now. Danger: person under construction.* It helps us make way for each other. It makes two-way, two-person travel possible. Once I thanked someone for being nice to me. He said, "I am *not* nice. Ask anyone who knows me well, and they will tell you that I am not a nice person." I saw what he meant. "True," I said, "and you can trust some people's 'not nice' much more than you can trust other people's 'nice.'" There's more to be said, but this isn't a book about marriage. Read Harville Hendrix, John Bradford, or Harriet Goldhor Lerner on fair, fruitful fighting.

Your children will lose it sometimes. Remember, they need to know that their anger can accomplish something but that it doesn't kill. Remember, they need the practice. Try to read the anger, to see what underlies it. Some of the things anger can mean: overtired, sick, frustrated, envious, afraid, oppressed, hurt, anxious, disappointed, sad, abandoned, growing, reaching a new stage, testing a new strength. What's trying to happen? What's needed?

As your children grow, help them learn to read and respond to their own anger. *What were you feeling? What do you think happened? We can't get rid of the baby, but what do you think would help?* One couple called me because their six-year-old daughter had started to have huge screaming unconsolable tantrums. I heard one that lasted for an hour and a half. They were really something. We talked about what might be going on with her: was it that she wasn't getting enough sleep? Was it that she was the middle child whose older sibling could do everything better and whose younger sibling was getting the most attention? Was it that she was anxious about starting first grade or that her mother had just started a new job? I don't know that we ever got to the root of the problem. Everything and nothing seemed to help. Not saying "why" and calling her "bad" helped.

Having private times with each parent and quiet times before earlier bedtime helped. But just when the parents thought the tantrums were over they'd start up again. We tried helping her find a place to be angry and something to do—a room to go to, a bat to hit a pillow with, and one clear rule: if she started to lose it at breakfast, instead of stopping everything and making everyone late, she would have to go to her angry place. "If you feel better you can come back. If not, I'll come and be with you when your sister gets off to school." Maybe that helped her to find some distance and control. Before long the tantrums stopped for good. Who knows what did the trick? Maybe none of these things, possibly all of them. Or maybe she just outgrew them. But it was lovely to see how they all lived and learned their way through it together.

No matter how hard you all try, your child will experience others' anger at times. A little dose of anger is good immunization. The important thing is not whether or not anger occurs but what happens when it does. It's not bad for our children to experience other people's anger even when it is unfair and out of control. If they never encounter anger at home they'll be devastated when they meet it in the world. It's good to learn that they can live through others' anger; it's good to learn that others can live through theirs.

Anger is one thing parents often disagree about and do differently, so it's often about anger (which includes discipline and setting limits) that parents fight. One parent may spend a lot of time trying to protect the child from the other's anger while not daring to fight fairly and directly with his or her spouse. About this I have two things to say: (1) Villainizing one parent is unhealthy for the child and the marriage. (2) Children need to learn to deal with all kinds of anger and with both parents. So as much as possible, get out of the middle and don't try to manage each other's relationship with the children. Controlled and out-of-control parents have controllingness in common. Avoid that. (See also "The Pugnacious Children of the Pacifist Parents," pages 293–295.)

If you're inclined to fear and suppress your anger while your partner is inclined to lose it and be verbally abusive toward your children, you may have to take a stand. But mostly it is better to stand back, stand by, and prayerfully recognize that there is something beyond self and other that supports you all and can help your child and your partner to work things out. Which way you need to respond at a particular time is something you can only sort out prayerfully. When children are very young they are entirely dependent on us to do this, but as they grow they need to learn to navigate on their own.

A-words may be pointed at one end, but they are open at the other. By opening ourselves prayerfully to deeper understanding of our own and others' anger we also open ourselves to fuller and more loving lives.

Practical Information for New Parents

The toys and materials covered here offer children material demonstrations and encounters with unity. They are presented roughly in progression from the most specific to the most general, the most concrete to the most open-ended and potentially abstract. Included are baby toys, puzzles and prepuzzles, blocks, construction sets, carpentry, gardening, play with water and sand, and science books—all things through which a child can make discoveries about fundamental unity and order.

Parts and Wholes

Among small unity toys a rattle is a whole composed of parts. Any infant hand toy with parts that do not come off demonstrates the parts/whole idea. *(It is apart from me, but I can pick it up.)* Anything with moving parts also demonstrates the parts/whole idea. *(It has parts, but it is one thing.)* Stack and nesting toys, puzzles, and pegboards are all wholes that can become parts, all parts that can become wholes. Blocks and construction sets are parts that can express the infinitude of the possibilities of unity. *(With the same set of parts I can make many different things.)* Tools implement the parts/whole idea. Mud, sand, and water are the most amorphous materials of all and are thus of the longest-lasting usefulness and the best teachers of both the fact and the infinitude of unity and reliability.

For Babies

It's silly to speak about what makes a good rattle or other hand toy for a little baby, yet even on this level there are toys that work and toys that don't. As with anything else, you have to pay attention to the baby—what she can do and what she's *trying* to do. To help her learn to grasp things, choose something that's easy for a tiny hand to hold. Dumbbell-type rattles are best for tiny babies—they can hold them before they know about holding. It is often the sound of a rattle in her hand that seems to call the baby's attention to the fact that the hand and rattle are there in the first place. For safety be sure your baby's toys are not sharp, breakable, soluble in the mouth, or small enough to swallow.

Don't buy redundant toys. Look for variety. Buy or make something that will help the baby learn to grasp, something bright colored to help her learn to use her eyes, something with a pleasant sound to help her learn to use her ears. Find one with moving parts, one that rocks, one that slides, one that rolls, ones in different shapes. Find something hard and something soft to mouth or handle. Most toys do/are several of these things; see if they do/are them differently.

Remember, you *really* don't have to buy anything. Your home is already full of inspiring things:

- An *empty film can* with some split peas inside.
- Some *big buttons* or *wooden spools* on a ring of nylon string.
- A *homemade cloth book* with four pages of bright shapes sewn on by machine. Use various textured materials (fake fur, wool, satin, corduroy, oilcloth).
- A *shape sheet,* that is, a few wonderful things like enormous round shiny buttons or a plastic costume jewelry bracelet sewn onto a small piece of sturdy cloth for the baby to hold. Or do the same thing around the edge of a larger quilt or blanket for her to lie on. Nothing small enough to choke on, of course.

Once you start, where can you stop? The possibilities are endless.

Prepuzzles, Parquetry, and Then Some

Gradually the child becomes ready for parts/whole toys that really come apart and can be put together. On the way to puzzles the following may be useful:

Pole and rings. Most children find the stacking of disks or doughnut-shaped rings around a center pole interesting at some point (one year old, more or less), though not for long. Ones with fewer rings are less trouble to pick up. A straight center shaft is better than a tapered shaft designed for learning seriation (the big one goes on first, the smallest one last). Simply removing and replacing the rings without regard to size is what appeals at first.

Stackable/nestable cups or boxes. Seriation is more easily learned with these than with stacking rings. And besides stacking and nesting, the cups and boxes are good for putting things in, out, on, and under.

Developmentally, inning and outing comes earlier than stacking. Games can be played with these such as hiding an object beneath an overturned box or cup and then guessing which one it is under. Here are two breeze-easy ideas for homemade sets:

A three-can *silver tuna tower* can be easily made from 3½-, 7-, and 13-ounce tuna cans. Check the inside of the cans and pound down any sharp edges. No need to decorate unless you want to; they look very pretty in natural silver, and some are gold inside. Box, gift-wrap, and present them to her when she wakes up from her nap.

A *super tower* can be made from stackable cat food cans with bottoms and tops removed. Cover with strips of different-colored contact paper, and you can help your child build a colorful tower taller than you are! For a sturdier base and an even taller tower, nail one can with its bottom intact to a board. Make a puzzle column by gluing a clown picture on a stack of cans to be scrambled and reassembled. For the older preschooler, these cans offer math fun. Build a two-can stack, a three-can stack, a stairway of stacks from one to ten.

Many *shape sorter* containers with geometrically shaped holes that admit only objects of the same shape are available. Some have too many holes and surfaces to work with. Try before buying to be certain of how hard or easy it is likely to be for your child at the time.

With tiny, tweezerlike fingers and surprising strength, the baby begins tweaking tiny patches of skin on your neck. Smile while you wince; he's developing dexterity. He is also checking things out. Do they come apart? Do you? *Pegboards* and pegs are for older preschoolers, but if you're willing to supervise, you may want one earlier. Briefly, well before a year, he will find simply picking out the pegs an absorbing challenge. At roughly a year and a half he may again be interested, this time in trying to maneuver the peg into position in his hands and then fit it into a hole. It's fascinating to watch. It looks the way it feels to unbutton a coat with freezing hands. A pegboard with regularly spaced holes and colored pegs is useful and will come in handy later for math, color, and design work. Older children sometimes enjoy having a design to follow. Copy the board on paper, draw one circle for each hole, photocopy, and make various designs and pictures by coloring in the circles to match the different-colored pegs.

Knobbed wooden puzzles made of plywood are ideal first puzzles. Some have geometric shapes; others have painted animals or objects.

They can be introduced soon after the baby can sit up alone and will continue to be of interest for a long time. A farm animal puzzle such as the one pictured here is fine to start with. For several months the newly sitting child simply lifts out the pieces. He'll also enjoy learning to recognize the animals' names and the sounds they make. After a while the idea of fitting the pieces back into the puzzle will dawn. At the end of a meal, help him with the puzzle in his highchair. (Turn it! Turn it! There it goes!)

We used the animals in the puzzle pictured here as play figures for making up and acting out stories and for simple hide-and-seek games.

One sunny day the duck and the hen went for a walk. [Child "walks" them around.] Dumtee-dum—teedum—teedum [a good strolling noise]. After a while they sat down to rest under a tree. [Child "sits" them down.] Next the cow and the crow decided to take a walk. Dumtee-dum—teedum—teedum. Soon they came upon the duck and the hen. What a surprise! So they all sat together in the shade. [This goes on until the child has seated all the animals under the "tree."] "I wish we had a picnic," they said, for by now they were all hungry. Just then the hen looked up, and said, "What do you know! We do not need a picnic, because this is an apple tree. And it is full of apples!" So the duck and the hen and the cow and the crow and the dog and the pig and the lamb and the sheep and the rooster and the cat and the goat and the goose and the rabbit had an apple picnic under the apple tree on the sunny day. Then, happy and full, they all went home.

Simple wooden picture puzzles, in which each piece is a whole part of the picture, are next. Lots are available but not all are equally suitable.

It is desirable that anything that is going to be worked over and looked at as much as these first picture puzzles should be lovely and sturdy. You don't need many. A few will be satisfying for quite some time if introduced soon enough.

First jigsaw puzzles. Difficulty depends on size, number, and distinctiveness of the pieces. Start with puzzles that have only a few large pieces, all easily distinguishable by shape. Work up gradually to smaller, more similar pieces, according to the child's readiness and enthusiasm. Good wooden ones are nice, but cardboard ones are adequate and more available. Older children won't work the same puzzle many times, because they have less to learn from doing so. At this point a whole boxful of cardboard puzzles is worth more than one or two wooden ones. Cardboard puzzles with a framed tray are more easily managed than those without.

Homemade jigsaw puzzles. Choose a magazine picture, photo, children's poster, or picture your child has made, pasted to a piece of cardboard, leaving a one-inch border around it. Cut the mounted picture out and into pieces appropriate in size and shape for your child. Make a tray for the puzzle by gluing the remaining cardboard border to a same-size piece of cardboard.

Parquetry. The official verb that describes this type of activity is "to tessellate," that is, "to form of small squares or blocks, as floors, pavements, etc.; form or arrange in a checkered or mosaic pattern." Many lovely, wooden, colored sets are available, from giant to pocket size. Parquetry tiles are good for simple random design or sophisticated studies of symmetry and optical illusion. Beautiful colored cards for matching designs of varying degrees of difficulty are available from educational suppliers. With or without cards, parquetry is an excellent activity in which unity becomes apparent and reveals itself as beauty. Worth buying, especially as they are difficult to make.

Tangrams. Every child should have a set of these ancient Chinese puzzle tiles that combine parquetry and puzzling in a remarkably versatile way. Magnetic ones are available for trips.

Construction

Construction Blocks

The youngest block builders are almost completely without skill. Nevertheless, as builders they are themselves models for us. They build without preconception—not to prove anything, not to impress, but to find out. If we teach our children to build towers for praise or a sense of power, we mislead them. But we can celebrate with them their small revelations of balance, stability, order. A few do's and don'ts. Don't channel, don't instruct, and when you build things, don't make them so spectacular that the child will feel discouraged. See what he is trying to accomplish with the blocks. Many children first "draw" with them, making long lines of blocks placed end to end. If you help, help him reach his objectives rather than imposing yours. A fun way to explore different ways of block building is for the whole family to build something together. Decide in advance how many blocks each person may add in each turn—two or three are about right. Let each person in turn add his blocks anywhere he likes. This activity is also good for learning to take turns.

Here are some worthwhile blocks and building toys:

Bright-colored one-inch wooden cubes designed for teaching math to three- and four-year-olds are also perfectly delightful for one- and two-year-olds for tabletop or highchair building and designing experiments. Little babies love them, too, so they can be bought early and used a long time.

Our four-year-old used them to invent and play wonderful games with his two-year-old brother. One was "You build what I build" (or the other way around), so patiently, block by block. "Is this the same? Is this? No, that's different. Which one looks like this?" He helped his brother learn colors ("Can you find another *red* one?"), numbers

("Now let's count them"), relationships ("Hey, let's build a stair!"), and patterns ("Here's a blue one, here's a red one, blue one, red one. Can you find the one that goes next?").

If you have room enough, corrugated *cardboard blocks* are lots of fun—large enough so that a stack of three is already rewarding, light enough to be managed, strong for climbing on, and no one gets hurt if they fall. Available in toy stores or from educational mail-order houses.

Wooden block sets. Small cubes and big cardboard blocks are adequate, but almost nothing compares with these. Various kinds, from small-piece tabletop to big-piece floor sets, are available. The latter are more satisfying but also more expensive. Buy a starter set and then add to it as needed. Make sure they are well sanded and have rounded or planed edges. And be sure to buy modular ones, with each block relating to the others in direct ratio. A really good block set is worth the investment.

Nonblock Construction Sets

Though a gaudy plastic toy may charm children for a few hours once or twice, they return endlessly to open-ended blocks, sand, clay, paints, and wood. One of the best things you can do for preschoolers is to let/help them learn to saw and hammer.

Wood scraps are more open-ended than blocks; blocks are more open-ended than construction sets. But in the whole hierarchy of manufactured toys, construction sets are more interest-sustaining than most, and contribute much to a child's pleasure, sense of spatial relationships, fine coordination, and repertoire of creative ideas.

In choosing a construction set, select the most open-ended one that fits your child's *present* skill level. Recommended are: Crystal Climbers, Tinkertoys, Bristle Blocks (or Multi-Fit), Lincoln Logs, and perhaps best of all, Legos. Large Legos exist for younger children.

Real Tools and Carpentry

There's nothing as nice for preschoolers as the real thing and real skills. A *pounding bench* is one of the best toddler toys around, good for children around age one, but by the time they are three, most girls and boys are capable of using a hammer and saw and drill on soft wood. A bag of nails, a hammer, a hand drill, and permission to go to work on the tree stump in the backyard is about all they need. Then, of course, there are beautiful tool benches available that are lovely to have if you *know* you will provide a steady supply of wood and a fair amount of help and guidance. Lumber yards have scrap wood to give away—choose only soft pine. Instead of buying a child's workbench, you can build a bench for her to stand on at yours. Or build a child's workbench yourself.

All you really need, besides a small twelve- to eighteen-inch *cross-cut saw* and a medium-sized *hammer* and maybe a *drill*, is a *vise* to hold the wood. A vise makes a big difference in preschoolers' sawing success, because they need both hands to saw. If woodworking vises are too costly, C-clamps will do. The advantage of vise over C-clamp is that the child can mount the wood in the vise by himself.

Teaching the proper care of tools is important whether or not a tool kit is purchased. Be sure to set up a good place for her tools and the ones you share with her.

Mostly the child will be happy just to hammer and saw. Give him some wire or rubber bands to entwine and stretch into designs on a board of nails. Hang up a "Bent Nail" original. And keep some glue available. When hammering and sawing become discouraging, gluing is glorious.

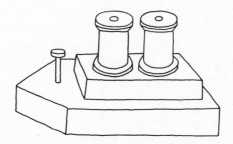

It is encouraging and satisfying to complete a few "real" carpentry products. A bath boat that really floats, a hook thing for neckties or kitchen utensils:

- The child cuts the board. (You may have to start the cut.)

- Together you sand it—perfectly (make the sanding the issue, not the child's willingness to stay with it).

- Supervised waxing and polishing.

- What a beautiful, smooth piece of wood this has become!

- Screw in the hooks (L-shaped) after careful measuring. You start and finish; he gives a few turns in the middle.

- Gift-wrap it for someone who will really hang and use it.

Like anything else, there's a time to help and a time to refrain from helping, a time to demonstrate and a time to refrain from demonstrating, a time for experimentation and (more rarely) a time for finished products. Be guided by what the child is ready for and what she wants to learn. Be open to your child's idea of what a finished product is. For a whole book full of doable woodcraft ideas for children, see *Easy Woodstuff for Kids,* page 155.

Mechanical Wonders

From small hardware items to tools and machines, mechanical things fascinate children and increase awareness of unity. Anything you can find that a child can safely work—*an eggbeater, a crank, a typewriter*—is happy and edifying for him. Hardware stores are full of toys for children. A great big nut and a bolt is a beautiful thing to a toddler.

Almost all children are fascinated by *keys.* They jingle nicely for babies and provide a growing challenge for the growing toddler who likes to fit things into things, and the older preschooler for whom opening and closing a padlock is a joy. Buy a good-size padlock and hide the extra key. Mount an assortment of latches on a board. Even better, cut a door in the board and attach it with real hinges. A better gift than two dozen junky toys.

Never miss an opportunity with your youngster to dissect an *old machine.* An old toaster or clock that is ready for the junkyard is a whole afternoon of investigation, the perfect opportunity to see, first of all, that things work, a little bit of how, and to practice using screwdrivers, pliers, and other real tools.

Water, Sand, and Mud

The more amorphous the material, the more can be done with it, the longer it will sustain interest, and the more can be learned from it. No toys for sale equals water, sand, and mud in entertainment and educational value, or long-lasting appeal. Like everything else in the world, these materials have symbolic meaning to be contemplated far beyond childhood.

Sandbox. Buy or build a wooden one (1-by-8–inch boards are about right), or make one from a half-sunk tractor tire, and just a washtub full of sand (or rice or cornmeal) and a few cups and spoons on the porch can be tremendously satisfying.

Sandpile. You don't have to have a sandbox at all. A mound/mountain of sand or soil in a corner of the yard may be even more fun to climb and work on. Just shovel it back together again from time to time to make it last a little longer.

Toy vehicles. While there are many beautiful wooden vehicles available, the most affordable and satisfying to children are the realistic metal ones. Among model vehicles, earth movers are the most fun, especially in a sandbox or pile of dirt.

Splish splash. Children don't need to be bathed every day for cleanliness, though regular bathing may be calming and soothing. But the bath is one of the best places for children to enjoy some quiet and uniquely private play. One mother tells of living in an apartment in which the only bathroom was off the kitchen. It was inconvenient in every way except one. She could fix dinner while keeping an unobtrusive eye on her child, and she found that all the best bath toys came from the kitchen. "I want da colander, please!" her two-year-old would call. Given a small trickle of running water to work with, the child played happily for nearly an hour each day before supper. Mother and child were equally refreshed by this period of quiet independence.

So take advantage of the bathtub, sink, a sand or water table, sandbox, the hose in that patch where the grass refuses to grow anyway, a rainy day, and the beach above all, amen.

Sticks, stones, and Popsicle sticks are more than enough equipment to keep a child busy with sand and water, but here are a few toys you might make or buy and some activities you might set up:

Sponge boats cut out of household sponges are good for scrubbing and sailing.

Plastic tube. Two feet of tube from any hardware store is good for blowing noisy bubbles in the bath.

Cups, colanders, ladles, funnels, and measuring cups from the kitchen are great for sand or water.

Bubble bath is fun for shoveling, modeling land- and seascapes, and for wearing.

Boats. Most cheap plastic bathtub boats are not a bargain because they capsize or sink. If they fill with water, they also mildew inside. A toy boat should be leakproof and buoyant. Buy or make a wooden one. Rubber-band-powered paddleboats are especially fun.

Bubbles. To make a *giant soap bubble,* rub a wet piece of soap along the side of your wet index finger and thumb. Close thumb tightly around index finger. Open slowly into a ring. Blow softly. If the ratio of water to soap is just right, you make a big bubble, equaled in size only by your child's wide eyes.

Water machine toys add to the fun and educational value of bath time. They come with small pumps and waterwheels and are mounted with suction cups on the side of the tub.

Gardening

Gardening is a wonderful thing to share with our children. The activity of growing things involves a concrete sort of praying together that makes divine providence evident. You begin by kneeling down and soon you have love and carrots sprouting up all over the place. At one and a half or two years old, a child can already enjoy and learn from planting, transplanting, and tending the garden. Even if you have no garden, on any spring walk, seedlings can be found pushing up last fall's leaves beneath the budding trees. Finding these sprouts under the soggy old brown leaves is a delight. Choose some promising ones and dig them up with a good clump of dirt. Take them home in an ice-cream cup or a pair of careful, small, bare hands. Plant firmly in small pots and water from time to time.

In autumn, maple seeds, acorns, and the seeds of pine cones can be harvested and planted. We grew a honey locust seed. Each night its leaves folded up; each morning they opened. Even indoors it had its autumn/spring cycle, complete with the falling and returning of leaves. At any season your child can tend an onion, potato, avocado pit, a knob of ginger root—there is no end to the wonders. Keep in mind that both the child and the plant are growing. If the plant appears to need water, you give it water; if it appears too wet, you refrain from watering it. If the child appears interested, encourage him; if he becomes bored, let him move on to the next thing, and you carry on with the plant. Let him help when he can and wants to, even if it's only in the finding of the sprout, the holding of it on the way home, the pressing down of the earth in the pot. Participation in growing things sustains interest, increases dexterity and botanical knowledge, develops the child's nurturing capacity—the patient waiting, the faithful caring, the joyful appreciation of growth, the mystery of it.

Some Good Growing Projects

• Set an *onion,* pointed side up, in the top of a glass or jar of water. The bottom of the onion should just touch the water. In only a few days it will send roots down and, soon after, leaves up. It grows with almost visible speed!

• Cut the tops off a couple of *carrots and beets* and put the tops in a flat dish of water. A few pebbles will help to keep them in place. New leaves will grow like crazy. It's an interesting way to demonstrate that different leaves grow from different plants.

• *Nasturtiums* are very satisfying for little children to cultivate. The seeds are big and obvious for little fingers to push into the soil. They can be grown indoors if placed in a window with lots of sun. They take quite a while to bloom (over a month) but meanwhile they produce many pretty leaves. From four or five seeds you may have as many as thirty blossoms open at one time. Pick them and more will follow.

• Plant, tend, and harvest *something edible* from seed—basil or carrots, for example. Carrots take a long time to grow—up to two weeks just for germination. But there is no hurry, and as a revelation of the miracle of growth and fruition, they are particularly wonderful for children. From the slow-growing seed so tiny and brown come the feathery green leaves up and at last the secret carrot down—to be tugged up all at once, so startlingly orange and crunchy.

For quicker results, sprout alfalfa seeds in a small, covered dish. Soak in lukewarm water overnight in a dark place. Drain and rinse with fresh, lukewarm water through a tea strainer or piece of cheese-cloth stretched over the dish. Continue to keep the dish covered and in a dark place, rinsing once or twice a day. In two or three days, when the seeds have sprouted and the leaves have opened, place the dish in a light window for a few hours to turn the leaves green. Now your child can eat them as a snack or in a sandwich, salad, or soup. Delicious and highly nutritious.

• Experiment with *seeds from your child's plate*—watermelon, apple, grapefruit, grape, squash, pear. Either green-thumb your way, hoping, or do a little research at the library. Some seeds need wintering. A day or two in the freezer is often enough to fool Mother Nature.

• Gift-wrap a little package of *narcissus bulbs* for your child to grow or give as a birthday gift for a playmate. Place bulbs on a bed of pebbles in a dish. Keep the pebbles in water up to the bottom of the bulbs. When the bulbs flower, place them near the child's bed so he can enjoy their lovely scent in the darkness and their pure glory in the morning.

Science Books

The early scientist/philosopher had one primary interest: to understand the nature of being. The old sage wanted to know what the facts meant. Nowadays we tend to think of philosophy and science as separate. Today the fellow who keeps a foot in both camps stands out as unusual. Children constitute the only large group for whom science and philosophy have always remained united. When a baby meets other living things—dog, insect—an earthquake happens in her. Hear her exploding laughter. "Eureka!" it exclaims. She may have no words, but you can see the marvel in her eyes. Give her the words!

In school she may not have "science" until third or fourth grade, by which time the world is divided into fiction and fact and she may already be pegged as a math/science or a language/literature "type." So it's up to us to help our children retain their innate sense that science and philosophy are just two sides of the same coin—being alive. Recognize her questions and help her find the words for them. Allow her life to be a scientific/religious experiment. And books—above all *books!* There are so many terrific ones to show a child amazing things and to give her the words for her amazing questions. What books? Let her interests guide you. Neither let interest die of neglect nor crush it by forcing. Just help her follow each interest as far as it goes. Library books are great for momentary scientific interests. Here are some books worth owning. (See also books on pages 155–158 and 336.)

Cooking up Learning, by Jackie Jundt and Lucy Rumpf. A wonderful cookbook for learning (science, math, social studies, life skills) and good times prepared by two nursery school teachers. Tested and found fabulous by scores of parents and children at home. Organized by season and perfectly tailored for the young child. A best must. Available for $5 from Jundt, 2340 St. Clair Ave., St. Louis, MO 63144.

The Children's Picture Atlas, The Children's Book of the Earth, The Children's Book of the Seas, by Jenny Tyler and Lisa Watts. Though not specifically designed for preschoolers, these three titles are excellent for family reference. Highly graphic and inviting presentations of a wealth of information in captioned pictures. Together a veritable encyclopedia. Usborne, 5 years and up.

The Cloud Book, by Tomie de Paola. "If you could hop on a bird and fly way up, you would see the whole earth covered with clouds." As much fun as a storybook. Increases a child's awareness and enjoyment of his environment. Scholastic, 4 years and up.

The Kids' Kitchen Takeover, by Sara Bonnett Stein. There is nothing quite so happy as an eight- or ten-year-old alone in the kitchen with this book, unless it's a preschooler and you in the kitchen with this book. Includes science, craft, cooking, and nature projects that encourage freedom and creativity. For example, "stir in a little milk until it gets as thick or as thin and gooey as you like." Workman, 4 years and up.

Mickey's Magnet, by Franklyn M. Branley and Eleanor K. Vaughan. The story of a small boy's discoveries with a magnet, including how to make one. A small magnet is included with the book. Scholastic, 3–8 years.

Science Toys and Tricks, by Laurence B. White. From bubbles in the sink to straws in wrappers—an introduction to the world as a science lab. Really easy directions for really easy science-powered tricks and toys. All are fun, none too elaborate, and each teaches. Addison-Wesley, 3–8 years.

The Science Book, by Sara Stein. As the jacket says, this book is "a feast for young science explorers." By the author of *The Kids' Kitchen Takeover,* who really knows how to talk to children about what interests them: about boys and girls and belly buttons, about people who can spread their toes apart, about molecules, and dog talk, and the shape of space. It's a book for older children—and for old children like me who want to bone up for their youngsters. Workman, 6 years and up.

Sharing Nature with Children, by Joseph Bharat Cornell. "A Parents' and Teachers' Nature Awareness Guidebook." If you're having a play group outdoors or if you just want your child to grow up with a reverence for nature, you may find the activities here helpful. Classified by age, type (e.g., calm or energetic), topic, equipment. Very thoughtfully prepared. Ananda, 2 years and up.

What Do People Do All Day? by Richard Scarry. Farming, mining, paper, electricity, the water cycle. This book, full of busy animal folk, is really an encyclopedia made fun and an indispensable introduction to the wider world. Random House, 2–6 years.

6

Beauty

i thank You God for this most amazing
day: for the leaping greenly spirits of trees
and a blue true dream of sky; and for everything
which is natural which is infinite which is yes

(i who have died am alive again today,
and this is the sun's birthday, this is the birth
day of life and of love and wings: and of the gay
great happening illimitably earth)

how should tasting touching hearing seeing
breathing any—lifted from the no
of all nothing—human merely being
doubt unimaginable You?

(now the ears of my ears awake and
now the eyes of my eyes are opened)

    —e. e. cummings, *Poems 1923–1954*

When Moses came down from Mount Sinai,
with the two tables of the testimony in his
hand as he came down from the mountain, Moses
did not know that the skin of his face shone
because he had been talking with God. And when
Aaron and all the people of Israel saw Moses,
behold, the skin of his face shone.

    —Exodus 34:29–30

Beauty is universally associated with goodness. But Me, Inc., who understands life only in terms of having pleasure (materialism) and exerting power, doesn't understand what beauty is. The Me, Inc. in us looks only to have and do beauty. Me, Inc. wants to have personal beauty and beautiful possessions. Me, Inc. envies beautiful and creative people, and associates beauty with visibility. As Me, Inc., we want to be visibly beautiful and creative and to have visibility in the eyes of others. Such motivations contaminate our way of being parents, reducing our children to art objects and projects of our own creation, valued only for how well they reflect on us. Me, Inc. involves parents with seeming rather than with seeing, and reduces family life to the staging of forced tableaus.

One man had always "been a good kid," completely accepting his position in the family tableau. As an adult he had continued to try to be what was expected and not to be what wasn't expected. But eventually his energy for doing that died until life seemed meaningless to him. With help he saw how he had been sculpted into something he wasn't, and he began to see who he was. One day in some old photo albums, he said, "I saw all these pictures of birthday parties, and they were all the same—the same family pose, the same birthday cake, the same stiff smiles, the same misery." A short time later his son had a birthday. "It was so beautiful," he said. "I wanted it to be fun, but I didn't know what he would like. So I asked him, and he planned the whole thing. He asked everyone to bring a joke to tell. And they all did. It was so great, and it was his own idea!"

Having and Doing Beauty

"Having" beauty translates into having good looks or things, including children that look good. Some of us spend fortunes to improve our appearance (and wind up looking worse than ever) or the appearance of our homes (and only wind up with clutter). "Doing" beauty translates into efforts to gain recognition as creative persons.

Here we suffer from such notions as lacking talent or not getting enough recognition. Failing to be personally creative, some of us seek recognition as connoisseurs of the arts, or attach ourselves to "beautiful people." All attempts at having and doing beauty have an artificial and superficial quality because the concern is with the appearance of goodness rather than with goodness itself.

As parents, Me Inc. seeks to use our children to have and do beauty for us. We want them to look good and to make us look good. We expect to get credit for our "little works of art." We doll them up, fuss over their hair, tell them to stand up straight and smile and be polite. In return they slouch and give limp handshakes and somehow manage to get their permanent front teeth knocked out or cut their own hair the night before Aunt LaLa arrives. We want to show off children who are talented. So without regard to their own interests, we give them lessons, and no matter how much they're made to practice, they make no progress. Celebrations like Thanksgiving or birthday parties become performances at which they whine, misbehave, or get sick, while we become witches or werewolfs and get migraine headaches.

> One man said that upon hearing of his mother's death, his first thought was *now I don't have to take piano lessons anymore.* Then he was sad about his mother, but first he was glad about the piano lessons.

As for the family, we have all these mental pictures of how our family is supposed to look—beautiful personal appearance, beautiful bodies, beautiful home, beautiful children, beautiful manners, beautiful relationships. Television sitcoms and commercials portray what we think we should be like and act like and how it should look. There is something awful about those ads. Because what if our children aren't *that* kind of beautiful? What if our relationships with each other aren't so beautiful? Shame on us.

Who's to say what's beautiful? Advertising agencies? And what gives a particular company the right to tell us what's beautiful? Me, Inc. does. More ugliness and unhappiness come from artificially trying to measure up to others' preconceived ideas of beauty than from any other source.

> A little girl with joy dancing in her eyes and news to share runs up to her mother.

"Your nose is running and your hair is a mess. First wipe your nose. Then tell me," says Mom.

So in a minute her nose is clean and her hair is fixed. But her eyes have died down and her shoulders are slumping and her mouth is hanging open.

"What did you want to say, dear?"

"I forgot."

By day, we nag children about their appearance, about doing better work. At night, when they are asleep and we sit quietly, their faces float before us like afterimages from a flashgun—so sweet and beautiful with mustaches of milk and jam. So the problem is not so much to bring about the beauty that should be but isn't. The bigger task is to recognize the beauty that is when we see it.

All Life as a Work of Art

One day a mother drew a picture of a child. She asked her two-and-a-half-year-old son if he'd like to add some clothes to the drawing. "I will draw a sweater for him," he said, and with a crayon he carefully drew a line around the whole drawing of the child.

When a young child saw a picture book illustration of the tail and hind legs of a dog, he frowned. "Oh, dear," he said. "He is broken. Where is the rest of him? Did it get cut off? How did it get cut off? Did he get deaded?" He did not infer that the dog was walking away until the page was turned. Then he could see the rest of the dog and that it was not dead, but going somewhere.

Beauty comes with seeing beyond the surface of what seems to be. The second child was not yet able to do that. It is something we have to learn. To appreciate the beauty of the first child's sweater drawing we have to see beyond the crude, inaccurate lines of her drawing to their significance. Rather than telling her how to fix her drawing, we see how perfectly and beautifully it expresses her sense that a sweater is warm and cozy and goes all around me.

The study of the beauty of art and music is called art and music *appreciation. Appreciate* means more than merely to like. It begins with valuing and is fulfilled in understanding. *Appreciation* is a synonym for *gratitude,* which is deeper than merely liking what shows on the surface.

It is often recommended that we take time to count our blessings, by which is meant the things we are glad about. But in true gratitude we appreciate the deeper significance of whatever presents itself to us. Recognizing that spiritual realization is the ultimate and only real blessing, our uppermost interest is to see what is so and what is not. Everything, good or bad, becomes a teacher and potential blessing, bringing further clarification of what is good and true—and what is not. Whether as hard lessons about what isn't or beautiful revelations of what is, both good and bad bring us "blessons" for which we are grateful.

A prerequisite and partner to gratitude is humility. With humility, even in the face of ugly appearances and discordant experience we are able to set aside our thoughts about what should or shouldn't be, and allow for the possibility that the only real problem may be ignorance. True gratitude is not possible without humility; humility is not possible without gratitude. Another name for this combination is prayer (gratitude) and fasting (humility). This is not sentimental religiosity. All life is a work of art. Every work of art expresses an idea that the artist has in mind about himself and life. Ugliness occurs when a false idea of who we are, or what life is, gains visible expression. At any moment each one's life is either Me, Inc.'s ugly artwork or a beautiful revelation of God. At any moment we can choose which to see and express.

> *For my people have committed two evils; they have forsaken me, the fountain of living waters, and hewed them out cisterns, broken cisterns that can hold no water.*
>
> —Jeremiah 2:13

Ugliness (ugly experiences, ugly situations, ugly moods) is the self-expression of Me, Inc. as something separate from God. Beauty, on the other hand, calls attention to something beyond itself. It takes shape whenever an individual Seeing Being through conscious awareness (oneness with God) becomes a vehicle through which God is expressed.

There are two artists shaping our lives. One is a faker. The other is the ultimate Old Master. The faker, Me, Inc., tries to paint a picture of itself as beautiful and brilliant in and of itself, and by contrast to everyone else. Its work is never of lasting value, because it can't compare with, or detract from, the Old Master's work. Only briefly does it dazzle, because it is phony and soon boring.

The most beautiful sights are those that force us to see beyond the seen to the unseen. True creativity is that sort of seeing. On a camping expedition a group of retarded adults camped and cooked out and rowed boats for the first time in their lives and had the most beautiful time—in the pouring rain. "I like camping," one camper told a reporter . . .

> . . . and the sheets of rain that streamed down on the bonfire seemed to touch some great fund of inner amusement in him.
> What did he like most, he was asked, the boating, the fellowship?
> "To be alive," he said, grinning as the raindrops dripped from his nose.
>
> —Glenn Collins, in the *New York Times*

In each individual the art of the master can be discovered. A seemingly retarded and homely camper nevertheless perceives and expresses his oneness with beauty, and in that moment is transformed into an unquestionably beautiful and creative individual. The beholder stands breathless as his first impression fades, revealing the hidden master's perfect work.

> How beautiful upon the mountains are the feet of him who brings good tidings, who publishes peace, who brings good tidings of good.
>
> —Isaiah 52:7

> For our light affliction, which is but a moment, worketh for us a far more exceeding and eternal weight of glory; while we look not at the things which are seen but at the things which are unseen: for the things which are seen are temporal; but the things which are not seen are eternal.
>
> —2 Corinthians 4:12–18

As any amateur painter quickly learns, an ugly appearance cannot be changed just by working on the surface. To find or express beauty, as with every good that we yearn for but cannot seem to bring about, we need first to understand what it is, and to recognize its source. The secret to realizing beauty is not doing or having but seeing. We are not here to look good but to see *and thereby be* good. The beauty is in the being.

The Single Eye

> *If my eye is to distinguish colors, it must first be free from any color impressions. If I see blue or white, the seeing of my eyes is identical with what is seen. The eye by which I see God, is the same as the eye by which God sees me.*
>
> —*Meister Eckhart,* trans. by R. B. Blakney

> *The five colors can blind,*
> *The five tones deafen,*
> *The five tastes cloy.*
> *The race, the hunt, can drive men mad*
> *And their booty leave them no peace.*
> *Therefore a sensible man*
> *Prefers the inner to the outer eye:*
> *He has his yes—he has his no.*
>
> —Lao Tzu, in *The Way of Zen,* by Watts

Since "beauty is in the eye of the beholder," it is the eye that must be trained, first to see, then to see beauty. Ultimately there is an inner eye with which to see inner beauty. The primary task in our quest for beauty is the discovery of this eye. To see anything clearly beyond the tip of one's nose, to see beyond the surface of a picture, beyond difficult circumstances, ugly personalities, moods and behavior, is an important step.

". . . *the eye* of the beholder." The use of the singular—*eye* rather than *eyes*—is important. The eye that beholds beauty is the single eye, the inner spiritual one rather than the physical two. Only the inner spiritual eye sees the beauty that is truthful, the truth that is so beautiful. What the spiritual eye sees of beauty, even in art and music, is beyond both sound and image. Spiritual truth consists of spiritual qualities—harmony, order, goodness, peace, grace, joy.

Even more valuable than what we see with the inner eye is what we become when we see it. In such a moment we become what we truly are—one with the One Mind, one with the infinite qualities of the One Mind, undivided from our source of being. When we perceive order we become orderly; when we perceive harmony we become harmonious. Perceiving spiritual reality, our lives become spiritual. Perceiving oneness, we become one, leaving no room for conflict. Perceiving truth, we become truthful. Perceiving beauty, we become beautiful. Whatever we see with the single eye finds expression in our lives.

How You Look Is How You Look

We are what we think
Having become what we thought
And joy follows a pure thought
Like a shadow faithfully tailing a man.

—*The Dhammapada,* trans. by P. Lal

The eye is the lamp of the body; if therefore thine eye is single, thy whole body shall be full of light.

—Matthew 6:22

I have never seen a spiritually alert individual who did not have beautiful eyes, with such spiritual qualities as kindness, merriment, and clarity. The look of our eyes conforms to our outlook. A conventionally beautiful person who lacks a loving, lovely perspective may strike us as not beautiful; whereas a so-called "homely" person with a beautiful outlook appears visibly beautiful as well. How we regard our children is how they will come to perceive themselves. How they perceive themselves is how they will appear.

Other People's Children

I had seen Bobby several times with his mother. She found him tiresome, trying, and hard to control, which she blamed on his supposed brightness. Like his mother, he was always impeccably groomed, with every hair in place. But he was demanding, brazen, and interrupted constantly—at once controlling and out of control. His eyes winced and flinched, evincing his own conviction that he was unacceptable.

Despite his physical handsomeness, at first I found him unattractive, too. Then one day I picked him up and gave him a lift home. "Nice day, isn't it, Bobby?" I said, secretly looking for the unique spiritual qualities that had to be there. "Oh, boy, is it ever!" he said, and began to tell cheerfully of his love of the early spring morning—the birds and chipmunks, the fresh smell of flowers and grass, the dew on the spider webs. His face was shining, and I was suddenly struck by what a beautiful, enthusiastic child he was. There, I thought, was a good place to begin.

The eye is not merely the instrument of seeing but also expresses and *calls forth* what is seen. Our lives can be transformed by our perspective on life—and other lives blessed as well. Therefore, in viewing both ourselves and our children we must learn to distinguish the superficial work of the faker and the deeper work of the Old Master—and thereby bring the real beauty to light.

Realizing beauty means affirming life's deeper goodness. It means we are interested to see goodness expressed; and when we see beauty to try to understand what goodness it is expressing, what particular spiritual qualities. Always if we see something truly beautiful we can find God behind it. It may appear in individuals or in homes, in our children, in works of art, in nature, but whatever beauty we see is some aspect of God, of love-intelligence coming to light.

To cultivate our ability to recognize and express and bring out beauty, we look at everything for what it signifies, to see what is of God and what is not. What are the qualities being expressed—divine spiritual ones? or not? And in seeking to express beauty ourselves, we look to see what spiritual qualities need expression in which circumstances. In this way we can recognize what will be lovely and beneficial.

> With three small children in a small apartment the family sometimes felt crowded and oppressed. They realized their need for peace and freedom. So they decorated their home around these qualities, emphasizing light and space with soft cool colors and white, with unmassive furniture that contributed a sense of peace and freedom. The result was surprisingly lovely and refreshing; the whole atmosphere changed, and people often commented on how spacious their apartment was.

What essential idea is being (or needs to be) expressed? If peace in the bedroom, perhaps joy in the kitchen? Or, with clothing, *what spiritual qualities am I meant to express in the world? What spiritual qualities are most called for in this particular situation?* We cannot impose a good appearance on each other or get "good taste" from each other by copying. The Old Master has a unique way of being beautiful in each life. It is an inner beauty that becomes outwardly visible through inner seeing—as an "outward and visible sign of an inward and spiritual grace." It is always original because it originates with the true origin of all beauty.

Creativity

Let your light so shine that men may see your good works and glorify your father which is in heaven.

—Matthew 5:16

I must be about my father's business.

—Luke 2:49

In seeking to fulfill our own creative potential and/or to help our children, it is good to remember that creativity is divine self-expression. This can protect us from apprenticing ourselves and our children to the faker, and can give us the privilege of watching and serving the Old Master at work.

Contrary to our usual impression that beauty is the artist's means of expressing himself, truly fine artists (composers, writers, dancers) are not interested in self-expression. It may start out that way as the personal ambition of child or parent, but along the way that self-ish motivation has to die until the artist becomes himself the tool through which truth expresses itself as beauty. Musicians must "lose themselves" in their music. Otherwise, even if they have the necessary discipline to learn technique, they will lack the inspiration to play or compose beautifully, or the needed assurance to present their gift to the world. Our task as Seeing Beings is to lose ourselves in love-intelligence.

A favorite toy of young children is the Play-Doh Fun Factory, an extruder through which amorphous modeling material is formed into a variety of shapes. Likewise when we are free of self-concern we become channels through which universal love-intelligence takes unique shape. Whenever we perceive a beautiful divine quality in some form, it becomes ours and can take new and unique expression in our lives. If at the ballet we appreciate grace, then, even without taking up ballet, we become more graceful, bringing grace into expression wherever we are, *and whatever we are doing*. We may live for years without recognizing the unique shape that God is trying to take in our lives or the lives of our children, unless we commit ourselves unconditionally to seeing and expressing love-intelligence. Then our unique purpose, and the unique individuality of our children, will take shape beautifully as well. But first we must give up our fixed ideas, whether about our own creativity or our children's.

Two Music Lessons

For years the boy dutifully studied viola. As was expected of him, he practiced and became quite skillful—good enough to play in a quartet and to impress the recital audiences of parents and children. Yet at fifteen, when his ability and need to make choices on his own burgeoned, he surprised everyone by giving up the viola. Someone asked him why, and whether he ever expected to take it up again. "No," he replied, "I couldn't see the good of it."

Attempts were made at music lessons, but the child religiously forgot to practice or, when made to, practiced without improvement, didn't show up for band rehearsals, and lied about his attendance. Parental disappointment and childish guilt and failure hung like gloom where music was supposed to have been. Finally defeat was accepted—well, almost. For months after the lessons were abandoned, just as the child had not been able to face practicing, the mother somehow failed to find time to return the rented instrument—the shiny horn remained in the front hall in its dusty black case.

Meanwhile something else happened, in three parts: (1) a new car, (2) with a tape deck, and (3) a commitment that placed mother and son together alone in the car each week—an hour each way. Otherwise, much of the time they were apart with separate busy lives, or together as supervisor and supervisee, dealing with daily shoulds—homework, meals, clearing the table, wiping the counters. It was an extremely busy time in both their lives, so the weekly trips proved to be an oasis between this and that and the other thing—and a very precious time together. With eyes on the road, neither here nor there, moving right along, these were shouldless times, characterized by mutual regard, a sense of refuge from the world, a time of freedom, joy, peace, laughter, and love. There was an assortment of tapes from the Beatles to Handel, according to the diverse tastes of the family. The mother steered the car, and the boy selected and played the tapes. Moving down the road, singing outrageously, he fell in love—with Pachelbel—and when they got home he dusted off his horn!

As the young ex-violist pointed out, the issue is to "see the good" of it. As the second child demonstrates, genuine recognition of the good cannot fail to bring about appreciation of its creative expression. We do not have to be concerned about what interest our children should pursue or what we are going to "make of their selves," but only with seeing the good.

So if as Seeing Beings we attend a concert, we are not looking enviously at what the other can do and wishing we, or our children, could do it too. And if as Seeing Beings we compose or dance or paint, we aren't thinking of how we look or what others are thinking of us or our children. Whether performing or creating or listening or looking, or mowing or cooking, our objective is simple: to see and become one with the good of God.

Artists

My father used to tell of a newspaper vendor in Chicago's University Station. Commuters went out of their way to buy from him. As the hurrying buyer extended his hand to pay, the vendor would slap a folded paper under his arm. In this way each transaction was made without the commuter even breaking stride. I have forgotten what I saw in museums as a child—I think this story did more to help me understand true creativity than all the trips we made to art museums put together.

Soda jerk was hardly a grand enough name for the master he was. He even placed our orders with flair. "Ham on rye—keep off the grass" meant hold the lettuce. But his best act was to fix a cola. Taking a glass in his left hand and scooping up a few ice cubes, he would then, with his right, pump in a little syrup, all of which was normal. The normality ceased and the marvel began as he threw the glass into the air in such a way that without spilling a drop it turned full circle, coating the entire inside of the glass with syrup before landing right-side-up in his right hand—just as his left was ready to pull the soda water lever down.

My grandmother passed on to me her beautiful grand piano, which then had to be transported across several states to my home. I did not expect to be transported in the process, but that is what happened. I hired a recommended piano mover and arranged to meet him at my grandmother's house. He proved to be a slight, almost fragile, elderly man. He arrived in a light pickup truck with an even older and frailer helper. With all of us so far from home, there seemed no way of backing out of the deal and sending the men home, but it seemed impossible that these two unhefty men could lift the hefty piano. "I used to lift pianos," the fellow commented quietly. "But I gave that up years ago."

With incredible precision and timing they obeyed and harnessed every physical law to maximum advantage. With only one brief exchange of words and no visible strain the two men removed the legs, swaddled the piano, and without even the benefit of a hydraulic lift, guided and glided the enormous piano onto their truck and secured it for travel in less than fifteen minutes. It was a ballet! A work of art! Pure love-intelligence did the job.

Sometime later three men, half as old and twice as strong, moved the same piano by brain and brawn. They removed more pieces from the piano to make it light, and with twice as much equipment and six times the muscle, succeeded in loading the piano onto their truck in four times as long. The piano was damaged in the process, and one of the men strained his back.

Parenthood and Creativity

Sometimes we experience parenthood as an interruption in our "creative" lives. But parenthood is an unmatched opportunity for growing in beauty and creativity.

Our children are models of how beauty takes place. They are drawn and driven by beauty. Thus they are naturally creative and, like Moses coming from the mountain, they are made radiantly beautiful by what they see. Even before they learn to speak in words, they talk in music. Dancing is not recreation for them; it's the only way to travel. Nothing is so beautiful as the way a child's face lights up at a sudden encounter with beauty.

As we strive to bring goodness to our beautiful children, we are forced to see more deeply, and thus to become more creative in expression. A special beauty comes of parental love and, whether or not we have previously identified them, our unique gifts are developed more and more.

A portrait-painter said, "I acquired most of the skill I needed years ago. But to be a real artist I had to come to see what makes a painting beautiful. Learning to love my children made all the difference."

Another spiritually alert artist was going to town on some errands with her three-and-a-half-year-old son along. She suggested to the child that they might look for beauty on their walk. "Perhaps you might collect some beautiful things and make a collage when we get home," she said. It was autumn. There were many beautiful things everywhere—leaves, acorns—and a crumpled red-and-white-striped package caught the child's attention.

As they trudged back up the hill toward home, the boy became increasingly awed by all the beauty-full things that lay on the ground for him to pick up. "Look, Mommy," he cried as he scrambled back and forth across the path. "This is beautiful. And this is beautiful. And this is beautiful. And this is beautiful! Why I could pick up everything for my collage." Suddenly his attention was lifted from the many beautiful things on the ground to an entire, outstandingly beautiful tree, aflame with autumn colors. He stood still and stared. "Oh!" he said softly. "The whole world is beautiful. There is nothing to be afraid of."

Perfect love casteth out fear.

—John 4:18

In an uplifted moment the child encounters, beyond the beautiful sights themselves, their deeper significance. Through beauty he encounters life as good, and the good is recognized as true, wiping away his fear that there is anything to fear. My book *Gently Lead: How to Teach Your Children About God While Finding out for Yourself* (HarperCollins Publishers) contains more examples of how a child can be introduced to God through nature. The above anecdote illustrates how spontaneously this happens.

As freedom is clearly related to fundamental intelligence, beauty is kindred to love. Freedom is a function of the fact that life is orderly; beauty expresses the fact that this order is good. Intelligence is cause, love its effect, beauty its aspect. Again consider the drinking glass, which gets its curved beauty through conforming to and expressing the inner purpose of the glass as a vessel. So does fundamental love-intelligence manifest itself beautifully and uniquely through each individual consciousness.

> When old age shall this generation waste,
>   Thou shalt remain, in midst of other woe
> Than ours, a friend to man, to whom thou sayst,
> "Beauty is truth, truth beauty,"—that is all
>   Ye know on earth, and all ye need to know.

—John Keats, from "Ode on a Grecian Urn"

Beauty and Spiritual Growth

Beauty occurs at the point where seeing becomes being. Once beauty is understood as the good of God, expressing beauty becomes a nonpersonal way of changing the subject from ourselves to God. We do not have to know how to do beauty, only to be aware of, and devoted to, expressing spiritual qualities. The simple commitment to recognizing and expressing goodness for the sake of goodness places us in the position where goodness itself can take charge and make itself plain. Beauty is the inevitable sign of an even greater blessing: the realization of our oneness with divine love-intelligence.

Moment by moment, we have the choice of expressing Me, Inc. or God. Whatever we put in charge of one moment determines the quality of the next. If ambition to look good is in charge, dishevelment, ugliness, and no creative inspiration ensues. But if love-intelligence is put in charge, beauty and creativity inevitably result. One beautiful love-intelligent moment leads to another.

The Parent as a Beautifying Influence

1. The Parent as a Model. The parent is a paintbrush through which God paints Self portraits. For such a parent, beauty, as evidence of God's goodness, is a high priority. A seeing parent endeavors to express beauty and to beautify the home through paying attention and calling attention to spiritual qualities, the good of God. Whether through personal appearance or creative activity or grateful enjoyment and appreciation, he expresses a constant love of beauty. He recognizes that expression of spiritual good is both the means and the meaning of beauty. He is characteristically grateful, joyful, gracious, lovely, loving, graceful, and thoughtful.

2. *The Parent as Beholder.* Insofar as we behold our children as Seeing Beings rather than as our own more or less pretty reflections and more or less talented creations, it becomes evident that each child is both uniquely beautiful and gifted. The essential spiritual goodness of the child is constantly kept in the forefront of our thoughts. Smiling to our children readily, and appreciating their beauty constantly, we assume, recognize, honor, and welcome forth this goodness, allowing it to take whatever surprising, unique, and beautiful shape it surely will.

3. *The Parent as Preparer of the Lovely Way.* Instead of being a slave to appearance or ambitious for creative recognition, the parent joins the child in recognizing and celebrating the good of God as it can be expressed in everyday activity. No task is regarded as uncreative. Every activity is approached not as a tableau or performance but as an opportunity to see, rejoice in, and bring spiritual values into expression as beauty. We look for and silently appreciate spiritual values in everything our children do and express our appreciation of them in our responses to them (not necessarily verbally).

4. *The Parent as Landscaper of the Beautiful Environment.* Everything in the home is designed to bring spiritual goodness to light as beauty. Whether in laying out their clothes or decorating the house or arranging their toys or serving meals, we seek to provide opportunities for our children to encounter and participate in spiritual values as beauty. Beauty is expressed not to impress others but to make God's love intelligible. Joy, simplicity, originality, variety, grace, order, peace, and love emerge as qualities of the home.

5. *The Parent as Teacher.* Creative activity is introduced as a medium for seeing and celebrating spiritual good. Music and art activities are approached not with the idea of making the child (or parent) look good but with the idea of helping the child encounter and see and participate in the good of God, and to discover her own individual

ways of expressing it. How to help becomes clear when we focus on the child's own spontaneous passions and interests.

Also evident in this light is the fact that it is as well to avoid much praise as it is to avoid criticism. In the beginning, at least, discovery is both the child's objective and her reward. The child does not seek *personal* praise at first; rather, all her activity is directed toward learning. Understanding and fulfillment are what delight her and will develop her unique talents. Personal praise is distracting. If we teach our children that praise is the reward, we impede their learning progress by encouraging self-consciousness and the growth of Me, Inc. Through praise we may be able to get them to *do* more, but only at the expense of perverting their motive.

Each time they turn *to* us for praise, they turn *from* their learning. And worst of all, in fostering a desire for self-acclaim, we introduce the possibility of self-doubt. In this way an appetite for praise and self-acclaim develops that will be less and less easy to satisfy as the child grows. Sooner or later it is inevitable for some of these motives to gain a hold in the child, but it is not necessary to introduce them prematurely, and it is possible to minimize them when they do come.

What then must we offer our children as they endeavor to learn (be it music, art, dressing themselves, or whatever)? Enthusiasm, love, gratitude! *Wonderful!* we can say. *That sounded so beautiful! You must be so happy to see it turn out that way! I love how bright that picture is! Thank you for showing me!* To the child, shared discovery and appreciation of what is beautiful in her work is worth ten times more than personal praise and actually furthers creative growth. (See also pages 131–132 and 217.)

6. The Parent as Art Supplier. The parent who is aware of the importance of beauty is able to supply the child with appropriate materials, equipment, and opportunities to help him grow in his ability to appreciate and express beauty. The two eyes and ears must be well trained before the true eye and the true ear can be awakened. See "Practical Information for New Parents" on page 268. Broken arbitrarily into separate sections on art and music, the main guidelines are invitation and letting be. There are not a lot of things to buy, though an abundance of art supplies and artwork, instruments and recordings, is good, since they are vehicles for invitation, education, and inspiration. Letting be is harder, but awareness of the child's quest for beauty can guide us in how to help without interfering.

Then I said, "I covet truth;
Beauty is unripe childhood's cheat;
I leave it behind with the games of youth";—
As I spoke, beneath my feet
The ground-pine curled its pretty wreath,
I inhaled the violet's breath;
Around me stood the oaks and firs;
Pine-cones and acorns lay on the ground;
Over me soared the eternal sky,
Full of light and of deity;
Again I say, again I heard,
The rolling river, the morning bird;—
Beauty through my senses stole;
I yielded myself to the perfect whole.

—Ralph Waldo Emerson, "Each and All"

I hearing get who had but ears,
    And sight, who had but eyes before,
I moments live who lived but years,
    And truth discern who knew but learning's lore.

I hear beyond the range of sound,
    I see beyond the range of sight,
New earths and skies and seas around,
    And in my day the sun doth pale his light.

—Henry David Thoreau, "Inspiration"

Practical Information for New Parents

This "Practical Information" deals with art, music, and poetry for very young children. Parents of older children may be interested in "No Such Thing as Tone Deaf" (page 279).

Art: Dwelling in Loveliness

When Nancy, our beloved high-school babysitter, returned from a trip to the Far East, she brought one of our sons a gift: an unusually beautiful, hand-made bamboo box with a lovely painting of a tiny bird on it. Every detail was exquisite. It was even lined with a polished veneer of bamboo. What an unusual gift for such a young child! On Nancy's next visit she took the child on a long walk in a city park. Some time after she had gone home, I happened to look in the box. Inside were two beautiful heart-shaped leaves from a beech tree. Now I understood what the box was for. It was given to help our son with an early, conscious appreciation of beauty.

Be sure to hang something pretty and moving over the crib and changing table—a lightweight *mobile*, out of reach, suspended from a cloth-backed stick'em hook. You can buy or make one. The more they move the better. And it's nice to change them from time to time. Give some thought to the baby's perspective. Many are nearly invisible when viewed from below. Either choose ones that are best seen from below or else hang them to the side or over the foot of the crib rather than directly above the baby. To add mobility to any mobile, tie it to a small swivel clip (used in fishing tackle). If you hang a swivel one within easy reach, it will be easy to switch mobiles from time to time without the use of a ladder.

Transparent plastic envelopes with safe, rounded corners are available from office supply stores. Put bright pictures or wrapping paper or photos inside and change them from time to time. With babies, high-contrast black-and-white designs are most easily perceivable and interesting. Great for the baby on his tummy. They won't roll out of reach, and they aren't uncomfortable if he tires and puts his face down on them.

Pictures on the wall: Some of the best windows to the world and beyond for wide, young eyes are the pictures on the nursery wall. Here, during those most private moments at both ends of a nap, children may take their first imaginary solo flights, examining and memorizing every detail of each picture, stepping through the frame and traveling into the world and beyond. Not all the pictures in a child's room need to be childish. Besides the many prints and posters available specifically for children, we can be grateful for the availability of reproductions of great masterpieces. Don't choose anything that might be scary, since the painting last viewed before the child's eyes close may accompany him into his dreams. Peace, beauty, joy, harmony—again, these are what to look for in selecting a painting or reproduction for a child's room.

The beauty that children live with becomes the beauty they appreciate when they grow up. A landscape painting can become the setting for stories you make up together, and perhaps for your child's dreams. Except for a few lovely pictures that may remain a permanent part of a child's room, it's good to change pictures often as the child learns all she can from them or moves to new interests. Hang pictures at her eye level. Hang some close to the floor in a hallway for the crawling baby.

Arts and Crafts

Though they sometimes require more parental supervision than toys, hardly anything is quite so fruitful, fulfilling, absorbing, and inexpensive as crayons, felt-tip pens, Play-Doh, paints, and glue. Crayons and Play-Doh can be introduced anytime beginning around one year, and the rest according to the child's readiness and your willingness to cope. Be willing. Set things up so that you don't have to be defensive about walls and furniture. This means either sticking close by or putting the child someplace where disasters are improbable. For the very young the highchair is good and augments concentration. Try the bathtub for fingerpainting. As he grows, having his own table will be handy, and an easel is wonderful. Many more ideas and instructions can be found in the books on pages 155–158 (especially, *I Saw a Purple Cow and 100 Other Recipes for Learning; Making Things; What to Do When "There's Nothing to Do"; Three, Four, Open the Door*). Here are a few ideas to get the ball rolling.

Crayons. Store these safely out of reach if you aren't fond of interior graffiti, but make them available any time after about one year. Don't make a big deal out of broken, peeled, or even chewed crayons. You and your child might decide to peel and break all crayons in half to begin with. A peeled half crayon can be used on its side for broad strokes of color. Good old crayons are fine. For preschoolers you may like the hexagonal ones that don't roll off the table, or extra-fat ones that make fat lines and can be fist-held.

Don't start by suggesting that the object is to draw something. Making a picture that represents something is a much later stage and will come (and perhaps also go) of its own accord. Just demonstrate things like dots! wiggles! lines! scribbles! If you take up a crayon at all, let it be to share with your child the discovery of *what happens when you do this with that?* Sometimes the child will be most interested in what he is doing with his hands; sometimes he will pay attention to the colors. After a while he will begin to *read* his pictures. "Hey!" said a two-year-old, "I drew many tiny fingers!" Try to see what he sees and celebrate the discovery.

Felt-tip pens are highly satisfying for preschoolers because they flow on so easily and brilliantly. Get the fat kind, and be sure the ink is washable. Washable doesn't mean that it comes off with a quick sponging or handwashing, but it does come off skin "by tomorrow" and off clothes in a washing machine. Teach your child to put the tops back on, but since felt-tips dry out quickly, be prepared to help a lot. If he is interested in his work, he will forget to put the tops on—be glad for the interest. For older children indelible markers are wonderful for decorating Easter eggs or drawing on wood.

Fingerpainting. To be honest, after a while I found fingerpainting at home too troublesome. But children do love it. Recipes for fingerpaint are included in several of the books listed at the end of Chapter 3. Small fingerpaint sets are generally not worth the money. You need lots of paint for each painting, and small sets are more box than paint. Maybe homemade paints are the answer, but quart and pint jars of fingerpaint are available for a good bit less than your time is probably worth. Glossy paper is needed—either special fingerpaint paper or freezer or shelf paper. At first many children hesitate to put their hands in the goo. Why, tell me, why? They are so willing to cover themselves with food! Don't insist. Just demonstrate the joys of fingerpainting yourself, put the paints away, and hang your painting up. You may even have to do this more than once before the child finally dares to dig in. Here's how:

- Wet the paper by dipping it in water or soaking both sides with a wet sponge.
- Place the paper on a large baking pan or edged cookie sheet to confine the mess.
- Spoon a tablespoon or less of different colors onto the paper.
- Spread the paint around with your hands and then paint in it (you could say "unpaint") with fingers. That's the conventional way.

Tempera paints may be more successful than fingerpaints with preschoolers at home. You can make these from dry pigments, but not very successfully unless you buy tempera medium and use a blender . . . once for each color—let's see now, that's—you figure it out. It may well be cheaper and easier to buy unbreakable plastic pints of pre-mixed paint. It's best to introduce tempera paints to a one-and-a-half- or two-year-old one color at a time. When more colors are used, provide a separate brush for each. It is also advisable not to put big jars before the child until the idea of not mixing colors in the jars is fairly well understood. Use smaller jars (baby food, junior size, is perfect), muffin tins, or paint pans.

Watercolors. For sheer pleasure, ease, and inexpensiveness hardly any paints equal a small cheap set of watercolors. It is surprising how early a child can learn to dip the brush in the water before touching it to a new cake of color. To make it easier, put a few drops of water on each color before the child starts to paint. The temptation to run the brush across the whole box of colors, playing it like a xylophone, is irresistible. The paints can be cleaned off with a damp paper towel rather than under running water.

Paper. If possible, never be in a position in which you have to refuse a child a piece of paper. Keep a small pad or notebook and perhaps some minipencils in your purse or glove compartment. Have a big pad of newsprint and a stack of construction or used computer paper at home. A big roll of shelf paper is great. Trace the whole child and let her decorate herself. Shelf paper makes good wrapping paper, adequate fingerpainting paper, and a giant surface for all kinds of creative activity on the wall or floor.

On a rainy afternoon invite another child over. Spread out enough shelf paper so that they can sit on it and make drawings all over the place. Draw a floor plan for playing with dolls, a landscape with railroad tracks for a toy train, fences to keep in toy animals, roads for cars, airstrips for airplanes. Build houses from blocks beside the roads. Hang a big sheet in the hall and let every member of the family or the birthday party add something to the mural. From smaller sheets of paper make books for your child to fill in. Offer to write down the stories she makes up beneath the illustrations she provides. Use newsprint, note cards, shirt cards, paper bags; brown wrapping paper is beautiful to paint on. Just don't run out of paper.

Easels. A good easel is a worthwhile purchase, if only because it makes painting so much easier on the parent and therefore more available to the child. Some are also chalkboards. Painting on a back-to-back easel is a pleasant way for two not-yet-quite-socialized young friends or siblings to be happily and busily together. Compact wall easels are also available. You can improvise (or buy) a modified version, trying to meet as many of the qualifications listed as you conveniently can.

Chalkboard. A chalkboard is a must, and the kitchen is a good place for it—with a high stool beside it. It's easy enough to draw a picture or write a message for the child while you're waiting for something to come to a boil, and she'll enjoy drawing and, soon enough, learning to form letters by your side.

Modeling materials. In the beginning (between one and two years) a soft play dough (commercially manufactured or homemade) is best, as most nonhardening clays are too stiff for young children to work with. Don't insist that he make something; just let him find out what he can do with the clay—squeeze it, poke it, pinch it, stick toys in it, cut it, scratch it. Make a clay slide that he can roll his clay balls down, or a nest for his clay eggs. Give him an egg slicer, rounded (never serrated or sharp) butter knife, rolling pin, apple slicer, and some of the Play-Doh Shapemakers and the Play-Doh Fun Factory, an extruder for forcing modeling dough into various shapes.

When, at around three years old, he wants to "make things," a slightly stiffer modeling material is nice, since dough models tend to slump and sag. Caran D'Ache makes soft clay in beautiful colors. There are clays that harden and can be painted with glaze for permanent keeping. Our son made a crèche of fist-squeezed figures as a Christmas present for one of our adult friends. She still sets it up each Christmas.

Printing with a pad. Printing with a stamp pad is fun. Large office-size stamp pads are more satisfactory than small ones, but the ink on them is indelible. Try brushing tempera paint onto the stamp. For stamps try anything. All kinds of vegetables are great (dry first with a paper towel). Press a leaf to the pad and then on paper. To avoid fingerprints, use two index cards: one to press the leaf to the stamp pad, one to press the inky leaf on the paper. Cards are also very nice for prints. If you use a big sheet of paper you tend to wind up with just a hodgepodge of stamped impressions, some good, some bad, but not worth hanging up. Also available are various stamp sets for kids, with washable inkpads.

Printing with a brayer. Cover a still-wet painting with a clean piece of paper the same size. Roll the brayer (or a rolling pin) back and forth to make a print. One picture may not be much, but (especially if each print is positioned differently), the two mounted and hung together may look terrific.

An alternative method is to use a pencil or nail to scratch a picture into a flat cake of soap or very soft balsa wood (available in quarter-inch-thick pieces from art supply stores). Roll the brayer in water-base printing ink (from an art-supply store) on a smooth surface (a sheet of stiff plastic or a metal tray). Thick paint can be used instead of printing ink. Roll the inked brayer over the etched surface of the wood (or soap). Use the inked wood (or soap) to make a print on a sheet of paper. Experiment. Usually it works best to put the paper onto the wood, but you can do it the other way around. Rub the back of the paper with a spoon or a clean brayer while it's lying on the inked block.

Printing with a screen. Cut the lid of a small cardboard box so that only the sides and a little bit of the top remain intact. Place a piece of window screen (larger than the opening) on it and staple the window screen securely to the sides of the lid. Place a piece of paper with a cutout or object in the bottom of the box and put the screen lid on. Scrub a toothbrush dipped in paint across the screen until the object has been silhouetted.

Rubbings. Go on a texture hunt with a piece of paper and a crayon or a pencil. Sidewalk, brick wall, wooden table, tree trunk, the bottom of a pair of sneakers, a leaf, or whatever looks interesting.

Skill building. An hour of cutting, folding, stapling, or paper-

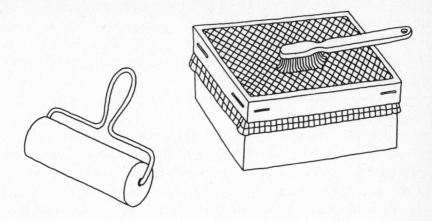

punching holes is fun and good practice. Scissoring is an activity in itself—not for making anything in particular, just cutting for the sake of cutting and the joy of simply using a tool. Fun and useful preparation for future art projects.

Trash-can sculpture. Make trains, houses, boats, and free-form sculptures by gluing saved-up cardboard tubes and boxes together. As another activity, paint or decorate them.

Wooden sculpture. A bag of wooden parts or some wood scraps from a lumberyard are fun to glue into structures or sculptures. The results are usually quite pretty. They may be left plain or, as another activity, painted. With a little extra parental help and some parts from a hardware store, a nice lamp for a child's bedside can be made this way.

Sand painting. Dye some sand with food coloring in paper cups. Spread the colored sand on baking pans to dry in the sun. Draw or paint with glue on paper, and sprinkle the colored sand over the glue (one color at a time). Shake off the excess sand. Dribbled glue drawings produce Jackson Pollock–type pictures. Brushed-on glue or paste yields more surface-covered pictures (à la watercolor landscape). This is a wonderful activity with beautiful results. Children as young as a year and a half can do it. It is so satisfying that it's worthwhile to dye enough sand in the summer to last through the winter.

Collage bin. Keep a bin of everything glueable—jar tops, beads, cartons, tree bark. Collecting and sorting these things can be fun, too. Try to arrange these items so that by age three, if he is interested, your child knows how to work with these materials without supervision.

- A table to work at and a covering to protect the table.
- An apron to protect clothing.
- A sheet of oilcloth or plastic to protect the floor.
- A sponge for spills and some training in wetting, wiping, rinsing, and squeezing out.
- A place to put finished works for drying.
- A place for trash.
- The obvious: glue, paste, scissors, paper.

Additional Activity. Try playing "The Squiggle Game," which my children enjoyed and which I have taught many others to play as well. All you need is paper and pencil. Close your eyes and make a short, simple scribble on the paper. Ask the child to look at it from different angles, and then, if she sees a picture in it, to complete the picture. Then invite her to close her eyes and make a squiggle for you to complete. For a discussion of how this game helps children to discover their own creative ability and the Beyond Personal source of inspiration, see my *Gently Lead*. A great activity for restless children in restaurants—can be played on paper napkins or the backs of paper placemats. Similar games could evolve using clay or paint, in which the players blindly squish lumps of clay or daub blobs of paint for each other to complete—"The Squish Game" and "The Blob Game."

The Whole Point Anyway

While creative freedom in artwork is crucial and should even be regarded as sacred, it is important that sloppiness not become a factor. Value beauty as it is sought and expressed in your child's work—not as accomplishment, not as pretty good for a little kid, but as beautiful. It isn't silly to say that the work of these little ones is beautiful. Spontaneous motion, brilliance of light and color, and striking form are often clearly present in the drawings and paintings of unhindered children.

If you see what is lovely in a particular picture, you will rejoice to hang it—not just to make your child feel good but because it is lovely and you would like to see it on your wall. The fact that you value your children's work enough to hang it encourages them to express beauty. Mount the child's painting so as to set off the beauty as clearly as possible. If your child is taking a birthday present for a friend, let her paint some wrapping paper for it, or wrap a gift in white shelf paper that she can decorate with felt-tip pens.

Sometimes after painting happily for a while, a child becomes aimless and sloppy in her work and begins messing around. Perhaps all she needs is a little companionship or help. If restlessness persists, it's time to stop. Always try to finish and thoroughly clean up while the spirit is happy.

It is one thing to make a pile of scraps while practicing how to use scissors, but when the objective is to make something, the end product should work. With crafts this involves careful planning and attention to the readiness of the child to do what's required to achieve a worthwhile result. When a project is undertaken with specific results expected, make sure that the activity is something the child can do and that the end product will satisfy. In a summer craft class for preschoolers the project one day was to make hats out of paper plates. The children worked all morning gluing things to the plates and painting them and decorating them according to their individual inspirations. But when the strings attached to the hats were tied under chins, the hats tore and fell off. A big disappointment. Lots of things can be done with scraps and trash, but the results should not be trashy.

Music: Going Forth with Joy

> For ye shall go out with joy, and be led forth in peace; the mountains and the hills before you shall break forth into singing and all the trees of the fields shall clap their hands.
>
> —Isaiah 55:12

Just Listening In

Crib bell. One family had a bronze wind chime from Japan hanging over their son's crib almost from the first day they brought him home. He loved its musical sound. The only thing they had found to hang it from was so low that the chime's paper sail was within reach of his foot. Soon he began accidentally ringing the bell by kicking, usually when he cried or was excited. This surprised and pleased him so much that he often stopped in mid-cry to listen. Eventually he discovered that there was a connection between his excitement and the lovely sound. The parents could see their son working on the problem. Gradually he discovered that general movement, and then specifically kicking, was what did the trick. Before long he could move around and grab the sail with his hand, so they hung a sturdier bell. From then on, he announced nearly all his wakings by ringing rather than by crying. Ding dong, guess who's awake?

Music box. It is nice to have one to wind up and play for stilling moments. (String-operated ones tend to break.)

Musical recordings are invaluable and unsurpassed for their many contributions to children. A lively tune inspires the child to dance, and it is through movement after all that the child can first really participate in, and feel, the music. Constant exposure to recorded songs not only helps develop musical skills and appreciation but also aids language and concept development. And through listening to recording, parents and children easily learn songs together. Recordings are better than television for eliciting active participation.

There are many musical toys and instruments for very small children (drums, pianos, horns, etc.), all fine at some point. But for babies, a bell and a music box seem sufficient. Wait until the real singing and dancing begin before adding other things.

Children especially appreciate shared times of singing and dancing when the harmony of music becomes the harmony of people together. It is special for a child to see his parents sing or dance together with others. Sometimes you can see a child's face become positively radiant with happy amazement upon witnessing such a wonder for the first time—at weddings or around campfires.

Private concerts. Ask (hire? invite?) neighboring grade-school children who are learning to play musical instruments to come and show their instruments to your preschooler and play a little tune or a scale. Ask the older child if he will let your child touch his instrument and perhaps even try to play it. Several families can get together—take turns performing and then have dessert. A Christmas concert with carol singing too? Tape it and play it back each year to hear the progress! We have very fond memories of our eighteen annual Christmas concerts. Toddlers played "Jingle Bells," teenage sitters played concertos, fathers sang "We Three Kings," parents and children played duets, and everyone clapped and sang along.

Chiming In

No Such Thing as Tone Deaf

When the boy was small he was fascinated by music, especially songs. Folk songs and musical comedies captivated him. He listened so intently that he would memorize entire records within only a day or so. Yet he did not carry a tune. His mother did not believe in tone deafness. She thought, *There is no such thing as tone deaf. He is perfectly endowed with every gift that God is.* Then she thought, *But if there were such a thing as tone deaf, he would be a perfect example of it.*

One day he said, "How come when everyone else sings, it sounds like singing; but when I sing, it sounds like talking?" That clinched it. There was nothing tone deaf about him. On the contrary, he clearly heard and appreciated the notes perfectly. But because he could not exactly match what he heard, he hadn't been trying. "Don't worry," Mom said. "It will come." Sure enough, very soon the tune "came in," and he has been singing and playing ever since.

Too many people labeled tone deaf as children remain so all their lives, never developing the skill of matching heard tones, never realizing the joy of music. Such a waste! To label a child tone deaf is like labeling a baby speechless when he can only say "goo."

Everyone knows that there's nothing like a verse or a song and the will to sing for turning a gloomy, boring, or struggling moment into a cheerful one.

A song at bedtime, a rhyme to shake hands by, a tune with ten verses for long trips—all have a cheering and harmonizing effect on our daily affairs with our children, and they all suggest that life is something worth singing about. When a child hears words that both rhyme and make sense, he finds order and harmony in a world that often must seem pretty helter-skelter. And when others sing with him or to him, he finds love. Repeated rhymes and songs aid a child's language development and help train his ear for an earlier, fuller experience of music. Even more, they add to his impression that joy and harmony are real possibilities and important priorities in life. All that—just for a song!

Poetry Books

Catch Me and Kiss Me and Say It Again, by Clyde Watson, illustrated by Wendy Watson. When you feed your child a snack, lift her down from a high place, pick her up from a tumble, a rhyme can always help to make light of it or make the most of it—whatever is called for. This book is full of rhymes to celebrate your youngster's life with a little extra love and joy. One Mother Goose–sounding rhyme for almost every ordinary thing a child might do. Indispensable. Collins, 0–4 years.

A Child's Garden of Verses, by Robert Louis Stevenson, illustrated by Erik Blegvad. Twenty-four of Stevenson's most charming and beloved poems about childhood made accessible to the young child through Blegvad's illustrations. Random House, 4–6 years.

Each Peach Pear Plum, by Janet and Allan Ahlberg. "Each peach pear plum. I spy Tom Thumb." And now *you* try to find Tom in the lovely full-color illustration. Children love to search the pictures to find favorite nursery book characters. Simple rollicking verse also tumbles easily into memory and can provide the basis for many "I spy" games with young ones. At first glance a quick and simple book, *Each Peach Pear Plum* has layers of value for the preschooler. Scholastic, 2–4 years.

Father Fox's Pennyrhymes, by Clyde Watson, illustrated by Wendy Watson.

Let the fall leaves fall
And the cold snow snow
And the rain rain rain till April;
Our coats are warm
And the pantry's full
And there's cake upon the table.

Whacky, joyful, grateful rhymes accompany charming pictures to depict the country life of a huge fox family. Written and illustrated by two talented sisters, *Father Fox's Pennyrhymes* contagiously transmits the happy spirit of their Vermont childhood. Definitely a book to grow up with. The perfect sequel to *Catch Me and Kiss Me and Say It Again.* Crowell, 4 years and up.

Nibble Nibble, by Margaret Wise Brown, illustrated by Leonard Weisgard.

One by one the leaves fall down
From the sky come falling one by one

And leaf by leaf the summer is done
One by one by one by one.

If you go to the library for a poetry anthology you will find many good ones to choose from, but you might not happen to meet this little collection of poems by Margaret Wise Brown, who knew almost better than anyone how to talk (in a whisper, of course) to little children. If you like her well-known *Goodnight Moon, The Sailor Dog, The Little Fur Family,* or *The Golden Egg Book,* try this collection. Young Scott, 4–6 years.

This Little Puffin, by Elizabeth Matterson.

Round and round the garden
(Run your index finger round the baby's palm.)
Went the Teddy Bear,
One step,
Two steps,
(Jump your finger up his arm.)
Tickly under there.
(Tickle him under his arm.)

Round and round the haystack
Went the little mouse,
One step,
Two steps,
In his little house.
(Repeat the same actions for the second verse.)

A good collection of musical games, action songs, and finger plays for all ages. The finger plays are especially useful with very young children and do not require musical skills on the part of the parent. Penguin Books.

Songbooks

If you don't read music, don't buy songbooks with many unfamiliar songs. On the other hand, you don't have to be able to play the piano or the guitar to use a songbook with your child. Just sit down on the sofa with an illustrated songbook and sing. A back carrier makes for wonderful singing and playing times at the piano with a very young child. Children are happy up there, where they can see comfortably and be rocked to the music. A lovely way to be lulled to sleep.

In choosing a songbook, size is not necessarily an advantage and may even be a drawback if you have to spend five or ten minutes between songs hunting for another that you know. Look for singable songs, with (if you also play) arrangements that are at once musical and easy enough for you to play and not too hopelessly out of your singing range.

Vast numbers of songbooks are available for young children. Some of the best are really better suited for groups. Most of the books listed below have been selected partly on the basis of their usefulness in the home.

The Fireside Book of Children's Songs, compiled by Marie Winn, musical arrangements by Allan Miller, illustrated by John Alcorn. An excellent selection of songs that appeal to children—sixty-seven of them divided into chapters: Good Morning and Goodnight, Birds and Beasts, Nursery, Silly, and Singing Games and Rounds. Guitar chords and easy piano arrangements. Simon & Schuster.

The Fireside Book of Folk Songs, compiled by Margaret Bradford Boni, piano arrangements by Norman Lloyd, illustrated by Alice and Martin Provensen. Alas, the best book of folk songs for the whole family that we have seen is out of print, but your bookstore may be able to find it by doing a book search. Includes traditional ballads, work songs, Christmas carols, marching songs, hymns, and spirituals. Easily playable, musical piano accompaniments and guitar chords. Simon & Schuster.

The Golden Song Book, selected and arranged by Katharine Tyler Wessells, illustrated by Kathy Allert. All the best-loved nursery songs, with pleasantly simple yet musical piano arrangements plus guitar chords. Golden Press.

Jim Along, Josie, compiled by Nancy and John Langstaff, illustrated by Jan Pienkowski. A perfectly superb selection of eighty-one singable, danceable, versatile folk songs and singing games for young children at home or in groups. Simple, *musical* piano arrangements by Seymour Barab. Guitar chords by Happy Traum. Lovely, unusual, black-and-white silhouette illustrations. Harcourt Brace Jovanovich.

Lullabies and Night Songs, music by Alec Wilder, illustrated by Maurice Sendak. Some of Sendak's finest work illustrates this lovely book of new and rearranged traditional lullabies. Harper & Row.

Playtime with Music, lyrics and text by Marion Abeson, music and arrangements by Charity Bailey, illustrated by Sally Michel. Sixteen fine songs just right for preschoolers to dance to and act out. Liveright.

Wee Sing, by Pamela Conn Beall and Susan Hagen Nipp. Two former music teachers compiled this excellent collection of more than seventy children's songs and finger plays, together with the actions and music. Sing your way through a whole childhood of car trips, rainy days, birthday parties, and other happy times. Price/Stern/Sloan.

There are a number of picture books that are simply illustrated editions of single children's songs. They are a source of great delight to young children who often do not understand the lyrics of the songs and who, in any case, enjoy learning more about them. Some fine ones to look for are:

The Erie Canal, by Peter Spier, Doubleday.
The Foolish Frog, by Pete Seeger and Charles Seeger, Macmillan.
The Fox Went out on a Chilly Night, by Peter Spier, Doubleday.
Frog Went A-Courtin', introduction by John Langstaff, Harcourt Brace Jovanovich.
Hush Little Baby, illustrated by Aliki, Prentice-Hall.
London Bridge Is Falling Down, by Peter Spier, Doubleday.
Old Macdonald Had a Farm, by Pam Adams, Child's Play.
People in My Family, by Jeffrey Moss, Golden Press.
To Market, To Market, by Peter Spier, Doubleday.
There Were Ten in the Bed, by Pam Adams, Child's Play.

The best songs may be those that you and your child make up together. Singing a song about anything, *especially* the most routine activities, reinforces the child's experience of life as harmonious, flowing, joyful. Lyrics don't have to rhyme; the tune can be different every time (or use an old tune). Narration or nonsense, one-line repeater or long-drawn-outer, a song relieves some situations and enhances others. A valuable sharing for you and your child.

Our family's best made-up song—from a winter walk:

Soft, soft snow is falling on my hair (face) (hand).
Soft, white snow is falling everywhere (every place) (on the land).
I hear the crow calling.
I hear the snow falling—soft, white snow.

7

Truth

In the beginning was the Word and the Word was with God, and the Word was God. He was in the beginning with God. All things were made by Him and without Him was not anything made that was made. In Him was life and the life was the light of men. And the light shineth in the darkness and the darkness comprehended it not. . . . That was the true Light which lighteth every one that cometh into the world. He was in the world, and the world knew him not. He came unto his own, and his own received him not. But as many as received him, to them gave he power to become children of God, even to them that believe on his name: which were born, not of blood, nor of the will of man, but of God. And the Word became flesh, and dwelt among us, and we beheld his glory, the glory as of the only begotten of the Father, full of grace and truth.

—John 1:1–4, 9–14

All of us, and all of our children, are words that God utters, individual points of divine self-expression, promises designed to come true. In Hebrew *words* are not just concepts or ideas to be looked up in dictionaries, but meeting places of speaking and hearing. If the word isn't spoken *and* heard, expressed and received, it hasn't occurred. For us and our children to come true we must truly meet each other in communication. As parents we must listen not only to what our children say in action, cry, word, and demeanor, but also to what God is saying as and through them. We need to pay attention to what we are saying not only in word and deed but above all through the way we are. What do our lives bespeak? What is our way of being expressing? Is it Me, Inc. or God who speaks through us? Are we trying to look great and be right, or are we seeking to come true and to help our children do so as well? Our children hear *how* we are better than what we say. So we must be seeing and *listening* beings, looking through all that confronts us to see what God is trying to show us, listening through whatever din of sound or fury surrounds us for what God has in mind.

But what we say, the words we speak, and how we communicate with each other are important, too. We all associate *truth, communication, ideas, language, speech, intelligence, understanding,* and *reality* with *words. Word* includes both concept and expression; it is the transition between *idea* and *expression,* the point where idea turns into event. *Idea* is the cause; *event* is the effect. *Word* is the transition between the two. So we recognize that language is important. We define our uniqueness as a species by the sophistication of our language. We know language development is important in children; communication is important in families. We recognize the power of the printed word when we say that "The pen is mightier than the sword." We know what we say can support and heal or psychically slay others.

Bridges

Some words are bridges, and after the bridge is crossed you don't need these words anymore. In this book, *Me, Inc., Seeing Being*, and *love-intelligence* are bridge words for helping us cross from some false understandings about ourselves and God to the shore of truer ones. It's a bit presumptuous to go around using coined words, but for crossing over they can be useful.

Me, Inc. and *Seeing Being* help us cross from who we aren't to who we are. *Love-intelligence* helps us to clarify what God is and what we are here for and what the good of it all is.

Why not just say *I* instead of *Me, Inc.*? Because it could mean either I/Me, haver and doer who is all wrapped up in itself, or the I that sees that I and my Divine source are one. *Me, Inc.* implies a self *in corpus* (in a body), incorporated, and calls attention to the fact that Me, Inc. is always in business for itself, and that it is often a nasty business. Me, Inc. is not a person, but it is a personal idea and a tricky imposter. It goes around looking for a place to call its own, convincing us that we are it—not only its place but *it,* its self.

Why not just say *God* or *love* or *truth* instead of *love-intelligence*? It is because they are loaded with many confused and confusing connotations. Sometimes Me, Inc. appropriates them for its own purposes, as keys for sneaking into our lives. Me, Inc. has a ring full of key words—want/will, have/do, right/wrong—which it misuses in the name of *love* and *truth,* and *good,* until finally Me, Inc. succeeds in getting *us* to impersonate *it!* even to believe we *are* it. This corporate takeover can ruin our lives if we don't watch out. But whenever we are watching out, the Seeing Being, which is what we really are, continues to wake up. When the Seeing Being is awake or at least on alert, Me, Inc. can't get a toe in the door or sit at the hearth of ourselves, because we are less confused by its confusions.

We have been observing Me, Inc. for some time now, and are fairly familiar with its tricks. So we are not surprised to find that Me, Inc., who approaches everything in terms of having and doing, looks to have and to do truth through using the word. To Me, Inc., words are vehicles of self-expression and the means to self-ish ends: what Me, Inc. wants and wills.

Having and Doing Truth

Me, Inc. the haver perceives words as sensational. Spoken words are sound effects. To Me, Inc., it feels good to talk. Whether words give Me, Inc. good or bad feelings, they make Me, Inc. feel that it is really something. Silence is intolerable because then Me, Inc. is not having any sensation—and no sound effects, no Me, Inc.

To Me, Inc. the haver, communication is a way of getting others to take care of our feelings. When our talk revolves around what we like and don't like. If we feel good when nice things are said about us and bad when bad things are said, we know Me, Inc. the haver is having its way with us.

With regard to intelligence, Me, Inc. the haver considers words to be containers of facts. He wants to feel that he has a good mind, and so is concerned with getting facts and storing them as information. He is a container corporation. He believes that words are fact capsules that are kept in his mind, which is his head. The more facts are stored the more Me, Inc. feels he has intelligence. He learns by rote. Sometimes he experiences not having a good memory, not grasping ideas. Sometimes he feels stupid.

As for communication within the family, Me, Inc. the haver wants to "have a say" and to "get a hearing." He uses speech to make demands for pleasure, whether directly as in "scratch my back" or indirectly as in paying compliments and hoping to get one in return. When these are our main concerns, Me, Inc. is in charge.

Concerning truth (the Word of God), Me, Inc. the haver regards truthful ideas either directly as experiences in and of themselves or indirectly as a means of bringing about pleasurable experience. Directly he may get "high" or have sensuous and emotional experiences from hearing "the Word." Indirectly he hopes to trade on the truth for pleasure. Viewing God as a source of potential pleasure, he may try to please God (meet God's demands) by giving up some pleasures in hope of gaining greater pleasures (having his own demands met). Me, Inc. is a believer. He believes in the power of belief. Just by believing "good" ideas, he expects to get good. He tries to incorporate the truth by rehearsing and repeating it. He tries to improve his experience by making positive affirmations. He expects thinking nice thoughts and words will produce nice experiences. When Me, Inc. the haver begins to suspect that his approach to life won't work, he imagines he is going crazy.

Me, Inc. the doer perceives words as powerful. He uses them as tools and weapons for bringing about what he thinks should be. Talking is a form of taking action and bringing about action. Me, Inc. talks to feel powerful and to exercise power. He often experiences the talk of others as exercising power over him.

For Me, Inc. the doer, communication often becomes verbal combat. His talk revolves around what he says should or shouldn't be. More than feeling good or bad, Me, Inc. the doer is overly concerned with being right. He feels strong and influential when people concur and comply with him. He feels great when people think he is right, devastated when they think he is wrong. Whether secretly or overtly, he tends toward (and experiences in others) bossiness, contention, argument, and persuasion.

Me, Inc. the doer, wants a powerful mind. Whereas Me, Inc. the haver views his mind as a container, Me, Inc. the doer views it as a generator or a weapon. To Me, Inc., words are power cartridges and formulas. Me, Inc. works with thoughts, flexing his mind to have the illusion of producing thoughts. Me, Inc. learns by figuring and calculating. He may appear certain, but he is subject to tremendous anxiety, doubt, dilemma, guilt, and indecisiveness, as by-products of the belief that his mind and what he says are, or ought to be, powerful.

Me, Inc. the doer uses speech to issue commands either directly, as in "Do what I say," or indirectly, as wit, in the hope of gaining recognition of his mental power. He seeks to gain command of the truth. He tries to master the Word of God and to do right in order to exercise control over life. He may view God's Word in terms of commands or techniques. He aims to use God's Word for personal power by being "in the right" and having "God on his side." He hopes that by doing what God commands he can make God do what he commands. He thinks that right makes might makes right.

Paul voiced the cry of Me, Inc., the doer of truth, when he said, "The good that I would I do not and the evil that I would not, that I do." When Me, Inc. begins to suspect his approach to life won't work, he experiences terrible powerlessness and the sense that life is meaningless.

Truth and Communication

We believe we are truly interested in truthful communication. Yet often we don't agree about the truth. We say we "aren't communicating." Parents complain of difficulties in communicating with their children. But when "communication problems" arise, it is wise to examine just what it is that is actually being expressed. Usually the problem is less with communication than with what is being communicated. (See also "A Word About Adolescence," pages 179–185.)

The Girl Who Said Kitty

There was once a little girl whose parents were eager for her to learn to talk. Diligently they spent much time trying to teach her the names of things. "Kitty!" they would exclaim—"Cup! Chair!"—trying to get her to repeat the words. The child was fascinated with the kitty, cup, and chair and she was entertained by her parents' animated behavior. But she did not learn to talk. Finally, one day when she saw the cat, she said, "Kitty." Great joy showed on the parents' faces. Hugs and kisses were bestowed on the child. She said "Kitty" again. More hugs and kisses.

A number of days went by and the little girl kept saying *kitty* but did not acquire any new words. The parents' enthusiasm for *kitty* waned noticeably, and suddenly the little girl began calling everything *kitty,* cup and chair included. The parents were dismayed and discouraged. "No," they said. "Not *kitty. Doggie.*" Eventually she said "Doggie," and the hugs and kisses were renewed. But with the coming of *doggie, kitty* disappeared. Now she called everything *doggie.* Even the cat.

As Me, Inc., we find ourselves trying to use our children to have and do truth for our own pleasure and sense of power. The girl who said *kitty* was getting the idea that the word is for pleasure. Because she had no idea what speech really is and does, she was not learning to talk. She thought speech was for getting hugs and kisses. Soon she would come to believe that learning was for praise—not for understanding.

The Boy Who Said Won't

A father expressed a desire for better communication with his son. Asked what he meant, he said, "Well, I have to teach him what he

TRUTH

should do, right? So I tell him to wash the dishes or take out the trash, but he ignores me or talks back. He says, 'Why should I? Who gave you the right to tell me what to do?' He won't do what he's supposed to do. So I want to know how to communicate better."

To him, as Me, Inc. the doer, communicating meant telling his son what to do. In a way the son was very obedient. He had adopted his dad's view that the issue in life and the purpose of speech was to exert power, so he communicated with his dad by saying "won't." They had plenty of communication around a mutual misunderstanding.

How Many Me, Incs. Does It Take to Change a Lightbulb?

While we all have different emphases at different times, we all behave as Me, Inc., both the haver and the doer of truth. Whether it enters through the ear or leaves by the mouth, whether it takes place between God and self or self and other, we all perceive the word as the junction of idea with effect. So we seek to understand the truth and bring it into experience by means of the word. Through the word we seek to bring to ourselves wanted pleasure and to bring about by ourselves what we will. It seems reasonable. Yet when we try to communicate our "reasonable expectations and demands" to others, we meet "unreasonable" opposition. And the more rational we try to be, the more irrationally we behave. Could our premise be mistaken? What premise?

In the comics when someone has a sudden understanding or gets an idea, this event is depicted by showing a lightbulb over the person's head. If our light-questing clown (pages 8, 20–21, 115, and 339–340) got his hands on the bulb, he would probably disconnect it, hoping to have it and to use it for himself. Dimwitted and futile as this would be, it is analogous to Me, Inc.'s misappropriation of words and *the* Word for himself. Only a lightbulb connected to its source can enable the clown to see and to be an intelligent Seeing Being rather than a bungling, grasping, grappling fool. The word, too, sheds light only when plugged into its source of power: God. The difference between Me, Inc. and the Seeing Being is in what is seen as the source and purpose of the word. As Me, Inc. we misperceive the word as the means for having our way with reality. As Seeing Beings we recognize that the word is the means whereby reality can have its way with us.

291

Connected to its power source, the word, like the lightbulb, becomes something illuminating to see by. This communion of word with source is the basis of communication. It is not the coming together of the seer and the word but rather the coming *to* light of the oneness of seer and word with their source. Light communicates through word and seer in unique ways, as illuminating guidance and inspiration and as seeing and being.

> *For with thee is the fountain of life;*
> *in thy light do we see light.*
>
> —Psalm 36:9

> *Thy word is a lamp to my feet*
> *and a light to my path.*
>
> —Psalm 119:105

> *My soul cleaves to the dust;*
> *revive me according to thy word!*
>
> —Psalm 119:25

> *My soul melts away for sorrow;*
> *strengthen me according to thy word.*
>
> —Psalm 119:28

The Child as a Truthful Model

> *Do not say things. What you are stands over you the while, and thunders so I cannot hear what you say to the contrary.*
> —Ralph Waldo Emerson, *Letters and Social Aims*

Young children develop language with astonishing speed and ease. They can master several languages simultaneously with perfect accents, very little mixing of them, no text, lessons, or tests. Some say it is the young brain that makes this possible and that in the entire rest of a human being's life it is never possible to learn languages as easily or as well as in childhood.

What is it about the young child's mind that gives it this facility for learning languages? I believe it is less what the brain has than what it lacks. The child does not at first think of having a mind, getting intelligence, doing well, being right, or having his way. He has something else on his mind. What is he primarily concerned with? With seeing and being.

Like computers, children at first learn language on a sort of on/off basis. The child's equivalent is true/false, question/answer, yes/no, *is/isn't*. Children do not successfully learn to talk in order to please or get praise, or even to exert power. They are motivated to understand and learn to talk in order to *find out what is and relate to it*. Once they understand the questioning and answering inflection of speech, language develops in a flurry. From "Peekaboo! *Where's* Mommy? *There* she is!" to "Is that the bear? No, that is not the bear. Yes, *that* is the bear!" the guiding and facilitating interest of children is in *what is so?* and *what isn't?* Their interest has little to do with pleasure or power. They learn speech to communicate, to come to conscious oneness with the truth of being.

That this is the way children learn is demonstrated negatively by both "The Girl Who Said Kitty" and "The Boy Who Said Won't." Both prove Emerson's paraphrased idea that "the way you are speaks louder than what you are saying." In both cases what the parents *said to do* was secondary in the child's mind to what they were *communicating about being*. Children approach everything with the assumption that by seeing what is real they can really be.

That this is a valid orientation in life is evidenced by the tremendous efficiency with which they learn and the extent to which their lives are transformed by their learning. Misled by their parents, the girl who said *kitty* and the boy who said *won't* demonstrate this efficiency negatively. But the vast number of children who, less distracted (or despite distraction), do master highly complex languages in so few years demonstrates positively that we are Seeing Beings for whom *seeing what is* is the best orientation.

Additional Reflection—The Pugnacious Children of the Pacifist Parents: During the discussion period following a lecture I had given, a lovely soft-spoken mother asked for some help. She explained that she and her husband were pacifists, and that they were doing their best to raise their children to be peace-minded, too, but that the children were fighting constantly. "And I don't mean really fighting," she said. "They are really violent! They say things like, 'I'm going to kill you,' as if they really mean it. We're pacifists, but we just can't seem to drive peace home." *Drive? Drive* gave me a clue. You can drive home a nail, a sword, a dagger, a home run, but you do not drive home peace. They were trying to *force* their children to be peaceful. But forcing begets rebellion, not peace.

Drive is an aggressive power word. These parents were not pacifists who valued peace above all. Rather they were people who feared aggression above all. So they always used soft voices and never acted angry even when they were angry, but they were very controlled *and controlling*. All their repressed anger and aggression was coming out through the wild children. The children were receiving the inadvertent yet loud and clear message and expressing it, loudly and clearly, back to the parents. The message was "the way to be is to dominate." That night the mother got the message, and began to reflect on *what* it was that she and her husband were communicating instead of on how to communicate more forcefully.

Pit Pat

So here comes little Pit Pat
up to us, listening
through those clear blue eyes
with 20/20 hearing
to every word we are.
She may or may not
understand the words we say;
But she listens carefully
to our much louder
pointing of view.
Her seeing hears every word
our being is saying.
She only sees in order to be,
and as far as she knows
the way we are
is telling it like it is. So
(regardless of what else
we are telling her to do
and how to do this

and why not to do that)
pit pat off she trots,
seeing being as we saw it;
saying her self
as we said ours;
being exactly
as she was told.
Poor little spitting image,
apple of my eye,
spitting at the sky.
But try as she may,
even with all our help,
Little Pit Pat can't
put out Old Sun.
Still, still it shines
and dries her face
and warms her hair
and lightens her way
and brightens her day.

* * *

For as the rain and the snow
come down from heaven, and return not
thither but water the earth,
making it bring forth and sprout,
giving seed to the sower and bread
to the eater,
So shall my word be that goes forth
from my mouth;
it shall not return to me empty,
but it shall accomplish that which I purpose
and prosper in the thing for which I sent it.

—Isaiah 55:10–11

Even a child is known by his doing,
whether his work be pure, and whether it be right
The hearing ear, and the seeing eye,
the Lord hath made even both of them.

—Proverbs 20:11–12

The Articulate Parent

1. The Parent as Word. The parent *is* the strongest statement that the child hears regarding what it means to be alive and real. More than what we say or do, the way we are expresses what we think it means to be alive. So the articulate parent is less a telling than a listening one. By listening inwardly to what is, we become to the child God's word about God. We are not Me, Inc.-expressive, but God-expressive. It is our questions more than our answers that lead to worthwhile communication So we rely less on what we think, and ask from moment to moment: *What is love-intelligent? What of God can be discerned or expressed here? How can the fact of love be evidenced? How can intelligent order be appreciably manifested?*

2. The Parent as Beholder. The child is God's word to the parent. By viewing the child as a word—for meaning and significance—we find we are being told what we need to hear. Whatever we discern of God in the child enlightens us. Whatever seems ungodly instructs us. The child's way of being "talks back" and explains to us our way of being is expressing to the child. We are thus guided by the idea of "first cast out the beam in thine own eye, and then shalt thou see to cast out the mote that is in thy brother's eye." Rather than defining and insisting on our own ideas of what the child should be, the articulate parent watches to see what God's idea of the child is. Constantly beholding the child as articulated to and by God, we distinguish the truth of the child from the false. As much as possible in thought and word we acknowledge and address ourselves to the true, ever turning the child over to God. We constantly behold our children as God's children and regard them as living and moving and having their being in God.

3. The Parent as Preparer of the Way. The best way to prepare the way is to get out of the way. With regard to communication, primarily this means to cease from "self-saying" and concerning ourselves less with two-way communication than with keeping open the channels for one-way communication. Thus we may help to preserve the child's natural inner hearing of God's "Still Small Voice." The Still Small Voice is always there to guide. It never ceases; it can only be drowned out.

> *A voice cries;*
> *In the wilderness prepare the way of the Lord,*

make straight in the desert a highway for our God.
Every valley shall be lifted up,
and every mountain and hill be made low;
the uneven ground shall become level,
and the rough places a plain.
And the glory of the Lord shall be revealed,
and all flesh shall see it together,
For the mouth of the Lord has spoken.

—Isaiah 40:3–5

4. The Parent as Preparer of the Truth-Centered Environment. Everything in the truth-centered home is oriented to discerning the expression of spiritual qualities. Attention is constantly paid to the question of *what divine quality is or needs to be expressed?* The atmosphere is shouldless, nonjudgmental. Space and time for quiet listening—both shared and private—are accorded high priority. Books, tapes, chairs, and lamps are thoughtfully located for effortless access. Reading, walking, and trips to the library may be frequent.

5. The Parent as Communicator. Communicative parents understand that true communication is conscious oneness, comm*union*, comm*uning* with truth. In speaking we aim not to control or tell so much as to bring the child, through conscious firsthand communion, to some aspect of truth. We no longer find ourselves saying, "How can I *get* him to eat? How can I *make* her behave?" Nor do we offer long verbal declarations or explanations of the truth. Nothing so cheapens the truth or closes the child's mind as preaching. As communicating parents we speak sparingly of "the truth," mainly only naming it when freshly inspired with what our whole being has already made plain to the child and what the whole child is clearly seeking to know.

Children respond much better to positive statements of what is and isn't than to negative ones of what should or shouldn't be. For example, instead of "Don't jump on the sofa," we might say, "The sofa is not for jumping. There is a better place for that. How about the mattress in the basement instead?" Or, "How would this be?" Parents who realize that conversation is shared participation in the discovery of truth and meaning more often ask than tell. "What do you suppose it means when the dog growls like that?" Not only words but also things and events are looked at for meaning. Whether or not God is mentioned, from evident blessings the child can learn to see that life is fundamentally ordered in favor of good. From apparent problems the child can learn to seek a lesson.

Communicating parents help their children learn to pray in the form of "listening to what God has to say" or "waiting" for a good idea or for love to "take place." It can be helpful to offer to wait prayerfully with your children during these times.

6. *The Parent as Supplier.* The articulate parent is guided in selecting and providing materials and experiences that can help the child grow in her ability to understand meaning and express truth, and to become aware that there is one love-intelligent mind constantly being expressed and that she can discern it directly. Primarily we seek to reinforce three convictions in the child: *(1) that life is fundamentally good and that she can continue to expect it to be so; (2) that problems can be seen through and transcended; (3) that she is not entirely dependent on us because guidance is directly available to her in moments of need.*

Such a perspective provides parents with love-intelligent guidelines for selecting good books for their youngest children and, as they grow, helping them learn to deal with so-called bad influences in the world. (See also pages 301–309 and 319–320.)

Truth and the Seeing Being

To the Seeing Being, words are turning points between idea and event. Seeing and hearing *through* the word with the inner, spiritual, or "single eye" and ear, the Seeing Being seeks conscious oneness with the One Mind. As money signifies, but is not, gold, so to the Seeing Being, the Word points to, but is not, God. Seeing Beings do not use speech merely to express themselves or to fulfill their wishes. To Seeing Beings speech is one way God uses them to express God. Waiting for inspiration from the still small voice is the Seeing Beings' way of letting God use them.

Being of No Mind—with the Father

As Seeing Beings we do not think we have minds of our own that generate intelligence. We understand that we are consciousnesses, which can receive guidance and inspiration from the One Mind. By taking time to set aside thoughts of future and past, wanting and willing, and what should or shouldn't be, we are prayerfully mindful of divine intelligence and receptive to inspiration, which can then be expressed as the living word, the word become flesh. Through such mindful attention we align our whole being with, and stake our life on, the idea that love-intelligence really is. We recognize the presence of God when our fretful state of mind gives way to establishment of a love-intelligent state of mind. We can recognize a divine idea by the fact that it is both surprisingly loving and surprisingly intelligent at the same time. If it is only *loving* but not intelligent, or if it is only *intelligent* but not loving, we are suspicious that Me, Inc. is lurking about.

> For though we walk in the flesh, we do not war after the flesh: For the weapons of our warfare are not carnal, but mighty through God to the pulling down of strong holds; Casting down imaginations, and every high thing that exalteth itself against the knowledge of God, and bringing into captivity every thought to the obedience of Christ.
> —2 Corinthians 10:3–5

All Life Is a True/False Statement

To the Seeing Being everything is a word. Like words themselves, the Seeing Being perceives everything as a symbol, as points where ideas become manifest. All people, all actions, all things, all feelings, all sights and sounds, all events are expressions of ideas and are therefore words or statements that may be true or false. All statements are self-expressive. True ones express God. False ones express Me, Inc. By looking at everything as meaningful words from this spiritual, true/false viewpoint, the Seeing Being keeps growing in consciousness, as everything both true and false increases awareness of God.

God's Word as the Seeing Being

The Seeing Being is herself a word of God—the turning point between divine idea and divine expression, between divine cause and divine effect, between intelligence and love. Becoming as a child, the Seeing Being understands that the whole point of seeing is not doing or having but being. And so it is that the Seeing Being with all her understanding is not after all preeminently knowledgeable but pre-eminently loving.

One word determines the whole world;
One sword pacifies heaven and earth.

> —Lao Tzu, in *The Gospel According to Zen,*
> ed. by Sohl and Carr

For the word of God is living and active, sharper than any two-edged sword, piercing to the division of soul and spirit, of joints and marrow, and discerning the thoughts and intentions of the heart.

> —Hebrews 4:12

Truth is always truth
untruth always untruth
this is what matters, this is right desire.

> —Buddha, in *The Dhammapada*, trans. by P. Lal

Through faith we understand that the worlds were framed by the word of God, so that things which are seen were not made of the things which do appear.

> —Hebrews 11:3

You must understand that One exists who is without not only speech but mouth itself, who lacks eyes, the four elements and the six roots of perception [in Buddhism the mind is a sixth sense]. Yet none can call him a void, for it is he alone that brought your body and mind into being.

> —Keizan in *Zen: Poems, Prayers, Sermons, Anecdotes,*
> *Interviews,* ed. and trans. by Stryk and Ikemoto

Words do not matter; what matters is Dhamma.
What matters is action rightly performed,
after lust, hate, and folly are abandoned
with true knowledge and serene mind,
and complete detachment from the fruit of action.

> —Buddha, in *The Dhammapada*, trans. by P. Lal

Influences: Good and Bad, True and False

As our children travel in ever wider circles and for increasingly longer periods of time away from home, we are inevitably concerned about outside influences. So-called "outside influences" invade our homes and our children like burrs on socks and radon, arriving by cereal box, fourth-class mail, Internet, and commercial-singing kids brandishing toy weapons on television. Television sponsors proposition children with everything from cosmetics to electronic games. Even educational programs that rely on fascinating sounds and animation not only teach children to read but also foster their dependence on constant entertainment. Some say it is "under the influence" of what they have seen on television or in movies that a child commits murder or a young man tries to assassinate the president of the United States.

We are shocked when drugs, alcohol, and guns turn up in grade school. We would like to withdraw our children from the world altogether when we find these horrors haunting even the lower grades. To the suggestion that it is only what we as parents cherish, fear, or hate that influences our children (see page 30), our first reaction is fearful denial. But a second look, from a spiritual perspective, makes this after all a hopeful and promising thought. If it is only our cherished beliefs and values that capture our children's interest, then they are not completely at the mercy of the world at large.

We can't change the whole world for our children or keep them from the world. But we can keep custody over our thoughts and values. While our children are barraged with all the world's mistaken ideas, it is only certain ones that "take." Honest self-searching of our own unconscious and unquestioned values can help us recognize and reevaluate these mistaken ideas. *If my child is not good at sports, will she be accepted? If he cannot beat others and be a winner, will he be a loser?*

Do we overly *cherish* acceptance by others? Do we secretly equate being worthy and loved with having what others have, doing what others do, belonging to what others belong to, looking as others look? As Me, Inc., we all fall prey to some of these ideas, and there is always some connection between our cherished, hated, or feared ideas and what our children cherish, hate, or fear. What truly holds *no* interest for us is unlikely to capture our children's attention—at least not for long. Sometimes the relationship seems contrary. If we overvalue success we may spawn either a breathless achiever or an individual dogged by lethargy and failure. If we are overconcerned with social acceptance we may spawn a child who is either an insincere "operator" or a wallflower.

Desire for acceptance is particularly prevalent and insidious. It is striking that in the addict's language a dose of narcotics is referred to as a "fix." Do all our loving attempts to "fix" our children so that they will be accepted only give them the idea that they are unacceptable and need to be fixed? Are a teenager's first experiments with drugs only attempts at being accepted? Is it only when having a "fix" that they find relief from the nagging sense of personal shortcoming and unacceptability? Sometimes what we are most against turns out to be our children's positive passion. When this happens we need to look deeper to see what we are inadvertently transmitting to our children. Remembering the mother who wanted to "drive peace home" (p. 294), consider the following example:

> In our son's nursery school carpool there was one boy who was fascinated by guns. The other children in the group could take or leave them, but when they went to his house they always played cowboys or cops and robbers or soldiers as he insisted. Guns were all that he wanted to play with, talk about, or read about. Yet his father was a pacifist who had done alternative military service as a conscientious objector. Both he and his wife were strenuously opposed to guns!

At least for young children, there is really no such thing as an "outside influence." The only influences on them are "inside influences." Sometimes when we want our children to leave us alone for a while, we actually influence them to watch too much television. In other words, to control our children we give them over to the control of others, many of whose values are horrendous.

Whether inside or outside influence, the basic idea of influencing is itself an insidious value. The desire to exert power, be successful, have what others have, to have "clout," impress, please, be in charge, be accepted and influential—all express a belief in the false value of *influencing.* As long as we attempt to influence our children to give us a break to shun this or choose that, we are teaching them that influencing (that is, exerting personal willpower over others' minds) is what life is all about. From such a standpoint the things we say we hate—crime, war, alcohol, narcotics—may seem attractive to our children as means of exerting influence over others.

Realizing that there is no such thing as an outside influence, we can also discern that no personal influence is a good influence. The Seeing Being parent comes to understand that *the only good influence is truth itself.* We learn to be less concerned with exerting a good, strong influence on our children than with what from moment to moment is influencing us. Our prayer is likely to be similar to Paul's: "Let that mind be in us which was also in Christ Jesus." When we are more concerned with being "in our right mind" than with having or putting across "right" thoughts, inspired ideas arise as needed to free our children from the influence of false ideas and to raise them to be uninfluenceable custodians of their own consciousness.

> In our town children referred to playing electronic games as "wasting quarters." "Hey," they asked each other, "want to waste some quarters?" While our sons were not encouraged to spend their money this way, one day while waiting for a take-out pizza I offered my son a quarter to play one of the games in the pizza parlor. "No thanks," he said, "I don't waste quarters anymore." "Good for you," I said, putting the quarter away. Then I thought about what kind of a statement I was making. Would I only give him money if he was going to "waste" it? A minute later I gave him the quarter to pocket.

Immunization Rather than Ignorance

Be ye wise as serpents and innocent as doves.
—Matthew 10:16

If each of three children in one family is allowed to select one half-hour TV program per day and to watch the others' selections, and if they watch two additional hours on weekends, then in fifteen years each will have spent more than a full year of twenty-four-hour days sitting in front of the television set! In many homes favorite programs govern activities, determine mealtimes, interrupt responsibilities, and weaken resolve. Some parents feel guilty about the amount of television their children watch. The Seeing Being realizes that TV or not TV is not the question, that even the good or bad content of shows is less important than the problem of mesmerism and addiction. The real issue is how to be conscious, addiction-free, discerning, and discriminating individuals.

Some families solve the couch potato problem by not having a television set. This can work, as can devices that preselect what and how much children watch. I say, good for them. But many children who feel "deprived" of television at home spend as much time as possible watching it in friends' homes. We can't protect our children from the influence of harmful values simply by turning off the television any more than we can keep them home forever or revamp the world before they get there. Merely keeping them in the dark is no protection and, in fact, can make them vulnerable to "forbidden fruit." In one family disposing of the television to make room for other things may be the way to go. In others the TV remains something to reckon with.

The principle of immunization is that injection of small, harmless doses of a disease rouses the system's defenses and strengthens it against further exposure. Mental immunization against unhealthy values can actually take place through watching television. Television mirrors the world's fantasies about itself. Popular shows reveal popular values. However crudely portrayed, it is the public's own secret desires that characterize successful shows. Many popular programs suggest that sex, power, and possessions are the most important things in life.

Our children will need to be able to move about in a world where such values are worshiped without actually falling prey to them. Thus, with all of its bad influences, TV can provide a fairly safe laboratory for confronting, seeing through, and thus being immunized against unhealthy values so as to be "in the world but not of it."

Who's in Charge?

I remember when I began to be aware that the TV habit had grown too large. I realized I had relied on TV to babysit our boys when I needed to get things done or have some time to myself. But this practice had gotten out of hand. I set some needed limits. I knew if I forbade them, then I would be in control, but that if I did nothing the TV would remain in control. Either way the children would be controlled, passive, gullible, and "under the influence" of one thing or another. I wanted them to learn to make good choices for themselves.

I reflected on what was so objectionable about excessive TV watching and presented it simply to my children: "When you are watching television you only get ideas that the television people want you to get. If you aren't watching TV you may get some other ideas—ideas meant just for you. Maybe they will be the best ideas you have ever had in your whole life. And they will come to you first-hand—they won't be somebody else's secondhand ones."

My sons were fascinated. "I'm going to try it," said one child, walking away from a favorite show. "Me too," said the other, all excited. "I wonder what ideas I'm going to get." They turned off the set and trotted off to their rooms, transported with enthusiasm and scientific curiosity. For several hours they played. Old toys were rediscovered, new games invented. One child began to write a play. They saw. They really saw something about how you have to be available to good ideas for them to occur to you. They learned something about mental hygiene. They saw that TV can interfere with inspiration. After that I still had to set limits, but I knew they had caught an important glimpse of their own capability to be inspired.

Try It, You'll Hate It

How manufacturers attempt to influence parents by influencing children in television commercials hardly needs to be discussed. Our children are programmed to plead with us to buy things. We can tell them it's junk, but to them it looks fabulous. We can say what goes and what doesn't, but wouldn't it be better if they could discern for themselves? Sometimes we just have to be firm, but sometimes we can recognize opportunities for letting our young Seeing Beings see for themselves.

The Ghastly Green Disappointment

Our children fell for a television commercial in which children were riding through a field on cute green inchworms. You could just picture yourself riding this friendly creature through a sunlit daisy field, conversing with chipmunks and rabbits. This time, instead of just saying no, we decided to test market the thing. Excitement was high as we drove to the store. Maybe we would bring one home!

Down rows and rows of toy-laden shelves we sought the coveted mount. At last in aisle six we found it. What a disappointment! Dwarfed by tall metal shelves, there on the drab linoleum floor drably stood the oh-so-plastic-and-lifeless inchworm. Having come this far the kids resigned themselves to a test ride. One noisy ride clinched it. However they'd thought it would look and feel, it was not like that. Though they'd seen it with their own eyes on TV, somehow something had been left out.

Even the toddler could tell that it would be tough, if not impossible, to ride through a field. "It's awful!" he said. The other didn't even bother to take his turn. After that they were less seducible. Marketing experts could aim all their weapons at them—sound effects, animation, and laughing children—but they were never completely convinced. "Wouldn't it be great if that was really great?" they'd say. "Could we take a look at that in the store and see if it's any good?"

The Best Thing in Life Is Life

Crummy toys and awful values aren't all that TV peddles. In itself the inclination to watch excessive TV expresses another, even worse value: that happiness is to be entertained by facsimiles of life. Real life, real active living, becomes associated with unpleasant effort and boredom, passivity with pleasure. Incredibly, we buy it. Next to TV our own lives look humdrum, so we watch TV for vicarious excitement, trading in our real living for the counterfeit lives on the "tube."

Our children can safely test out the crummy toys that are advertised, but we don't want them to test out all the false values they see. Will they have to become junkies or get pregnant or wind up on Skid Row to find out what isn't "the life" after all? Will they have anguish about not being sexpots, superstars, superjocks, or superheroes before realizing that these weren't such great goals to begin with? There must be a better way. Finding a better, truer, truly fulfilling way of being is the key.

If you've already eaten, you aren't hungry. Often, disgusted, we say, "Can't you find something better to do than watch that dumb show? Turn it off and find something better to do." Grumbling, they obey, but are bored. A room full of toys and he's bored? In fact, he's lying on the dining room floor, rocking back and forth, humming to himself—just waiting for life to happen to him. So turning off the TV is not, in itself, the answer, because the problem isn't TV so much as the false belief that happiness means being entertained; it's the lack of a truer, better idea of what it means to be alive.

This brings us to question our own values again. Do we equate pleasure with being passive or have we some lively interest? Are we helping our children develop their interests by providing time and supplies as needed each day?

> Our children went through a Mommy I'm Bored period, which coincided noticeably with a particularly busy time in my life when I had little time for anything except work and putting meals on the table. So for a while we began to set aside the last half hour of every day for "something creative." We made things with clay, painted, drew, and had puppet shows together. No matter what "had to be done" we made sure to protect this special creative time. I admit that we didn't keep it up, but the idea was planted and its benefits sampled. After that, sometimes the children would even walk away from a favorite show to "do something I've really been wanting to do and now's my chance."

Especially helpful is a good reading habit. After years of bedtime books most children develop an enthusiasm for reading. It is not uncommon for book-loving children to turn away from what's on TV in favor of finishing a book.

> "Mom, are you busy? If you are, could I watch TV? If you're not, could we do something together?"

Putting "first things first" is a good best way to deal with any ignorant values that rise to capture our attention or seemingly influence our children. Putting first things first is the same as what is meant by the first commandment: "Thou shalt love the Lord thy God with all thy heart and with all thy strength and with all thy mind—and thou shalt have no other Gods before me." For Seeing Beings this means valuing and having no priority ahead of love-intelligence. That's not just religious gobbledygook; it is a way of letting truth take charge of our lives. When *what is* is in charge, *what isn't* has little influence.

Earlier we saw that the necessary and practical are points of contact with the essential and spiritual. Here we see it again. At any moment that we stop to consider and commit ourselves to whatever is love-intelligent, love-intelligence takes over. Homework, practice, clean room, table setting—whatever the mandates in any family may need to be are put first with only some exceptions. And when priorities are set intelligently on a first-things-first basis, other things find their proper place.

Given a healthy set of priorities, most children are too busy to spend much time sitting before the tube. Helping them discover that they have better things to do immunizes them against false values—whether presented on television or in "real life." The child who finds fulfillment in music or reading or cooking or swimming or writing or drawing is less easily convinced that he needs recognition or power or possessions to feel worthwhile and good. TV or not TV, outside or inside, right or wrong, good or bad influences—these are not the questions. To be or not to be is the question.

Additional Reflection—Reading, Self-Esteem, and Spiritual Practice

A good reading habit teaches children that they are good company. Learning to be peacefully alone with oneself facilitates confidence for being with others. While a book can be a place to hide from the world it can also be a launching pad for being in the world. A child who knows herself to have real interests has something to share with others. A child who is comfortable alone with herself is also comfortable with others. A child who discovers her expansive space imagination is also able to play imaginatively with others.

The capacity to "lose oneself in a book" also develops a child's capacity for spiritual practice. If she sees that a quiet read in the middle of an anxious, upsetting, or boring day brings peace, calm, refreshment, and inspiration, she has encountered firsthand what it means to prayerfully reorient oneself in a larger, spiritual context than self and other. For more about this, see my *Gently Lead*.

Seduction of children by mindless and harmful television programs, video cassettes and games, films, Internet "chat rooms," and so forth is not only harmful because of the often inappropriate content and values, but because addiction to constant passive entertainment inhibits individual, creative, psychic, and spiritual life. It teaches children to fear silence, solitude, and peace, and it cripples them socially.

Good films, whether on television, VCR, or in a movie theater, are wonderful, but when the value of a good "read" is lost, much more than reading and intellect is lost as well. If love of reading is undeveloped or lost, the individual development and self-discovery it affords are also lost. The situation is even worse today than when *Whole Child* was first published. The sinking of children's selves and lives into hours and hours of television has reached psychically and spiritually dangerous, if not disastrous, proportions. So, please, read, read, and read some more to your children! Start early and don't stop.

Practical Information for New Parents

Babies, Books, and Learning to Talk

Many are surprised to hear that books can be used with children under a year old. In fact, the right book may be worth a dozen toys even for a child who can't crawl yet. You know your little striver is tired, yet when you try to hold him close, he struggles out of your arms and wriggles away. Just snuggle him into your lap, open a big book around him, and see what happens. After hours of looking at nothing but the floor without craning his neck, here suddenly is the world in Vista Vision—a whole new view of it on every page, with everything he couldn't get to on his own coming to him instead! Experiment early—around five or six months of age. Try different books at different times. No interest? Try again soon. Never insist, but don't give up too quickly either.

What's the hurry? It is not to push our children or fill them with information or qualify them for Harvard. Language is the thing. Books are a gateway to the freedom of speech. A common assumption is that books aren't for children until they can talk. But a good picture book can help a child learn to talk. Through learning to talk the child gains freedom to find out what he needs to know, to orient himself and navigate in the world, and above all, to seek and find meaning in life.

As soon as a baby can play peekaboo she is ready for her first book. A way to tell if you are starting books soon enough is whether or not she tries to eat them. If she thinks a book is something to eat, you are starting right on time. First she must do a taste-and-tussle test. A cloth book to chew, an old telephone book to tear, will do for a start. (Doctors assure us that no child can be hurt by the amount of telephone book she tries to consume.) The telephone book is a disposable practice book for the child to use by herself. A big urban one will outlast its usefulness no matter how much it gets torn, crumpled, eaten, drooled, scribbled, or painted on. To the child it is a wondrous block that turns out to be made of a thousand smooth, flat, thin things that she can flip and that sometimes flop back delightfully by themselves.

The first time you show her a picture book she may try to pick up the things pictured on the pages. But after a few times she will switch to simply patting the pictures. What a revelation for a six-month-old— those round-looking things are flat! Those flat things look so round! She may also try to grab the book and tear or chew the pages. You just have to be on hand, protecting the book until, having explored all its physical properties, she learns to turn pages and knows books are for looking.

Learning to Talk

By the time our babies are three or four months old, it is good to talk to them in phrases, especially ones that help them discover the idea of question and answer. Just naming things is not the point. "Do you see the fish? Is *that* the fish? *Yes,* that's a *fish!*" Hide-and-seek and peekaboo games help, too. "*Where's* Daddy?" "*There* he is!" She discovers that *"where is?"* and *"what's that?"* mean seeking, and that *"there it is"* or *"yes! that's a . . ."* means finding.

Suddenly our question and answer inflection begins to make sense. The question expresses her desire to understand. The answer celebrates her finding out. A few single words may come first, but the question will come quickly. "Whassa?" "Dassa!" "Deresa!" Once she has cracked the code, there's no stopping her. Don't overcorrect pronunciation. If she points to a telephone and says, "Dophone," and you say, "No, it's a *tele*phone," she may think, "Oh, that's not a telephone?"

Instead, say, "Yes [i.e., I understand what you mean and it's true], that *is* a *tel*ephone." Words of more than one syllable often get the sounds scrambled. When our son jumped out from beneath the bed, shouting, "B'kee!" we realized he was trying to say *peekaboo*. "Yes! *Peekaboo,* we see you!" we answered. *B'kee* grew into *buh-ka-pee* and finally *peekaboo*.

If we can teach them that speech is the means of formulating their endless questions, and if we can learn from them to sincerely ask questions, our children will talk sooner and learn more; we will talk less and learn sooner (and more).

Story Times Shared and Private

An immediate benefit of an early introduction to books is cozy times they give us together. Reading can provide some of our most inspired and happy times together. It's not only what's in or comes through the books but what happens between us when we share a book together—the mutual growing awareness, the communication. Reading takes our minds off each other by refocusing on something else. Books are vehicles for relaxed and refreshing travel together.

Odd Times

Some days are just wrestled away. The parent plans to play with the child "just as soon as my housework is done." But the housework is endless, the phone keeps ringing, the child keeps messing up the house and whining, and the more you try to get her to wait the less she can. Children don't have to come first all the time, but sometimes they need to be reminded that they are high on our list of priorities and that love is always available. Sometimes we need to be reminded to put love first, and after we do, things go more smoothly.

A quick story can be helpful. Ten minutes of reading, right off the bat at the beginning of the day, may free you both to go separate ways for a time. If she's writhing on the floor wrapped around your ankles, before you feel like running away from home, try a book. "And when we finish the story, what are you going to do while I vacuum?" That bedtime is storytime is obvious. But try books at odd times, too—

at the end of a nap or at a meal. A great way to change the subject when the subject needs to be changed.

Private Times

The child who is read to becomes a child who can enjoy private time. *If I get ready for bed now, will I still have time for a book? Oh, good, tomorrow's Saturday and I can stay in bed longer and read. While you buy the groceries, may I wait in the bookstore?* We know that books are an unmatched resource for providing concepts, information, and entertainment, but the book habit per se can be an important mental hygiene practice. Here are some ways that a good book habit contributes to a child's mental health.

• *Peace.* In our society many people find even a few moments of peace and quiet uncomfortable. Yet Seeing Beings *need* peace. Peace is an opportunity for inspiration, a time to reestablish conscious contact with God. To take the time to read a book, we must first drop many of Me, Inc.'s concerns. The child who enjoys a quiet, private read is also cultivating an appreciation of, and tolerance for, peace.

• *Discipline.* When you tell a misbehaving child to stop, often he is unable to. So we realize a little discipline is in order. Discipline means teaching. When a child is misbehaving he is being a disciple to a mistaken idea. Before he can stop, the mistaken idea must be replaced. The old-fashioned tactic of sending him to his room is not bad. But let him choose a book on the way. Losing himself, even briefly, in a joyful, funny, or lovely book may be all it takes to put joy, good humor, and love in charge of him again. For little Seeing Beings this shifting of viewpoint is a good preliminary exercise in prayer.

• *Self-esteem and assurance.* These days the overemphasis on relating to others leads to a tendency to feel lonely and unsure when there are not others around or to be anxious and attention-seeking when they are around. Ease with others is desirable, but its prerequisite is ease with oneself. Books are a doorway to appreciation of solitude. The child who discovers the joy of quiet book times has a refuge from both loneliness and excessive interaction.

Read-Ins

In our house Friday night was the most shouldless time of the week. No homework pressed and there was plenty of weekend ahead for chores. On Friday night life made fewer demands on us, and we made fewer demands on each other. So on these evenings we had more time for, and found it easier to be with, each other. Instead of games, movies, or television, sometimes we had "read-ins." Sometimes we read stories aloud together, sometimes different ones to ourselves. "Is it a quiet read-in or an out-loud one?" the boys would ask. Long before they actually learned to read, for a "quiet read-in" they'd choose stacks of books, maybe ten apiece, to "read" to themselves by quietly studying the pictures and thinking over the familiar stories. So even when they were very young we had quiet read-ins, and even when they were older we had out-loud ones, from long books that kept us in suspense from week to week. We didn't do this as often as we meant to, but there is no question that read-ins are to be counted among our best family memories.

Reading Stories to Preschoolers

Many picture books with real stories are too complex for children under five. But with a little help, much younger children can use these books to more advantage and for longer periods than the older child. A storybook can serve first as a word book, then a concept book, only eventually becoming a connected story adventure. While an older child may soon wander off on his own firsthand explorations, the lap-sitter, less free to roam, benefits greatly from the discoveries he makes in books about what's what and how it all adds up. Simple techniques for reading aloud to pre- or barely verbal children:

• *Read the child more than the book, the pictures more than the text.* At first you may merely have off-the-cuff conversations about the pictures. *Do you see the truck? Yes! Vrmm, vrm—there it goes! Oh, what a nice soft puppy! Yes, you are patting the puppy!* See what interests her, what she does and does not understand. Speak in whatever terms she can understand and only as long as she remains interested. It's easy to tell when she loses interest because she begins to wriggle away. Talk about clear communication!

- *Let your fingers do the talking.* Pointing may not be polite in society, but when reading to little children, always point. Even tap audibly on the pictures. At least half of what we say probably means nothing to her. If there are twenty-five animals on the page and you want to say something about the mouse, point to the mouse. You can play hide-and-seek or peekaboo this way, too. Ask *"Where's* the bear?" Then, pointing and tapping with your finger (or the child's), ask, "Is *that* the bear? No, that's *not* a bear. It's a *dog.* Can you find the bear? Is *that* the bear? Yes, *that's* the bear!" This is both clarifying and fun. "I see a mouse on this page, do you? Can you point to the mouse?" Sometimes we "walked" our fingers all over the page looking for things "Yes! There's the mouse! What is the mouse *doing? Sleeping? Eating?"*

- *Storytelling.* Once the child is familiar with basic words and concepts in a book, he may be ready to understand the story. Unless the text is exceptionally simple, it's usually best at first to boil the story down into words and sequences he can understand. Gradually introduce him to the idea that one thing leads to another by summing up key events. Announce each one clearly.: *and now . . . and then . . . and suddenly . . . and after that . . . and then what do you think happened?*

- *Finger telling.* Finger dramatics are also helpful for introducing children to discover story continuity. Tracing events as you read, pointing to the characters and showing, for example, who threw the ball and where it went, also helps to explain the appearance of the same character in several pictures. Unless we show with our fingers that this bear who walked out the door with his hat on is the same bear who is now putting on his pajamas, children may think that the book is full of many bears that just happen to look alike.

- *Pantomime.* Simple acting out of words and events makes all the difference in whether or not the child knows what's going on. She may know the word *throw,* but have no recognition of it in the past tense. A throwing gesture when you read "He threw the ball" makes it clearer and more fun.

- *Question and answer.* Simple questions encourage the child to verbalize and help him discover that books are means of finding out. Through question and answer you also discover what he does or doesn't understand, and what does or doesn't interest him. From simple "Where is the—?" you can move to unspoken questions, pausing silently and inviting the child to fill in the blank. Sometimes children are also drawn in by intentional misreadings that invite them to make corrections.

- *Expression.* Reading with lively expression makes the reading more interesting and provides clues to the meanings of pictures and words.

- *Abbreviation.* Some say not to speak to children in less than full sentences. But short brief phrases may be clearer. You can fill in more words as she is ready to understand them.

- *Filling in the rest of the story.* Once the tracks have been laid and you are sure the child has a general idea of the story's direction, you can begin to run the whole train over him, adding car after car at whatever pace is appropriate. Eventually you may be able to read the full text. Once he is clear about what is happening in the story, he may happily listen to even the most sophisticated words and details. Even words you don't explain will eventually become clear. He'll guess many from their context, and the rest will be decoded later, perhaps from hearing them used in other situations.

Selecting Books

The books recommended in earlier editions of *Whole Child* were selected from among thousands reviewed. I believe they were among the best available at the time and can still be regarded as prototypically good. So I have not substantially changed this list—not only because too many books have been published since then but also because the books already listed I had the opportunity to test on young children. Until the publication of *Whole Child,* all books for young children were lumped into the category of K (kindergarten)–3 (third grade). I believe my system of classifying books, specifically for preschoolers and, more specifically, for preverbal to talking and reading children, was the first of its kind. For choosing and using your book selection (and helping older children to do so), and for deciding which to buy and which to borrow from the library, I hope the following guidelines will be helpful:

- *Truthfulness.* Good questions to ask are: *What is this book saying about life? Will it augment or diminish the child's sense of enthusiasm, com-*

petency, assurance, confidence, humor, peace of mind, kindness, understanding, and freedom as he goes forth into the world? Every book makes some sort of a statement about life. The best do so in an unspoken way while telling an entertaining story. Better to borrow rather than buy those that offer important messages but not in a sufficiently entertaining way to be reread many times. Sometimes a child chooses books with really awful values. By reading and talking them over together, we can help him discover healthier ones.

• *Artistic value.* Is this a well-written and -illustrated story that will enhance the child's appreciation of good language, literature, and art? *In both art and text does it foster the child's awareness of beauty by being well crafted and designed, graceful, original, beautiful?* For preschoolers important qualities of beauty are clarity, simplicity, vitality, brightness, and joy. Finding actual stories that very young children can enjoy is especially difficult. In many books the text is only a flimsy excuse for the pictures, or too sophisticated, or just boring. Children lose interest in such books after only a few readings. Comprehensible interest grabbers and holders such as *Goodnight Moon* are rare and priceless.

• *Educational value.* In assessing nonfiction books a good question to ask is: *Does this book offer skills or information the child needs or craves and couldn't pick up more easily, cheaply, or satisfactorily elsewhere?* On this basis I exclude most counting and ABC books, but include "passion books" (e.g., dinosaur, truck, horse books for children with special interests), activity books, and only those concept books with a little something extra, such as Spier's *Fast–Slow High–Low.*

• *Entertainment value. Will the child like it and enjoy it? Will it effectively sustain her interest?* We may think it's good *for* her, but if it doesn't seem good *to* her, buying it is a waste. Is the ratio of text to picture appropriate, or will she be bored before it's time to turn the page? If it seems worthwhile but too long, can it be simplified while reading aloud?

• *Dollar value.* All things considered, *is this a good purchase, a better borrow, or an oh-forget-it?* Many fine books are available as reasonably priced paperbacks. Especially for preschoolers who don't yet get around much, it is good to have many books. Even some mediocre ones are worth having to give the child freedom of choice. Some are worth buying in hardcover no matter what. I felt that way about *Little Pear* and *The Poppyseed Cakes.* Consider probable mileage, long- and short-range value to the child, your child's individual preferences. When in doubt, head for the library to try before you buy.

Books and Buoyancy: Values in Children's Books

It is commonly known that things often happen to us according to our expectancy. The person with a sunny outlook tends toward a sunny life experience. Free of suspicion and fear, he moves with assurance, friendliness, and good humor, thereby attracting predominantly pleasant responses from the world. Difficulties roll off his back and he makes his way through adversity with strength and assurance, learning from even bad experiences. The fearful person is always on guard, approaches others with suspicion, and interprets difficulties personally as discouragement, failure, or persecution. Such attitudes tend to be self-perpetuating and self-fulfilling.

But don't we have to teach our children to be realistic? Don't they need to learn the hard facts of life? Don't worry, they will. Positive thinking and whitewashing is no solution. But painting a black picture is also false and troublesome. When selecting books for children, the most realistic ones are those that help children *realize* their potential for a full and meaningful life. From stories children derive ideas of what to expect in life and how to respond to what comes. Well-meaning problem-solving books address such issues as sibling rivalry head-on, but many of them only create fear and anxiety in children about situations they would otherwise take a step at a time.

Sometimes children catch from these books the very problems they were designed to solve, as well as a subtle general message that life is a problem with which they may or may not be equipped to deal. In this sense, so-called "realistic" books may, in fact, be the least so. Especially on the preschool level it is best to look for stories—whether "realistic" or "fantastic"—that reinforce the child's positive expectancy of life and his confidence in his ability to respond to it. This is less a matter of providing answers to specific problems than of letting him know that he's capable, that even problems are likely to bring revelations of some new good.

The arrival of the helpful policeman in *Make Way for Ducklings* may give your child a sense of trust that if problems arise, help will be there. The resourceful character in *Pippa Mouse* may give him confidence in his own ability to discern and carry out intelligent ideas. Let him know that life will support him even when he makes mistakes, as with the duck in *The Story About Ping*.

Even rather gruesome fairy tales about evil creatures and people can help a child deal with "bad" fears and angry feelings. From them he learns that these things can be lived through, that even after terrible losses life goes on, that even if he makes awful mistakes, he will be supported and forgiven. In short, let your child's books increase his sense of buoyancy—his own buoyancy coupled with the buoyancy of life. Let him know that he is *see-worthy* and that weighing anchor does not mean sinking or being adrift.

Good Books for Children

A good children's book is like an onion, with layers and layers to be discovered. Young children enjoy endless readings of one book, if they keep finding new things to understand in it. Once they have gotten the answers to all their conscious and unconscious questions, interest tapers off suddenly. They ask for a favorite story, but before you have read three pages they begin to wriggle away. It's time to retire that book and find another. Sometimes the retirement is temporary and in a few months they're ready to discover a new layer of meaning. Sometimes years later a book they loved as little children will suddenly come to mind, bearing an important and needed message.

Here, in four groups of increasing sophistication and difficulty, are some of the best storybooks we found for preschoolers. Not all of these books are in print. They come and go. Hopefully you can find them or new and equivalent ones in the library if not in the bookstore.

Stage One Stories

These books are for the child who has a vocabulary of single words (twenty-five badly pronounced ones will do for a start). At first they can be used as word books, then as connected ideas, and finally most of them can be used as real stories. These pre- and first stories introduce connected ideas and prepare the way for real stories. Most are set close to home. They are good for an almost endless number of readings.

Best Word Book Ever, by Richard Scarry. If you had to buy only one book for the first two years, this would be a good one—1,400 lively captioned pictures of things, actions, and animal people, grouped helpfully around such topics as getting dressed, the airport, and so forth—and full of little almost-stories. Useful from as young as six or seven months as a word book until the child is three or four years old as a storybook encyclopedia. One of the first books our children "read" to themselves, immersing themselves in the pictures, and coming up for air only to ask questions. Random House, 6 months–4 years.

Big and Little, by J. P. Miller. This artist portrays animals for tiny tots better than anyone else—bright, bold, friendly ones. In this case his animals present opposites: fat/thin, few/many, tall/short animals of various sorts to talk over with the very young child. Random House, 1–2 years.

The Early Bird, by Richard Scarry. A little bird sets out to find a worm for a friend. A funny idea that captivates children. They love to see the different ways that Early Bird and his friend do all the same things they do. This was the first book in which Scarry's best-loved Lowly Worm character appeared. Random House, 1–2 years.

500 Words to Grow On, by Harry McNaught. Five hundred basic words, contextually grouped (e.g., kitchen words, people words) and illustrated with very realistic, beautifully rendered paintings. Perfect for the child who is just breaking forth into speech. Neither confusingly cluttered nor too simple-minded. A gem at a very low cost. Random House, 1–2 years.

Go Dog Go! by P. D. Eastman. A very first storybook for a two-year-old, a very first reader for the older child. This zany book combines the clear presentation of paired concepts (in/out, over/under, up/down) with the purely cuckoo. Random House, $1^1/_2$–6 years.

The Golden Egg Book, by Margaret Wise Brown. When he can't crack open an egg he finds, little bunny finally falls asleep. Now the duckling hatches, but *he* can't get that bunny to wake up. Or can he? Darling illustrations with a funny story. Golden, 6 months–4 years.

Good Morning, Chick, by Mirra Ginsburg. The first funny adventures of a chick. How he hatches, meets a huge cat, falls into the puddle of a fat laughing frog, and finds refuge under his huge mother's wing. Perfectly timed to get youngsters to join in; perfectly designed to show that the unexpected isn't the disastrous. Greenwillow, 1–3 years.

Goodnight Moon, by Margaret Wise Brown. Just the best, coziest good night ever. The bedtime book of all bedtime books, by the master of the gentle whisper. Harper & Row, 5 months–2½ years.

Is This the House of Mistress Mouse? by Richard Scarry. Well, is it? Put your finger in the hole and see if *you* can guess what that furry thing is. If it isn't Mistress Mouse, who is it? Golden, 1½–3 years.

Jamie's Story, by Wendy Watson. "I open my eyes. The sun is up. Mama comes." From waking to dressing, to playing, to eating, Jamie tells and shows it "like it is" when you are more or less one or two years old: colorful, bright, simple, impressive, wonderful. A story about Jamie and for your child maybe "a story about *me!*" Philomel, 6 months–3 years.

Jump, Frog, Jump! by Robert Kalan. How did the frog catch the fly? How did the frog get away? Let's hear it for the frog! *Jump, Frog, Jump!* Let's hear it for a book during which a really young child will sit still but not keep quiet. Greenwillow, 1½–4 years.

Lois Lenski's Big Book of Mr. Small. Set in sunrise to sunset terms a child can understand, the daily routine of Mr. Small as old-time farmer, cowboy, and policeman is still the perfect introduction to the idea of a story line. Youngsters like the sunny, peaceful mood and identify with the friendly child-faced man. From time to time other single stories about Mr. Small are also available. Walck, 6 months–4 years.

Lowly Worm's Word Book, by Richard Scarry. Of all of Scarry's animal folk, Lowly Worm is the most intriguing. With a shoe on one end, a hat on the other, Lowly Worm hides out in Scarry's big books for children to find him. Here he is in his own book of first words: holding a toothbrush, kicking a ball, and doing other things in his own unique way. A handy, fist-sized, block-shaped book of heavy cardboard. Random House, 1–2 years.

Pat the Bunny, by Dorothy Kunhardt. This old-timer is a uniquely happy introduction to books for the very littlest ones. The children in the book can pat the bunny, play peekaboo, look in a mirror— *and so can you!* Golden, 1–2 years.

Pigs Say Oink, by Martha Alexander. Any new talker loves learning animal sounds and meeting the animals that make them. *Pigs Say*

Oink is full of animals sounding off and making friends with children. The pictures are sweet but not saccharine. Pleasing, educational, and affordable. Random House, 1–2 years.

Sam's Car, by Barbro Lindgren, illustrated by Eva Eriksson. When Sam won't let Lisa play with his car, Lisa smacks him. Then Sam smacks Lisa. Now they both feel sad and don't know what to do. This is a real-life drama with which a really young child can identify. Simple, absorbing, exciting, and reassuring. Morrow, 1–4 years.

Sam's Cookie, by Barbro Lindgren, illustrated by Eva Eriksson. Sam's dog wants Sam's cookie, which makes Sam mad, which makes the dog growl, which makes Sam scared. Another very young real-life predicament presented simply and dramatically. Morrow, 1–4 years.

Sam's Teddy Bear, by Barbro Lindgren, illustrated by Eva Eriksson. Sam loves his teddy bear and plays happily with him in his crib. Sam's dog loves Sam and plays happily on the floor with Sam's slippers. Sam's bear falls out of reach and into a terrible predicament. This makes Sam sad and gives his dog a chance to be a big hero. Funny, exciting, unpatronizing. Morrow, 1–4 years.

Springtime for Jeanne-Marie, by Françoise. A little girl and her sheep have a hard time finding their lost friend, a little white duck. This text of many words can be reduced to a few at first. The story stays interesting to children for several years. Scribner's, 1–3 years.

The Three Birds, by Hilde Heyduck-Huth. "By the river there was a town. In the town there was a garden. In the garden stood a tree. Among the branches was a nest. In the nest there were three blue eggs. From the eggs came three little birds. The three little birds flew over the house. A boy watched the birds from his window. He saw the three birds fly home to the nest." A sturdy cardboard book with a story that doesn't need to be boiled down. Harcourt Brace Jovanovich, 1–2 years.

See also *Catch Me and Kiss Me and Say It Again* (page 284). And be sure to have a book of Mother Goose rhymes. Although the stories they tell are often incomprehensible, Mother Goose rhymes are part of our culture and a good collection amuses and fosters language and musical development. Rhyme, rhythm, and repetition help children master basic speech sounds; and through picture and context, children can build their vocabulary of words and concepts. These verses provide first experiences in story continuity and some general exposure to the wider world.

The most useful Mother Goose anthologies have lots of illustrations for children to "read" to themselves while you read the verses aloud. Look for one in which each rhyme is illustrated with at least one picture. Long before the rhymes are understood, a heavily illustrated Mother Goose can be used as a word book. Find and talk about familiar objects in the pictures and name the unfamiliar ones. Most enjoyable are the ones that you rehearse over and over as part of your daily doings. Our children loved singing and acting out "Misty Moisty Morning" with its handshaking *"How do you do and how do you do and how do you do again?"* Take your pick from the many good big collections, as well as from smaller ones that treat a single rhyme in dramatic detail (e.g., Spier's *To Market, To Market*).

Stage Two Stories

Some of these have lots of words, but they are all composed of concrete events that can be told in a few words. It doesn't matter if children don't get the main point at first. They enjoy the story sequence and the discovery that events are connected.

Anybody at Home? by H. A. Rey. What do you think is in this hole or hive or tank? Make a guess and then unfold the page to see. Houghton Mifflin, 2–4 years.

Are You My Mother? by P. D. Eastman. If *you* hatched when *your* mother was out, how would you recognize her? Designed for beginning readers, baby bird's quest makes a charming story to chuckle over for new listeners as well. Can be carefully abridged—*Is the kitten his mommy? No! Is the dog his mommy? Naah! Is the boat his mother?*— and gradually developed into a full story. And before you know it: "Hey, remember how I used to love this book? Well, listen! Now I can read it!" Random House, 2–6 years.

A Boy, a Dog, and a Frog, by Mercer Mayer. After skillfully outwitting the efforts of a boy and dog to catch him, a lonely frog trails his would-be captors to a joyful bathtub reunion. There is no text— only delightful pictures for story-telling adventure. Dial, 2–5 years.

The Country Noisy Book, by Margaret Wise Brown, illustrated by Leonard Weisgard. Muffin the dog goes to the country with his family and hears many new sounds. Children identify happily with the little dog who, traveling in a box, has no idea of where he is going or what will happen next. They love to guess what makes each sound that Muffin hears. HarperCollins, 2–5 years.

Feed the Animals, by H. A. Rey. Another Rey guessing book with fold-out surprise pages. Guess which animal the zookeeper is going to feed next? Houghton Mifflin, 2–4 years.

Goodnight, Richard Rabbit, by Robert Kraus, illustrated by N. M. Bodecker. Richard Rabbit can't go to sleep because he is imagining things. But fear by fear (and excuse by excuse) his patient mother shows him what really is and isn't there until at last Richard Rabbit is fast asleep. Reassuring and charming illustrations. Windmill, 2–4 years.

The Little Fireman, by Margaret Wise Brown, illustrated by Esphyr Slobodkina. A big and a little fireman respectively put out a big and a little fire in their big and little ways. But falling asleep at last, the big fireman dreams a little dream, while the little fireman dreams a great big one. Scholastic, 2–4 years.

The Little Fur Family, by Margaret Wise Brown, illustrated by Garth Williams. "The fish didn't have any fur and they didn't have any feet and they swam around under the river. The little fur child watched them for a long time." The wonderful simple adventures of a furry fellow who dares to go forth in the bright world all by himself, and finds his way home again just when it's getting too dark. Reassuring and loving—an ideal bedtime story. Harper & Row, 2–5 years.

Little Gorilla, by Ruth Bornstein. "Once there was a little gorilla, and everybody loved him." Just who loved little gorilla, and how, is this book's charmingly simple story. That he kept on being loved even when he grew huge is its special message. Scholastic, 2–4 years.

The Runaway Bunny, by Margaret Wise Brown. When a little rabbit imagines going away and becoming something else besides his mother's son, Mrs. Rabbit wisely reassures him that love will be there with him in some other form, too. "If you become a bird and fly away from me," she says, "I will be the tree that you come home to." This amazing story reassures children *and parents* that wherever they go, even when they part company, they'll find love taking new shape to meet their new needs. Harper & Row, 2–4 years.

Whither shall I go from thy spirit?
Or whither shall I flee from thy presence?
If I ascend up into heaven, thou art there.
If I make my bed in hell, behold, thou art there.
If I take the wings of the morning,
and dwell in the uttermost parts of the sea,
Even there shall thy hand lead me,
and thy right hand shall hold me . . .

—Psalm 139:7–10

See the Circus, by H. A. Rey. Yet another of the Rey fold-out books. Houghton Mifflin, 2–4 years.

The Snowman, by Raymond Briggs. A boy and a snowman share a wonderful night of adventure in each other's worlds. As soundless as snow itself, Briggs's lovely pictures are better than words. A gentle, charming fantasy. Random House, 2–6 years.

The Snowy Day, by Ezra Jack Keats. A city child wakes to find that mountains and mountains of snow have fallen. Striking pictures convey the momentousness of every child's first snowfall. Viking, 2–4 years.

Sunshine, by Jan Ormerod. From the moment the sunshine wakes the little girl to the hilarious departure of the whole family for school and work, the message of this book is that sunshine makes sunshine. A book for parents as well as children to wake up by. A wordless book with lovely, loving, and funny pictures. Lothrop, 2–6 years.

The Winter Bear, by Ruth Craft, illustrated by Erik Blegvad. In these days of television and electronic games it is distressingly possible for a child to grow up without discovering the mystery and beauty of long walks. That's what makes this superbly illustrated book about three country children such a treasure. From a pattable cow to a lovable toy bear caught in a tree, this story/poem is a tempting invitation to the joys of a winter walk. Atheneum, 2–4 years.

Stage Three Stories

Longer than Stage Two stories, these also range farther from home yet are still quite concrete. By now the child is ready for fewer repetitions. A great time for trips to the library and the children's corners of bookstores.

Blueberries for Sal, by Robert McCloskey. A little girl and a bear cub get all switched around and wind up with the wrong mothers while harvesting blueberries. A gentle suspense story that resolves itself with reassuring smoothness. Children love recognizing the mixup before the book characters do. Viking, 3–5 years.

Caps for Sale, by Esphyr Slobodkina. When a hat peddler angrily tries to make a bunch of monkeys return his stolen caps, they seem to make fun of him. Only when he flings down his own cap in disgust do the mimicking monkeys throw down his wares as well. Captivating, funny, and wise. Scholastic, 3–5 years.

Chicken Forgets, by Miska Miles. Little chicken is on a mission for blackberries, but will he remember what he is supposed to get? Doubt becomes suspense as one creature after another confuses the suggestible chicken. Any child who's ever been asked, "Are you old enough to . . ." will find this a cliffhanger—and a big relief. Little, Brown, 3–6 years.

The Christ Child, illustrated by Maud and Miska Petersham. Selections from the Bible tell the story of Jesus from the prophecy of his birth through childhood. The lovely illustrations and traditional text make this an ideal book for Christian children. Doubleday, 3 years and up.

Clipper, by Debbie L. Carter. Clipper keeps a lighthouse and wishes for company to share his nice but slightly lonely life. At last a storm brings him a wet, green friend who is only too happy to share shelter, friendship, and hot chocolate with Clipper. Simple and with charming pictures, *Clipper* presents the value of companionship. HarperCollins, 3–5 years.

The Goblin Under the Stairs, by Mary Calhoun, illustrated by Janet McCaffery. To the child who spies him through a knothole in the wall, the boggart is a "wee frisky man," a playmate. To the mother he appears "a good servant elf," to the father "a house-plaguing goblin." The most violent predictions prevail until the father gives up trying to get rid of the boggart his way, and the mother serves up the hospitality a tidy servant elf deserves. This lively story has a good underlying message that who we are is many things and that how we perceive and treat each other makes a big difference. Morrow, 3–5 years.

The Happy Lion, by Louise Fatio, illustrated by Roger Duvoisin. The beloved lion of a French zoo is bewildered by the startled and unfriendly response he receives when taking a stroll among friends outside the zoo. Only the zookeeper's son greets him in a kindly way and saves the day. McGraw-Hill, 3–5 years.

Jack Kent's Book of Nursery Tales, illustrated by Jack Kent. Every event in each of seven nursery classics is illustrated with a lively picture, making this the best first nursery tale book. Soon the child can learn to "read" the pictures and tell himself the familiar story. And then you can move on to the wealth of good nursery tale books with more traditional illustrations. Included in Kent's book are "The Three Little Pigs," "Little Red Hen," "Three Bears," and "Chicken Little." Random House, 3 years and up.

The Little Engine That Could, by Watty Piper, illustrated by George and Doris Hauman. Adults tend to find this story slightly sugary, but children adore it and are evidently encouraged by the little engine who pulled the broken-down train full of toys over the mountain, saying, "I think I can, I think I can." Grosset, 3–5 years.

The Little House, by Virginia Lee Burton. Children love to hear again and again the story of the nice little house in the country that became a city house and got rescued. Houghton Mifflin, 3–6 years.

The Little Island, by Golden MacDonald (really Margaret Wise Brown), illustrated by Leonard Weisgard. On the surface this is a pleasant story of an island day by day, season by season, plant by plant, and creature by creature. But tucked away is the amazing thought (which a kitten must take on faith) that the island that seems separately afloat is really a part of the land and, like the kitten himself, is simultaneously "a part of the world and a world of its own." Doubleday, 3–5 years.

The Little Red Lighthouse and the Great Gray Bridge, by Hildegarde Swift and Lynd Ward. A small lighthouse is relieved to learn that its usefulness is not over when a towering bridge with a huge beacon is built over it. "Quick, let your light shine again. Each to his own place, little brother." A tremendous favorite with youngsters. (The lighthouse still stands beneath the George Washington Bridge in New York City.) Harcourt Brace Jovanovich, 3–6 years.

Make Way for Ducklings, by Robert McCloskey. Children who are also little and new in a huge strange world love this tale of a duck family in busy Boston. Everything is just right for preschoolers in this exciting yet comprehensible adventure. Tops among the classic McCloskey books. Viking, 3–6 years.

Midnight Moon, by Clyde Watson. In rich yet simple poetry, Watson places your hand in the sandman's and sends you to visit the Man in the Moon. He'll play you tunes, show you his trick dog, and tell you stories of the earth, before sending you back—just in time for Mother Sun to wake you up. Collins, 3 years and up.

Pippa Mouse, by Betty Boegehold and Cyndy Szekeres. Six just-right stories about a little girl mouse who wants to try things and does. From making a door to keeping out the rain to sleeping out overnight, the results are a fifty-fifty mixture of success and failure that any child will happily call adventures. Pantheon, 3–6 years.

The Poppyseed Cakes, by Margery Clark, illustrated by Maud and Miska Petersham. Two children always get into trouble when left alone—and they're always forgiven in the end. Any preschooler who ever gets into trouble is filled with suspense when these two do—and vastly relieved when they are rescued. Beautifully written and illustrated. This book and *Little Pear* provide a bridge from picture books to longer classics. A must. Doubleday, 3½–6 years.

The Sailor Dog, by Margaret Wise Brown, illustrated by Garth Williams. When Scuppers the sailor dog got shipwrecked and needed a house, he built one. When he needed tools, he found some. When he needed supplies, he fixed his ship and sailed after some. "And here he is where he wants to be, a sailor sailing the deep green sea." Wonderful pictures, wonderful story. Inspires children with a sense of order, possibility, and self-confidence. Golden, 3–6 years.

The Story of Babar, by Jean de Brunhoff. How Babar the elephant grew up and went to the city and came home in clothes to be crowned king and marry Celeste. The classic beginning of a storybook elephant civilization that has lasted through two authors (father and son), more than a dozen sequels, and thousands upon thousands of enthusiastic children, including me and mine. Random House, 3–6 years.

Wake Up, Bear . . . It's Christmas, by Stephen Gammell. Having set his alarm clock for Christmas, Bear wakes up just in time to trim a tree and spend an amazing evening with a remarkable little stranger in red. (Guess who?) The gentle mood and beautiful pictures carry small listeners right into the starry sky with Bear and his friend. Lothrop, 3–6 years.

Stage Four Stories

Some of these are longer than those in Stage Three. Others are not necessarily longer but conceptually harder.

Bravo Ernest and Celestine, by Gabrielle Vincent. To earn enough money to fix their leaking roof is a big problem, but Ernest, with little Celestine's help and encouragement, finds a wonderful way. Working together brings many more benefits besides the needed roof. All the books about this improbable pair, a childlike mouse and a fatherly bear, are marvelously illustrated and call to mind the tenderest and funniest moments we share as parents and children. Greenwillow, 3–6 years.

The Camel Who Took a Walk, by Jack Tworkov, illustrated by Roger Duvoisin. A beautiful camel out for a walk on a beautiful day remains oblivious of, yet mysteriously protected from, a lurking hungry tiger. The suspense is terrific and the surprise ending both hilarious and meaningful. Dutton, 4–6 years.

Ernest and Celestine, by Gabrielle Vincent. When Celestine loses her beloved toy bird and it finally turns up wet and ruined in the snow, Ernest tries everything to cheer her up. Greenwillow, 3–6 years.

Ernest and Celestine's Picnic, by Gabrielle Vincent. When it rains on their picnic day, they have a rainy-day picnic; when accused of trespassing, they befriend their accuser. As with each of the other books about these two, this one has a lovely, loving atmosphere. Greenwillow, 3–6 years.

The Fire Cat, by Esther Averill. A little bully of an alley cat becomes a skillful important firehouse cat, and then must still learn to be kind. He reflects, "Once I chased a little cat up a tree. Oh me! Oh my! Why did I do that?" Loving, accepting. Dismisses badness as ignorance. HarperCollins, 4–6 years.

The House on East 88th Street, by Bernard Waber. The story of a citified crocodile who terrifies, charms, and wins the love of everyone he meets. Fanciful and entertaining, with just enough "real" world to set a child's imagination perking. There are more stories about beloved Lyle Crocodile, all available in both recorded and book form. Houghton Mifflin, 4–6 years.

Katy and the Big Snow, by Virginia Lee Burton. The enthralling tale of a red crawler tractor that plowed out a whole town after a snowstorm. A big bonus in this book is its little picture catalog of many other kinds of road machines. Houghton Mifflin, 4–6 years.

Little Pear, by Eleanor Frances Lattimore. Sooner than you think, the child who has been thoughtfully exposed to books is verbal enough to enjoy a story without seeing many pictures. There are no two better to start with than *Little Pear* and Margery Clark's

328

Poppyseed Cakes. In *Little Pear* a Chinese child's curiosity gets him into one scary and hilarious predicament after another. And time and again he is lovingly rescued, scolded, and forgiven. Another must. Harcourt Brace Jovanovich, 4–6 years.

Little Raccoon and the Thing in the Pool, by Lilian Moore, illustrated by Gioia Fiammenghi. On his first solo trip to the pool, Little Raccoon is warned by many animals about the "thing" he will find there. When he arrives, sure enough, the fearful thing stares back at him from the water. After all his efforts to scare the thing fail, he runs home and learns from his mother that the way to tame the "thing" is to smile at it. McGraw-Hill, 4–6 years.

Mike Mulligan and His Steam Shovel, by Virginia Lee Burton. Mike Mulligan and his steam shovel Mary Ann are being put out of business by more modern diggers. At last they nab a job digging the foundation for a town hall, for pay if they can do it in one day, for nothing otherwise. They succeed with the job, but in their haste, they dig themselves into their own deep hole. All problems are solved by converting the steam shovel into a furnace and Mike Mulligan into the superintendent of the new town hall. Houghton Mifflin, 4–6 years.

Moon Mouse, by Adelaide Holl, illustrated by Cyndy Szekeres. A small mouse goes to see what the moon is made of and, at least to his satisfaction, finds out that it is delicious. Lovely illustrations. Random House, 3–5 years.

My Box and String, by Betty Woods. A boy makes something from a box and learns that the real fun is in the making and sharing, not only in the having. Scholastic, 4–6 years.

Our Animal Friends at Maple Hill Farm, by Alice and Martin Provensen. From Max the Cat, who is clever and hates snakes, to Whiney the Sheep, who is dumb and confused and faints from fear when she gets sheared, to Goat Dear, who is very gentle and likes people, all the animals at Maple Hill Farm have personality and are appreciated—faults and all. Highly original and entertaining. Helpful for learning to accept all kinds of people and all kinds of feelings. Random House, 4 years and up.

Smile, Ernest and Celestine, by Gabrielle Vincent. When little Celestine secretly explores the drawers of fatherly Ernest and finds a bundle of photographs, she is overcome with jealousy. But gentle Ernest knows just what to do with her complaint that "there's not a single picture of me." All children who have ever sneaked peeks at their parents' things, as well as many foster, adopted, and stepchildren, will find this book special. Greenwillow, 3–6 years.

The Story About Ping, by Marjorie Flack. Rather than receive a spank for being the last on board his Chinese junk home, a yellow duckling chooses to stay behind. After an exciting adventure and a narrow escape he finds his boat again and opts to return, spank or no spank. This tale of a daring duckling who disobeys and survives can be helpful to parents and children as they try to deal with freedom and discipline. Viking, 4–6 years.

The Tale of Peter Rabbit, by Beatrix Potter. Every home library needs at least one of Beatrix Potter's beautifully illustrated books—and if only one, then surely *Peter Rabbit.* His dangerous adventure in Mr. McGregor's garden snares, scares, delights, and turns out all right. Frederick Warne, 4–6 years.

Three Grimm's Fairy Tales, illustrated by Bernadette. A boxed set of three classic Grimm's tales presented, almost miraculously, in simple enough terms for young children. In "The Fox and the Geese" a gaggle of not-so-silly geese outfox a hungry (and silly) fox. In "The Magic Porridge Pot" a little girl is the only one who can save a whole town from drowning in porridge. In "The Silver Pennies" a poor but generous child gives away all she has on earth and receives more than she needs from heaven. Mysterious, meaningful, and magical. Lays groundwork for more fairy tales. Little, Brown, 4–6 years.

The Tiger in the Teapot, by Betty Yurdin, illustrated by William Pène du Bois. After all the threatening, ordering, bribing, and pleading of the rest of the family fails to induce an unwelcome tiger to leave their teapot, it is the littlest girl, gracious and graceful, who finally succeeds. Holt, Rinehart and Winston, 4–6 years.

A Personal Selection

I wish every child could own:
Goodnight Moon
Midnight Moon
Make Way for Ducklings
The Poppyseed Cakes
Little Pear
Jamie's Story
Catch Me and Kiss Me and Say It Again

The Little Fur Family
Good Morning, Chick
Jump, Frog, Jump!
The Sailor Dog
The Country Noisy Book
Father Fox's Pennyrhymes
Our Animal Friends at Maple Hill Farm
The Runaway Bunny
What Do People Do All Day?

Toddler-Told Tales

If besides being chief cook and bottle washer, you are willing to be your children's occasional scribe, you can begin to foster their literary and artistic creativity, as well as their appreciation of books. Telling tales is tops for toddlers; making books is even better. The time we take to make little books of our children's ideas contributes to their sense of worthiness and creative ability. Here are a few suggestions for getting started:

• Offer to write captions for your child's artwork. Don't ask "What is it?" because maybe it isn't a what—maybe it's a feeling or an exploration or some other kind of happening. Just try, "Tell me about your picture and I'll write down your words." Sometimes the answers are pure poetry.

• Help the child cut out a picture from a magazine and glue it on a piece of paper. Invite her to tell you about it. Write down her "story" below the picture. At first maybe she'll just say what it is; later maybe she'll make up a story about what is taking place in the picture.

• Divide a piece of paper into squares for recording stories in comic book fashion. This can help a child to look at a story in terms of a sequence of events. Depending on the child, either of you may draw the pictures. Or maybe you can work on them together. Good old stick figures are just fine.

• Fold some pieces of paper in half to make a little book with pages that really turn. Maybe she has a story in mind. Or maybe she hasn't a clue of how or where to begin. Help with leading questions. Once there was a—who went—when suddenly—. How did it feel? What did it look like? Did anything happen after that?

Reference Books

Children's questions can be so difficult—especially the simple ones, such as, "What does *nevertheless* mean?" Easy, until you try to explain it in words that your four-year-old can understand. And so the cranky expression comes out instead, "Stop asking so many questions! Can't you see that I'm busy?"

Take a minute to look it up together. Keep a dictionary some-place where it can lie flat and be left open. Better than a children's dictionary is a big unabridged one with plenty of illustrations and charts. Keep lists of words and facts that you and your child want to look up, and set aside time to do so. A dictionary also makes a won-derful picture book in which to poke around at random with a child. And how about an atlas, a one-volume encyclopedia, and a Bible? Besides the obvious educational benefits, a look-it-up habit brings long- and short-term benefits to the mental health of the whole fam-ily. The family that can find things out together can also talk things over together. And when our children are teenagers, they will more readily turn to us with their more troublesome questions if we *don't* claim to have all the answers. Other good books for family reference are *What Makes It Go, Work, Fly, Float?* by Joe Kaufman (Golden Press); *The Children's Picture Atlas, The Children's Book of the Earth,* and *The Children's Book of the Seas,* by Jenny Tyler and Lisa Watts (Usborne).

Cassette Recorders

"A gawk! Dassa gawk!" pipes a tiny, remarkably familiar voice.

"Right!" says a fatherly voice. "So then the dog went to sea on a—what did he go on?"

"In da waff."

"Yes. Right! He went on a raft."

"Is that me?" says the now big boy. "Did I really say 'gawk' for dog?" He seems proud of that somehow. And we are touched. His voice is already so much deeper, but the resemblance to the little pipsqueaking on the tape is unmistakable.

A tape recorder's usefulness and potential contribution to family life is vast, especially with preschoolers. When you read a story repeatedly you develop a certain way of doing it, which to the child becomes part of the book—the way it's meant to sound. Tapes of such readings can be listened to over and over by the child—not as a substitute for, but as a supplement to, the shared times.

Quite early children can learn to operate cassette recorders alone and childproof ones are available. They can take a book and our recording of it and privately "read" it at will. The same goes for the songs you sing together and the stories a child makes up. Such recordings become treasured memorabilia. One of our favorite recordings is of an entire bedtime—the story, some songs, our one-and-a-half-year-old's gradual acceptance of "Night, night," and his final babblings to himself in the darkness as he drifted off to sleep.

8

Love

. . . and the Word became flesh and dwelt among us.

—John 1:14

For I am persuaded that neither death, nor life, nor angels, nor principalities, nor powers, nor things present, nor things to come, nor height, nor depth, nor any other creature shall be able to separate us from the love of God which is in Christ Jesus.

—Romans 8:38–39

Love. Oh, boy, do we want love! Give me love, we say. Love me because I am nice. Love me because I am smart. Love me because I am beautiful. Love me because I am rich and strong. Love me because I am poor and helpless. Love me because I am sweet and dumb. Love me because I am smart and tough. Love me because I am competent. Love me because I am funny. Love me because I am cute. Love me because I am a good mother or father. Love me because I say so.

Love me by approving of me. Love me by accepting me. Love me by touching me. Love me by *not* touching me. Love me by agreeing with me. Love me by liking what I like. Love me by looking up to me. Love me by taking care of me. Love me by letting me take care of you. Love me by giving me gifts. Love me because of the gifts I give you. Love me by doing me favors. Love me by letting me do favors for you. Love me by picking up your socks.

Talk to me. Confide in me. Let me confide in you. At least look at me when I talk to you. Love me because I am a wonderful husband. Love me because I am a wonderful wife. Love me because I am a wonderful parent. Love me because I am such a great kid.

Oh, well, then just notice me. See, I'm over here! Do you see me? Me me me me me me me. Hear that? I *ex-iiiiiiiist!* Don't you love it?

If you don't love me, I'll die. See? I'm dying. I'm not kidding— this time I really mean it! Aren't you worried? It kills me when you don't love me. . . . At least *say* something. "Okay, something." That was mean. Oh, well, go ahead and be mean. I don't care what you do, just so long as you don't ignore me. *I can't stand that.* When you ignore me, I could just scream. Love me or else.

Now then, let's be reasonable. How about this? I'll love you, and then you love me! I'll even go first. See? I just loved you. Now it's your turn to love me back. What do you mean you don't feel like it? Not in the mood! No fair. You can't quit in the middle. I hate you for not loving me. Do me good, bay-baby, *or I'll die.*

Rock-a-bye baby
on the tree top.
When the wind blows
the cradle will rock.
When the bough breaks
the cradle will fall,
and down will come baby—
cradle and all.

—Traditional nursery rhyme

Ashes ashes
we all fall down.
Ashes ashes
we all . . .

—Traditional nursery rhyme

For he is like a refiner's fire.
But who may abide the day of his coming,
and who shall stand when he appears?

—Malachi 3:2

He that loseth his life for my sake shall find it.

—Matthew 10:39

As Me, Inc. we are desperate for love. Getting love is our whole life, and we will go to any amount of trouble to get it. We grow up, get married, have children—anything to get love. We never doubt that love is something between people, something interpersonal. *You mean, it isn't? Of course it is!* First it was supposed to come from our parents; now we're supposed to give it to our children. They'll love us in return; we'll all love each other. Maybe we'll even go public and get the world at large to love us. *(Personally, I've never loved a president yet.)* *(I'm running for the school board, so I'll just pretend I didn't hear that.)* We completely blind ourselves to the fact that even if we succeed in getting love from each other, each other is going away. *(I'd rather not continue this conversation.)* The children are growing. Soon they'll be going. And they aren't the only ones. *(I said I'd rather not talk about this!)* . . .

Even with a spiritual perspective, the pitfall remains that we will continue to go about love in general, parenthood in particular, with the idea of doing it right so we can get what we want from each other, which is after all not a loving but an exploitative idea. We keep deceiving ourselves. *(Now I get it! This book shows how to be loving parents. The spiritual way! This is really going to work.)* But parenthood is not an arena for proving ourselves loveworthy by successfully turning human children into human adults. It is for awakening both parents and children to their individual and shared oneness with the God who *is* Love. We—parents and children together—are a result that God is achieving, or bringing into being. We are in fact not separate selves but individual aspects of God's self. How much easier it would be if we understood that! Not understanding that, we keep trying to use our children to prove ourselves.

See how patient I am? I'm being good. I'll think good and I'll do good. That'll be good. Now look—I'm being strong and disciplined and self-sacrificing and brave and faithful. And I'm a wonderful parent. Now do they love me? Mom and Dad, do you still love me? See how good I'm doing? Do you love me *yet?* (No answer.)

Me, Inc.: *God? . . . Are you there?*

Still Small Voice: *God is . . . You're not.*

Me, Inc. [gulp]: *But what about love? Don't we have to love each other?*

Still Small Voice: *Each other. This message does not compute.*

Me, Inc. [incredulous]: *Just let me run this through again. I said e-a-c-h-o-t-h-e-r. Me + you = LOVE.*

Still Small Voice: *Each, other, me, you? Does not compute.*

Me, Inc.: *I don't feel so good. I'm not doing so good.*

Still Small Voice: *Don't feel, not doing? Does not compute.*

Me, Inc. [fading]: *. . . what then?*

So Me, Inc. comes to the end of its sleep and the beginning of its life. We used to be just plain old havers/doers. Then we became seeing/doers. But at long last we begin to question ourselves and to discover that we are Seeing Beings. Gradually, in fits and starts, we discover this means not getting or doing love, but being loving. Because now Still Small Voice is whispering to us.

Before Abraham was I am.

—John 8:58

Son, thou art ever before me.
All that I have is thine.

—Luke 15:31

I have loved you with an everlasting love.

—Jeremiah 31:3

We love because he first loved us.

—1 John 4:19

After all, love is not something that we get or do but something that we are. Always were. Always will be. To himself, the clown of our story is Me, Inc. (pages 8, 20, 115, and 291); everyone (and everything) else is to use to give himself pleasure *(When I'm with you, I feel warm inside. When I'm with you, I feel warm all over)* or to shed light on his personal importance and power *(You make me feel ten feet tall. When I'm with you, I feel on top of the world)*. His version of love is utilitarian. In perceiving himself as an entity he also objectifies everyone else. He regards and approaches everyone else as his private utility, and "loves" only whatever he deems useful for warming himself and for spotlighting him.

Each of us struggles in vain to get the other to live on his terms. *I'll be me and you be it. No, you're it. I was it the last time.* So we try to take turns, compromise, swear over and over to "stop playing games," even feign to refuse to play games with each other, boycott each other's games—still pining for love. We have to come to terms. My terms? No, *my* terms. To terms with each other? Impossible.

Finally we have to come to God's terms, to recognize that we cannot, need not, get love from each other, but that we can be loving together. This means being *in* love.

Intelligence	Cause	Idea	Truth	Seeing
Love	Effect	Expression	Good	Being

These two sets of ideas are parallel, belong together, are one. So as Seeing Beings in relation to other Seeing Beings, we can say the same about expressing love as about communicating truth.

Love is not the coming together of self and other, of clown and lightbulb, but rather the coming to light of the oneness of both with the force *and* goodness of light. Love-intelligence expresses itself through clown and bulb, through everyone in unique ways, as seeing and as illumination, as intelligence and love. Through its oneness with the light each life is fulfilled and enhanced and thereby also enhances the life of the other. The awakened clown through seeing sheds light on the value and worth, the goodness and purpose, of the bulb. The bulb through shining sheds light on the value, the worth, the goodness and purpose of the clown. And both express the one great *fact and force and goodness* of the light.

> *And God saw the light and, behold, it was very good.*
>
> —Genesis 1:4

> *Let your light so shine that men may see your good works and glorify your father which is in heaven.*
>
> —Matthew 5:16

One Plus One Is One

> *In the higher realm of true Suchness*
> *There is neither "self" nor "other":*
> *When direct identification is sought,*
> *We can only say "not two."*
>
> —*Buddhist Scriptures,* selected and translated
> by Edward Conze

So it comes down to the point where Me, Inc. has to let go of itself, and with itself others, in favor of something truer. Most of us do not do this all at once, but over and over until death. But it helps to see that this is necessary. And it helps to know that it has always been so and wasn't just one person's idea of how to get comfortable in, or at least used to, life. And it helps to hear that this is not only the difficult and hard way, but after all the easiest and best and only way.

Zen Buddhists tell of a student who could not speak Japanese. Therefore, instead of speaking with him, his master gave him a drawing to meditate on to help enlighten him regarding the truth of being. The drawing was a simple circle with a dot in the center. After a long time the student brought the drawing back to the master to demonstrate his understanding. He had erased the circle. The master indicated that while this was a fine beginning, it was not sufficient. So the student went away—again for a long time. This time when he returned he had erased the dot. He was enlightened. The dot stood for self. The circle for others. He had discovered that there was only one mind—one self.

Jesus said, "Hear, O Israel, the Lord our God is one Lord; and thou shalt love the Lord thy God with all thy heart, and with all thy soul, and with all thy mind and with all thy strength. This is the first and great commandment, and the second is like unto it; thou shalt love thy neighbor as thy self."

—Matthew 5:43

The two commandments are the same. There is nothing arbitrary about the first or sentimental about the second. They are not even commandments, but they form a statement about what is.

Both the two-commandments-that-are-one and the story of the Zen student describe the path most of us take toward the realization of wholeness as oneness. In the early days of parenthood, we try to erase the self to serve the other (the baby). We can all attest to the benefits of learning to put someone else first. But it isn't enough and, since it isn't really the truth, in the long run it isn't sufficient. As Jesus' second commandment indicates, the true nature and worth of both self and other has to be clearly seen. As the Zen story explains, both self and other as distinct from the One Mind have to be erased. God is the only I AM.

Before Abraham was I AM.

—John 8:58

We are here for what God is. We are here *as* what God is. We are God's self-expression. This is our life. This is our love. Some think that erasing the dot and circle, self and other, leaves nothing. That is what makes it so hard. Will we be nothing? Will there be no love? But it is not possible to be a loving (or loved) separate self any more than one wave can float a boat or, for that matter, even be a wave by itself. In proportion, as self and other are erased (the second commandment), love as conscious oneness with good (God, love-intelligence) is expressed (the first commandment).

Three Sisters

I received a telephone call from a grandmother, a lovely woman who was concerned about her daughter. "For two years I have watched my daughter devote herself with infinite patience to her baby. Nothing has been too much trouble for the sake of that baby—and the baby is as sweet-tempered and alert as can be. But she is a full-time job for the mother because she cannot be left with anyone else. Today my daughter called, finally sounding a little desperate about when she will ever have any time for herself again. She really can't do anything without the baby. The baby has never been left with a sitter. When she is left she becomes unhappy. I know it is really my daughter who has not let go of the baby, not that the baby won't let go of her. I was wondering if there is anything helpful that I might tell her."

"Well," I said. "Often parents and children cannot tell each other anything. Somehow we all have to get over this idea that we are each other's parents and children first. Whether we are thinking of ourselves as parents of our children or children of our parents, eventually we have to come to see that both parent and child are children of God—and that it is God who is raising us and teaching us and bringing us along together."

"Oh!" I could hear recognition in her voice. "Maybe I have to let go of my daughter! Perhaps *I* need to see that she is God's child and that I don't have to tell her anything!"

A few hours later the wise grandmother called again. "Something wonderful has happened! My daughter just called. For the first time today she was able to leave her baby. She said the child acted as if nothing was happening. She didn't even seem to notice that her mother was gone. It was the very first time she has ever been happy with a sitter!"

When Israel was a child, I loved him, and out of Egypt I called my son. The more I called them, the more they went from me; they kept sacrificing to the Baals, and burning incense to idols. Yet it was I who taught Ephraim to walk, I took him up in my arms; but they did not know that I healed them as one who eases the yoke on their jaws; and I bent down to them and fed them.

—Hosea 11:1–4

Letting Go

Behold what love the Father hath given us, that we should be called children of God; and so we are. Therefore the world knoweth us not, because it knew him not. Beloved, we are God's children now; it doth not yet appear what we shall be, but we know that when he shall appear we shall be like him, for we shall see him as he is. And every man that hath this hope in him purifieth himself even as he is pure.

—1 John 3:1–3

We are what we think,
having become what we thought.
And joy follows a pure thought,
like a shadow faithfully tailing a man.

—Buddha, in *The Dhammapada*, trans. by P. Lal

As soon as we have conceived, we have to start letting go of our children. In fact, for some people letting go of the idea of *having* children is a prerequisite to conception. Often when couples who have had difficulty conceiving finally turn to adoption, they suddenly discover that the pregnancy they sought to achieve is under way.

Maybe the moment of conception coincides with a shift in our motivation from the desire simply to "have a child of our own" to the desire to become parents regardless. Maybe it is when the parental motive slightly edges out the purely possessive one that the idea of a child (which is conceptually dependent on the idea of a parent) can occur. The child is conceived as the parent is conceived.

But this is only the beginning. We must keep on and on, letting go—letting our children be born, letting them sleep, letting them mature. We have to let go of the diapers, let go of the mistakes, and sooner or later we have to let go of the children altogether, let them walk right out of our lives to the care of a sitter, to a first overnight at Grandma's, to nursery school for half a day, to grade school, to college, to marry, to live in another part of the world. It can all be very painful, very hard and sad if we do not understand what all this letting go is for.

Having struggled so hard to learn to love them, we must let them go. But what is the good of the love if the beloved goes away? The fact is that true love, the truth that love *is*, does not come to us until we let go of our beloveds (beloved self, beloved beloved). The real loss in letting go is the loss of two, the two that is you and me, self and other, lover and beloved, revolving around each other in the nothingness, protecting each other from the nothingness, exchanging our nothingness for nothingness. If we *have* each other we *lose* each other, an event so painful that we wonder how we ever could have thought the having would be worthwhile. If we do good to each other, we also do bad to each other; if we help, we also hinder. So what is it all worth? As two (not only separate from each other but separate, two, from *everything*) it is all a fifty-fifty proposition—50 percent of the time you win, 50 percent of the time you lose. It all averages out to nothing. Two cannot become one. So losing this twoness is no loss at all.

When Abraham and Sarah were old and childless, they had to let go of their belief that they were old (persons) and childless (persons) who could not *have* (by personal means) a baby (person). But that wasn't all. Letting go of their sense of personal adequacy/inadequacy, they also acknowledged that there was One who could and would fulfill them. Two Me, Inc.'s could not produce a baby, but the One (Mind) could and did. Sarah conceived and bore a son. When they let go of their sense of personal power and powerlessness they discovered divine power. When they let go of wanting/having a child, they *became* parents. And although they were old before they started, they lived to be—how old? Well, they remained young a long time after they had grown old. So, by giving up a little of their twoness, they discovered that God is intelligence, that God is creative power.

Then they went about the same sublime/ridiculous business of parenting in which we are involved, since of course they were as young as parents as Isaac was young as a child, newborn in the first, most ignorant sense of the word. Isaac must have slept and cried, pleased, perturbed, worried, and made them proud. They must have struggled to learn to love just as we do. Like us, they must have loved their son—cherishing him, wanting to protect him and hold him close. They, too, may have dreaded the inevitable, that he must (for his good if not for theirs) move away from them to become a man instead of a child!

Existence having born them
And fitness bred them,
While matter varied their forms
And breath empowered them,
All created things render, to the existence and fitness they depend on,
An obedience
Not commanded but of course.
And since this is the way existence bears issue
And fitness raises, attends,
Shelters, feeds, and protects,
Do you likewise:
Be parent, not possessor,
Attendant, not master,
Be concerned not with obedience but with benefit,
And you are at the core of living.

—The Way of Life According to Lao Tzu,
trans. by Witter Bynner

Give up what is before, what is behind,
Give up what is now, and cross the stream.
Then will your mind be free,
then will you cross birth and old age.

—Buddha, in *The Dhammapada*, trans. by P. Lal

And he said, Take now thy son, thine only son Isaac, whom thou lovest, and get thee into the land of Moriah, and offer him there for a burnt offering upon one of the mountains which I will tell thee of.
—Genesis 22:2

So Abraham was called upon to sacrifice Isaac. He loaded Isaac up with the kindling wood for his own sacrificial fire and, knife in hand, climbed the mountain with his son—his cherished, precious, dearest son—prepared to kill him in obedience to God. This time he was prepared to sacrifice the two for the One. In his consenting thought he had already done so. So, of course, such a thing was not necessary. God did not want him to kill his son, only his *own* son, his *having* of a son. But Abraham didn't know that until the last minute.

This time in sacrificing the twoness—his role as a lover (the father person) of the beloved (the son person)—he discovered another aspect of the One. As long as he knew God only as the creator, he was able to imagine (unable not to imagine) God the destroyer. But in surrendering once again his attachment to twoness he discovered this aspect of the One—that God is Love. In the slaughtering of both father and son, neither father nor son is lost, except as insufficient, slaughterable persons. Instead there is revealed infinite love which is no less available to one than to the other. Both father and son are revealed to be *in* love; both are seen to be children of God. Sacrificing *his* child, Abraham discovers that Isaac is God's well-protected child. Sacrificing himself as parent (the desire to protect and defend), he discovers that God is parent. The experience of sacrifice may be enormous, but the revelation of truth is that there was never anything to sacrifice, no sacrifice at all, in the first place. There is only love sustaining the only loving.

We all go through this. Each letting go is experienced as a sacrifice—first of ourselves to the child, then the child to the sitter, to other children, to the teacher, to the freedom to make mistakes and be terribly wrong and unhappy. We even supply our children with errors. While we are learning to behold the eternally perfect qualities in our children, we have to teach them the finite. We must teach them worldly, material concepts in what we finally begin to see is a spiritual universe. In educating our children to be successful and competitive we pit them against others. In the very process of learning ourselves to see with a single inner eye, we teach our son or daughter that he or she has two outer ones. Concepts of quantity, time, space, corporeality—all ultimately false—are necessary for living in the world and become kindling for the fire at which the grown child will ultimately have to sacrifice his own material sense.

> *And Abraham took the wood of the burnt offering, and laid it on Isaac his son; and he took in his hand the fire and the knife. So they went both of them together. And Isaac said to his father Abraham, "My father!" And he said, "Here am I, my son." He said, "Behold, the fire and the wood; but where is the lamb for a burnt offering?" Abraham said, "God will provide himself the lamb for a burnt offering, my son." So they went both of them together.*
> —Genesis 22:6–8

This is such a beautiful detail of the story. Abraham does what he has to do (the laying of the kindling on his son's back), but he *speaks* to him only of God (the spiritual, the true). While doing *as if* for a God who takes away (demands this sacrifice), he speaks of God as the provider. He does not try to carry either his son or his son's burden up the mountain. The son climbs himself, bearing his own burden of error to the summit. But Abraham walks beside him, keeping silent about the sacrifice, the evil, the grief, and the horror, teaching only that God is good (an idea he is not even sure of himself). At the same time that he supplies his son with the kindling for material sacrifice, he endeavors wholeheartedly to kindle his son's interest in spiritual reality.

As the son climbs the material mountain, the father ascends the spiritual one. Both child and man are sacrificed upon the mountain. As the child is sacrificed, the man is born; Abraham relinquishes his mental holding of Isaac to childhood. As the man is sacrificed, the child is born; in giving up his possessive, protective, defensive selfhood, Abraham becomes as innocent, as trusting, and as pure as his son. For Isaac to be born a child, Abraham had to conceive of parenthood. For Isaac to be born a man, Abraham must become a child again.

What really happens in this second birth of Abraham is that, through the loss of both (two) material father and son, the spiritual fatherly/sonly, loving/humble One is born (realized in Abraham's consciousness). There is no loss of individuality, but rather the fulfillment of individuality. Abraham and Isaac do not become one with each other, but rather each is seen to be individually one with the father.

Thus it can be seen that in losing there is no loss. In sacrificing the material son, Abraham gains and sets free the spiritual one. This son, the perfect, spiritual child of God, eternally in the care of infinite, fathering love, can never be lost to him. Now he and his son share sonship. Having seen the unslaughterable, perfect spiritual identity of his son, Abraham can see it in everyone. And sacrificing his finite fatherhood to see the unslaughtering, perfect spiritual identity of the infinite Father, he becomes truly fatherly. Thus it is that Abraham sires more children than the stars in the sky. He becomes at one with the Father of the spiritual children of God. He is fatherly with the Father and a son with the sons. The twoness of loss is erased when thus the father and son are one. "Son, all that I have is thine."

So it is with us and our children. On the one hand, we *do* for them, and teach them how to get along in the material world, but at the very same time we sacrifice our notion of them as finite selves, our notions of our *own* personal responsibilities, and our own personal *having/needing* selves. At the same time that we deal with and seem to be material selves, we behold the spiritual, relinquishing errors, lacks, and problems as nothing (fasting, forgiveness) and maintain in consciousness the spiritually perfect (prayer, atonement). At the same time that we let our children go from us forth into the world, we acknowledge that there is only one father/mother/parent—infinite, omnipresent love never withheld, only to awaken in.

In letting go of our children it is helpful to know that, although we are releasing them into the world, we are not turning them over to the world. Instead, constantly, consciously, we are turning them over to the one loving Father ("Not I, but the father in me," "I and my father are one," "In him we live and move and have our being"). This is the secret of our redemption and the healing of our grief and at the same time a vital protection for our children.

There is nothing to be lost but loss. Our loss of a sense of finitude yields awareness of eternity; loss of the sense of power and powerlessness, creative power; loss of the material, awareness of the spiritual; loss of the beloved, awareness of love; loss of personhood, awareness of love-intelligence. In becoming at one with the Father, instead of striving to become one with each other, both we and our children become channels for, and recipients of, the infinitely various spiritual qualities of beauty, truth, creativity, and love.

Jesus had no children, yet in recorded history there is no man who ever saw more clearly that each of us is a child of love, born of love, in essence and through consciousness at one with love. It is notable that this most parently of individuals was known above all as God's son, a fact that by itself suggests what parenthood really is.

> *As the truly parently parent is the childlike parent,*
> *As the truly nourishing parent is the nursing parent,*
> *As the truly teaching parent is the learning parent,*
> *As the truly freeing parent is the obedient parent,*
> *As the truly unifying parent is the unified parent,*
> *As the truly beautifying parent is the truthful parent,*
> *As the truly creative parent is the beholding parent,*
> *As the truly communicating parent is the listening parent,*
> *So is the truly loving parent after all no parent at all, but only*
>   *the loved child of God.*

Seeing is being. Intelligence expresses itself as love. Awareness expresses itself as being. Understanding is loving. Loving is understanding. Intelligence is the only cause, love its only effect. Whether we begin by seeing the truth and become loving, or begin by being loving and then see the truth, one love-intelligent moment leads to another.

> *The more we see that seeing is the issue in life,*
> *the more we look at everything for what it has to teach us.*
> *The more we look at everything for what it has to teach us,*
> *the more we see that we are being taught.*
> *The more we see that we are being taught,*
> *the more we know that we are loved.*
> *The more we know that we are loved,*
> *the more lovingly we are seeing.*
> *The more lovingly we are seeing,*
> *the more loving we are being.*
> *The more loving we are being,*
> *the more we see that seeing is the issue in life.*
> *[start over]*

Afloat

Finally my grandmother died. For more than three years she had barely been here, hanging on to her old Me, Inc. and refusing to take her nap. Somebody said, "Thank God it's over for her. Now she can rest in peace." I thought, *Rest in peace? I was just thinking, Thank goodness, now she can finally get on with her life!*

Even before she died, some said my grandmother was gone, floating, didn't know what was going on. But I remember the last thing she said to me, and to me it sounded like a lot was going on. She had already slipped way back inside, and I had to rub her hands with my hands and her cheeks with my cheeks to bring her back to look out of her eyes like windows. "Oh, Nana," I said. "You're wonderful." "Ha!" she laughed. Slowly, barely, she got out the words, "I ... don't ... see ... whasso ... wuful. ... " But the laugh was her same old laugh. "Well," said I, "you have a great sense of humor." Again the words came slowly but this time they were very clear: "A sense of humor helps a lot in a dreary situation."

Me, Inc., the would-be complete Me, whole child/whole self, hangs on to itself for dear life. It is as if we were waves trying to pull ourselves together, to gather ourselves up under ourselves—and succeeding only in cutting ourselves off from everything. Me, Inc. hangs on to this and that and to this one and that one. But no matter what it gets its hands on and wraps itself around, it is still simply hanging on to itself. Me, Inc.'s all, we come and we will go. The great art in life is learning to let go gracefully—at every birth, at every bedtime, at every transition. Each time Me, Inc. lets go of something it is trying to do or wants done, or of something it has or wants to have, it lets go of a little bit of itself. This is when God gets a word in edgewise. And the word is love. When Me, Inc. has come and gone, I expect we'll all be shrugging and shaking our whatever is left, saying, *How funny that I ever fought so hard to hang on.* Because we will have found that all the love we have been wanting so badly and doing so hard was all the time what we were. Me, Inc. struggles in vain to last forever, but the Seeing Being is here for good.

> *Further, I say that if the soul is to know God it must forget itself and lose consciousness of itself, for as long as it is self-aware and self-conscious, it will not see or be conscious of God. But when for God's sake, it becomes unselfconscious and lets go of everything it finds itself again in God, for knowing God it therefore knows itself and everything else from which it has been cut asunder in the divine perfection.*
>
> —*Meister Eckhart,* trans. by R. B. Blakney

> *love is a place*
> *& through this place of*
> *love move*
> *(with brightness of peace)*
> *all places*
>
> *yes is a world*
> *& in this world of*
> *yes live*
> *(skilfully curled)*
> *all worlds*
>
> —e. e. cummings, *Poems, 1923–1954*

Just as a blue, red, or white lotus grows in stagnant water, but rises clear and unpolluted out of it, a truth finder grows up in the world but overcomes it and is not soiled by it.
— *The Dhammapada,* trans. by P. Lal

It isn't something we can do, but rather a point we are brought to, a wonder quietly taking place—like flowers blooming on a pond while the traffic is roaring by. Our strategies are exhausted, agendas thinned, and out of desperation, awareness grows and blooms into love. Drifting away is *Why should I? After all he . . .* , and *Why shouldn't he? After all I . . .* Bubbling up is *What is there to lose? What better is there for me to do? What is more important anyway than love?*

Like the first time we let go of poolside or parent or neck-craning dog paddle, there comes a moment (no one else sees it) when we let go of everything we think should be or else. Instead, mid-trivia, we rest, staking our very lives on love—just being loving for the sake of goodness. Does one lotus blossom get something from the other? Teach the other? Obey the other? Change for the other? No, the long stems of each run to deep roots, and it is the deep that flowers at the surface. And the whole pond is beautified. And each flower is enhanced by the presence of those nearby. And the roots run deep.

It is so very different from what we imagined. There is no thought of trade or gain. We stop gathering ourselves under ourselves and relax in the presence of infinite love-intelligence as if we already knew that it is and always has been.

And then realization is taking place. Hey, what do you know, it's true. I really don't have to struggle to keep from sinking. I don't have to rely on someone else. I am not on my own. God, love, is. In love I live and move and have my being. Love is and lives my being. Loving is it. Now, wantlessly, I can be here for good, can truly love. What quiet, grateful, peaceful, pure joy.

In thy presence is fullness of joy
and at thy right hand are pleasures for ever more.
—Psalm 16:11

As far as I know it doesn't happen all at once. Well, maybe all at once, but not once and for all. Over and over we come to it and it comes over us. But each time we reach this point, it is forever after easier. Increasingly we notice the change. Fear and bitterness have some-how shrunk. And as often as they arise, worries subside. Loud accusa-tions drown themselves in silent never-minds. Less gets our goat. More strikes us as funny. More touches us with beauty. We are more often moved by gratitude, tenderness, generosity. We are less critical, more compassionate. Less anxious. More peaceful. Forgiving? What's to for-give? We are less nervous. More assured. Sometimes inspired. And more and more we marvel. Afloat in, blooming in, love.

It doesn't happen all at once, but it always happens now and can again anynow. It may not last forever, but now we sense the possibility and are aware that there's a choice. We may not yet choose it often, but in case we're ever interested, now we know it's there and that now is the acceptable *and possible* time and that one love-intelligent moment really does lead to another.

Bon Voyage

Someone I know is going away.

I was thinking about how I don't want him to go,
and how it is sad to be left behind.

Then I found a card.
There is a beach in the foreground
with huge tracks like a land machine's
going down toward the sea.

At the end of the tracks is no land machine,
but after all a huge turtle
just heading into the sea—
the endless sea that stretches before him.

So this card calls to mind the fact that
where the land ends and the sea begins
the turtle ceases to be a grave, ungainly
plodding creature,
and becomes something graceful and free
that can go on effortlessly forever.

Inside the card said: Bon Voyage
which, it suddenly came to me,
means Good Seeing!—

not traveling from this place to that
and leaving anyone behind—just a Good Seeing.

He was going to sea—going to see.
And right here so am I.
And right there so are you.
And everywhere so are our children.

Beneath the greeting the card said:
(And don't forget to write).

Bon Voyage!
Good seeing good!

Index

Author photograph © 1996 by Jerry Bauer.

POLLY BERRIEN BERENDS is a spiritually oriented psychotherapist who has lectured, taught, and led workshops at many institutes, churches, and schools in the United States. Her adult books *Whole Child/Whole Parent, Gently Lead: How to Teach Your Children About God While Finding Out for Yourself,* and *Coming to Life: Traveling the Spiritual Path in Everyday Life* reflect her lifelong personal journey and over twenty-five years of experience as a therapist and parent. She is widely acclaimed for her unique ability to reveal the connection between spiritual truth and everyday practical concerns. Berends is a graduate of Union Theological Seminary with training in Jungian analysis and existential psychotherapy, and has done additional advanced studies in psychiatry and religion at Union Theological Seminary and the New School for Social Research. She lives in Hastings-on-Hudson, New York.